D1766430

RACE, COLOR, IDENTITY

Race, Color, Identity

Rethinking Discourses about "Jews" in the Twenty-First Century

Edited by

EFRAIM SICHER

berghahn
NEW YORK • OXFORD
www.berghahnbooks.com

Published in 2013 by
Berghahn Books
www.berghahnbooks.com

Library of Congress Cataloging-in-Publication Data

Race, color, identity : rethinking discourses about "jews" in the twenty-first century / edited by Efraim Sicher.
p. cm.
Includes bibliographical references and index.
ISBN 978-0-85745-892-6 (hardback : alk. paper) —
ISBN 978-0-85745-893-3 (institutional ebook)
1. Jews—United States—Identity. 2. African Americans—Relations with Jews. 3. Race—United States. 4. Jews—Great Britain. 5. Muslims—Relations with Jews. 6. Jews—Africa—Identity. 7. Genetics. 8. Europe—Ethnic relations. 9. Jews, Ethiopian—Israel. 10. United States—Ethnic relations. I. Sicher, Efraim.
DS143.R13 2013
305.800973—dc23
2012032931

British Library Cataloguing in Publication Data

A catalogue record for this book is available from the British Library

Printed in the United States on acid-free paper

ISBN 978-0-85745-892-6 (hardback)
ISBN 978-0-85745-893-3 (institutional ebook)

Jews are like everyone else, only more so.

(ascribed to Chaim Weizmann)

Contents

Part II. Jews as Blacks / Black Jews

Part III. Discourses of Racial and Ethnic Identities

Acknowledgments

This book is the result of discussions and debates among scholars around the world in anthropology, ethnography, history, literature, and sociology; no attempt has been made to resolve differences of opinion between the various contributors. The editor wishes to express his appreciation to Elizabeth Berg, Melissa Spinelli, Lauren Weiss, and all the team at Berghahn Books for their steadfastness and efficiency in getting this book out. Last, but not least, thanks to Danielle Rubin for assistance with the index.

Foreword

Sander L. Gilman

Race, Color, Identity is an important document in the ongoing debates about the relationship of older and contemporary discourses of race in the age of modern genetics that have seemingly recycled the debates of the first age of biology in the late nineteenth century. Our second age of biology seems to be repeating the claims (albeit with substantially different evidence) of the first. But, as usual, the Greeks know best: Plato noted in the *Cratylus* (402a), "Heraclitus, I believe, says that all things go and nothing stays, and comparing existents to the flow of a river, he says you could not step twice into the same river." The river, the role of race in defining human difference, is today not at all the same river in which Darwin waded.

Today we are in a new, social science debate about race and its meanings which parallels that of the biological sciences. David Theo Goldberg, in his *The Threat of Race: Reflections on Racial Neoliberalism,* argues that in neoliberalism there is a silencing of race as a long-term process, embedded in the gradual demise of scientific racism and the associated explicitly biological theories of race.[1] After the Holocaust, as thinkers of the 1960s such as Stephen J. Gould argued, race cannot matter.

However, the real question is not what meanings race takes on, but empirically which group is used as the litmus test for race. Thus Peter Wade argues that Goldberg's approach privileges an overly institutional presence for race and thus loses sight of the real and continuing presence of race in contemporary societies, especially notable in biotechnological and genomic contexts.[2] For him race is not about biology, but about a constant movement between nature and culture, mediated by classifications of Others based on histories of Western colonialism and postcolonialism. Wade goes on to argue that in Latin America racialized difference is, if anything, made more explicit in the context of what Charles Hale has labeled "neoliberal multiculturalism."[3] So it does matter if you look at Latin America and biology rather than, as in the United States, a "postracial" world of politics.

Yet with race everything is political and all science, as objective as it may wish to be, grapples with the political use and implications of its claims. Here we can turn to Mitchell Ash, who proposes that historians and sociologists of science should adopt a dynamic view of the relationship between science and politics in which each serves as a resource for the other. Science may serve as a "cognitive, rhetorical or institutional resource"; it also transforms the very content or practice of science in that political context.[4] But as in real estate, the bottom line is always location, location, location.

In twenty-first-century United States, race is defined by African American bodies, not Jewish ones. When the first patent was granted to BiDil on October 15, 2002, as a combined medication deemed to be most effective for a specific race (African American) for a specific form of heart failure, the ongoing debate about the effect of the older category of race was renewed. BiDil is a combination of two drugs, hydralazine and isosorbide dinitratre. These drugs are vasodilators that dilate blood vessels in order to diminish the stress on the heart as it pumps blood.[5] They were seen to be most effective among African Americans to ameliorate the impact of a specific form of heart failure.

Race in the United States is defined by the creation of African Americans as a biological or genetic collective. But many saw the use of race as being too controversial. The irony is that when in November 2005 a letter appeared online in *Nature Genetics* that provided some further data on the BiDil claim of effectiveness, the authors wrote of "ethnicity-specific risk of myocardial infarction."[6] By 2005, not race but ethnicity seemed to be the key to risk for a higher rate of heart disease among African Americans. Yet the label of ethnicity is an odd one for a genetic cohort..Indeed, this has nothing to do with ethnicity as a means by which an individual understands being in a cohort. The German sociologist Max Weber (1864–1920) defined ethnicity as "the belief in group affinity, regardless of whether it has any objective foundation, can have important consequences especially for the formation of a political community."[7] But such a belief in one's own ethnicity is belied by the authors of the Helgadottir and colleagues study who "corrected for potentially misclassified individuals by excluding from the study self-reported African Americans with < 20 African genetic ancestry." With this pattern of exclusion, they claim an objective (genetic) basis for ethnicity. Here the category is not truly ethnicity, but also is not quite race.[8]

In twenty-first-century Germany, historically it is still the Jews who define a race. Thilo Sarrazin, then a prominent member of the Social Democratic Party, former senator of finance for the state of Berlin from 2002 until 2009, and in 2010 a well-respected member of the executive board of the Deutsche Bundesbank, published a best-selling screed, *Deutschland schafft sich ab!* ("Germany is doing away with itself"), against German multiculturalism. In it he decried the dilution of German society by the reproductive capacity of a permanent and inassimilable underclass of Muslim immigrants in Germany.[9] Yet it was his comment that "all Jews share a particular gene [that] makes them different from other peoples" that caused an international uproar,[10] and Sarrazin was forced to resign from the Deutsche Bundesbank in September 2010. This claim became the focus of much of the German, as well as international, engagement with Sarrazin. It was most crudely articulated in an interview with *Welt am Sonntag* following the publication of his book in which he stated, "[A]ll Jews share a certain gene as all Basques share a certain gene that distinguishes these from other people."[11] But this theme was present not merely in the interview.

In his book, Sarrazin also clumsily links his argument about the danger of Muslim immigrants to the German nation by writing about the average higher intelligence of the Jews passed through a Jewish gene. He thus sought to escape the charge of racism by praising the Jews as a race, a telling gesture of philo-Semitism with a long history, as the German-Jewish journalist Henryk Broder was quick to point out.[12] This recycling of nineteenth-century claims of Jewish particularism struck a deep chord. Ironically, Broder's praise of Jewish superiority seemed to overshadow the substance of his attack on the Muslim immigrants in Germany. In Germany this notion of a Jewish genetic identity was read as a clearly political statement about discredited notions of race: "Whoever tries to define Jews by their genetic makeup, even when it is superficially positive in tone, is in the grip of a race mania that Jews do not share," said Stephan Kramer, secretary general of the Central Council of Jews in Germany.[13]

The nineteenth century, the age of biological racism, replaced the notion of religious conversion (as partial as it was) with the notion of the indelibility of race. Jewish converts were never to be accepted in the first age of biology as they could not convert out of their race. The popular understanding of such shifts of identity mirrored in the meanings attached to science has a radically different implication today. On the religious right in Israel, this has a different tone in 2010: "A convert, if he converts through the Orthodox, he has the Jewish gene. If he doesn't convert through the Orthodox, he doesn't have the Jewish gene. As simple as that." This quote is taken from an interview the interior minister of the Jewish state and the Shas Party leader, Eli Yishai, gave to the editor of the *Jerusalem Post,* David Horovitz, explaining why only Orthodox conversions were acceptable.[14] And the Jewish gene was proudly cited by Sephardic singer and actor Yehoram Gaon. On his weekly radio program on Israel state radio's second channel (Reshet Bet), he told listeners about a scientific study that shows that the Palestinians have a Jewish gene and some of them were even graced with the Cohen gene.[15] The Cohen Modal Haplotype model has been found in Y chromosome testing among some groups of self-identified Jews. Its existence, scope, and meaning remains highly contested although it is often evoked as proof of some level of Jewish genetic homogenity. In Israeli public discourse, the use of genetics for the purpose of establishing social or political positions has been criticized, and the claim of shared DNA sequences among Jews has been seen as dangerous.[16]

The discourse of the Jewish gene in Germany and Israel has radically different implications. Here is a salient passage from joint research by a genetic anthropologist and a human evolutionary geneticist at University College London, a historian at the School of Oriental and African Studies, University of London, an American geneticist, and two Israeli medical experts:

> According to Jewish tradition, following the Exodus from Egypt, males of the tribe of Levi, of which Moses was a member, were assigned special religious responsibilities, and male descendants of Aaron, his brother, were selected to serve as Priests (*cohanim*). To the extent that particular inheritance has been followed since sometime around the Temple period (roughly 3000–2000 years before present), Y chromosomes of present-day Kohanim and Levites should not only be distinguishable from those of other Jews, but—given the dispersion of the priesthood following the Temple's destruction—they should derive from a common ancestral type no more recently than the Temple period. Here we show that although Levite chromosomes are diverse, Cohen chromosomes are homogenous. We trace the origin of Cohen chromosomes to about 3000 years before [the] present, early during the Temple period.[17]

Thus the Cohen chromosome claim for a Jewish genetic marker is tied to a specific place and time (no diasporic experience even in the light of the biblical narrative of Egyptian and Babylonian exiles can be reflected in this fantasy of the Jews' genetic makeup.) So, on the one hand, the Jews are one big family (with exceptions) as this literature views the main groups of Diaspora Jews as genetically related to each other:

> For more than a century, Jews and non-Jews alike have tried to define the relatedness of contemporary Jewish people. Previous genetic studies of blood group and serum markers suggested that Jewish groups had Middle Eastern origin with greater genetic similarity between paired Jewish populations.... Two major groups were identified by principal component, phylogenetic, and identity by descent (IBD) analysis: Middle Eastern Jews and European/Syrian Jews.... Thus, this study demonstrates that European/Syrian and Middle Eastern Jews represent a series of geographical isolates or clusters woven together by shared IBD genetic threads.[18]

On the other hand, the claim that such inbreeding leads also to Jewish diseases is countered by some recent work that argues the contrary, that the Ashkenazic Jewish population is genetically more diverse than people of European descent, despite previous assumptions that Ashkenazic Jews have been an isolated population. The analyses of disease-related genes of higher prevalence in the Ashkenazic Jewish population indicate that only a minority of traits show signs of positive selection.[19] Researchers looked for close to one million single nucleotide polymorphisms (SNPs): common alternative spellings in the genome, analogous to alternate American and British spellings of words such as organize or organise. One measure of genetic diversity in a population is heterozygosity, or how many of the SNPs inherited from the mother and father are different; a more-inbred population has less heterozygosity. "We were surprised to find evidence that Ashkenazic Jews have higher heterozygosity than Europeans, contradicting the widely-held presumption that they have been a largely isolated group," said first author Dr. Steven Bray in an interview that I undertook.[20] Only six of the twenty-one disease genes that they examined showed evidence of selection. This supports the argument that most of the Ashkenazic-prevalent diseases are not generally being selected for, but instead are likely to be a result of a genetic bottleneck effect, followed by random drift.

Is the category biological or cultural?

Even biological arguments reflect ever more complex reconstructions of what Jewish identity means: "Our study represents the largest cohort of Ashkenazic Jews examined to date with such a high density of genetic markers, and our estimate of admixture is considerably higher than previous estimates that used the Y chromosome to calculate European admixture at between five and 23 percent."[21] The notion that there is a "Jewish-by-disease" aspect of any definition of the Jews and on the status of claims to identify a gene for descent from Jewish priests, the Cohen Modal Haplotype, remains highly contested.[22] Subsequently, there has been compelling evidence that the Cohen Modal Haplotype may not exist as a singular marker for a Jewish identity, as it seems also to be found in other populations, for example it was used as a claim for Jewish identity among the Lemba, a Bantu-speaking tribe in southern Africa, yet their descent, though possibly Middle Eastern, may not necessarily be Jewish.[23] The disease model has also been answered in the use of BRCA1 and BRCA2 genetic markers for cancer to identify people as Jews. The national attitude concerning the meaning of such markers toward creating the category of the precancerous shapes the choices undertaken by those so defined. Thus the discoveries in 1995 of a higher rate of the BRCA1 mutation among Ashkenazic (Eastern European) Jews—usually defined as Jewish women, though male breast cancer, while rare, does exist and is seen as having many of the same genetic markers as in women (including the BRCA1 mutation); this led in the United States to wide-scale commercial screening sold through Jewish community congregations. Significantly, this screening was undertaken in the context of a heightened anxiety in the Jewish community about the presence of Jewish genetic diseases, as well as the prodding, as Ilana Löwy shows, on the part of the company that owned the patent on the test and its "multisite 3 analysis" because this cohort's risk became one of its major moneymakers.[24] The fact that most cases of cancer in this self-defined population was of a nonfamilial form and that the frequency of the mutation did not translate into a higher rate of cancer was ignored. Such prognoses may lead directly to surgical interventions. In France, this ethnicization of breast cancer did not occur. For the French there is no corollary that is obvious between belonging to a specific cohort and risk for breast cancer. Women who consult an oncogeneticist are not asked whether they come from an Ashkenazic family.[25] As a result, the attendant anxiety is less and, one assumes, there are lower rates of prophylactic mastectomy.

Scientists must be responsible for the meanings of the language they use. As a recent study of the sociology of race in science noted, "One respondent, who was involved in studies on Jewish populations, mentioned that his research was likely to be misinterpreted and misused by some, but insisted that it was out of his hands. He said that people used to approach him and ask whether it could be 'genetically' tested if they were Jewish. He was adamant to stress that being Jewish was not about genetics and it was wrong that this research was interpreted this way, but claimed that he had no control over these types of 'popular' representations of his work."[26] Science does have a responsibility in terms of the implications inherent in the presentation of findings; all science is ideological—though some science is less tendentious than others. In the twenty-first century, we are confronted with new data through the new genetics that needs models of analysis. Sadly, some of the models revert to older patterns or to older belief systems with unfortunate, sometimes unintended, but often quite tendentious claims. Modesty cannot be expected with the riches of information now pouring out of genetic laboratories across the globe, but some sense of the problematics of the application of this science should be hoped for. This is where the present volume may offer a clearer, more-nuanced perspective.

Notes

1. David Theo Goldberg, *The Threat of Race: Reflections on Racial Neoliberalism* (Oxford and Malden, MA: Wiley-Blackwell, 2009).
2. Peter Wade, "The Presence and Absence of Race," *Patterns of Prejudice* 44, no. 1 (2010): 43–60.
3. Cited by Wade, "The Presence and Absence of Race": 47.
4. Mitchell Ash, "Wissenschaft und Politik als Ressourcen fur einander," in *Wissenschaften und Wissenschaftspolitik. Bestandsaufnahme und Perspektiven der Forschung,* ed. Rüdiger vom Buch and Brigitte Kadera (Stuttgart: Franz Steiner, 2002), 32–49.
5. Peter Carson et al., "Racial Differences in Response to Therapy for Heart Failure: Analysis of the Vasodilator-Heart Failure Trials," *Journal of Cardiac Failure* 5 (1999): 178–187.
6. Anna Helgadottir et al., "A Variant of the Gene Encoding Leukotriene A4 hydrolase Confers Ethnicity-Specific Risk of Myocardial Infarction," *Nature Genetics,* no. 1 (January 3, 2006): 68–74; published online, November 10, 2005, DOI:10.1038/ng1692.
7. Max Weber, *Economy and Society: An Outline of Interpretive Sociology* [1922], ed. Guenther Roth and Claus Wittich (Berkeley: University of California Press, 1978), volume 2, 389.
8. Helgadottir et al., "A Variant of the Gene."
9. Thilo Sarrazin, *Deutschland schafft sich ab!: Wie wir unser Land aufs Spiel setzen* (Munich: Deutsche Verlags-Anstalt, 2010), 95.
10. Judy Dempsey, "Comments by German on Minorities Are Criticized," *New York Times,* August 29, 2010.
11. "Gibt es auch eine genetische Identität?" "Alle Juden teilen ein bestimmtes Gen, Basken haben bestimmte Gene, die sie von anderen unterscheiden." Andrea Seibel, Hajo Schumacher, Joachim Fahrun, "'Ich bin kein Rassist' (Interview mit Thilo Sarrazin). *Welt am Sonntag,* August 29, 2010; "Thilo Sarrazin, Bundesbank-Vorstand und früherer Berliner Finanzsenator, über seine These, muslimische Migranten hätten größere Probleme als andere Einwanderer," *Welt am Sonntag,* August 29, 2010, p. 4. See also Stephen Lowman, "German Politician Stirs Controversy with His Inflammatory Views on Muslims and

Jews," *Washington Post,* August 31, 2010; and Michael Woodhead, "'All Jews Share a Certain Gene': German Banker Sparks Outrage with 'Stupid' Comments," *Daily Mail,* August 30, 2010. Sarrazin does not see any problem with these earlier remarks, as he recently stated in an interview: "Sarrazin: ... aber ich hatte mich so viel mit genetischen Fragen beschäftigt, dass ich die Sache gar nicht als dermaßen explosiv verstand, wie sie sich dann herausstellte. Welt Online: Sonst nichts? Sarrazin: Nein. Ich habe mir die kritischen Passagen öfter angesehen und nichts Falsches oder Anstößiges gefunden." *Die Welt-online,* January 28, 2012, http://www.welt.de/politik/deutschland/article13805710/Thilo-Sarrazin-geisselt-die-Wut-der-Pharisaeer.html

12. "Debatte um Thilo Sarrazin: Henryk M. Broder im Gespräch mit SPIEGEL TV," http://www.spiegel.de/video/video-1082930.html
13. Quoted in Dempsey, "Comments by German on Minorities Are Criticized."
14. David Horovitz, "Editor's Notes: The Rabbi's Dutiful Deputy PM," *Jerusalem Post,* August 8, 2010.
15. Quoted in Akiva Eldar, "'Jewish Gene' Theories Make Waves In Germany, Go Unnoticed In Israel," *Haaretz,* August 31, 2010.
16. Eldar, ibid.
17. Mark G. Thomas et al., "Origins of Old Testament Priests," *Nature* 394 (1998): 138.
18. Gil Atzmon et al., "Abraham's Children in the Genome Era: Major Jewish Diaspora Populations Comprise Distinct Genetic Clusters with Shared Middle Eastern Ancestry," *American Journal of Human Genetics* 86, no. 6 (2010): 850–859.
19. S. M. Bray et al, "Signatures of Founder Effects, Admixture, and Selection in the Ashkenazi Jewish Population," *Proceedings of the National Academies of Science,* 107, no. 37 (September 14, 2010):16222–27; published online, August 26, 2010.
20. "Analysis of Ashkenazi Jewish Genomes Reveals Diversity, History," posted on *Reporting on the Middle East, Science, and Education,* http://cnpublications.net/2010/08/29/diversity-of-jewish-genes/
21. Bray, quoted ibid.
22. Michael F. Hammer et al., "Extended Y Chromosome Haplotypes Resolve Multiple and Unique Lineages of the Jewish Priesthood," *Human Genetics* 126, no. 5 (2009), DOI: 10.1007/s00439-009-0727-5; Anatole Klyosov, "Comment on the Paper: Extended Y Chromosome Haplotypes Resolve Multiple and Unique Lineages of the Jewish Priesthood," *Human Genetics* 126, no. 5 (2009): 719–724, DOI:10.1007/s00439-009-0739-1. But see also Michael Hammer et al., "Response," *Human Genetics* 126, no. 5 (2009): 725–726, DOI: 10.1007/s00439-009-0747-1.
23. L. Fernando Mendez, et al., "Increased Resolution of Y Chromosome Haplogroup T Defines Relationships among Populations of the Near East, Europe, and Africa," *Human Biology* 83, no. 1 (2011): 39–53.
24. Ilana Löwy, *Preventative Strikes: Women, Precancer, and Prophylactic Surgery* (Baltimore: Johns Hopkins University Press, 2010), 191.
25. Ibid., 193.
26. Julia Egorova, "DNA evidence? The Impact of Genetic Research on Historical Debates," *BioSocieties* 5 (2010): 348–365.

INTRODUCTION

Rethinking Discourses about "Jews"

Efraim Sicher

Against Binaries

Over twenty-five years have passed since Henry Gates published *"Race," Writing and Difference,*[1] but in the second decade of the twenty-first century the concept of race is back in the center of academic and ideological discussion. Of course, "race" is a mythical construct and socially constructed. Advances in genetics have renewed the controversies over inherited characteristics and the pathology of congenital diseases, as well as the linking of Ashkenazic Jews with high intelligence.[2] While there may be obvious benefits of premarital screening among Jews for hereditary diseases, genetic testing opens up a number of ethical and social issues, such as the construction of a community or population of potential carriers of defective or abnormal genes, or the identification of certain diseases with ethnic groups such as the Jews.[3] The discourse in the media and in science has returned us to biological links for ethnic and cultural bonds, for example in attributing inherited physiological attributes to certain ethnic groups or in the use of DNA testing to determine biological links with ethnic ancestry.[4] Isolation of the 185delAG mutation in BRCA1, for example, detected both in familial breast and ovarian cancer found among Ashkenazic and Iraqi Jews, but also independently among non-Jews, has enabled oncogeneticists to identify a founder mutation carrier predating the dispersion. Similar genetic investigations have laid claim to Jewish ancestors from Spain following the expulsion among populations of New Mexico and Latin America, but geneticists and folklorists have questioned these findings[5] Columbia University anthropologist Nadia Abu El-Haj has critiqued the epistemology of this research on the grounds that genetic testing may reveal a post facto determinism; her critique, however, places the genetic discourse in the framework of race and politics.[6] Indeed, the public as well as academic discourse on genetics has focused on the question of the biological origins of Jews in ways that seem to return us to biological claims to a common ethnicity that recall stereotyped images in establishing a common pathology or that bolster political agendas by attempting to disprove the common identity of a Jewish people. An anti-essentialist argument might lead us to assume there was no common Jewish heritage or collective memory and have us believe in a patchwork of mismatched superficial experiences that have no deep or lasting value or cohesion.[7] To the contrary, sociobiology and psychological evolution theory have looked to the Bible, Jewish beliefs and practice, and comparative religion, as well as to genetic and medical evidence, to explain the continuity of the Jewish people despite adverse demographic and historical conditions, through a process of evolutionary selection.[8]

This book contributes to that discussion by opening up previously locked concepts of the relation between the terms "color," "race," and "Jews" in the global discourse of multiculturalism, hybridity, and diaspora. It is not merely a question of whether we acknowledge that Jews are interracial, but how we address academic and other discourses that continue to place Jews and others in a racial or color category. This shift in perspective should allow us to reexamine how Jews were racialized by twentieth-century anthropologists and ethnographers and force us to confront the difficulties faced by practitioners in the field today, as well as to question basic assumptions of theory and methodology. The limitations of quantitative research, for example, are evident when we analyze narratives of self-identification or discourses about the "Jew," that is the figure or the social construct of the Jews, and recognize the gap between statistical data and perception, or between demography and cultural identity of real Jews. The "Jew" is a shifting and ambivalent signifier in the dominant social discourse about nation or empire that defines the Other, not to be understood outside the historical and ideological context, but also not a means to overdetermine the discourse as anti-Semitic.[9] Since this book deals with *discourses* and does not pretend to analyze trends of Jewish identification or survey patterns of assimilation, it is important to keep in mind this distinction.

The synchronic and diachronic context of local history can frequently complicate the binary model of Jewish identity and posit multiple options or introduce ambiguities and ambivalences (for example, in Jewish populations with high rates of exogamy), not to mention complex cultural, religious, and political attitudes toward Israel and complicated family and ancestral ties. By introducing a nonbinary perspective on the Jewish case we intend to uncover undercurrents of racial or even racist thinking and persistent stereotypes in perceptions of the "Jew." Ideally, the study of the mutual perceptions of Jews and Others should free us from the racialized thinking that persists in Western scholarship and politics and open up multidisciplinary investigation of the function of the "Jew" in debates over national, ethnic, personal, sexual, and gender identities in these troubled times.

The eminent British sociologist Paul Gilroy prefaces his study *Against Race* with a familiar excerpt from Frantz Fanon's *Black Skin, White Masks,* to which we will return later in this book.[10] It is the passage in which Fanon recalls his philosophy professor, a native of the Antilles, telling him that an anti-Semite is inevitably anti-Negro.[11] Gilroy then opens his book by noting that the modern times that W.E.B. Du Bois had called the century of the color line had passed, but racial hierarchy was very much with us. His own understanding of the complexities of what he calls "raciology" grew as he pondered the Jewish historical experience in the Holocaust and affinities between Blacks and Jews.[12] Gilroy thus reinforces the complex self-perception of Blacks in terms of Jewish history and anti-Semitism, while separating them from Jews, whom, it will be recalled, Fanon identified as the intellectuals feared by the Whites, just as the Black was feared by the Whites as a sexualized Other.

The interrelationship of African American and American Jewish self-perceptions and the history of their mutual fears has been studied in the framework of African American and American Jewish political alliances or confrontations, as well as the history of Jewish immigration and assimilation in the United States.[13] However, increasing attention has been paid to the common discourse of American race relations, where Jews and Blacks may share or compete for victimhood, yet where the "Jew" and the Black have been constructed as sexual and gendered Others.[14] In the first quarter of the twentieth century, the "Jewish" body was pathologized in medical discourse just as much as the Black body. Indeed, Jews were described as having high levels of immunity to tuberculosis, in contrast to Blacks, perhaps because of their long endurance of persecution, which says much about the racialized views of the body, whereas in Europe tuberculosis was perceived as the "Jewish" disease.[15] Moreover, however marginal Blacks may be within the narrative of American Jews, Blacks have often perceived Jews as Whites and identified them with the dominant White society that enslaved and segregated them, or viewed them as models of modernization and upward social mobility. Yet both Blacks and Jews must be understood in the changing discourse of race in the United States of America, which is far from becoming "postracial," despite the hopes invested in the first American president of mixed race, as so dramatically indicated in the arrest of Black Harvard professor Henry Gates for breaking into his own home.[16] Indeed, it is questionable whether a raceless America is possible or desirable. Post-9/11 racial tensions have complicated the discourse of race and the identity politics of ethnic groups that are otherwise well integrated in American society, while globalization and a borderless cyberspace have seen formation of new ethnic and racialized spaces for collective non-White identities.[17]

Moreover, there is some confusion in contemporary race discourse as to whether one should regard Jews as White, or whether they are a race or a religion.[18] President Obama, in an apparent attempt to define Jews as a religion rather than as a race, adopted an evangelical phrase and lauded the survival of this "band of believers," whose history was a testing of their faith.[19] In his celebrated speech on race relations on March 18, 2008, "A More Perfect Union," during his campaign for candidacy as Democratic presidential nominee, Obama quoted from his memoir, *Dreams from My Father: A Story of Race and Inheritance* (1996), to describe the moment of faith during a church service when the pastor's voice carried the congregation to heights of ecstasy: "People began to shout, to rise from their seats and clap and cry out, a forceful wind carrying the reverend's voice up into the rafters … And in that single note — hope! — I heard something else; at the foot of that cross, inside the thousands of churches across the city, I imagined the stories of ordinary Black people merging with the stories of David and Goliath, Moses and Pharaoh, the Christians in the lion's den, Ezekiel's field of dry bones. Those stories — of survival, and freedom, and hope — became our story, my story; the blood that had spilled was our blood, the tears our tears; until this Black church, on this bright day, seemed once more a vessel carrying the story of a people into future generations and into a larger world. Our trials and triumphs became at once unique and universal, Black and more than Black; in chronicling our journey, the stories and songs gave us a means to reclaim memories that we didn't need to feel shame about … memories that all people might study and cherish — and with which we could start to rebuild."[20] In his speech, Obama condemned the Black supremacism of his pastor, Reverend Jeremiah Wright, but could not disown his origins, which formed his identity as a multiracial American and may explain his attitude toward Jews, as well as toward race relations. There was much Jewish support for Obama (as Ibrahim Sundiata tells us in chapter 2), and many Jews were moved by an identification with him as a Black.

For Jews, the Black as another Other has been an enticing image, as in the fantasy of Black-Jewish brotherhood in Bernard Malamud's short story, "The Angel Levine" (1955), but more often Jews perceive Blacks as being on the other side of the color line, something that is challenged in Art Spiegelman's provocative 1993 Valentine's Day cover for the *New Yorker,* after the Crown Heights stabbing incident, showing a West Indian woman and a Hasidic Jew kissing.[21]

Black and White, it seems, are buttons that ignite red lights for many who are insecure about identity—their own and others'—while stereotypes and myths disseminated in the media and the Internet continue to circulate in the popular imagination despite the discrediting of race as a biological category. Jews themselves in the past have engaged in racialized discourse when combating anti-Semitism and have adopted some of the discursive practices in the social sciences in debating identity and assimilation.[22] As Eric Goldstein has shown, the color of Jews was an ideological issue, relating to social acceptance, rather than a racial or physiological question; the perception of Jews as "Black" during the waves of immigration at the turn of the twentieth century was replaced by a hard-won "whiteness" in the postwar period.[23] In the age of Obama, Jews can be Black again, only now any Black-Jewish alliances have to be renegotiated from opposing political sides, given anti-Jewish hostility in the Nation of Islam and other fundamentalist groups, which identify after 9/11 with the jihad against the West and the Jews, or identify Jews with the White privileged classes.

Passing Jewish / Passing White

To what extent identity has in the past been determined by race consciousness in the United States can be seen in narratives of mixed-race life stories in which Jewish origins are colored ambiguously and identity is confused. In James McBride's *The Color of Water: A Black Man's Tribute to his White Mother* (1996), the Black-White binary makes his Jewish mother an object of curiosity in a Black neighborhood as a White woman riding a bicycle (a symbol of her precarious standing in a Black community), who abandoned her religious immigrant family and abusive father to marry a Black and accept Jesus (who is the "color of water"). Her kinship with Blacks is presented as something that comes with always being on the run when growing up in a segregated town in the South during the thirties. Black Power brings with it a surge of militant ethnic solidarity, and McBride fears for his mother, who is the "wrong color." She remains aloof, hiding the past, yet her immigrant experience bred in her an instinctive sympathy for Blacks and hatred of racists, as well as a paranoiac distrust of authority, though she thought anything Black was somehow inferior and she sneered at Black parvenus. As a "token Negro" bussing to predominantly Jewish public schools, McBride perceived Jews to be different from other Whites, some supportive of the Civil Rights movement, others racist. There is a similar dissonance in McBride's account of his mother's exposure to anti-Semitism at school and her parents' prohibition of any relations with Gentiles.

The past is no less unstable and fluid for Rebecca Walker (daughter of the well-known Black writer), who similarly grew up in a dysfunctional mixed-race family. Her confused identity is a nagging anxiety in *Black, White, and Jewish: Autobiography of a Shifting Self* (2001). Her body feels none of the certainty that her peers feel about their color, and she seeks protective refuge in sex and drugs from the constant racial gaze that constructs her ethnically, culturally, and sexually. It is as if her "Jewish folk" were a safe cosmopolitan space between colors that is free of this anxiety. This is her father's world, where she can feel pride and a sense of empowerment in identifying with her great-grandmother's pogrom experience and with Anne Frank.[24] In her reading of memories by biracial/ multiracial authors of Jewish descent, such as James McBride and Rebecca Walker, Helene Meyers argues that the "whiteness" of Jews was never a given and that American Jews sometimes defended their social acceptance as Whites by adopting dominant social attitudes that differentiated them from Blacks, but also from more traditional religious Jews (the stereotyped "dirty" Jews), so that vis-à-vis both Whites and Blacks Jewish identity is erased or repudiated. At all events, Meyers concludes, in this color triangle it is difficult to escape mutual racialized perceptions.[25]

In America, Jews have passed as White to such an extent that a Black passing as White might easily be taken as a Jew, thus exposing the ambiguity of the Jew's color and race. Passing provides an entry ticket to American whiteness—and with it the envied stereotypical intelligence, power, wealth, and sexual passion of the "Jew." In Philip Roth's comic novel *The Human Stain,* set in 1998 against the background of the Lewinsky affair, a New England college professor named Coleman Silk is caught up in a scandal involving his racial identity and sexual behavior. After signing up as a White in the American Army, he is taken to be Jewish. His success in passing, however, rebounds on his family after his tragic death in an automobile accident after a relationship with a Vietnam vet's wife. Coleman Silk's sister tells the writer/narrator, Roth's habitual alter ego Zuckerman, "If Coleman was intent on keeping his race his secret, then the price he should have paid was not to have children. And he knew that. He had to know that. Instead, he planted an unexploded bomb."[26] Passing as White is to become "Jewish" in more than a metaphorical sense, but the fake identity carries risks and responsibilities. As a professor at a provincial college and positioned as "White," Coleman Silk finds himself entangled in accusations that he made a racist remark. A misinterpreted language usage costs him his job and sets off a series of misadventures that leads to his death. Identity is rendered fluid and indeterminate, but at the same time, Silk's "Jewish" identity relies on externalization of stereotypes associating Jews with sexual and intellectual prowess. Roth shows how Jews negotiated assimilation through whiteness and parodies overdetermined role-playing.[27]

Passing is more than just deception; it blurs the boundaries of identity markers and demonstrates the complexities of Jewish identity.[28] It is also a way of negotiating one's ethnic difference through the allo-Semitic figure of the "Jew."[29] In America, becoming Jewish means being American, or so a young Chinese American teenager in Gish Jen's *Mona in the Promised Land* (1996) believes. Mona is one of the Woodstock generation, in rebellion against her immigrant parents who are helpless when faced with American freedoms and who try to stop their daughter converting to Judaism, promiscuity, and hash. This Judaism (or its local Reform variety spiced up by a radical rabbi) stands for social action and universal love, but after Mona and her boyfriend shack up with some African American drop-outs, they discover they are on the wrong side of the color line when it comes to Black pride and resistance to "Jew-daddy" money. The explanation Mona comes up with for why a Chinese woman can turn Jewish but not Black is that "Black" is "a race, not a religion."[30] But changing religions does not make the difference that Mona dreamed about. Her friend Barbara Gugelstein has had a nose job at her mother's insistence, and urges her that it is OK to be Jewish but not too Jewish, especially when Jews are in danger and terrorists are killing Jews at the Munich Olympics.[31] Mona's Jewish partner, Seth Mandel, is a hippie libertine, but also a traditional Jewish predator—he is the shadow, if not the double, of an assailant who tried to rape Mona and has been harassing her in the guise of a Japanese admirer. Even before ethnicity became big, identity politics did not allow Jews to get away from their inherent stereotypes or perceived social status, and, while Jews and Blacks seem to have confused perceptions of each other's ethnicity, color, and race, Jews can also serve as models in a hierarchy of race and color for other ethnic minorities.[32]

In Achmat Dangor's *Kafka's Curse* (1997), Oscar Khan, like Coleman Silk, sees that to be a successful White means passing as a Jew. Just as Jews shed their Jewishness to survive in wartime Europe, passing as blond Aryans, Omar Khan found that full social life and liberty to be whoever he wanted were denied to him as a "colored" Muslim in South Africa: "I changed from Omar Khan to Oscar Kahn, fair-skinned and curly-haired. A beautiful hooked nose … enabled me to cross an invisible divide. It was like leaving one dimension of the world for another, where time and place remained the same, but their surfaces had different textures."[33]

The release from the township and from murderous nocturnal eyes to the safety of middle-class suburbia is liberating. Omar-turned-Oscar becomes someone else, sitting comfortably on the Whites-only bus and hating the hybrid South African Yiddish of his boss, Meyer Levin, but enjoying his tutelage that will make his career as an architect. Yet, while the subtle change in his name affects the desired change in his identity and he successfully enters the White business world and weds a White woman, for whom a Jew may be a desirable and acceptable Other, his Semitic body betrays him. Although Anna finds pleasure in sucking his Semitic nose, after proper blowing and cleaning, the overbearing and uncontrollable sexuality of the Semite proves a barrier to bedding down with his wife who recoils at his monstrous erections. His circumcision, the ritual curb on the unbridled lust of the Semite, is mirrored in the rusted statue of the naked David in the garden, whose circumcised penis is mutilated beyond repair, surely an allusion to Oscar's thwarted attempts at procreation. Moreover, he suffers from "Kafka's Curse," a respiratory dysfunction that leaves him with a fatal "Jewish" disease, formerly associated with ghetto poverty and constructions of Jewish emasculation, as if his pretended Jewishness was now becoming a literal infliction.[34] Eventually he vegetates alone in his house as a tree starts growing through the floorboards, just as in the cautionary Arabian fable about the tragic fate of Majnoen and Leila who defied the strict rules of social division; what remains of his body is reclaimed by his devout Muslim brother, Malik. Not only has he existed precariously between real and fantasized identities, but his family, too, has a variegated history of hybridity in its Afrikaner, Indian, and Cape Muslim origins, reflected in the fragmented and contradictory narratives of the various characters. They are also tainted (as is Anna's pure White family) by a history of incest and sexual transgressions.

Malik, a respected communal leader, gets entangled in an adulterous affair with Omar/Oscar's therapist, Amina Mandelstam, daughter of a Muslim businessman and married to a Jewish paraplegic, a woman who has reputedly given both refuge and bed to opponents of the apartheid régime. Estranged from his hirsute and unsatisfying wife, Malik allows himself to be seduced into the Shangri-la of secret hedonistic freedom and sensual pleasure. He, too, must experience how will succumbs to fate.

Dangor's novel uncovers how apartheid had imposed hierarchal boundaries on a racial and cultural heterogeneity that did not comply with the Black-White bifurcation imposed by the state but was rippled with nuanced ambiguities that demonstrated the instability of all identities. The Jew's performance of racial identity becomes the racial signifier itself, exposing the arbitrariness of essentialized cultural or physical markers of identity and the complex realities beneath the social masks that are bequeathed to post-apartheid South Africa.[35] The question posed by Sander L. Gilman, "Is the Jew White?", peers out below passing and fake identities and undermines the markers of racial difference.[36] Indeed, in South Africa at the beginning of the twentieth century Jewish immigrants from Eastern Europe were officially classified as Black, yet under apartheid Jews were accepted, albeit grudgingly, as White. Passing interrogates rules of social acceptance beyond the South African experience and engages with both representation and self-perception of Jews.[37] Another example of such playing around with the fluidity of sexual, gender, and racial identities is *My Life as a Fake* (2003), by Australian novelist and Booker Prize winner Peter Carey. In this parody of English anti-Semitism, it is a negatively stereotyped Jew, David Weiss, who is the victim of the fake, but whose story (based on a true incident) sparks off a series of exposures of fake stories, fake identities, and fake authors. These question assumptions about gender, sexuality, skin color, and, above all, biological and literary paternity, and blur any line between fabricated lives and the real bodies that are scarred by pain and disease (like Tina's, the daughter of Christopher Chubb, a despicable literary hoaxer).

These examples from North America, South Africa, and Australia show how postmodern figures of the "Jew" highlight the ambiguity of all identities. In multicultural societies, we no longer are to consider minority group identity in terms of center and periphery; instead, we should think in terms of "frontier selves" negotiating for ethnic space with other minorities and defining difference as a subject position within and, in a sense, opposed to multiculturalism. As Sander Gilman has suggested in *Multiculturalism and the Jews,* the figure of the "Jew" is a key to understanding the very nature of the multicultural society represented in cultural texts.[38] Gilman's study looks at the question as an issue in Jewish self-identification and Jewish cultural history, beginning with enlightened German Jewish intellectuals in the nineteenth and early twentieth centuries and continuing through the debate over cultural pluralism versus a competitive difference in the Diaspora in the early twenty-first century. The Holocaust is seen in this scheme as a radical marker of difference, marking the Jew as both victim and witness. The radical marker of extermination has given rise to the figure of the vanishing Jew as the figure of post-Holocaust survival, whose identity is determined by erasure of prewar East European Jewish culture. The trope of the Jew as universal victim leaves the real Jews as an empty category.

Jews as Europeans

Hannah Arendt used to speak of Jews as the ultimate Europeans, and various intellectuals from Milan Kundera to George Steiner have idealized the Jews as essential Europeans. While Jews may offer a model for the management of European diversity, the upsurge of anti-Semitism and racism also offers evidence of adversity in European history of genocide and in hostility to immigrants from the Third World. We should recall that the concept of Jewish race in the West was connected to simultaneous constructions of "Arab race," under the rubric of the Semitic in the nineteenth and twentieth centuries, and to a very old history of linking Islam and Judaism, or Muslims and Jews, in the Western and Christian traditions. In a complex, far-from-straightforward transformation through biological thinking, the race concept has replaced a theological category, and it outlives any confessional faith that may originally have motivated constructions of the image of the "Jew." After the Holocaust, moreover, racial (and, on the far right, racist) constructs of the "Jew" have not disappeared, and European political and academic discourse is not an exception.

In Britain, for example, ethnicity entered sociology in the 1980s and is inextricably bound up with culture. The discourse about ethnic identity is invariably inflected with racialized categories that complicate the religious and communal ties of immigrant communities and that are countered by competing, sometimes confusing, values and terms in an attempt to reconfigure a cohesive national identity amid security fears and Islamophobia.[39] One can see how unstable meanings of difference are generated in discourses about ethnic minorities and national identity by looking at a paradox that confronts anyone who tries to understand the perplexing and persistent phenomena of race today in Europe. On the one hand, in genetic terms, the physical or biological differences between groups defined as races have been shown to be trivial. Yet, racism still remains a widespread and intensifying fact of many people's lives. Reiterating that "there's no such thing as 'race'" offers only the frail reassurance that there *should not* be a problem.[40]

From a cultural materialist perspective, race can be understood only as a manifestation of the power hierarchy, but discursive practices often occlude any simple opposition of multiculturalism and racism. The attempt to divorce ethnicity from religion and nationality in some (as yet nonexistent) European multinational harmony is reflected in a nonaffiliated secular European Jewish identity that has been floated by Nick Lambert in *Jews and Europe in the Twenty-First Century*.[41] Carole Fink, by contrast, warns of the growing ethnic adversity in Europe, as well as the resurgence of anti-Semitism and Holocaust denial, and concludes that, despite the creation of European Jewish cultural spaces, there seems little promise of some integral European Jewish revival independent of Israel.[42] The discourse of ethnicity could no longer be ignored as Europe reeled from terror attacks, social unrest, and street violence and turned inwards to national identities and integrationist models of citizenship. Anti-Semitism was hitting record levels in some Western countries, and familiar tropes were circulating on both the right and the left. In Russia, a revived race theory promoted the superiority of the Russian nation, betrayed by Bolshevik Jews, who were once more the scapegoats responsible for all evil, and who were perceived as sexual predators whose bodies were deviant and deformed, at once emasculated and dangerous.[43]

The British sociologist Zygmunt Bauman (who himself was forced out of Poland as a Jew) has spoken of the "liquid" globalized world, where the state is finding it difficult to weld itself to a fixed concept of nation, and indeed, in the postmodern era, fluid or surface identities have proved not to be sustainable, stable anchors for cohesion between individuals or between communities, but have revealed fractures and masks that did not always match content.[44] In Europe, where the Holocaust has erased the prewar center of Jewish life, the presence of the vanished Jew is felt in literary, social, and political discourse. Real Jews find themselves faced by specters of themselves in the "Jewish" klezmer culture celebrated every June in Kraków, as well as in tourist sites, museums, and anti-Semitic discourses.[45] Ethnicity, it turns out, is itself an invented category that has generated measures of "authenticity" (a romantic idea, as Werner Sollers has reminded us), which complicates any simple opposition of assimilation and pluralism.[46] On the other hand, among Jewish groups who practice purity laws and traditional family values, reproduction has shot up since the Holocaust and *haredi* sectors look to soon shift the balance of demographic distribution within Jewish communities, while outside Israel secular Jews are not even reaching replacement levels.

Redrawing Boundaries

For too long, discussion of Jewish identity has been dominated by a Black–White polarity and inflected with the terminology of American race discourse. This book offers the opportunity to reconsider Jewish identities as multiple, hybrid, and global communities of different colors and racial make-up—indeed, a large percentage of Jews in Israel and many in other parts of the world are persons of color. A 2011 poll conducted by the UJA-Federation of New York Jewish Community Study found that a quarter of respondents identified themselves as Sephardim or non-White.[47] There are also many American Jews who have bifurcated or multiple identities (such as the Cuban American journalist and novelist Achy Obejas or anthropologist and film maker Ruth Behar) that defy a single color or race classification. On the other hand, in CUNY Diversity Action Plans for 2011 and again for 2012, groups reclassified for purposes of eligibility for affirmative action included "White/Jewish," eliciting protests when the story hit the *New York Post*.[48] The East–West axis is also fallacious and misleading, no doubt a product itself of Orientalism and cultural or racial typologies imposed upon the Jews. Sephardim were originally the *Westerners* of the Iberian Peninsula, whereas the Jews under Christian rule in Provence and Germany (Ashkenaz) were later driven *east* by persecutions and expulsions and became the *Ostjude* denigrated by assimilated German Jews. The *mizrakhim* ("Oriental Jews"), who immigrated to the land of Israel in the nineteenth century from Yemen and elsewhere, or arrived there en masse after expulsion from North Africa and other Arab countries following the establishment if the Jewish state, become associated with the Levant, and have been labeled "Arab–Jews," a category appropriated by Ella Shohat and others to oppose what they present as an Ashkenazic Zionist hegemony.[49] Sephardic Jews, who have a long history of settlement in Israel and boast their own distinct heritage and language, are often lumped together with "mizrakhi" or "Oriental" Jews as victims of an Ashkenazic–Zionist discrimination.[50] Some have attempted to "color" these ethnic divisions, citing the Israeli Black Panthers, who spoke of "Black" consciousness (ignoring the ideology and anti-Semitic views of their counterparts in Harlem), as the vanguard of the struggle for social justice in the 1970s, identifying them with a

Third World uprising against a colonialist regime,[51] though in fact the empowerment of the "mizrakhim" in the turn to the right in the 1977 elections and the rise of the Sefardi uktra-religious party Shas belies such easy politicized oversimplifications. In fact, Jewish communities in Israel that originated in Aleppo, Baghdad, Cochin, Gundar, Saloniki, and Yemen make up a complex ethnic map that crisscrosses sectarian and political divides in contemporary Israeli society—not to mention the Tat Jews of Central Asia (in the former Soviet Union), whose ethnic status has been disputed, although some shared the fate of their Ashkenazic brethren under German occupation, while Bukharan Jews form a unique cultural and ethnic group in Jerusalem and New York.[52]

The influx to Britain and Israel of Jews from Baghdad, Calcutta, Cochin, and Mumbai; the presence of African American and Caribbean Jews in the United States; and the growing number of racially mixed marriages in America should all alert us to the fallacies of speaking of Jews as if they were "White" or European. In particular, Ethiopian Jews or the various diminished communities of Jews in India provide case studies of preservation of Jewish memory through rituals and customs that may be unfamiliar to Jews elsewhere and that tell remarkable stories of interaction with surrounding communities that reflect the influence of local cultures—as Indian Jewish artist Siona Benjamin (originally from Mumbai, now living in the United States) demonstrates in her startling combination of Indian artistic forms with Sephardic and modern Jewish motifs.[53] The immigration of Ethiopian Jews to Israel allows us to study the dynamics of their changing identification vis-à-vis other Jews and their racialization in social discourse and practice.[54] Meanwhile, shifts in Israeli culture and demography have encouraged Ethiopian Jews to negotiate their integration into a multicultural mainstream and claim their ethnic identity, establishing political protest groups and an Amharic theater. Some of the lost Jewish tribes, such as the Bnei Menashe of northeast India (a small tribe among the Kuki-Chin-Mizo), have also returned home to Israel, or wish to do so, and may have to adapt to a normative rabbinic Judaism, in order to fulfill expectations of what constitutes Jewish identity. African tribes who claim Jewish descent or who have adopted Judaism similarly challenge the discourse about Black Jews and alter our perception of criteria for determining Jewish identities, as will be seen in chapter 9 by Jonas Zianga and chapter 10 by Edith Bruder.

Significantly, the claim of Jewish ancestry was used in Enlightenment discourse to argue for an original natural religion and to bolster a comparativist understanding of contemporary Indian and African cultures that would claim natives were not inferior to White Europeans; it was also an argument conducive to conversion of Africans to Christianity while preserving their indigineity.[55] This merely reminds us that the political construction of a unified stable Jewish identity is a fairly recent phenomenon, but also makes us reexamine what, remarkably, the Jews have preserved of their common heritage and values, as well as what they have accrued from other cultures or developed during nearly two millennia of exile. Examining those admixtures can illuminate the ethnographic study of social and cultural transformation over time.

In America and Europe, new ways of talking about Jewish identities (or, rather, the rediscovery and reinvention of Jewish diversity and pluralism) are reflected in the development of alternate and multiple forms of identifying as Jews or with Jewishness, ranging from New Age kabbalah to a return to more traditional and messianic mysticisms, such as the Lubavitch and Bratslav Hasidic movements, from experimentation across ethnic and gender lines to secular "cultural Judaism." The tolerance or acceptance of racial, ethnic and religious minorities in a multicultural society has also made it more hip to do the Jewish thing; it has even become "hip to be Hebe"—as in the adoption of hip-hop by Jewish musicians, such as Matisyahu, or the penitent Moshe-Levi ("Harper") Shayne, and its adaptation to a Jewish message. Y-LOVE, an African American Orthodox Jewish hip-hop artist from New York City, premiered a new music video, "This Is Unity," in 2011 that called for the inclusivity of the racial and ethnic diversity of the Jewish people. And while some Jews of color complain about not feeling welcome in Jewish communities in the United States and London,[56] the documentary film *Punk Jews* (USA, 2012) promoted alternate spaces for Jews who did not fit into religious or racial categories. Against the backdrop of a postmodern breakdown in kinship and communal affiliation, such experimentation in a musical genre associated with the African American experience provides a globalized space for renegotiating Jewish identities and particularly their relation to blackness.[57]

Jewish Bodies

After World War II, social anthropologists and psychologists in the United States tried to disprove racist theories by testing differences between Gentile and Jewish faces (which assumed there was a "Jewish" face in public discourse about Jews and in social practice). Against the background of the recent revelations of the liberated concentration camps in Europe, Arthur Miller's novel *Focus* (1945) and Laura Z.

Hobson's movie *Gentleman's Agreement* (1946) countered perceptible anti-Semitism in America by following the adventures of a Gentile passing as a Jew. But from the 1970s, American Jews have flaunted their "Jewish" features in an effort to win back their ethnicity, even to the extent of internalizing and performing anti-Semitic stereotypes (a subject of much humor and parody, for example, in the American adult magazine *Heeb*). In modern dance and performance art, there have been experimental and often provocative explorations of stereotypes of the Jewish body as weak, grotesque, or aberrant, which work through fantasies of degradation, feelings of shame, and uneasy complexes associated with identification with other Jews, the Holocaust, and Israel (for example, Rebecca Pappas' 2009 show, *Monster*), or which amplify anti-Semitic images of the "Jewish" body as effeminate and sexually perverted (as in Stephen Cohen's outrageous performances on Vienna streets).[58] There have been Jewish body awareness weeks in California, and in November 2010 Hadassah's *(614)* magazine ran a special issue encouraging women to love their "Jewish" bodies. It may be that, in the face of successful assimilation to the point where Jews have become almost invisible in the larger population, secular Jews in the Diaspora are still concerned about being seen as "too Jewish," but they also may feel the need of social practices that mark them as "Jewish." Indeed, one golden-haired daughter of Israelis resident in the United States has recorded her testing of passing as a shiksa among Ashkenazic males with amusing but all-too-predictable results. Her experience testifies to strategies among secular Jews for identification of members of their perceived ethnic in-group (for dating and other social purposes) when outward signs (such as head covering, clothes, and beards) or cultural and religious practice have long vanished.[59]

The "Jew" has entered body politics, as Jews reposition themselves among other previously marginalized ethnic and sexual minorities. For example, tattooing, a biblical prohibition and (especially after the Holocaust) taboo among Jews, has become "cool" as a Jewish body art, with Jewish symbols marking the body in an individual configuration of personal sexual, gender, or ethnic preferences.[60] As a token of surface or skin identity, tattooing paradoxically returns us to epidermal identification familiar from racist discourses, but in a way that attempts to move across race and color to ethnicity. For some young Diaspora Jews, tattoos make a visible statement of identification, commitment, comic irony, and oppositional transgression; some boast concentration camp numbers on their arms as a way of making their bodies a living memorial (a practice parodied in Emily Prager's 1991 novel *Eve's Tattoo*), while photographer Marina Vainshtein has inscribed Holocaust graphics on her body and, in her exploration of sexuality, Californian artist Rachel Schreiber has inscribed "Jude" on her shaven pubis.[61]

However, as Sander L. Gilman has shown in his prolific and penetrating studies of Jewish stereotypes, the "Jewish" body has long been a construction of Western medical, political, and social discourses.[62] Male circumcision, which is common to a third of American men, has come under approbation in some liberal progressive circles in Europe and the United States as a form of infant genital mutilation that puts Jews and Muslims beyond the pale of civilized behavior; it has often been fantasized as a Jewish threat to the body. Freud thought anti-Semitism could be explained by fantasies of castration.[63] Following Max Nordau's study of Jewish degeneracy, the trope of the emasculated or femininized "Jew" was countered by "muscular Jews," who obsessively displayed their masculinity, thus projecting their anxiety about their sexuality.[64] Jews have internalized stereotypes of the Jewish body as oversexed or undersexed, as we see in Philip Roth's and Woody Allen's parodies of the neurotic Jewish intellectual, or in Howard Jacobson's comic novel *Kalooki Nights* (2007). One of the new "Generation Я" of Russian American Jews, Gary Shteyngart, has shown in his comic novel *Absurdistan* (2006) how troubling the "Jewish" body can be for today's assimilated Russian Jews who had thoroughly erased their Jewish identity under social and political pressure a generation previously, but were identified by Russian anti-Semites as a danger to the body of the nation.[65] Predictably, the myth that circumcision was meant to bridle uncontrollable Jewish lust has been internalized by Jews: the Gargantuan son of a Russian Jewish oligarch Misha Vainberg has his mixed-race Puerto Rican girlfriend (another Other) resurrect his organ, damaged by the rabbis who have circumcised him. Misha is constantly anxious about the state of his phallus as he staves off threats from all directions to his cultural identity. In this parody of the new Russian Jew, Misha, the "good Jew," despises the Hasid on the Austrian Airlines plane, the "bad Jew" who refuses uncertificated food and will not shed his rituals or traditional dress. Misha, on the other hand, is a would-be rapper hooked on antidepressants and sex, who has sold out to American hedonism and multiculturalism, which, he declares, cannot be reconciled with the Bible or belief in God. There is no word for multiculturalism in Russian, Misha reminds us. When he is caught up in a civil war in Absurdistan, a former Soviet republic on the Caspian Sea, the local rulers want to use this Jew to "talk to Israel" and get American aid, but he remakes himself into a minister for multiculturalism with plans to build a Holocaust museum to cater for Diaspora Jews' ideas of their identity. In the end, he is rescued by the most antediluvian, traditional Mountain (Tat) Jews, but even their offspring hanker for the American paradise, where you could play basketball with Blacks on the streets.

As for the Jewish woman, she is generally stereotypically voluptuous, and her large breasts invite the émigré Chinese playwright in Nobel Prize laureate Gao Xingjian's novel *One Man's Bible* (2003) to lose his painful memories of the Cultural Revolution in her *white* body, only to discover that she, too, carries personal and collective memories of pain and violence. Traumatic memories are what the Chinese and the Jews have in common, though it is her Jewishness that makes the woman (with the Faustian name of Margarethe) who attracts the Chinese intellectual in Xinguan's novel erotically compassionate in the candid sharing of suffering in a hotel room in Hong Kong (where East meets West).[66] The Chinese, after all, have themselves been persecuted as Asia's "Jews."[67] At the same time, some Muslims consider themselves the new "Jews" and may regard real Jews as racist Zionists; in the discourse about Jews in India, for example, Jews are identified by Muslims with Hindus and racist violence.[68]

The Postcolonial Turn

The postcolonial turn initiated by Daniel and Jonathan Boyarin[69] has been taken up by the Australian sociologist Jon Stratton and others who oppose essentialist positions on what defines Jews, culturally, ethnically, biologically, and geographically, on the somewhat questionable grounds that separatism bars knowledge of the Other and excludes the human.[70] The Jews could be seen themselves as colonial subjects within European states who reclaimed their ancestral homeland from the British after the Holocaust, yet the ambiguity of their status in the Diaspora has sometimes caused resentment of exclusivity and particularism, as well as reawakening suspicions of conspiracy to undermine the economy or control the press. In a postcolonial view of things, Jews are both the ultimate cosmopolitan migrants and also collectively associated with exploitation (as a wealthy plutocracy) and oppression of the Third World (represented by "Palestine").

There existed, already in the 1960s, a fundamental ambiguity in the link between sympathy evinced for Jews as victims of the Holocaust and the solidarity with the struggle against colonialism, such as the Algerian war for independence from France. That solidarity was felt by French intellectuals such as Simone de Beauvoir, who recalled how the French police rounded up Algerian demonstrators and sent them to the Vel' d'Hiv' stadium, just as they had done to the Jews in the 1940s: "The police waited for the Algerians to come up out of the metro stations, made them stand still with their hands above their heads, then hit them with truncheons.... Corpses were found hanging in the Bois de Boulogne, and others, disfigured and mutilated, in the Seine.... Ten thousand Algerians had been herded into the Vel' d'Hiv' [stadium], like the Jews in Drancy once before. Again I loathed it all—this country, myself, the whole world."[71] Certainly, the "double legacy" (in Colin Shindler's phrase) that drove Jean-Paul Sartre to identify with the Algerian independence movement in the same way he identified with the Jews deported in wartime France was weakend by the Suez crisis of 1956 (when Israel was allied with imperialist forces), and in the generation of 1968 the New Left did not share the same sympathies with Israel or the Jews.[72] Moreover, postcolonial theory tends to detach the Holocaust from the history of anti-Semitism and to inscribe the Nazi Final Solution as a product of European colonialism, whose first laboratory was the Belgian Congo and which was part of a universal discrimination against gays, Gypsies and others.[73]

Anti-colonialism set a dilemma for Jews on the left such as French postcolonial writer and critic Albert Memmi, whose faith in universalism was shattered by the Holocaust and France's own collaboration in deportation of the Jews. As he writes in *Portrait of a Jew* (1962), when Zionism was excluded from postcolonial discourse as a colonizing force, Memmi, a supporter of the Tunisian liberation movement, was forced to look for Jewish solutions to universal issues, rather than universal solutions to the Jewish problem.[74] Memmi concluded in *Portrait du colonisé, précédé par Portrait du colonisateur* (1957; translated as *The Colonizers and the Colonized,* 1965) that the Jews were trapped in an ambiguous position between Arab nationalists in a liberation movement, which was ostensibly freeing them from oppression, and the colonizers, with whom they wished to assimilate and thus escape Jewish difference.[75]

Edward Said contributed to Gates's collection *"Race," Writing, and Difference* with an analysis that effectively racialized the Arab-Israeli conflict by asserting that Zionism had rigorously separated Jew and non-Jew; he looked to a narrative that would humanize Palestinian Arabs.[76] Said prefaces his classic document of postcolonial theory, *Orientalism,* with an interesting remark. The history of Orientalism, he writes, in its Islamic branch has mirrored the history of anti-Semitism; this, he says, is for a Palestinian Arab like himself an irony since he regards Israel as the colonial occupying power.[77] In the common falsification of history, as Ivan Davidson Kalmar and Derek Penslar have pointed out in their collection of essays, *Orientalism and the Jews,* the so-called Zionist myth is treated as *only* a form of colonialism, never *also* as a national liberation movement.[78] Contemporary postcolonial discourse echoes Arnold Toynbee's neo-Paulite position that the Jews were "a fossilized relic" of an extinct civilization, who, because of their economic conflict with Western Gentiles and their incompatibility with a homogenous community, had suffered a tragedy in three acts. Toynbee castigated the sinister and demonic nature of Zionism, that grew with the rise of Nazism in Germany and that proved the point that "Jewish" characteristics derived not from racial origins but from the peculiar conditions of the Diaspora, which, Toynbee declared, the Israeli Jews were now destroying. Toynbee accused the Israeli "colonizers" of persecuting and dispossessing the Arabs as the Jews had been dispossessed by the Nazis: they were settling the land in the same spirit as the Puritans in America and the Boers in South Africa, inspired by the biblical books of Exodus and Joshua and smitten with the sin of nationalism.[79]

For Paul Gilroy, as we have seen, colonialism is to be seen as a parallel with racial anti-Semitism in a comparative study of the history of persecution of minorities, particularly Blacks. As a result, Jews are no longer regarded as unique, though their history may be paradigmatic for other colonized or enslaved peoples; since they are no longer identified as a persecuted minority, however, they can also be considered as guilty of racism or oppression as Zionists or capitalists. In fact, postcolonial discourse operates within an attempt to think through globalized identities and their relation to the new gospel of human rights. The struggle against racism and war places the blame for suffering and exploitation on nineteenth century mythicization of land as nation, which is regarded as antediluvian in a globalized world of transnationalism based on solidarity with the victims of occupied territories in a new cosmological sense of a shared, imperiled biosphere.[80]

Anti-Semitism is increasingly recognized in textbooks on race as a model of European racism, arising from the promotion of the nation-state as a totalitarian ideology in the twentieth century. This development is introduced as an explanation of political Zionism, that, in a cruel paradox, is depicted as itself guilty of nationalism and held responsible for the refugee problem after the Arabs rejected the UN Partition Plan and five Arab armies attacked the fledging Jewish state. The ethnic cleansing that is alleged to have occurred illustrates for scholars of race discourse the way Zionism turned from portraying Jews as outsiders in Europe to becoming itself a typically European colonial project, characterized by racial superiority and territorial expansion.[81]

The mantra that Zionism has turned into a colonizing force ignores the irony that the tiny state of Israel could be considered a threat to radical Arab nationalism (a favorable ideology that grew out of a revolt against European colonialism).

Some Marxist-Leninists would contend that Jews do not count as a nation, and some liberal progressive thinkers would deny Jews' aspirations for sovereignty on the grounds that the nation-state was the root of all evil, responsible for racism and all forms of violence in the twentieth century. Following his own historical dialectic, John Hutnyk, professor of cultural studies at Goldsmiths College, University of London, has decided that there is no Jewish nation but rather that there are diverse Jewish peoples (in the plural) who were dispersed prior to the destruction of the First Temple in Jerusalem by the Babylonians—so that there could conceivably not be any common political or ethnic entity such as "the Jews" who (falsely) claim their forced exile justifies a return to Zion.[82] This redefinition of diaspora, naturally, has implications for the discourse of race and Otherness that are elaborated by Hutnyk in his assertion that "the dialectic between whiteness [*sic*] and Otherness is succinctly expressed in the formation of the Israeli nation-state (created as a compensation for the Holocaust of the Second World War), but it has effectively become a representative of White supremacy with strong backing from the US government and a sanctioned systematic oppression of displaced Palestinians."[83] In other words, the Zionist deceit that conceals supposed Israeli racism is the primal sin against the real Others, the Jews' "Jews," the Palestinian Arabs. The parallel being constructed here is with America, because the Whites have driven natives from their land, a characteristic move in such reductive demagogy that imperceptibly robs Jews of their victim status and makes them appear historically as perpetrators with an ambivalent place in the racial hierarchy. Significantly, and this is commonplace dogma in Arab propaganda constructions of Zionism, it is the Holocaust that is the moral standard of the injustice done to Others. Jews can be recognized as victims of the Holocaust and at the same time as perpetrators because of the Holocaust.

The Jews, in this view, are no longer seen as the exemplary diaspora. The reconfiguration of diaspora, especially relating to the hybrid identity of African Caribbeans, has been formulated by Stuart Hall, a leading British sociologist of race, as a metaphorical figure for heterogeneity, ruling out the Jewish historical experience as a false "backward-looking" diaspora bound to a sacred homeland that was regained by forcing out the Arab Palestinians.[84] As Jonathan and Daniel Boyarin have noted, the disqualification of the Jewish experience as a paradigm of diaspora requires that the Zionist diaspora must be removed.[85] We might say more precisely that postcolonial discourse tends to think of diaspora in terms of a transnational community of global migration. This displaces the historical understanding of the Jewish Diaspora as the dispersion of Jews in the Babylonian captivity and the Roman exile that would end with the reestablishment of a Jewish state in the land of Israel.[86] Indeed, some recent Jewish discourses about postnational diaspora identities have insisted on Judaism's intrinsic extraterritoriality and values based on radical activism that are assimilable to a human rights agenda.[87]

Cultural studies (at least in their British mutation) have not always recognized Jews as subaltern or not taken Jews into account when race became the dividing social marker.[88] The "Jews" are often associated with the Judeo-Christian civilization that is held by such reputable scholars as Henry Gates and Edward Said responsible for colonialism and capitalism, the scourge of the world's oppressed, despite the fact that Jews were rarely accepted in British imperialist society under that category.[89] The problem may be with the reductiveness of analogous thinking in a discourse that has tried very hard to transcend conventional boundaries of race and ethnic difference. When distinguished cultural theorists such as Homi Bhabha dutifully voice their identification with the correct global causes, these risk being reduced to analogous cases—for example, when Bhabha generalizes blackness into the marginal status of all outsiders who come late to White European modernity. In the conclusion of *The Location of Culture,* Bhabha thinks of Frantz Fanon's story of the "Dirty Nigger" in "The Fact of Blackness" whenever he hears angry words about, among others, "the Jew in the *estaminet* of Antwerp, or of ... the Palestinian on the West Bank, or the Zairian student eking out a wretched existence ... on the Left Bank."[90] This kind of rhetoric tends to flatten out different situations into "a chain of subalternity," and the Palestinian becomes an archetype of the "jew" in T. S. Eliot's poem, "Gerontion" (1920).[91] In a revision of this view, Bhabha has written, "[T]he 'Jew' stands for that experience of a lethal modernity, shared by the histories of slavery and colonialism.... In the half century since the Shoah, we have had to stand too often with, or in place of, 'the Jew', taking a stance against the spread of xenophobic nationalism. To stand today besides the Palestinians, the Bosnian Muslims, the Black South Africans, or the Indian Dalits, is to occupy a position from which the very discourse of modernity is eviscerated and needs to be rewritten from a place other than its enlightened or 'civilisational' origins."[92] In this way, the Jew is displaced by the Muslim and the Black as archetypal victims in a revised history of imperialism and neocolonialism. On the other hand, the image of the "Jew" in postcolonial criticism is often benign or ambiguous, as the archetypal cosmopolitan transnational migrant, at home everywhere, with roots nowhere. A good example is Bhabha's critique of Salman Rushdie's *Satanic Verses* (1988) at the end of *The Location of Culture,* where he identifies the Armenian Jewish Mimi Mamoulian's mimicry as the "siren song" of postcolonial global migrancy.[93]

Postcolonial theory has tended to marginalize Jews, while inscribing its own politicized narrative, that constructs Zionists as European Whites who imposed modernity and Western civilization on inferior Muslim inhabitants of the Middle East. David Theo Goldberg has constructed a model of a racialization of Israeli "Whites" who are locked in an endless and senseless struggle with the local Philistines (though the latter actually have no connection with Palestinian Arabs) in a Samson complex, powerful but blind in Gaza. Goldberg's global model of racialization of ethnic difference thus reintroduces color and race into the representation of Jews who are placed in a politicized hierarchy of oppression, which he calls the "Palestinization" of race.[94]

Multiculturalism has, indeed, brought with it a competition for victimhood.[95] When we analyze the discourses about the "Jews" as a construct of the Western imaginary, an ambivalent figure emerges that is familiar from modernist constructs of the cosmopolitan who is uneasy in modernity, but who represents the latecomer to modernity who must confront its history of violence.[96] At the same time, familiar stereotypes recur that go back to the Middle Ages in Europe or Soviet anti-Zionist propaganda and are reimported in the politically correct new anti-Semitism of our days, in an increasingly hostile atmosphere of hate speech, demonization of Israel, harassment on college campuses, murderous attacks by jihadists in Mumbai and Toulouse, and threats of genocide by Iranian leaders.[97]

Mapping the Discourses

This is a multidisciplinary study that interrogates the construct of the Jew" in ethnography, anthropology, history, literature, and cultural studies. We hope to show how rethinking methodological approaches could give us a fuller understanding of the discourses about Jewish identities and the complex perceptions behind them. The book demonstrates that the former boundaries set by American race discourse and European identity politics no longer hold, or perhaps were always false or misleading representations of Jewish identities.

We begin in Part I in the United States with two reassessments of Black-Jewish relations—one by a Jewish historian, the other by a Black Muslim scholar, who consider from their personal perspectives the changes that mutual perceptions of Jews and Blacks have undergone, both historically and in the era of Obama's presidency. We then consider the racial politics of reading novels by Philip Roth in the context of Jewish-Black relations, before looking back to the positioning of Blacks and Jews in the early twentieth century to see what we can learn from a gendered analysis of Jewish and Black American novels. The complex relations of Zora Neale Hurston with her mentor and patron, Franz Boas, when juxtaposed with her novelistic as well as ethnographic practice, raise a number of disturbing questions about ethnographic constructions of Blacks and Jews.[98] Racialized stereotypes of Jews are embedded in popular American culture, and an examination of their parody in a television comedy series such as *Weeds* tells us much about Jewish self-images, constructions of masculinity, and sexuality. Jews are here not just subjects of representation, but also its testing ground.

Part II focuses on Black Jews, first reexamining race in the identity of interracial or mixed-race Jews and Jews of color in the United States, positioned between anti-Semitic discourses coming from Black Muslim leaders and racist attitudes or statements among Jews. We will then study "extrinsic" racism in public discourse and the media regarding Ethiopian Jews in Israel before considering how other African groups have formulated a Jewish identity, as well as how their identities have been constructed in academic and Jewish communal discourses.

In part III of the book, we look at both academic and public discourses about the "Jews" in anthropology, sociology, and genetics. Amos Morris-Reich reveals the resurfacing of old tropes of anti-Semitic racial typology in anthropological discourse in Germany after 1945. On the one hand, Noa Sophie Kohler demonstrates how a historian comes to the minefield of genetics and can reap evidence for Jewish social history, while, on the other hand, Klaus Hödl assesses Sarrazin's attempt to field the "Jewish gene" myth in the immigration debate in a country where stereotyping of the "Jewish" body is taboo. Fran Markowitz, by contrast, returns us to the discussion earlier in the book about ethnographic practice and shows that "full-bodied" ethnography is one way to help rethink the discourse of Jewish identities in various societies, thus opening up definitions and self-identifications of Jewishness.

The turbulent times of the early twenty-first century have had a particular impact on discourses about the "Jews" in Europe, where diversity does not always mean an end to ethnic strife, but often adversity and new troubles for Jewish communities, here illustrated by the complex dynamics of race relations in Britain that reveal fissures in national identity and the contradiction between integration and respect for ethnic difference. Turning to European perspectives on the "Jew" in sociology, Glynis Cousin and Robert Fine demonstrate the connections in sociological thinking between anti-Semitism and racism in contemporary discourses about "Jews" in Europe.[99] Ivan Kalmar concludes with a review of the historical development of the link between religion and race in Western imaginings of Jews as a nation that shows the developing perception of the Jewish Other and the interdependence of Christian notions of religion and race.

There is much that could not be covered in this volume, not least the story of Chinese Jews from Kaifeng, the situation in South Africa, or the adoption of the caste system and local customs or rituals among Indian Jewish communities. A separate volume at least would be needed to approach the complexities of race and color in Israel, touched on briefly here in the chapter by Steven Kaplan on the "extrinsic racism" in the discourse about Ethiopian Jews. Yet we hope that the present discussion of the discourses *of* Jews and *about* the "Jews" will contribute to the renewed debate over the relations of Israel and the Diaspora, the tensions between pluralism and the normative, and the parameters of Jewishness in a transformed space and time of globalized societies, as well as the tensions between localized and globalized identities; for example, thriving international communities of Port Jews in Shanghai, Beijing, Singapore, or Warsaw have transformed Jewish identity into a global concept with ties to local communities.[100] Yet, how are we to understand secular diasporic Jewish identities in a global transnational culture, when "diaspora" no longer implies exile from a sacred land but a permanent state of migration? Is the Jewish Diaspora any longer unique, or has it become another cosmopolitan ethnotransnational grouping with little connection with an ancestral homeland?[101]

While this book is not concerned with critiquing or defending any one practice of Jewish identity, we need to reexamine how and with what assumptions we come to study those cultural and social formations that represent Jews or set out to define Jewishness. We must take account of the instabilities and interrelationships of identities—real and imagined, fake and constructed, multiple and invented, hybrid and denied. Diaspora identity is being renegotiated as secular assimilated Jews confront stereotypes in their performances of the Jewish body, hip-hop music, and installation art that challenge boundaries of race, color, gender, and sexuality. It is time to take the debate over Jewish identities out of its American or Eurocentric framework and work beyond binaries to examine how race discourse affects the way Jews see themselves and others, and are themselves perceived, whether through ambivalent appropriation by other Others or hostilely in an intersection of race discourse with resurgent anti-Semitism.

Notes

1. *"Race," Writing, and Difference,* ed. Henry Louis Gates was first published as a special issue of *Critical Inquiry,* 12, no. 1 (Autumn 1985).
2. E.g., Gregory Cochran, Jason Hardy, and Henry Harpending, "Natural History of Ashkenazi Intelligence," *Journal of Biosocial Science* 38, no. 5 (September 2006): 659–693; Kiryn Haslinger, "A Jewish Gene for Intelligence," *Scientific American,* September 21, 2005. Despite inconclusive results and errors in research methods, these studies have received much publicity. See Sander L. Gilman, *Smart Jews: The Construction of the Image of Jewish Superior Intelligence* (Lincoln: University of Nebraska Press, 1996). For a survey of common myths about the Jews' racial difference in constructions of "Jewish" intelligence, diseases, and genes see Raphael Patai and Jennifer Patai. *The Myth of the Jewish Race,* revised edition (Detroit: Wayne University Press, 1989).
3. Sander L. Gilman, "Private Knowledge," *Patterns of Prejudice* 36, no. 1 (2002): 5–16 (special issue on The New Genetics and the Old Eugenics: The Ghost in the Machine, edited by Sander L. Gilman); *Race in Contemporary Medicine,* ed. Sander L. Gilman (London and New York: Routledge, 2007).
4. *See* Sander L. Gilman's foreword and chapter 12, by Noa Sophie Kohler and Dan Mishmar, in the present volume. For a critique of popular sociobiology, see Richard H. Thompson, *Theories of Ethnicity: A Critical Approach* (New York: Greenwood Press, 1989), 21–48. See also on the discourse on genetics within the American Jewish community, Susan Martha Kahn, "Are Genes Jewish? Conceptual Ambiguities in the Genetic Age," in *Boundaries of Jewish Identity,* ed. Susan A. Glenn and Naomi Sokoloff (Seattle: Washington University Press, 2010), 12–26.
5. See Wesley K. Sutton, et al., "Toward Resolution of the Debate Regarding Purported Crypto-Jews in a Spanish-American Population: Evidence from the Y Chromosone,"*Annals of Human Biology* 33 (2006): 100–111; but see also Eitan Friedman et al., "Haplotype Analysis of the 185delAG BRCA1 Mutation in Ethnically Diverse Populations," *European Journal of Human Genetics,* advance online publication July 4, 2012; doi: 10.1038/ejhg.2012.124.
6. Nadia Abu el-Haj, *The Genealogical Science: The Search for Jewish Origins and the Politics of Epistemology* (Chicago: University of Chicago Press, 2012). See, by contrast, Harry Ostrer, *Legacy: A Genetic History of the Jewish People* (Oxford: Oxford University Press, 2012).
7. Such arguments often rest on two well-known discredited attempts to disprove the existence of a common origin of the Jewish people: Arthur Koestler's *The Thirteenth Tribe: The Khazar Empire and its Heritage* (London: Hutchinson and

New York: Random House, 1976); and Shlomo Sand's *The Invention of the Jewish People,* translated by Yael Lotan (London and New York: Verso, 2009).

8. See Rick Goldberg, ed., *Judaism in Biological Perspective: Biblical Lore and Judaic Practices* (Boulder, CO: Paradigm Publishers, 2008); Melvin Konner, *Unsettled: An Anthropology of the Jews* (New York: Viking, 2004).
9. Cheyette, "Neither Excuse nor Accuse: T.S. Eliot's Semitic Discourse," *Modernism/Modernity* 10, no. 3 (2003): 433. For discussion of this usage, see Efraim Sicher and Linda Weinhouse, *Under Postcolonial Eyes: Figuring the "Jew" in Contemporary British Writing* (Lincoln: University of Nebraska Press, 2012), xi–xiii.
10. Paul Gilroy, *Against Race: Imagining Political Culture beyond the Color Line* (Cambridge, MA: Harvard University Press, 2000).
11. Frantz Fanon, *Black Skin, White Masks,* trans. Charles Lam Markman (London: MacGibbon & Kee, 1968), 122. See chapter 16 in this volume.
12. Gilroy, *Against Race.*
13. See Katya Gibel Azoulay, *Black, Jewish, and Interracial: It's Not the Color of Your Skin, but the Race of Your Kin, & Other Myths of Identity* (Durham: Duke University Press, 1997); Karen Brodkin, *How Jews Became White Folks and What That Says about Race in America* (New Brunswick, NJ: Rutgers University Press, 2000); Eric L. Goldstein, *Price of Whiteness: Jews, Race, and American Identity* (Princeton, NJ: Princeton University Press, 2006); and Matthew Frye Jacobson, *Whiteness of a Different Color: European Immigrants and the Alchemy of Race* (Cambridge, MA: Harvard University Press, 1998).
14. On sharing or competing for victimhood see, e.g., Stephen J. Whitfield, "Black Like Us," *Jewish History* 22 (2008): 353–371. On the Jew and the Black as sexual and gendered Others: see, e.g., Jeffrey P. Melnick's study of American Jewish musicians' projections of Black homosexuality in blackface performances, *A Right to Sing the Blues: African Americans, Jews, and American Popular Song* (Cambridge, MA: Harvard University Press, 1999) and Melnick's essay, "Some Notes on the Erotics of 'Black-Jewish Relations,'" *Shofar* 23, no. 4 (2005): 9–25. See the essays in this volume by Cheryl Greenberg and Adam Zachary Newton; and see Newton, *Facing Black and Jew: Literature as Public Space in Twentieth-Century America* (Cambridge: Cambridge University Press, 1999); Emily Miller Budick, *Blacks and Jews in Literary Conversation* (Cambridge: Cambridge University Press, 1998).
15. On racialized views of the "Jewish" body: see Klaus Hödl, "The Black Body and the Jewish Body: A Comparison of Medical Images," *Patterns of Prejudice* 36, no. 1 (2002): 17–34. On tuberculosis as the "Jewish" disease: see Sander L. Gilman, *Franz Kafka, the Jewish Patient* (New York: Routledge, 1995).
16. See Gerald Early, "The Two Worlds of Race Revisited: A Meditation on Race in the Age of Obama," *Dædalus* (Winter 2011): 11–27. For a discussion of how much a role race played in Obama's election and in his presidency see the special issue of *Patterns of Prejudice* 45. no. 1–2 (2011), "Obama and race," edited by Richard H. King.
17. See Dara N. Byrne, "The Future of (the) 'Race': Identity, Discourse, and the Rise of Computer-Mediated Public Spheres," in *Learning Race and Ethnicity: Youth and Digital Media,* ed. Anna Everett (Cambridge, MA: MIT Press, 2008), 15–38.

18. See Eric L. Goldstein, "Contesting the Categories: Jews and Government Racial Classification in the United States," *Jewish History* 19 (2005): 79–107.
19. President Barack Obama, addressing a delegation of high-ranking American Jews at the White House to mark American Jewish Heritage Month, May 17, 2011; transcript and video recording, http://sfjcf.wordpress.com/2011/05/18/Jewish-leaders-at-white-house
20. Transcript of Obama's speech, http://www.politico.com/news/stories/0308/9100_Page2.html For another reading of this passage see chapter 2 in the present volume.
21. See Budick, *Blacks and Jews;* Newton, *Facing Black and Jew;* Eric J. Sundquist, *Strangers in the Land: Blacks, Jews, Post-Holocaust America* (Cambridge, MA: Harvard University Press, 2005).
22. Mitchell B. Hart, ed., *Jews and Race: Writings on Identity and Difference, 1880–1940* (Lebanon, NH: University of New England / Brandeis University Press, 2011). See also Hart, *Social Science and the Politics of Modern Jewish Identity* (Stanford, CA: Stanford University Press, 2000); John Efron, *Defenders of the Race: Jewish Doctors and Race Science in Fin-de-Siècle Europe* (New Haven: Yale University Press, 1994). On the early twentieth-century work on "Jewish" race by Fishberg and Jacobs see Ostrer, *Legacy*, 1–22.
23. Eric L. Goldstein, *Price of Whiteness;* Matthew Frye Jacobson, *Whiteness of a Different Color.*
24. James McBride, *The Color of Water: A Black Man's Tribute to his White Mother* (New York: Riverhead Books, 1997); Rebecca Walker, *Black, White, Jewish; Autobiography of a Shifting Self* (New York: Riverhead, 2001).
25. Helene Meyers, *Identity Papers: Contemporary Narratives of American Jewishness* (Albany: State University of New York Press, 2011), 125–137.
26. Philip Roth, *The Human Stain* (Boston: Houghton Mifflin, 2000), 320.
27. Meyers, *Identity Papers,* 167 See chapter 3 in this volume.
28. See Jennifer Glaser, "The Jew in the Canon: Reading Race and Literary History in Philip Roth's *The Human Stain," PMLA* 123, no. 5 (2008): 1465–1478.
29. See Jonathan Freedman, "'Who's Jewish?' Some Asian-American Writers and the Jewish-American Literary Canon," *Michigan Quarterly Review,* 42, no. 1 (2003): 230–254.
30. Gish Jen, *Mona in the Promised Land* (New York: Knopf, 1996), 49. For a comparison of assimilation and whiteness among Jewish and Chinese immigrants, see Cathy J. Schlund-Vials, *Modeling Citizenship: Jewish and Asian American Writing* (Philadelphia: Temple University Press, 2011).
31. Jen, *Mona in the Promised Land,* 222.
32. For an account of Jewish perceptions of Blacks from the Bible to the early modern period, see Abraham Melamed, *The Image of the Black in Jewish Culture: A History of the Other* (London: Routledge, 2003).
33. Achmat Dangor, *Kafka's Curse* (New York: Vintage Books, 2000), 33.
34. See Gilman, *Franz Kafka.*
35. Ronit Frenkel, "Performing Race, Reconsidering History: Achmat Dangor's Recent Fiction," *Research in African Literatures* 39, no. 1 (Winter 2008): 155. See also Milton Shain, "Ethnonationalism, Anti-Semitism, and Identity Politics: The North American and South African Experiences," in *Jewries at the Fron-*

tier: Accommodation, Identity, Conflict, ed. Sander Gilman and Milton Shain (Urbana: University of Illinois Press, 1999), 335–350.

36. Gilman, *The Jew's Body* (New York: Routledge, 1991), 169–174.
37. Loren Kruger, "Black Atlantics, White Indians, and Jews: Locations, Locutions, and Syncretic Identities in the Fiction of Achmat Dangor and Others," *South Atlantic Quarterly* 101, no. 1 (Winter 2001): 111–143. See also Gilman, *The Jew's Body,* 169–177; and Melanie Kaye/Kantrowitz, *The Colors of Jews: Racial Politics and Radical Diasporism* (Bloomington: Indiana University Press, 2007), 1–32; and Jacobson, *Whiteness of a Different Color,* 171–199.
38. Sander L. Gilman, *Multiculturalism and the Jews* (New York: Routledge, 2006).
39. See Alice Bloch and John Solomos, eds., *Race and Ethnicity in the 21st Century* (Houndmills and New York: Palgrave Macmillan, 2010).
40. James Donald and Ali Rattansi, "Introduction," in *Race, Culture and Difference,* ed. Donald and Rattansi (London: SAGE, 1992), 1.
41. Nick Lambert, *Jews and Europe in the Twenty-First Century: Thinking Jewish* (London: Vallentine Mitchell, 2008).
42. Carole Fink, "Jews in Contemporary Europe," in *Ethnic Europe: Mobility, Identity, and Conflict in a Globalized World,* ed. Roland Hsu (Stanford, CA: Stanford University Press, 2010), 212–239.
43. Henrietta Mondry, *Exemplary Bodies: Constructing the Jew in Russian Culture since the 1880s* (Boston: Academic Studies Press, 2009), 244–270.
44. See Zygmunt Bauman, *Identity: Conversations with Benedetto Vecchi* (Cambridge, England, and Malden, MA: Polity Press, 2004), 26–28.
45. See Magdalena Waligórska, "A Goy Fiddler on the Roof: How the Non-Jewish Participants of the Klezmer Revival in Kraków Negotiate Their Polish Identity in a Confrontation with Jews," *Polish Sociological Review* 4, no. 152 (2005): 367–382; Ruth Ellen Gruber, *Virtually Jewish: Reinventing Jewish Culture in Europe* (Berkeley: University of California Press, 2002).
46. Werner Sollers, "Introduction," in *The Invention of Ethnicity,* ed. Werner Sollers (New York and Oxford: Oxford University Press, 1989), xiv.
47. UJA-Jewish Federation of New York survey of New York, 2011, http://www.ujafedny.org/get/196904/; pdf.
48. Peter Wood, "Counting Jews," *Chronicle of Higher Education,* June 5, 2012 http://chronicle.com/blogs/innovations/counting-jews/32699; Susan Edelman, "New minority label at CUNY: 'Jewish'," *New York Post,* June 3, 2012, http://www.nypost.com/p/news/local/new_minority_label_at_cuny_jewish_orJZewejNjoC1c1cLA2d5J
49. See, for instance, Ammiel Alcalay, *After Jews and Arabs: Remaking Levantine Culture* (Minneapolis: University of Minnesota Press, 1993). See also Harvey Goldberg and Chen Bram. "Sephardi / Mizrahi / Arab Jews: Anthropological Reflections on Critical Sociology in Israel and the Study of Middle Eastern Jewries within the Context of Israeli Society." *Studies in Contemporary Jewry* 22 (2007): 227–256.
50. See for example, Ella Shohat, "Sephardim in Israel: Zionism from the Standpoint of its Jewish Victims," in *Dangerous Liasons: Gender, Nation, and Postcolonial Perspectives,* ed. Anne McClintock, Aamir Mufti, and Ella Shohat (Minneapolis: University of Minnesota Press, 1997), 39-68; David Theo Gold-

berg, *The Threat of Race: Reflections on Racial Neoliberalism* (Oxford and Malden, MA: Blackwell, 2009), 117.

51. E.g., poet, and activist Sami Chetrit, *Intra-Jewish Conflict in Israel: White Jews, Black Jews* (New York: Routledge, 2010).
52. On Tat (Mountain) Jews, see Chen Bram, "Immigrant Jews of the Caucasus in New York and Moscow: Ethno-Cultural Identity and Community Organization," *Between Tradition and Modernity: The Plurality of Jewish Customs and Rituals* (Sociological Papers volume vol. 13) (Ramat-Gan: Sociological Institute for Community Studies, Bar-Ilan University, 2008), 1–16; Mikhail Zand, "Notes on the Culture of the Non-Ashkenazi Jewish Communities under Soviet Rule," in *Jewish Culture and Identity in the Soviet Union,* ed. Yacov Ro'i and Avi Becker (New York: New York University Press, 1991), 378–441. On Bukharan Jews, see Alanna Esther Cooper, *Negotiating Identity in the Context of Diaspora, Dispersion and Reunion: The Bukharan Jews and Jewish Peoplehood,* Doctoral Thesis, Boston University, 2000 (Ann Arbor, MI: UMI, 2000).
53. Another example is the Indian Jewish novelist Esther David. See Shalva Weil, "On Origins, the Arts and Transformed Identities: Foci of Research into the Bene Israel," in *Indo-Judaic Studies in the Twenty-First Century: A View from the Margin,* ed. Nathan Katz, R. Chakravarti, B. M. Sinha, and Shalva Weil (New York and Houndmills: Palgrave Macmillan, 2007), 147–157; Weil, "Esther David: The Bene Israel Novelist who Grew Up with a Tiger," in *Karmic Passages: Israeli Scholarship on India,* ed. David Shulman and Shalva Weil (New Delhi: Oxford University Press, 2008), 232–253.
54. See Hagar Salamon, *The Hyena People* (Berkeley: University of California Press, 1999); and Salamon, "Reflections of Ethiopian Cultural Patterns on the 'Beta Israel' Absorption in Israel: The 'Barya' Case," in *Between Africa and Zion,* ed. Steven Kaplan, Tudor Parfitt, and Emanuela Trevisan Semi (Jerusalem: Ben-Zvi Institute, 1994), 126–132.
55. See, e.g., claims of Ibo ancestry or affinity with Jews in Olaudah Equiano's spiritual autobiography-cum-antislavery tract, *The Interesting Narrative of the Life of Olaudah Equiano, or Gustavus Vassa, the African* (1789). Carlo Ginzburg has argued that the comparison of Jews and Indians characterized Enlightenment discourse in his "Provincializing the World: Europeans, Indians, Jews (1704)," *Postcolonial Studies,* 14, no. 2 (2011): 135–150, a response to Dipesh Chakrabarty's *Provincializing Europe: Postcolonial Thought and Historical Difference* (Princeton, NJ: Princeton University Press, 2000). See also Jonathan Boyarin, *The Unconverted Self: Jews, Indians, and the Identity of Christian Europe* (Chicago: University of Chicago Press, 2009).
56. For example, Frances Abebreseh, "One People Means Including Me, and All People of Color, Too," *Haaretz,* June 5, 2012; Erika Davis, "Talking Honestly About Jews and Racism," *Forward,* June 13, 2012; http://blogs.forward.com/sisterhood-blog/157719/talking-honestly-about-jews-and-racism/; Wayne Lawrence and Molly Langmuir, "The Black Orthodox: Double-consciousness and the Pursuit of G-d," *New York Magazine,* December 23, 2012; http://nymag.com/news/features/black-jews-2012-12/.
57. Kristy Warren, "Twenty-First Century Jewish Journeys in Music," *Jewish Culture and History* 11 (2009): 172–183; Dani Kranz, "Living Local: Some Remarks

on the Creation of Social Groups of Young Jews in Present-Day London," *European Review of History* 18, no. 1 (2011): 79–88; see also Jeff Chang, *Can't Stop, Won't Stop: A History of the Hip-Hop Generation* (New York: St. Martin's Press, 2005).

58. See Rebecca Rossen, "Jews on View: Spectacle, Degradation, and Jewish Corporeality in Contemporary Dance and Performance," *Theatre Journal* 64, no. 1 (March 2012): 59–78.
59. Daria Vaisman, "My Life as a Shiksa Jew: What It's Like To Be Jewish in a Gentile Body," Jewish Student Press Service, http://www.shmoozenet.com/jsps/stories/0998Daria.shtml. Also see Susan A. Glenn, "'Funny, You Don't Look Jewish': Visual Stereotypes and the Masking of Modern Jewish Identity," in *Boundaries of Jewish Identity,* ed. Susan A. Glenn and Naomi Sokoloff (Seattle: Washington University Press, 2010), 64–90.
60. See Kate Torgovnick, "For Some Jews, It Only Sounds Like 'Taboo,'" *New York Times,* July 17, 2008, http://www.nytimes.com/2008/07/17/fashion/17SKIN.html?pagewanted=1&sq=judaism tattoos&st=cse&scp=1
61. See, e.g., Dora Apel, "The Tattooed Jew," in *Visual Culture and the Holocaust,* ed. Barbie Zelizer (New Brunswick: Rutgers University Press, 2001), 300–320. On *Eve's Tattoo,* see Rob Baum, "'And Thou Shalt Bind Them as a Sign upon Thy Hand': *Eve's Tattoo* and the Holocaust Consumer," *Shofar: An Interdisciplinary Journal of Jewish Studies,* 28, no. 2 (2010): 116–138; and Susan David Bernstein, "Promiscuous Reading: The Problem of Identification and Anne Frank's Diary," in *Witnessing the Disaster; Essays on Representation and the Holocaust,* ed. Michael Bernard-Donals and Richard Glejzer (Madison: University of Wisconsin Press, 2003), 141–161.
62. Sander L. Gilman, *The Jew's Body* (New York: Routledge, 1991). See also Melvin Konner, *The Jewish Body* (New York: Schocken, 2009).
63. For a history of the circumcision debate see Leonard B. Glick, *Marked in Your Flesh: Circumcision from Ancient Judea to Modern America* (Oxford: Oxford University Press, 2005); Gilman, *The Jew's Body;* Konner, *The Jewish Body.*
64. See Todd Samuel Presner, *Muscular Judaism: The Jewish Body and the Politics of Regeneration* (London and New York: Routledge, 2007); Neil Davison, *Jewishness and Masculinity from the Modern to the Postmodern* (New York: Routledge, 2010).
65. For a study of the "Jewish" body in modern Russian culture and race discourse, see Mondry, *Exemplary Bodies.*
66. Chinese people tend to venerate Jews for their enduring cultural memory and for their success; see M. Avrum Ehrlich, *Jews and Judaism in Modern China* (London and New York: Routledge, 2010). In the pre-communist period Jews were sometimes perceived to be victims of the White race; see Zhou Xun, *Chinese Perceptions of the "Jews" and Judaism: A History of the Youtai* (Richmond: Curzon, 2001). In Japan, where there has similarly been in modern times little contact with Jews other than as Western traders, there are fears of a Jewish conspiracy and negative, as well as positive, stereotypes; see Rotem Kowner, "On Ignorance, Respect and Suspicion: Current Japanese Attitudes toward Jews," *Papers on Analysis of Current Trends in Antisemitism,* no. 11 (Jerusalem: Vidal Sassoon International Center for the Study of Antisemitism, Hebrew University of Jerusalem, 1997); David G. Goodman and Masanori Miyazawa,

Jews in the Japanese Mind: The History and Uses of a Cultural Stereotype (New York: Free Press, 1995).

67. E.g., in Thailand, where Hitler's genocidal policies were favorably cited as an example for dealing with ethnic Chinese, *The Jews of the East* was the title of a pamphlet by King Vajiravudh attacking the wealthy Chinese merchants as cheating money-grabbers; see Yuri Slezkine, *The Jewish Century* (Princeton, NJ: Princeton University Press, 2004), 37.
68. See Julia Egorova, *Jews and India: Perceptions and Image* (London: Routledge, 2006).
69. Jonathan Boyarin and Daniel Boyarin, eds., *Jews and Other Differences: The New Jewish Cultural Studies* (Minneapolis: Wisconsin University Press, 1997).
70. Stratton, *Coming Out Jewish.*
71. Simone de Beauvoir, *Force of Circumstance,* trans. Richard Howard (New York: Putnam's, 1965), 599; see Michael Rothberg, *Multidirectional Memory: Remembering the Holocaust in the Age of Decolonization* (Stanford, CA: Stanford University Press, 2009), 227–266.
72. Shindler, *Israel and the European Left: Between Solidarity and Delegitimization* (New York and London: Continuum, 2012), 213–214. See Rothberg, *Multidirectional Memory;* Stef Craps, *Postcolonial Witnessing: Trauma Out of Bounds* (Houndmills and New York: Palgrave Macmillan, 2013).
73. David Theo Goldberg, *Threat of Race,* 154–164.
74. Albert Memmi, *Portrait of a Jew,* trans. Elisabeth Abbott (New York: Orion Press, 1962), 3–8.
75. Memmi, *The Colonizer and the Colonized,* trans. Howard Greenfeld (Boston: Beacon Press, 1965), 15–16. See Colin Shindler, *Israel and the European Left,* 218.
76. Edward Said, "An Ideology of Difference," *Critical Inquiry* 12, no. 1 (Autumn, 1985): 38–58.
77. Said, *Orientalism,* 25th anniversary edition (New York: Vintage, 1994), 27–28.
78. Ivan Davidson Kalmar and Derek J. Penslar, "Orientalism and the Jews: An Introduction," in *Orientalism and the Jews,* ed. Kalmar and Penslar (Waltham, MA: Brandeis University Press / Hanover, NH: University Press of New England, 2005), xxxv–xxxvi.
79. Arnold J. Toynbee, *A Study of History* (New York: Dell, 1965), volume 2, 192–200. For a critique of Toynbee's writings on Israel and the Jewish people see Anthony Julius, *Trials of the Diaspora: A History of Anti-Semitism in England* (Oxford: Oxford University Press, 2010), 412–414.
80. Paul Gilroy, *After Empire: Melancholia or Convivial Culture?* (London: Routledge, 2004), 89–92.
81. Clive J. Christie, *Race and Nation: A Reader* (London: I. B. Tauris, 1998), 175.
82. John Hutnyk, "Home and Away: Social Configurations of Diaspora," in *Diaspora & Hybridity,* ed. John Hutnyk, Virinder S. Kalra, and Raminder Kaur (London: SAGE, 2005), 9–10.
83. John Hutnyk, "Journeys of Whiteness," in *Diaspora & Hybridity,* ed. Hutnyk, Kalra, and Kaur, 119.
84. Stuart Hall, "Cultural Identity and Diaspora," in *Identity: Community, Culture, Difference,* ed. Jonathan Rutherford (London: Lawrence and Wishart, 1990), 235.

85. Jonathan and Daniel Boyarin, *Powers of Diaspora: Two Essays on the Relevance of Jewish Culture* (Minneapolis: University of Minnesota Press, 2002), 11–13.
86. For a reconsideration of these terms from a post-Zionist perspective, see Jon Stratton, "Historicising the Idea of Diaspora," in his *Coming Out Jewish: Constructing Ambivalent Identities* (London: Routledge, 2000), 145–163.
87. See, in particular, Daniel and Jonathan Boyarin, "Diaspora: Generation and the Ground of Jewish Identity," *Critical Inquiry* 19, no. 4 (Summer 1993): 693–725.
88. Jon Stratton, "Speaking as a Jew in British Cultural Studies," in his *Coming Out Jewish,* 35–36.
89. Bryan Cheyette, "Neither Black nor White: The Figure of the Jew in Imperial British Literature," in *The Jew in the Text,* ed. Tamar Garb and Linda Nochlin (London: Thames & Hudson, 1995), 31–32.
90. Homi K. Bhabha, *The Location of Culture* (London: Routledge, 1994), 236.
91. Rebecca Stein, "The Ballad of the Sad Cafés: Israeli Leisure, Palestinian Terror, and the Post/colonial Question," in *Postcolonial Studies and Beyond,* ed. Ania Loomba (Durham, NC: Duke University Press, 2005), 331. Stein is in fact arguing that the Palestinian Arabs lose out in this equation.
92. Homi K. Bhabha, "Joking Aside: The Idea of a Self-Critical Community," in *Modernity, Culture, and 'the Jew'*, ed. Bryan Cheyette and Laura Marcus (Cambridge, England: Polity Press, 1998), xv–xvi.
93. Bhabha, *The Location of Culture,* 320.
94. Goldberg, *Threat of Race,* 106–150.
95. See David Biale, Michael Galchinsky, and Susannah Heschel, eds., *Insider/Outsider: American Jews and Multiculturalism* (Berkeley: University of California Press, 1998).
96. Sicher and Weinhouse, *Under Postcolonial Eyes,* xxi–xxii.
97. See Kenneth L. Marcus, *Jewish Identity and Civil Rights in America* (Cambridge, England: Cambridge University Press, 2010).
98. For a useful discussion of the development of race in the Boasian school and its context of the constraints of an assimilationist discourse in Germany and America, see Gelya Frank, "Multiculturalism, and Boasian Anthropology," *American Anthropologist* (New Series) 99, no. 4 (1997): 731–745.
99. For a discussion of the relation of classical sociological theory to anti-Semitism in fin-de-siècle Germany, France, and Hungary, see the special issue on modern anti-Semitism and the emergence of sociology, guest edited by Marcel Stoetzler, *Patterns of Prejudice* 44, no. 2 (2010).
100. For a historical study of Port Jews, see David Sorkin, "The *Port Jew:* Notes Toward a Social Type," *Journal of Jewish Studies* 50 (1999): 87–97; David Cesarani and Gemma Romain, eds., *Jews and Port Cities 1590–1990: Commerce, Community and Cosmopolitanism* (London: Vallentine Mitchell, 2006).
101. See Sergio DellaPergola, Uzi Rebhun, and Mark Tolts, "Contemporary Jewish Diaspora in Global Context: Human Development Correlates of Population Trends," *Israel Studies* 10, no. 1 (2005): 61–95; William Safran, "The Jewish Diaspora in a Comparative and Theoretical Perspective," *Israel Studies* 10, no. 1 (Spring 2005): 36–60; and Gabriel Sheffer, *Diaspora Politics: At Home Abroad* (Cambridge, England: Cambridge University Press, 2003).

PART I

JEWS AND RACE IN AMERICA

CHAPTER 1

"I'm Not White—I'm Jewish"

The Racial Politics of American Jews

Cheryl Greenberg

The election of an African American to the U.S. presidency in 2008 prompted Americans to reflect on the changing roles of race and color in the United States. Is there something about American Jews' relationship with color and race that might be instructive for scholars of race in America? Is there something about the changing roles of race and color in the United States that might be instructive for scholars of American Jews? In the United States, a nation without a history of Jewish persecution and a nation that from its inception guaranteed religious freedom, Jewish immigrants found themselves remarkably free to choose their own lifestyles. And yet they were caught in a thicket of racial definitions shaped by the historical context of slavery that did not lie comfortably within traditional Jewish self-understanding. The problematic and shifting status of Black people in the United States led to a rigid and binary structure of American race relations—the division of American society into two groups, White and Black. Yet Jews have never defined themselves in such terms. So, in the American context, the question becomes whether—and how—Ashkenazic American Jews consider themselves White people, and in what ways racialized self-understanding has shaped American Jewish history.

Jewish identity, or the way Jews understand themselves as a group, is complex and shifting, constituted by social and residential ties, friendships, community interests, a shared sense of history, and religious and cultural practices. But in the United States, at least, Jewish identity is also related to questions of race and color because both have been central in determining access to power. So I want to look, in that context, at Jewish understandings of race and color and how they interact with other factors such as religion and ethnicity, and then assess the impact they have on our understanding of Jewish history and of race in America. I begin this inquiry by addressing the question of Jewish whiteness in a nation where race largely determined destiny, a topic that leads almost inevitably to the subject of the American Jewish community's relationship with African Americans. The essay then explores changing notions of the salience of race, color, ethnicity, and religion in recent U.S. history, and concludes with some preliminary thoughts about American Jewish identity and race.

Race and Color in the American Context

When Eastern and Southern European Jews came to the United States during the tidal wave of migration from 1880 to 1920, they arrived in a nation polarized by a racial binary. In the United States a person was either Black (Negro) or White. Individuals deemed White enjoyed substantial legal, social, civic, and economic benefits not available to those considered Black. Slavery embodied this division, of course, but emancipation did not erase it, as Jim Crow segregation and racial discrimination continued to constrain non-White life chances in similar ways. It was not always clear to White Americans where immigrant groups fit within that racial schema. The Irish, for example, who arrived primarily in the mid-nineteenth century, faced substantial employment and social discrimination. Whites born in the United States could not decide whether the Irish fully qualified as White. In response, many in the Irish community took great pains to identify with whiteness, in part by espousing a racism of their own.[1] Indeed, embracing whiteness proved a popular strategy for any immigrant group that could claim that status. Natives of India or the Caribbean, Chicanos from the American Southwest, mixed-race individuals and others from groups not clearly recognized as either White or Black petitioned the courts (not always successfully) to be recognized as White people.[2] If one were considered either Black or White in the United States, early immigrants, including Jews, embraced whiteness.

Both the Jewish immigrant populations prior to the 1880s, Sephardic and German Jews, identified with the White community, for much the same reason other groups did: being seen as White paid off in the sense of both an economic and a "psychological wage," to borrow a phrase first used by W.E.B. Du Bois and popularized by David Roediger.[3] In any case, these Jews identified with the Europeans among whom they had lived, and some made their living, either directly or indirectly, from the slave trade. The only Jew prominent in the abolitionist movement was a recent immigrant, August Bondi. Rabbi David Einhorn, who preached a sermon against slavery—in Baltimore in 1861—was run out of town by his own congregation.[4] Indeed, Jews had racially assimilated so thoroughly that a Jew, Judah Benjamin, served as vice president of the Confederacy.

The large influx of new immigrants from Eastern and Southern Europe beginning at the end of the nineteenth century intensified the nativism of many Americans of Western European descent, who looked with suspicion on these allegedly swarthy newcomers. They feared what they termed the mongrelization of their nation and demanded full assimilation into Anglo-Saxon culture and norms—if indeed these were White people at all. The choice of color-specific terms was not accidental in a society where color still defined racial boundaries and therefore access to power. Increasing numbers of court cases regarding racial identification, persistent economic exclusion, and social hostility made it clear that, in the words of John Bukowczyk, these new immigrants were "not-quite-White."[5] Similar skepticism was evident even within the American Jewish community, as German Jewish organizations from social clubs to the American Jewish Committee closed ranks against their Eastern European coreligionists and called for "more polish and less Polish."[6]

Obviously these attitudes sprang, at least in part, from German Jews' fear of losing their hard-won social status by being associated with these newcomers whom other Americans often believed were either degenerates or dangerous. New and public expressions of anti-Semitism followed close on the heels of this Eastern European Jewish immigration, including restrictive quotas at many colleges and universities and the social exclusion of Jewish elites from clubs and social registers. Wealthier and more-established American Jews particularly felt the repercussions of such attitudes. The rhetoric of these German Jews suggests that race and color played a part in their attitudes toward their Eastern European coreligionists. These new immigrants were "miserable darkened Hebrews," according to the *Hebrew Standard;* a German Jewish newspaper referred to them as "wild Asiatics."[7] Color lines also hardened with the growing migration of African Americans from the rural South into northern and urban areas. The Great Migration contributed to heightened segregation in the nation's cities, the explosive growth of the Ku Klux Klan, and a number of White-on-Black race riots.[8]

In such a racist and nativist atmosphere, most of the new immigrant populations from Eastern and Southern Europe not surprisingly embraced a White identity, as others had done before them. Self-interest lay in making clear their membership in the dominant group.[9] Yet many Eastern European Jews hesitated to define themselves in the same way. While earlier German Jews had by and large understood themselves as Germans first, these newer immigrants rarely identified with the nations from which they had emigrated. They had more trouble seeing themselves as White. After all, Whites in Central and Eastern Europe had always identified them as outsiders and Jews had endured a long history of violence at their hands.

A number of these new American Jews tried to restructure contemporary notions of race and assimilation, thus challenging the binary choice between Black and White that their immigration posed. Anglo-Jewish playwright Israel Zangwill popularized the term "melting pot" in his 1908 play of that name, calling on native-born White Americans to stop insisting that immigrants give up their own identities to become, in the term of the day, "100 percent Americans." Rather, he suggested, each new group made its own unique contributions to the national culture. Advocates of a melting pot argued that rather than corrupting America, immigrants added their own spice to the American cultural mix, thereby enhancing it. Still, in the end, melting pot advocates believed immigrants would willingly and inevitably shed their cultures, their backgrounds, and their historic baggage to become fully American in this new, broader, cultural sense. Zangwill's play ends with the marriage of a Jew whose mother had been killed in a pogrom to the daughter of the Russian army officer who spearheaded the violence. In the new world, the past became unimportant. Corporations that hired immigrants also embraced this vision. Ford Motor Company's English instruction classes featured a play in which program graduates in traditional dress entered a huge mock cauldron and emerged in American suits and ties.[10]

Other critics of nativism argued for a different understanding of diversity in America. Pluralism, a term coined by Jewish sociologist Horace Kallen, rejected the image of a stew yielding a single, bland pablum. Rather, pluralism called for accepting, even celebrating, private differences among communities because they all shared the same basic American values: fairness, justice, love of family, commitment to community, and morality. The immigrants' varied cultural expressions, then, were simply different ways of saying the same thing, and posed no threat to the American way of life. Immigrant populations, pluralists explained, were "ethnic groups," a linguistic term that distinguished them from the more pernicious label of races.

Although early pluralists, including Kallen himself, were not sure where such cultural differences originated, they quickly unified around the assertion that these differences were not innate but rather learned and therefore voluntary. This neatly resolved the question of whether immigrants could be fully absorbed into American life or whether they had to be excluded as permanently inferior races. Not surprisingly, many African American thinkers such as Alain Locke embraced pluralism because it challenged prevailing notions that racial characteristics were innate—or that they even existed.[11]

The emphasis by advocates of pluralism on ethnicity rather than race, history rather than biology, and shared rather than subversive values, made little impact in the early part of the twentieth century. But within a generation it emerged as the central understanding of American culture. After Pearl Harbor, to promote wartime unity in the fight against Hitler and the Axis, armed forces propaganda films began featuring the all-American platoon of Irish, Italian, Jewish, and other soldiers—sometimes even Black and Hispanic—bonding happily in a muddy trench, fighting together for the American way. More sobering, the liberation by American forces of concentration camps exposed the genocidal slaughters that were the consequences of racially based ideologies. And the Cold War that followed made American egalitarian and antiracist rhetoric a political strategy to woo nonaligned, non-White nations. By mid-century, then, pluralism had become the dominant theory defining the ideal American civic community.

The irony of a nation embracing a pluralist vision while living a racially segregated reality was not lost on liberal and progressive scholars and activists and spurred civil rights efforts both in the streets and the academy. Journalists such as Carey McWilliams insisted Black and White Americans were "Brothers under the Skin"; the newly organized Congress on Racial Equality gave these beliefs substance in its public campaigns against segregation.[12] Pluralist theory extended into intellectual explorations of race relations as well. In his path-breaking book on slavery, *The Peculiar Institution,* historian Kenneth Stampp explained that "innately Negroes are, after all, only White men with black skins, nothing more, nothing less."[13] Stampp insisted that he was not negating the distinct cultural heritage, shaped by slavery and racism, that Black people shared. Rather, he explained, he was arguing that save for color there were no meaningful differences between racial groups.

Blacks and Jews Together?

The theories of the melting pot and pluralism both offered ways to understand and legitimate Jewish and other cultural differences without resort to racial language. But of course if Ashkenazic Jews were not considered, and did not consider themselves, fully White by race, certainly they were white by color. That is, regardless of theoretical claims of origin, most Jews' skin color resembled that of native-born Whites more than that of most African Americans. And this useful distinction between race and color, explored by Thomas Guglielmo in the case of Italians, made all the difference.[14]

Because most Jews were white by skin color, they were able to take advantage of economic and civic opportunities available only to White people in early twentieth-century America. As Oscar Lewis wrote in his memoir, *La Vida,* "I am so white that they've even taken me for a Jew, but when they see my Spanish name they back right off."[15] The white skin privilege gave Jews access to higher education, loans, and other building blocks for success. With their skills and training, they became shopkeepers, teachers, traders. They accumulated savings and moved to nicer neighborhoods.

But because Jews did not consider themselves White racially, they did not feel the need to embrace a virulent racism to demonstrate or reinforce their whiteness. While Jews absorbed the racism of the culture that surrounded them, many were more willing than most White Americans to serve Black clients and maintain stores in Black communities. As marginal business operators, Jews also seized available opportunities to establish entrepreneurial niches. Because many White people avoided jobs that required working among African Americans, Black communities provided one such niche.[16] Ashkenazic Jews therefore engaged with Blacks far more readily than most Whites, although given their economic disparity, these encounters were almost exclusively hierarchical with Jews as patrons, property owners, or employers, and African Americans as clients, tenants, or employees. This inevitably created class-based resentments that too often were translated into anti-Semitism in the Black community, or heard as anti-Semitism in the Jewish community. Jews tended to be less racist and more willing to interact with Black people, but their relations with Blacks were often more strained as a result.[17]

Jews were not the only ones who believed they were not racially White. White anti-Semites continued to treat them as standing outside the circle of privileged whiteness. As a result, many Jews came, albeit hesitantly, to identify with African Americans' plight as a despised minority. Sometimes recognizing their shared vulnerability led Jews to minimize their own risk by avoiding, as one Jewish community leader put it, "tying ourselves up with another minority group ... whose difficulties ... are even more deplorable than our own."[18] Over time, however, especially after the Holocaust, more Jews concluded that, as fellow victims, they had a stake in fighting for full equality for all. "The Klan is a threat today," read one Anti-Defamation League pamphlet from 1941. Although the Klan was then targeting only African Americans, Jews must nevertheless fight it because "when any minority race or faith is attacked, other minorities inevitably become the targets of hate."[19] In other words, the real threat came from not recognizing the universality of the struggle for equality and security. If one group could be discriminated against, Jews understood this would give license to anti-Semites to do the same to them.

African Americans also felt a sense of kinship with Jews. African American history was replete with metaphors of slaves as Jews and of emancipation as the arrival of the Israelites into the Promised Land. Some Black Christians may have absorbed anti-Semitic attitudes circulating in certain American Christian circles. This sense of identity with biblical Jews, however, made African Americans more open to engaging with Jews they encountered in their daily lives. Black–Jewish engagement, then, was mutual—a subject crucial to any understanding of Black-Jewish relations, but only of tangential significance to our discussion here, which focuses only on reasons for American Jewish involvement with Black civil rights.

The historical reality that these Jews were white by color, even when they were not fully understood as being White by race, helps explain what otherwise would appear to be contradictions in the historical record. By the middle of the twentieth century, Jews increasingly identified themselves as allies in the struggle for Black equality and took pride in making up the largest population of non-Black participants in the civil rights movement. African American activists and leaders embraced such staunch colleagues and supported Jewish causes in their turn. At the same time, however, many of the direct engagements between Blacks and Jews were patently unequal, sometimes even exploitative. From the perspective of the Black community, Jewish store owners who charged high prices, Jewish housewives overworking Black domestics, Jewish impresarios profiting from Black talent, were White, or no better than other Whites. For Jews, the distinction between race and color allowed them to align themselves with the Black freedom struggle and deny any identification with the White race, all the while benefiting from the privileges granted those whose color was white. It helps explain how Jews were able to proclaim race blindness and trust in merit, yet fail to recognize the power of White privilege and structural inequality.[20]

The overlapping yet distinct categories of race and color also help explain the decline of Black-Jewish cooperation by the mid-1970s. With the rise of Black Power and the increasing nationalism of the Black struggle, many Black activists rejected Whites, including their White allies. Most Jews, who, after all, constituted a disproportionate number of those movement allies, interpreted it rather as anti-Semitism (which was occasionally the case, given the presence of anti-Semitism in the African American community, or racism in the Jewish community).

More fundamentally, because most American Jews were Ashkenazim and therefore apparently white by skin color, they by and large accepted without adequate interrogation the basic system that had admitted them. They often did not recognize the structural difference that color still made to opportunity in America. The souring of relations between Blacks and Jews, in other words, occurred not only because African Americans saw Jews as White, but also because Jews responded as Whites to threats to the social order. Jews were more White than they knew.

Multiculturalism, one result of these debates over the nature of race and social structures, largely replaced pluralism in the popular imagination in the last quarter of the twentieth century. Often likened to a salad bowl, the multicultural model valorized minority cultures but reasserted the impermeability of these structural racial boundaries. In this way, multicultural models reified race once again, coming close to a racial essentialism that scientists and pluralist scholars had rejected. With multicultural divisions based largely on skin color, multiculturalists generally placed Jews within the category of European American whiteness. Jews, generally uncomfortable with the salad-bowl approach in which cultures comingled yet never affected one another, and dismayed to find themselves lumped together with European groups that despised them, felt like both insiders and outsiders, both critical of multiculturalism's insistence on apparently permanent racial distinctions and excluded from the pantheon of celebrated cultures.[21] The contradictions between race and color had not been erased.

Ethnicity and Religion: A Way Out?

While the debates over race raged in both civil society and intellectual circles, Jews as a group held tightly to pluralism, seeking to find ways to fit into the ever-shifting understanding of American culture without reference to race. Despite the pressures of 1950s conformity or late 1960s ethnic chauvinism, neither complete assimilation nor an isolationist nationalism that called for severing ties to the larger community attracted many. Rather, Jews sought ways to acculturate effectively enough to become full members of American society while maintaining as many of their own cultural practices and beliefs as they wished. The extent of cultural retention varied, of course, yet none but the Hasidic communities from Eastern Europe sought total cultural segregation, and relatively few sought the path of intermarriage or conversion.[22] A majority, however, sought to maintain the social and residential proximity that had enhanced a sense of Jewish identity in earlier years, from immigrant ghettos to the suburban "gilded ghettos" of the next, more successful generations. They established not only synagogues, but also Jewish community centers, social clubs, political organizations, and the like to keep younger Jews connected.[23] But how could this desire for social self-segregation be understood in the more open American context? Because pluralist American Jews could not plausibly defend their desire to maintain a sense of community by identifying as a separate race, they instead followed American trends regarding religion and ethnicity to stake their claim.

During the 1940s and 1950s, American public discourse sought to heighten the contrast with communist regimes by emphasizing the importance of religious faith. The deep insecurities of the atomic age sharpened the perceived need for divine guidance and assurance that America's path was the correct one. Maintenance of religious practices was therefore deemed both important and legitimate. It was in this era that the phrase "under God" was placed into the Pledge of Allegiance, a God clearly understood to be of the Judeo-Christian sort. At the same time, placing too much emphasis on ethnic differences could itself threaten an American social stability. Both the Holocaust and the increasing visibility of the struggle for racial equality made ethnic heritage an illegitimate and dangerous ground for distinction.

While refusing to marry outside one's ethnic group was seen as narrow or bigoted, few objected to seeking a spouse of the same religion. In such a case, it made sense for Jews to describe themselves not as a racial or ethnic group, but as a religious community. Religions could legitimately stay separate but still deserve full civic equality. Think of Will Herberg's *Protestant, Catholic, Jew,* published in 1955, in which he suggested that American society was best understood not as a single melting pot, but rather as three religious melting pots, each of which had its own hierarchies and structures.[24]

The same commitment to defining Judaism as a religion underlay arguments made in the Jewish community for support of Black civil rights. Judaism teaches us that we were strangers in the land of Egypt, as the rabbis preached and Jewish institutions emphasized, therefore we are particularly admonished to care for those who are downtrodden and excluded.[25] While such teachings are indeed in the Torah, the Hebrew prophets' compelling call to social justice cannot explain Judah Benjamin's support of slavery in the South, or why American Jews had only recently turned to issues of universal human rights. Nor can a Jewish religious tradition of social justice explain the later falling-out between Jewish and African Americans on a number of highly publicized political issues, such as affirmative action. Furthermore, using religious teachings to explain the disproportionate Jewish presence in the civil rights movement would give the false impression that Christianity lacked comparable arguments for justice and egalitarian practice.

Rather, emphasizing Judaism's call for universal justice to defend Jews' commitment to Black civil rights was historical and contingent. Redefining their Jewish identity as rooted in ethics more than ritual helped American Jews solve two challenges simultaneously. Many Jewish immigrants—or more typically their children—understood that ritual practices such as *kashrut* (dietary law observance) or strict Sabbath observance interfered with the process of social integration. How to balance the maintenance of Jewish identity with a commitment to full engagement in the larger world? And how to demonstrate Jews' commitment to American values while maintaining ties to their separate community? If Judaism was at its root a call to ethics, one could remain Jewish without so many restrictive rituals. At the same time, this understanding of Judaism provided a means to endorse the American commitment to a universalist pluralism through Jews' own particularism. One was a good American *because* one was a Jew. Jews could safely remain separate as a religious group; it was far harder to defend community borders on the ground of ethnic heritage.

In the 1960s, however, ecumenism challenged religious separatism and it became more difficult to legitimate religion as a reasonable justification for exclusivity. At the same time, thanks largely to the civil rights movement, ethnicity became a matter of pride. This produced a broad cultural shift toward an embrace of ethnic identity: Black is Beautiful, ethnic is in. Now it was acceptable to take pride in one's heritage, and to be public about it. "Kiss me, I'm Irish," read a popular button seen on St. Patrick's Day. Ethnic pride was especially powerful for Jews after the remarkable Israeli victory in the Six-Day War. This renewed muscular Jewishness, enhanced by solidarity with Israel, was understood primarily in ethnic rather than religious terms by Jewish and non-Jewish Americans alike.

By the 1970s, then, American Jews had largely shifted their self-description from a religious community to an ethnic one. Now only ethnic identity could legitimate their maintenance of separate communal structures while demanding full acceptance into the broader society. This ethnic identity was more visible among the more numerous Ashkenazic Jews, but the smaller number of American Sephardic and Mizrakhi Jews, too, embraced their distinct ethnic heritages. The heightened awareness and valorization of ethnic distinctiveness helps explain why Jews have embraced as well as resisted multiculturalism. More recently, however, race has reentered the debate. Not only do most multicultural approaches reify race as an inescapable category with deep social ramifications, but also the allegations of identity politics have made such affiliations public. The widespread assumption that people act politically, based on their race, sex, or sexual identity makes biological difference a predictor of individual activity.[26] In such an atmosphere, I suggest many American Jews are returning to a self-definition that includes race. American Jews have identified themselves differently at different times, while holding fast to the same goal: maintaining their distinct community while protecting their open access to all America has to offer. American Jews have always navigated uneasily between religion and ethnicity, race and color. They have never existed comfortably within America's binaries.

American Jews and Race

The fact that American Jews straddle many boundaries offers insights into broader questions about how Americans understand themselves as both united and diverse. These border skirmishes also provide hints about the nature of Jewish self-conception in contemporary America, because the nature of American Jewish identity today remains strikingly complex and fluid: sometimes understood primarily as a religion and sometimes primarily as an ethnic group, in some aspects shaped by race and in others shaped by color.[27] Let's examine each binary in turn.

On the one hand, the emphasis of most of the organized American Jewish community today, from local Jewish Community Relations Councils to national Jewish organizations, is on Judaism as a religion, and I would argue that this is true also of many American Jews themselves, particularly those outside the large cities. Much of Jewish political and organizational life operates through and around congregations rather than, say, the Yiddish theater or *landsmanschaften* frequented by the immigrant generation, or secular Jewish cultural groups of today. The oft-expressed warning from pulpits and Jewish community leaders that intermarriage is a threat to a Jewish future makes most sense if understood in a context of religious practice, and the many congregational, community, and campus programs addressing what they have called "continuity" since the National Jewish Population Survey of 2000 demonstrated the broad-based concern felt in the American Jewish community. Yet an estimated half of all self-identified American Jews do not affiliate with synagogues or conduct any, or many, religious rituals. They presumably consider themselves Jewish in some ethnic or cultural sense. What can "kosher style" possibly mean other than affinity with an ethnic group?

Regarding the question of race and color, Jews still reflect Guglielmo's useful distinction between phenotype (skin color) and political concepts of race as biological ancestry. Most American Jews today still do not consider themselves Whites, whereas their economic and political status and their high rate of intermarriage with non-Jewish Whites all reveal that they quite clearly are. As Bible Raps, a Jewish rap group that performed at my suburban synagogue a few years ago insisted,

> I'm not White, I'm Jewish.
> I'm not White, I'm Jewish.[28]

How can we understand this assertion? Phenotypically, the way that is relevant for opportunity in America, most Jews are regarded as White. Some Black Jews have reported ignorant or unwelcoming comments from White Jews and say it is sometimes easier to be Jewish in the Black community than to be Black in the American Jewish community.[29] Jewish racism comes from Jewish whiteness in the sense that there are American Jews who apparently do see themselves as members of a racial group—in the bad, racist sense—even if they do not admit it. Yet, given the distinction between color and putatively biological race, the rappers are not altogether wrong. Emotionally, historically, in the ways that are most relevant in the shaping of identity, Jews have never considered themselves White. Nor do they consider themselves Black, or a subset of any other racial group. This does not mean Jews have rejected the idea of race. Rather, I would argue, in some inchoate and generally unexamined way, most American Jews have understood themselves as a separate race (although they may not use that language) without being a separate color. More research needs to be done on this question of American Jewish conceptions of race; my thoughts are entirely speculative and are offered as issues to ponder, or as potential new directions for research, rather than as definitive arguments.

Regardless of whether European American Jews see themselves as primarily an ethnic or a religious group, I suggest that much of their identity as Jews is actually predicated on older notions of race, in the sense of biology or ancestry—not color, but still biology. In other words, while scholars understand that race is a social construct, the product of a history of power distinctions based on presumed (but false) biological differences, there is evidence to suggest that most Jews actually seem to hold the more traditional view that race exists as a biological fact. Races, as a biological definition, are discrete populations within which the range of genetic diversity varies less than the range between that group and others. By this definition, one can plausibly divide human beings by thousands of characteristics (e.g., height), virtually none of which correspond to traditional understandings of racial divisions. Furthermore, thanks to continual intermixing of populations and because genetic variations such as melanin content (determinants of skin color) are not discrete but rather occur along a continuum, most scientists concur that race in the traditional sense as a grouping by color is not a meaningful biological concept.[30]

Jewish law itself places significance on biology, arising from the fundamental understanding that God made a covenant with Abraham and designated Jacob's descendants to be His people, a people apart. This covenant is biological in the sense it is inherited through the lineage of Jacob. Certainly outsiders may join this community, yet doing so requires severing existing biological kinship and establishing a new lineage within the Jewish people. If not born to a Jewish woman, a person who wishes to be Jewish must have a ceremonial rebirth in a ritual bath (*mikvah*). When called to the Torah or other ritual duty they are referred to as "son (daughter) of Abraham (Sarah)." Even Reform Jews, who have expanded the notion of who is a Jew from those born of a Jewish mother to those born of a Jewish parent of either sex, still focus on the question of biology. DNA, but not adoption, is still an automatic "in" to membership in the Jewish community; adopted children must still go through the ritual of conversion. Being raised by Jews, culturally and religiously, is not enough, even for this liberal Jewish religious branch.[31] Religious Jewish membership is even more biologically driven than American citizenship, which is granted automatically not only to those with an American parent, but also to anyone born on American soil. In that sense, American Jews not only see themselves as a separate people, but also see that separateness as essentially biological, and therefore problematic in an American political discourse that is based on egalitarianism and antiracism.

I would go further—and here I speak only from what I have seen in my own engagement with American Jewish congregations and communal organizations—and suggest that, in the United States at least, these biological convictions also permeate more secular aspects of Jewish self-understanding. The signs are all over American Jewish popular culture, from, "funny he doesn't look Jewish" to identifying Jews as "the Tribe." Even among educated Jews, regardless of level of religious observance, a surprisingly large number believe that Jews are intellectually superior, and that this superiority is genetic.[32] Such sentiments are meant benignly and in a spirit of pride. But they should also be cause for concern: they are elitist and reflect a racial essentialism that Jews, more than most other groups, know can be lethal. After all, if we have superior genes, then some other group has inferior genes. And that leads down a path no rational person would wish to take.

Race in Contemporary America

If these assertions about the importance of biology or race to American Jewish identity are true, does it have any relevance for the understanding of race in America? If the Jewish conception of race is a relatively benign one—that is, a generalized self-satisfaction and sense of pride—then it may offer a model for African Americans. While older forms of segregation were imposed by the White community in order to maintain their own hegemony, some forms of racial separation now prevalent in our society appear to be driven at least in part by desires of many within the Black community. In recent years, calls for all-Black, Afrocentric public schools, opposition to transracial adoptions, lamentations about interracial dating, criticism of Whites moving into traditionally Black neighborhoods like Harlem, and the shift in litigation from racial integration of schools to resource equality across predominantly White and predominantly non-White schools have come more often from African American than White activists and organizations.[33] (This is not to erase or excuse continued racial discrimination by White people and institutions that remain a dreadful reality in a "postracial" American society.) That is, while calls for racial separateness in certain facets of American life remain, the reasons for them have changed. If race is best understood as an encapsulation of historical experiences and cultural traditions shared by a group of common descent, then race and not racism underlies the current desire of many African Americans to remain separate. Even if the calls for separation sound a great deal like racist arguments of previous years, one could argue they are actually motivated by a different agenda entirely. This may well be a new articulation of race for African Americans, one that is seen as a legitimate reason for segregation, in contrast to older, more pernicious reasons for it.

American Jews, however, have long made such a benignly racial argument, insisting that it is desirable and appropriate to advocate for exclusively Jewish social and cultural institutions, to oppose intermarriage with non-Jews, to live in their own neighborhoods if they choose. They believe such interests and desires are legitimate because Jews are different in some fundamental, meaningful way—although not, they insist, in a negative way. Jews must be permitted to separate themselves, but they may not legitimately be separated by others. This is the position of groups like the Anti-Defamation League, which opposes any attempt by external forces to compel segregation or exclusion but does not oppose, for example, voluntary decisions by Hasidic or Amish communities to live together. In that sense, one can argue that Jews have led the way to a newer understanding of race in America. Just as Jews have been cosmopolitan, hybrid, and global long before others took up the call, so too have American Jews led the way in defining race as a positive rather than a negative reason for community.

Understanding American Jewish conceptions of race would also change historians' sense of how American Jews have seen themselves. One interpretation of current expressions of biologically based identity is that while Jews' sense of community remained the same, their understanding and articulation of it has changed over time. Jews in every period have sought a justification for group cohesion that works within the society in which they live; this has been as true in the United States as it has elsewhere in the Jewish Diaspora. By this reasoning, American Jews have always believed they were distinct, but had to defend that belief in terms acceptable to the broader community of the time. Implying that Jews are in some sense biologically set apart would not be tenable in a culture that uses biology to allocate opportunity, so until the 1960s American Jews argued instead on the basis of religion or ethnicity.

Since the civil rights movement, however, American culture has changed. A Black pride movement emphasized the formation of a positive racial identity, a reinterpretation of African American experience rooted in historically enforced biological distinctions. Multiculturalism validated this transformation of biologically transmitted difference from an unacceptable justification by those in power to exclude others into a reasonable justification by those out of power to be exclusive. If such a reinterpretation of biology as a politically useful strategy for group cohesion is valid, it could explain the changing notions of Jewish identity from religious to ethnic and back again over the course of the twentieth century. It would also explain why Jews might now feel freer to make more openly biological and particularistic arguments. Jews, like other groups, define themselves according to what the society can bear.

American society and multicultural materials both primarily focus on what divides rather than what unifies groups. In such a context, how can Jews best describe themselves? They identify as neither White nor Black, neither oppressor nor oppressed. Perhaps a racialized Jewish identity serves as that marker, a way to ensure that Jewishness is asserted in these non-Jewish spaces. On the other hand, perhaps Jews have been arguing all along for a racialized understanding of identity that others have only now come to. While framed in the past in terms of a religious covenant, a commitment to the Jews lost in the Holocaust, or the ever-present threat of anti-Semitism, perhaps at its root American Jewish understanding of identity has always been biological in nature, the notion of race without the related notion of color. Such a durable understanding would fit well with what we know of twentieth-century American Jewish history, particularly Jews' commitment to civil rights despite their enjoyment of White privilege, their support of Black equality alongside expressions of racism that sounded a lot like those of many Whites.

But can claims of race ever be truly benign? As I suggested above, there also is a more pernicious side to this concept of Jews as a race. If the root of American Jewish identity is biology, then does this not reify biological claims that biologists and scholars of race have been combating for so long? Does it not potentially reinforce the negative aspects of race—that is, might it not potentially legitimate the use of race as a force for exclusion or discrimination by those with the power to do so? It is important that we consider what the implications of a positively described biological or racial identity are—for American society and for American Jews. Or to put it in more traditional terms my grandparents would understand: Is it good for the Jews or bad for the Jews?

Notes

1. See, e.g., David Roediger, *Wages of Whiteness*, rev. ed. (New York: Verso, 1999); Noel Ignatiev, *How the Irish Became White* (New York: Routledge, 1995).

2. There were more than fifty such cases between 1878 and 1952, when racial restrictions were lifted from immigration statutes. For more on the subject, see Ian Haney Lopez, *White by Law* (New York: New York University Press, 1996; reprint 2000); Teresa Zackodnik, "Fixing the Color Line" *American Quarterly* 53, no. 3 (September 2001): 420–451; Richard Delgado and Jean Stefancic, eds., *Critical Race Theory: The Cutting-Edge,* 2nd ed. (Philadelphia: Temple University Press, 2000).
3. Roediger, *Wages of Whiteness,* 12; W. E. B. Du Bois, *Black Reconstruction in America* (New York: Harcourt, Brace, 1935), 700–701.
4. For more on Jews and abolition, including Bondi and Einhorn, see Peter Hinks, John McKivigan, and R. Owen Williams, eds., *Encyclopedia of Antislavery and Abolition* (Westport, CT: Greenwood, 2007), 38; Bennett Muraskin, *Let Justice Well Up Like Water* (New York: Cong. of Secular Jewish Orgs,. 2004), 29–32.
5. John Bukowczyk, *A History of the Polish Americans,* 2nd reprint ed. (New Brunswick, NJ: Transaction Press, 2008). Roediger, in *Toward the Abolition of Whiteness* (New York: Verso, 1994), 184, altered the phrase to "not-yet-White," which has a slightly different meaning. There is a large and growing literature on whiteness. Some of the best, especially regarding Jews and whiteness, include Jacobson, *Whiteness of a Different Color;* Brodkin, *How Jews Became White Folks;* Goldstein, *Price of Whiteness;* David Roediger, *Working toward Whiteness: How America's Immigrants Became White* (New York: Basic Books, 2005); Melnick, *A Right to Sing the Blues,* 1999; George Lipsitz, *The Possessive Investment in Whiteness* (Philadelphia: Temple University Press, 2006); Ruth Frankenberg, *White Women, Race Matters* (Minneapolis: University of Minnesota Press, 1993); Michael Rogin, *Blackface, White Noise* (Berkeley: University of California Press, 1996); Thomas Guglielmo, *White on Arrival* (New York: Oxford University Press, 2004). Also see James Barrett and David Roediger, "Inbetween Peoples," *Journal of American Ethnic History* 16, no. 3 (1997): 3–45.
6. There are many studies of late-nineteenth-century Jewish American history: see Gerald Sorin, *A Time for Building* (Baltimore: Johns Hopkins University Press, 1992), especially 51, 68.
7. On "darkened" and "Asiatics," see Cheryl Greenberg, *Troubling the Waters* (Princeton, NJ: Princeton University Press, 2006), 33.
8. On the Great Migration and its impact on racial attitudes and violence see, e.g., James Grossman, *Land of Hope* (Chicago: University of Chicago Press, 1989); Arnold Hirsch, *Making the Second Ghetto* (Chicago: University of Chicago Press, 1983); William Tuttle, *Race Riot* (1970; republished Urbana: University of Illinois Press, 1996); Nicholas Lemann, *The Promised Land* (New York: Knopf, 1991); *The Great Migration in Historical Perspective,* ed. Joseph Trotter, Jr. (Bloomington: Indiana University Press, 1991); W. Fitzhugh Brundage, *Lynching in the New South* (Urbana: University of Illinois Press, 1993).
9. See note 5 for recent books on early twentieth-century immigration and whiteness in America that have in many ways defined the field.
10. Israel Zangwill, "The Melting Pot" (1908), in *From the Ghetto to the Melting Pot: Israel Zangwill's Jewish Plays,* ed. Edna Nahshon (Detroit, MI: Wayne State University Press, 2005), 265–364; Jeffrey Mirel, *Patriotic Pluralism* (Cambridge, MA: Harvard University Press, 2010), 82; Philip Gleason's *Speaking of Diver-*

sity (Baltimore: Johns Hopkins University Press, 1992), esp. chaps. 1, 2; John Higham, *Send These to Me* (1975; rev. ed., Baltimore: Johns Hopkins University Press, 1984), chap. 9; Milton Gordon, *Assimilation in American Life* (New York: Oxford University Press, 1964), 88–114.

11. Horace Kallen, *Culture and Democracy in the United States* (New York: Boni and Liveright, 1924); Kallen, *Cultural Pluralism and the American Idea* (Philadelphia: University of Pennsylvania Press, 1956); Alain Locke, "The Legacy of the Ancestral Arts," in *The New Negro,* ed. Alain Locke (New York, 1925); Locke, "The Concept of Race as Applied to Social Culture," in *The Philosophy of Alain Locke,* ed. Leonard Harris (Philadelphia: Temple University Press, 1989) ; Johnny Washington, *Alain Locke and Philosophy* (Westport, CT: Greenwood Press, 1986). For more on pluralism, see Gleason, *Speaking of Diversity,* esp. chaps. 3 and 6; Werner Sollors, "A Critique of Pure Pluralism," in *Reconstructing American Literary History,* ed. Sacvan Bercovich (Cambridge, MA: Harvard University Press, 1986), 250–279; Higham, *Send These to Me* and Higham, *Hanging Together* (New Haven, CT: Yale University Press, 2001); Gordon, *Assimilation in American Life;* Stanford Lyman, *Color, Culture, Civilization* (Urbana: University of Illinois Press, 1995); Daniel Greene, *The Jewish Origin of Cultural Pluralism* (Bloomington: University of Indiana Press, 2011). In its own way, ethnic theory reified racial ideas as well as challenged them, by redrawing the line of race from within the European continent to outside it; see on this Michael Omi and Howard Winant, "Racial Formations," in *The Social Construction of Difference and Inequality,* ed. Tracy Ore (New York: McGraw Hill, 2003), 23.
12. Carey McWilliams, *Brothers under the Skin* (Boston: Little, Brown, 1943). For more on Congress on Racial Equality (CORE), see August Meier and Elliott Rudwick, *CORE* (Urbana: University of Illinois Press, 1973); this is still the most thorough exploration of the organization's early history.
13. Kenneth Stampp, *The Peculiar Institution* (New York: Vintage Books, 1956), viii. Many later historians, while accepting his explanation, still point out that this negation of race occurred at just the moment that an intentional racial consciousness was emerging among Black people in the United States, and thus contributed to an erasure of identity.
14. Guglielmo, *White on Arrival.* See note 5 and Greenberg, *Troubling the Waters,* for more on the discussion that follows regarding the ambiguous nature of American Jewish whiteness in terms of color and race.
15. Oscar Lewis, *La Vida* (New York: Random House, 1966), 180–181.
16. For a closer look at Jewish entrepreneurial niches in one community, see Ewa Morawska, *Insecure Prosperity* (Princeton, NJ: Princeton University Press, 1996).
17. Economic tensions plagued Black-Jewish relations throughout their long collaboration on civil rights, a point emphasized by most scholars of Black–Jewish relations from Melnick, in *A Right to Sing the Blues,* to Herbert Hill, "Black–Jewish Conflict in the Labor Context," *Race Traitor* 5 (Winter 1996): 72–103. James Baldwin made the same point in "The Harlem Ghetto: Winter 1948," *Commentary* 5, no. 2 (February 1948): 165–70. See also Greenberg, *Troubling the Waters.*

18. Philip Frankel, Anti-Defamation League, to Richard Gutstadt, September 2, 1943, Anti-Defamation League Microfilm: "Yellows 1943, Negro Race Problems," Anti-Defamation League Archives, New York.
19. "The Klan Is a Threat Today," Anti-Defamation League pamphlet, 1941, American Jewish Committee vertical files: "Anti-Semitism: ADL," AJC library, New York. For more on this, see Greenberg, *Troubling the Waters.*
20. See, e.g., Bernard Rosenberg and Irving Howe, "Are American Jews Turning to the Right?" *Dissent* (Winter 1974): 30–45; Leonard Fein, "Thinking about Quotas," *Midstream* 19, no. 3 (March 1973): 13–17; Nathan Glazer, "Negroes and Jews: the New Challenge to Pluralism," *Commentary* (December 1964): 29–34; Stephen Whitfield, "The 'Bourgeois' Humanism of American Jews," *Judaism* 29, no. 2 (Spring 1980): 160–66; Arnold Wolf, "Remarks," in (and responding to) Fein, *The Negro Revolution and the Jewish Community* (New York: Synagogue Council of America, 1969), 22–24; Eli Ginzberg, "The Black Revolution and the Jew," *Conservative Judaism* (Fall 1969): 3–19; Ben Wattenberg and Richard Scammon, "Black Progress and Liberal Rhetoric," *Commentary* (April 1973): 43–44; Greenberg, *Troubling the Waters,* 236–242.
21. Biale, Galchinsky, and Heschel, eds., *Insider/Outsider.* Also see David Theo Goldberg, ed., *Multiculturalism: A Critical Reader* (Cambridge, MA: Harvard University Press, 1994).
22. The rate of intermarriage has accelerated in the past generation and now approaches 50 percent, but even in these cases there are no definitive studies of how many of these families have abandoned all Jewish practice. National Jewish population studies have been conducted in 1971, 1990, and 2000. The most recent, "National Jewish Population Survey 2000–2001," by United Jewish Communities, was released in October 2002, and is available online through the North American Jewish Data Bank, http://www.jewishdatabank.org/national.asp. Also see Barry Kosmin and Seymour Lachman, *One Nation Under God* (New York: Harmony Books 1993); and Barry Kosmin and Ariela Keysar, *Religion in a Free Market* (Ithaca, NY: Paramount Publishing, 2006), both of which interpret the findings of ARIS (American Religious Identification Survey) studies. See also Egon Mayer, Barry Kosmin, and Ariela Keysar, eds., *American Jewish Identity Survey* (New York: Center for Cultural Judaism, 2003).
23. See, e.g., Jeffrey Gurock, "The Depth of Ethnicity: Jewish Identity and Ideology in Interwar New York City," *American Jewish Archives Journal* 61, no. 3 (2009): 145–161; Deborah Dash Moore, *At Home in America* (New York: Columbia University Press, 1981); Judith Kramer and Seymour Leventman, *Children of the Gilded Ghetto* (New Haven, CT: Yale University Press, 1961).
24. Will Herberg, *Protestant, Catholic, Jew* (Garden City, NY: Doubleday, 1955).
25. The number of articles in Jewish journals and magazines, "race relations" sermons both published and preached, synagogue civil rights programs, pamphlets written and directives sent from Jewish religious and political agencies on this point since the 1940s is remarkable. See, e.g., Greenberg, *Troubling the Waters,* 114–168; Lynn Landsberg and David Saperstein, eds., *Common Road to Justice* (Washington, DC: Religious Action Center for Reform Judaism, 1991); Henry Cohen, *Justice, Justice* (New York: Union of American Hebrew Congre-

gations, 1968); and Marc Schneier's unabashedly celebratory *Shared Dreams* (Woodstock, VT: Jewish Lights, 1999).

26. To cite one recent example, the decision of many Connecticut Jewish Democrats to support their own party's non-Jewish candidate Ned Lamont over independent Jewish candidate Joseph Lieberman was apparently so striking and unexpected that the *Hartford Courant* ran stories about it, e.g., Leonard Felson, "Joe and the Jewish Vote," *Hartford Courant,* October 1, 2006.
27. See, e.g., Deborah Dash Moore, ed., *American Jewish Identity Politics* (Ann Arbor: University of Michigan Press, 2008).
28. The Bible Raps Project, a Jewish educational outreach band, performs around the United States and has a number of albums; see http://www.bibleraps.com. See the discussion on hip-hop in the introduction to the present volume.
29. Excluding communities identifying as Black Jews or Black Israelites (see chapter 7 and note 31. On views of African American Jews, see autobiographical works, including Hettie Jones, *How I Became Hettie Jones* (New York: E. P. Dutton, 1990); Azoulay, *Black, Jewish and Interracial*; Lise Funderburg, *Black, White, Other: Biracial Americans Talk about Race and Identity* (New York: W. Morrow, 1994); Rebecca Walker, *Black, White and Jewish: Autobiography of a Shifting Self* (New York: Riverhead, 2001); Yelena Khanga, *Soul to Soul: A Black Russian Jewish Woman's Search for Her Roots* (New York: Norton, 1994); Julius Lester, *Lovesong: Becoming a Jew* (New York: Bullfinch Press, 1988). Also see Trymaine Lee, "Black and Jewish and Seeing No Contradiction," *New York Times,* August 27, 1910. An entire 2011 issue of *Transition,* No. 105 ("Blacks, Jews and Black Jews"), is devoted to this topic. There is also a growing scholarly literature on African American Jews, both those who consider themselves full members of an interracial and international Jewish community, and those who define themselves as a separate group. Also see, e.g., A. Paul Hare, ed., *The Hebrew Israelite Community* (New York: University Press of America, 1999); Yosef ben-Jochannan, *We the Black Jews* (Baltimore: Black Classic Press, 1983); Janice Fernheimer, *Arguing Black Jewish Identity: Hatzaad Harishon and Interruptive Invention* (Birmingham, AL: University of Alabama Press, 2013); Yvonne Patricia Chireau and Nathaniel Deutsch, *Black Zion: African American Religious Encounters with Judaism* (New York: Oxford University Press, 2000); Marla Brettschneider, *The Family Flamboyant* (Albany, NY: State University of New York Press, 2006); Tudor Parfitt and Emanuela Trevisan Semi, *Judaizing Movements: Studies in the Margins of Judaism* (London and New York: RoutledgeCurzon, 2002).
30. For a fuller discussion, see American Anthropological Association, "Statement on Race," adopted May 17, 1998; Omi and Winant, "Racial Formations," 19–29; and their book-length treatment of the subject, *Racial Formation in the United States from the 1960s to the 1990s,* 2nd ed. (New York: Routledge, 1994). Many (if not most) claims about biological race go further, linking specific skills, temperaments, or abilities with these putative genetic variations. See, e.g., Richard Hernstein and Charles Murray, *The Bell Curve* (New York: Free Press, 1994). Gilman, *Smart Jews* also discusses such biological linkages regarding Jews.
31. "The Status of Children of Mixed Marriages," Report of the Committee on Patrilineal Dissent, adopted by the Central Conference of American Rabbis

March 15, 1983. Many communities of Black Jews or Black Israelites emphasize their own racial ties to Judaism (I refer here to communities of practicing Jews, not those Black groups who do not practice Judaism but rather espouse various anti-Semitic positions.) See note 29 and Zev Chafets, "Obama's Rabbi," *New York Times,* April 2, 2009.

32. Sander L. Gilman has traced beliefs held by both Jews and non-Jews that Jewish difference is biological in *Smart Jews.* Hernstein and Murray, in *Bell Curve,* also briefly discuss groups on the high end of their putatively biological curve, including Jews. A number of those intermarried Jews interviewed by researchers espouse biological positions, e.g., "You do the traditions because that's what you are, not because of what you believe," quoted in Jennifer Thompson, "'What You Are' or 'What's in Your Heart,'" unpublished paper presented at the American Jewish Studies Annual Meeting, Washington, DC, 2008. See Gilman's foreword to the present volume.

33. Regarding Black attitudes toward intermarriage, see, e.g., Erica Childs, "What's Class Got to Do with It?"; and Jenifer Bratter, "The 'One Drop' Rule through a Multi-Racial Lens," both in *Multiracial Americans and Social Class,* ed. Kathleen Korgen (New York: Routledge, 2010), 22–29, 184–202. Regarding school integration, see, e.g., John Brittain, the lead counsel for *Sheff v O'Neill,* the 1996 CT Supreme Court case challenging racial segregation in schools, later withdrew in part because he came to believe it was racist to argue that Black children could learn better only when seated beside White children. At least one Black Hartford School Board member agreed. See Stan Simpson, "A Decade of Half Measures," *Hartford Courant,* July 23, 2006; Rachel Frank, "A Shift of Views on *Sheff,*" *Hartford Courant,* November 5, 2007. For the fierce debates over the creation of a Black (and all-male) Afrocentric public school in Detroit, see Sonia Jarvis, "*Brown* and the Afrocentric Curriculum," *Yale Law Journal* 101, no. 6 (April 1992); Carolyn Talbert-Johnson, "The Political Context of School Desegregation," *Education and Urban Society* 33, no. 1 (November 2000): 8–16. On opposition to transracial adoption, see National Association of Black Social Workers, "Preserving African American Families," affirmed in 1994 and subsequently reaffirmed several times. Regarding Harlem, see Timothy Williams, "In an Evolving Harlem, Newcomers Try to Fit In," *New York Times,* September 6, 2008.

CHAPTER 2

"The Stolen Garment"

Historical Reflections on Blacks and Jews in the Time of Obama

Ibrahim Sundiata

They have stolen our garment.
Conrad Muhammad

Barack Obama, elected forty-fourth president of the United States in 2008, may well be the beneficiary of an ongoing African American–Jewish alliance. One of the president's Chicago supporters hyperbolically exclaimed, "Jews made him. Wherever you look there is a Jewish presence."[1] Another supporter, Rabbi Arnold Jacob Wolf, who died in 2010, believed the president is "embedded in the Jewish world."[2] This may be exaggerated, but it is undeniable that Obama has long had a coterie of Jewish friends and associates. More significantly, in 2008, 78 percent of Jews voted for Obama as compared with 43 percent of the White vote in general.[3] Four years later, however, the percentage of the Jewish vote for Obama had slipped to 69 percent.[4]

Nevertheless, it would be disingenuous to argue that no dissonances have crept into the Black-Jewish relationship since the 1960s. Today, lingering mistrust remains, not so much over changing neighborhoods or the abuse of domestic workers, but rather over historical space. A nagging question is how to square African American and Jewish narratives of suffering. When this question is globalized, it can be perceived as an issue of Western imperialism and non-Western peoples. More specifically, is Zionism to be considered a late and variant form of European colonialism or a national liberation movement? Diverse commentators, such as Norman Podhoretz and Obama's former pastor, Jeremiah Wright, arrived at very different answers. Obama himself points out the need to transcend claims for the primacy of a certain group's suffering. In this way, he breaks with some bedrock assumptions of the African American historical narrative. He also pulls away from the idea that "the West" always has agency and that "the rest" are always victims.

Black–Jewish conflict is not about the narcissism of small differences per se.[5] More simply, in the Manichean social imaginary that characterizes the United States, Blacks are black and, therefore, the polar opposites of Whites. Often in the American telling of it, slavery in the United States was the worst form of psychosocial degradation in human history. Jews claim the same ideological and historical terrain. Tension is partially caused by the achievement of the American Dream on one side of the color line and the hobbling of it on the other. As Ralph Ellison observed, "Being a Negro American has to do with the memory of slavery and the hope of emancipation and the betrayal by allies. It involves, too, a special attitude toward the waves of immigrants who have come later and passed us by."[6] Brutally put, the issue is often reduced to who has suffered more.

Blacks have been and are the North American outcaste par excellence. They create whiteness through their blackness and they become the standard of the most abject misery. For most of U.S. history, Blacks have been a caste group, in-marrying and residentially segregated, removed from the mainstream and without any hope of ever entering it. Slavery is the nation's original sin. However, Jews remind us of a time before whiteness, before the presence of the Black. And this is disconcerting for all concerned, because the national psyche accepts Black Otherness as the starting point for discussions of collective suffering. If the United States is a "White man's country," Jewish cosmic suffering is, in many Black minds, fanciful. Henry Louis Gates once wrote of a confrontation at a Black-Jewish forum in New York in the early 1990s. The organizer, Melanie Kaye/Kantrowitz, "her voice quavering with emotion," expressed her most abject shame for the past five hundred years of Black suffering. Gates asked, "Should the Melanie Kantrowitzes of the world, whose ancestors survived pogroms and, latterly, the Nazi Holocaust, be the primary object of our wrath?"[7] Indeed, the wrath is historically misplaced.

Obama plays against a historical backdrop in which Black shame and blame are asserted and contested. In May 2010, Gates asked that the blame-game surrounding the Atlantic slave trade cease: "President Obama, the child of an African and an American ... is uniquely placed to publicly attribute responsibility and culpability where they truly belong, to White people and Black people, on both sides of the Atlantic, complicit alike in one of the greatest evils in the history of civilization."[8] We might go further and reason that, since there is no unique White guilt, there is no specific Jewish guilt. However, this is different from asserting that Jews did not participate in White privilege. In the United States, American Jewish suffering definitely pales in comparison with the experience of African Americans. To maintain that the oppressions were equal is fatuous. But the United States is not the world and the world of the United States is not static. The danger does not lie in making comparisons between Black and Jewish experiences. It lies in ripping events from their contexts and then making them stand alone as stand-ins for some universal pain. We can say that both arch-segregationist Senator Theodore Bilbo of Mississippi and Adolf Hitler were racially obsessed. At the same time, we can recognize that neither the focus of their rage, nor the consequences, were the same.

Israeli historian Yaacov Shavit sees American Blacks as living with a historical deficit. Only African Americans, he argues, "found themselves without a recognized historical past, without ancient historical written records, and without Holy Scriptures."[9] True, but all groups create myths of their own selfhood. These claim historicity, but are beyond the scope of historical questioning. African Americans have a past that contains slave narratives, musical traditions, family genealogies, folktales, Bible stories, abolitionist tracts, and the shared memory of the civil rights struggle. Interestingly, in 2008 the literary scholar Charles Johnson critiqued the resultant collective Black American narrative. Enslavement, slavery, and segregation were truly an unholy trinity of oppressions, he said, adding, "It simply is no longer the case that the essence of Black American life is racial victimization and disenfranchisement, a curse and a condemnation, a destiny based on color in which the meaning of one's life is thinghood, created even before one is born." Johnson believes that the popular African American view of the past "fails because it is conceived as melodrama, a form of storytelling in which the characters are flat, lack complexity, are either all good or all bad, and the plot involves malicious villains and violent actions."[10] This may be true, but it is doubtful that many American Blacks are going to abandon the image of their travail as the ultimate in human suffering. It is this fixity of vision that abrades other narratives. When Nobel laureate Toni Morrison dedicated her novel *Beloved* (1987) to the "sixty million" taken in the slave trade, she knew that a multiple of six has power.[11] In a biting critique, the literary critic Stanley Crouch observed,

> Yet perhaps [*Beloved*] is best understood by its italicized inscription: "Sixty Million and More." Morrison recently told *Newsweek* that the reference was to all the captured Africans who died coming across the Atlantic. But sixty is *ten* times six, of course [emphasis in original]. This is very important to remember. For *Beloved,* above all else, is a blackface holocaust novel. It seems to have been written in order to enter American slavery into the big-time martyr ratings contest, a contest usually won by references to, and works about, the experience of Jews at the hands of Nazis. As a holocaust novel, it includes disfranchisement, brutal transport, sadistic guards, failed and successful escapes, murder, liberals among the oppressors, a big war, underground cells, separation of family members, losses of loved ones to the violence of the mad order, and characters who ... have been made emotionally catatonic by the past.[12]

Strangely, the African American narrative does not arouse a widespread movement for reparations. Obama is not likely to ask for them, even though the United States was the most powerful patron of the *illegal* slave trade in the half-century following its abolition in the United States in 1808. The role of Blacks in constructing a nation occupied by later immigrants takes a backseat to stories of degradation. The fact that African Americans produced 60 percent of U.S. exports and 80 percent of the world's cotton in 1860 is almost forgotten. Instead, there is the bodice-ripping dramaturgy of the abolitionist tale. The African American narrative can be that absolute before which all other narratives are relative. That 20 million Chinese peasants died in the Taiping rebellion between 1850 and 1864, while roughly 4 million Blacks toiled in the Old South, is an irrelevancy. That 1 million people died in the Paraguayan War (1864–1870), a war that shook the foundations of Brazilian Black slavery, dims in significance. That the tsar liberator freed more than 23 million White people in Russia in 1861 is hardly credible. The African American activist and singer Paul Robeson singing the songs of the Volga boatmen and comparing them to slaves on the Mississippi is pure sentimentality. The African American narrative can be a jealous narrative.

In the 1990s, a member of the Nation of Islam remarked that Jews had "stolen our garment" of Black suffering.[13] That image may serve as a metaphor for both the current state of Black-Jewish relations and the underlying struggle of two disparate peoples to occupy the same historical space. In June 2010, Louis Farrakhan, leader of the African American religious movement, the Nation of Islam, wrote to the leaders of more than a dozen major U.S. Jewish groups and demanded reparations.[14] While it would be a mistake to see Farrakhan's views as typical, they have received a wide hearing. The leader of the Nation of Islam thundered, "We could charge you [Jews] with being the most deceitful so-called friend, while your history with us shows you have been our worst enemy." He offered a steel olive branch—"an offer asking you and the gentiles whom you influence to help me in the repair of my people from the damage that has been done by your ancestors to mine." Farrakhan charged that Jews "present reality is sitting on top of the world in power, with riches and influence, while the masses of my people ... *are in the worst condition of any member of the human family* [italics added]."[15]

Farrakhan's letter was accompanied by two books from the Nation of Islam Historical Research Team. He said they showed "an undeniable record of Jewish anti-Black behavior."[16] The first of these books, *The Secret Relationship between Blacks and Jews,* Volume 1, is a Rorschach test of race relations in the present-day United States.[17] It says little about the history of comparative slavery, but everything about the ways in which we conceptualize racial hierarchy. Whites in general were guilty of the crime of the slave trade, but a special group, Jews, were central. Indeed, if the slave trade was *all* about race, *any* Jewish involvement exposes as myth the Black-Jewish alliance. The final chapter, listing Jewish slave owners in the South, is provocatively called "Jews of the Black Holocaust." The *Secret Relationship* is a mirror in which present-day Black-Jewish relations play out before a background that is a historical pastiche. The work has had a varied career. Professor Tony Martin of Wellesley College created a furor in the early 1990s by using the book in one of his classes. When challenged, Martin issued a broadside, *The Jewish Onslaught at Wellesley,* blaming a cabal of Jewish professors for his travails.[18] Several leading historians, as well as other social scientists, did critique *The Secret Relationship.*[19] The Anti-Defamation League published its own retort, *Jew Hatred as History,* a pamphlet that meticulously goes over every major argument in the book. The critiques were nearly unanimous in pointing out that many of the facts in the book had been wrenched from their context.[20]

The debate on the history of Black oppression became embrangled in larger issues. In the 1990s, slavery in Muslim Africa often became the second front in a propaganda war. A reply to the charge of Jewish culpability in slaving was one of Arab or Muslim culpability. When the Nation of Islam's newspaper, *The Final Call,* called charges about slavery in Sudan an attempt "to divert attention from the role Jews played in the slave trade in America," Nat Hentoff asked whether Farrakhan would be willing to go on television and debate slavery with Sudanese refugees from slavery.[21] Jeff Jacoby said that the slavery in Africa seemed almost purposely ignored.[22] Charles Jacobs, ardent Zionist and organizer of the Anti-Slavery Group, averred, "Every schoolchild in America knows that women have been raped in Bosnia.... Everyone knows the whales have to be saved. But no one seems to realize you can buy a Black woman as a slave for as little as $15 in Khartoum." Jacobs complained that groups he would have considered as allies were lukewarm.[23] An officer of the Islamic Council of New England, Abdul Cader Asmal, riposted, "At this time, however, [there] are only allegations that have been repudiated as anti-Sudanese, anti-Islamic propaganda."[24] Louis Farrakhan himself struck back at those who linked Islam and slavery in Africa.[25] The minister queried, "If there was slavery going on in this country where I live [in Louisiana and Texas], that I didn't know about, how can I be expected to know about conditions in a country, where, during the last 10 years, I've been five times?"[26] When the National Association for the Advancement of Colored People (NAACP) took up the issue of slavery in the Sudan, the Nation of Islam saw the focus as proof of conspiracy: "Most people did not realize that Kwesi Mfume [the executive-secretary] was brought in to prop up the NAACP after the Million Man March [of 1995] put the Black nation outside the control of the Jewish power structure."[27] Such statements make it clear that accusations of slaving can be used as a cudgel with which to beat competing groups in the rough-and-tumble of American ethnic politics. In 2001, Ronald Segal published his semipolemical *Islam's Black Slaves, the Other Black Diaspora.* Segal lamented that slavery in Islamic lands "is not condemned or even recognized, because it is outside the historical confines of the Atlantic Trade and the survival of racism in American society."[28] African Americans were not about to shift their gaze from the American South to the Sudan.

Jews and African Americans have long been involved in telling and debating the Black story. Who is to tell it, control it, and, most important, profit from it? Far more popular than *The Secret Relationship* is Alex Haley's epochal 1975 *Roots, the Saga of an American Family.*[29] In 1977 a serialization of the book became one of the most watched series in the history of American television. An estimated 130 million Americans viewed at least one episode of the eight-part series; at least 250 colleges began offering credit courses based on it. *Roots* purports to be the story of Haley's ancestors from mid-eighteenth century Maryland to modern Tennessee. The book answered a need; Jim Sleeper noted that Haley's "intent was to weave sub-Saharan Africa's diffuse cultural threads into a Western myth of 'exile' and 'pilgrimage' for a Black American audience that had internalized such notions from the Old Testament and Christianity, and for other Americans who needed to understand, in both Christian and liberal-Enlightenment terms, what their own forebears had perpetrated and suborned."[30] However, problems with the work soon emerged. In 1978, Harold Courlander, a Jewish anthropologist and novelist, sued Haley in U.S. District Court in New York for copyright infringement. Courlander's lawyers found eighty-one passages taken from Courlander's 1967 novel, *The African*. A settlement was finally reached and Courlander was paid $650,000. The plaintiff seems to have agreed to keep the matter quiet and died in 1996, outliving his renowned rival by three years. Henry Louis Gates summed up scholarly opinion well when he said, "*Roots* is a work of the imagination rather than strict historical scholarship."[31] More acerbically, Oscar Handlin observed, "Historians are reluctant—cowardly—about calling attention to factual errors when the general theme is in the right direction. That goes for foreign policy, for race, and for this book."[32] *Roots* claims to speak as racial memory—Black racial memory. Who actually gathered the material for the African section of the book is secondary. Alvin Poussaint, an African American professor of psychiatry at Harvard Medical School, remarked, "There was a larger truth that he [Haley] captured: That we were brought here against our will, we were mistreated, we progressed, we had survived, we were a strong people who could keep going, despite this experience, and become part of America."[33] More forcefully still, Askia Muhammad, foreign editor of the Nation of Islam's *Final Call,* asked, "Did he [Haley] lie?" The response was: "I don't give a damn."[34] The position might be stated as, "We wear the garment of suffering; who stitched it together is secondary."

There is nothing inevitable about Black-Jewish collaboration or conflict. During slavery in the United States, one group was geographically restricted to the South and the other had yet to immigrate. The pogroms and the lynchings of the late nineteenth century are far better analogues than the frequently cited slave trade and the Holocaust. Both pogroms and Southern White terror reflected, in part, the birth pangs of societies in which millions were moving off the land. When Blacks and Jews did meet in urban America, both were newcomers and both entered a society already defined by whiteness (or, in other words, non-Negroness). Their human capital was different and so were their life-chances. In 1892 alone, 66,544 Jewish immigrants arrived at Ellis Island. In the same year, there were only sixty thousand African Americans in the entire city of New York.[35] Between 1881 and 1914, more than 2 million Jews left Russia, Romania, and Galicia for the United States. While Jews poured into American urban ghettos, African Americans largely remained in the South where segregation and, worse yet, mob violence, were increasing. Between 1877 and 1919, more than

3,000 African American men and women were hanged, shot, burned, or mutilated in the United States. Many more were terrorized or forced from their homes.

There were reverberations of these horrors on both sides of the Atlantic, some touching on American race relations and comparative suffering. One instance is the 1903 pogrom in Kishinev. The mob terrorism resulted in the death of forty-nine and the injury of five hundred Jews. Following this massacre, President Theodore Roosevelt forwarded to the tsar a B'nai Brith petition denouncing the killing and looting. Booker T. Washington, the leader of African American opinion, spoke out publicly for the victims.[36] However, solidarity was not the only note. Following Kishinev, African Americans could not help but sourly observe that the protest was also signed by prolynch law Mississippi senators and by the mayor of Evansville, Indiana, a town from which more than a thousand Blacks had just been driven.[37] *The Freeman,* published in Indianapolis, ironically asked, "Shall the Negroes look to the Tsar of Russia for protection, since neither the President of the United States nor the Mayor of Evansville seem interested in protecting them?"[38] Russia, indeed, did respond. Foreshadowing later exchanges between the United States and the Soviet Union, Roosevelt was advised to busy himself with abuses in his own country. The American president was reminded that while "in Russia the members of the mob, to the number of 500, have been imprisoned and punished, in America even the leaders of the lynching mob have been permitted to go free."[39] The aftermath of the pogrom did not immediately draw the groups together. Indeed, in some cases, a rather pathetic appeal to whiteness was used to differentiate the two cases.

By the second decade of the twentieth century, Jews and African Americans were in far greater contact than ever before. More than 90 percent of Blacks in America lived in the South in 1900. With the decrease in European immigration after 1924 and the avid recruitment of Southern Black replacements by Northern industries, Blacks poured out of the South. During the years 1910 to 1920, more than 500,000 African Americans moved North and 903,000 more had followed by 1930.[40] Migration out of the South slowed during the Great Depression, but it still added 400,000 people to already crowded Northern ghettos. In 1930, only one Northern city had a Black population above 100,000; by 1935, there were eleven cities with more than 100,000 African Americans.

Jews could have bought into the prevailing virulent Negrophobia. Indeed, avoidance rather than fellow-feeling would have abetted their whitening process. Early on, the arguments were there. An 1863 article in *The Jewish Record* could have been the tact taken: "We know not how to speak in the same breath of the Negro and the Israelite. The very names have startling opposite sounds—one representing all that is debased and inferior in the hopeless barbarity and heathenism of six thousand years; the other, the days when Jehovah conferred on our fathers the glorious equality which led the Eternal to converse with them, and allowed them to enjoy the communion of angels."[41] Abolitionism was a plague and an "insult to God Himself, in endeavoring to reverse the inferiority which he stamped on the African, to make him the equal, even in bondage, of His Chosen people."[42] Forty years later, Solomon Cohen, leader of the Philadelphia B'nai Brith, argued that it was irresponsible "to contrast the advanced stage of intellectual and moral development of the Jews in general with the limited progress that the masses of Negroes in America have made."[43] In 1943, in the midst of the Holocaust, Philip Frankel of the Anti-Defamation League wrote, "The difficulties facing the Jews as a minority group are sad enough without tying ourselves up with another minority group of less influence."[44]

On the other side of the color line, some African Americans found Jewish claims of suffering to be, even if justified, narrow. Reacting directly to Kristallnacht in 1938, the Black nationalist Marcus Garvey sympathized with Zionism, but also felt the need to foreground Black oppression. All minorities should beware: even if Jews in Germany had been "uppermost in the intellectual, industrial and financial groups," the blind bias of the majority would trample them. The time would come when "the Negro, irrespective of his cry for help, will as a minority, get the club in his neck and there will be no world sympathy for him, even as the Jew has had some kind of sympathy expressed by other nations."[45] Six years later the leading African American intellectual, W.E.B. Du Bois, read the Declaration of Human Rights (circulated by the American Jewish Committee after the Dumbarton Oaks conference) and wrote to Joseph Proskauer, President of the American Jewish Committee:

> I have received your declaration of human rights and want to say frankly that I am greatly disappointed. You say under paragraph two of your creed: "No plea of sovereignty shall ever again be allowed to permit any nation to deprive … these fundamental rights" … you appeal for sympathy for persons driven from the land of their birth, but how about American Negroes, Africans and Indians who have not been driven from the land of their birth but nevertheless are deprived of their rights? In other words, this is a very easily understood declaration of Jewish rights but it has apparently no thought of the rights of Negroes, Indians, and South Sea Islanders. Why then call it the Declaration of Human Rights?[46]

The Jewish community in the United States was, on the whole, loath to employ the ideological capital provided by "the wages of whiteness." There was indeed racism among American Jews (as there was anti-Semitism among American Blacks). However, few Jewish organizations openly embraced racism in a racist America. Rabbi Abraham Joshua Heschel, a collaborator of Martin Luther King Jr. in the 1960s, argued that tolerance stemmed from the central tenets of Judaism: "A person cannot be religious and indifferent to other human beings' plight and suffering. The essence of a Jew is his involvement in the plight of other people, as God is involved."[47] Historian Lawrence Fuchs located the substrate of Jewish antiracism and general liberalism in the Hebraic religious tradition of *tsedakah* (charity).[48] Perhaps so, but other faiths urge tolerance among their members (for example, the Roman Catholic Church). Norman Podhoretz has nevertheless argued that the commandment to give charity is particularistic; traditionally, *tsedakah* began at home with the Jewish community.[49] In a somewhat dyspeptic opinion, following the interpretation of conservative rabbis, he comes to the view that "the Torah of Judaism is at variance with the [social justice] 'Torah' of contemporary liberalism."[50]

Yet there is no denying the philanthropy of some Jews to those outside their community. For example, early in the twentieth century, the Chicago businessperson Julius Rosenwald helped educate more than one-fourth of all the Black children in the South.[51] The premier African American educationalist, Booker T. Washington, received aid from several affluent Jews, among them Jacob and Mortimer Schiff, James Loeb, Felix Warburg, Joseph Pulitzer, Jacob Billikopf and Julian Mack. The original sponsors of the NAACP were upper-class German Jews and WASP reformers, who were inspired by the ideals of the Progressive Era. Representative of privileged Ashkenazic leadership was Arthur Spingarn, who served as the head of the NAACP's legal committee soon after its formation and who worked without compensation until 1940. His brother, Joel, was NAACP chairperson after 1913. Other examples of Jewish philanthropy included Felix Frankfurter and Louis Marshall, jurists with a keen interest in African American legal education. Apropos of these connections, historian David Levering Lewis contends that, in the period 1910–1930, "a small number of socially powerful and politically privileged Jews and Afro-Americans embraced an ideology of extreme cultural assimilationism."[52] Lewis believes they saw the common enemy of African Americans and Jews as "a species of White gentile." These elites needed one another: "Theirs was a politically determined kinship, a defensive alliance, cemented more from the outside than from within. Believing themselves at the threshold of full acceptance by mainstream America, then knocked off balance by an unwelcome population infusion, becoming frightened and dismayed by the eruption from below of nationalisms, the privileged Ashkenazim reached for the Afro-American leadership and even helped to create it."[53] Political and cultural cooperation between Blacks and Jews was, in this reading, only an elite phenomenon and belied deep divisions.

Elite collaborations undoubtedly existed, but it is hardly the whole of the story. Two other factors come into play: the persistence of a Jewish narrative of suffering and a tradition of oppositional activism. Other immigrants might backdate their whiteness; the Old Country might be perceived through a mythopoeic prism of memory so that even Ireland or Herzegovina might be reimaged as idyllic. For the Jews this was not possible. For instance, in 1926 Louis Marshall, president of the American Jewish Committee, spoke to the NAACP and told the group that he belonged to "a race which has had even longer experience of oppression." The Jews of Europe had been subject to "wholesale massacres, not mere individual lynchings" and his race had suffered "indignities in comparison to which to sit in a 'Jim Crow' car is to occupy a palace."[54] Julius Rosenwald informed a Black audience, "If it is any consolation to you, I want to say that there are White people who suffer a great deal more. The Jewish race, which dates back thousands of years and like yours dates back to a time when they were known to be in slavery."[55] Unlike other ethnics who might reconfigure and reimagine Europe, twentieth-century anti-Semitism would not permit the luxury. However, by acknowledging their "garment of suffering," some Jews threatened to rend the national myth of a seamless White American identity. Ironically, to disenfranchised Blacks such acknowledgement often appeared disingenuous.

While the majority of both the Jewish and African American communities warily viewed each other across a racial and religious divide marked by rent strikes and shop boycotts, Jewish activists, ranging from members of the Communist Party to liberal reformers, tried to breach the color line. The frequent pro-Negro positions of the Yiddish-language *Forverts* and the Communist Party were not the result of dame charity, but the trans-Atlantic reverberations of Old World Jewish activism. The Communist Party was one place where Blacks and Jews could meet as equals. Some of the latter saw their salvation in the modern secular and universalist state in which race, religion, or class would be irrelevant. Joseph Brodsky and Samuel Liebowitz, the leftist Jewish attorneys who took on the Scottsboro Boys Case in 1931, were far from both New York Jewish elite philanthropy and the NAACP. They did not represent the majority of Jews, nor did they resemble the German Jewish philanthropists who funded the Black so-called Talented Tenth. Norman Podhoretz is right when he, with some distaste, observes, "Although the Jewish radicals added up to only a tiny segment of the Jewish population as a whole, they do seem to have formed a disproportionately large percentage of the various factions on the Left working to overthrow the Tsarist regime.... As such, they all played a crucial role in the formation of the political culture of their American descendants—even unto the fourth generation."[56]

One could argue that a broad-based Black-Jewish coalition did not really materialize until after World War II and that its high point was between the *Brown v Board of Education* decision of 1954 and the Voting Rights Act eleven years later. The march on Washington in the summer of 1963 took place in a golden summer of seeming goodwill. More than two hundred fifty thousand people marched on the National Mall; sixty thousand of them were White, and more than half of those were Jewish. In the Freedom Summer voter registration drives in Mississippi the next year, Jewish students made up two-thirds of the Whites involved. However, the alliance seemed to peak and wane. By the late 1960s, Black–Jewish relations had taken a turn for the worse. Under the leadership of Stokely Carmichael and others, "Black Power" emerged as a term and an organizing principle by 1966. The following year, Martin Peretz, a long-time contributor to the civil rights movement, founded the New Politics Convention. The group was designed to solidify a Black–Jewish coalition; instead, Peretz walked out when some participants denounced Zionism and what they perceived as Jewish organizational dominance. In 1968, a bitter fight over community control of schools in the Ocean Hill–Brownsville section of Brooklyn resulted in a face-off between Black and Hispanic parents and the largely Jewish teachers' union. During the controversy, a Black Power poem declaimed, "Hitler's reign lasted for only fifteen years / For that period of time you shed crocodile tears / My suffering lasted for over 400 years, Jew boy."[57] The assassination of Martin Luther King Jr. in the same year silenced one of the chief proponents of the interethnic or interfaith alliance. Other Black voices, like Bayard Rustin, continued to urge unity, but were increasingly marginalized. In January 1969, *Time Magazine* dedicated an issue to the topic: "Black vs. Jew, A Tragic Confrontation."[58] Twenty-two years later relations seemed to have reached their nadir when, in 1991, the Brooklyn neighborhood of Crown Heights erupted in violence after a the death of a seven-year-old Black child in a traffic accident in which a Hasidic driver was involved. Rioting climaxed with the murder of a Hasid visiting from Australia.[59]

In 1998, a survey of African American opinion by the Anti-Defamation League indicated that Black Americans were much more likely to hold extremely anti-Semitic views than were Whites (37 percent versus 9 percent).[60]

It is possible to overemphasize supposed African American anti-Semitism. Such attitudes have never been at the center of Black American life, confronted as it is by chronic unemployment, drug addiction, police violence, and continuing broad-based societal racism. In spite of dire prognostications in the 1990s, African Americans and Jews have not become opposed communities. During the 2008 campaign, Bernard Avishai noted that "Obama's campaign is an implicit opportunity for a new leadership to emerge, a contemporary equivalent of Rabbi Heschel locking arms with Dr. King. The campaign has given the Jewish majority a new way to focus their political energies, which looks much like their former way—organized work toward a tolerant commonwealth."[61] In 2009, 70 percent of Jews were in favor of policies specifically aimed at helping African Americans, but only 58 percent of non-Jewish Whites were in favor. Sixty-four percent of Jews, as compared to 53 percent of non-Jewish people, believed that the condition of the African American community was the result of discrimination rather than its own social practices and work ethic.[62] In the wake of the 2012 election, it was obvious that the majority of Jews were still liberals on matters racial and otherwise. Indeed, the Republican Party garnered a 64 percent unfavorable rating from Jewish voters compared to just 26 favorable, according to one Democratic survey.[63] During Obama's reelection campaign, the survey found that the economy and health care ranked were overriding concerns for Jews, topping issues like Iran's nuclear program and Obama's tepid relationship with Israeli Prime Minister Benjamin Netanyahu.

In 2009, Obama reminded an audience at the American Israel Public Affairs Council of the halcyon days of the alliance: "We must not allow the relationship between Jews and African Americans to suffer. This is a bond that must be strengthened. Together, we can rededicate ourselves to end prejudice and combat hatred in all of its forms. Together, we can renew our commitment to justice."[64] This might be dismissed as political posturing were it not for the fact that Obama, more than previous Black candidates for the presidency, has a very solid core of Jewish supporters and adjutants. For instance, Obama met his chief campaign strategist, David Axelrod, a former *Chicago Tribune* reporter and Democratic Party consultant, in 1992 while working on Chicago's Project Vote. Other Jews in the constellation around the rising politician were Lester Crown, Jack Levin, Abner Mikva, Judson

Miner, Newton Minow, Gidon "Doni" Remba, and Ira Silverstein. On entering the White House, Obama appointed Rahm Emanuel, then an Illinois representative to Congress, as his first chief of staff. Early in Obama's political career, Bettylu Saltzman was especially active. She met the future president when he was thirty and concluded, "[T]here was something about him that was clearly destined to be something very special.... I said to my husband and a lot of other people, he is going to be our first Black president."[65] Saltzman supported the budding politician in his 1996 campaign for state senate and in his failed bid for Congress four years later. In 2002, she introduced him to a group of Chicago women who called themselves "The Ladies Who Lunch." A year later she invited him to speak at a downtown rally against the Iraq War.

Suspicions remain, however. On one level, Jews and African Americans continue to argue, almost subliminally, over historical space. The issue of policy in the Middle East is much more overt. In the summer of 2009, an email circulated that claimed to have discovered the Black nationalist origins of the president's thought. Claiming an insider's view, a Black anti-Obama cleric raged, "The question is whether Obama, given his Muslim roots and experience in Farrakhan's Chicago, shares this antipathy for Israel and Jewish people. [Obama] was comfortable enough with Farrakhan ... to attend and help organize his 'Million Man March' ... a future President was in the crowd giving Farrakhan his enthusiastic support."[66] This reaction is extreme, but many Jews who opposed the president were suspicious that he was weak on Israeli security. The suspicion has had a long genesis, one long predating Obama's appearance on the political scene. For well more than a generation, some African American activists and leaders have been wary of the Jewish state. In 1973, Israel stepped up relations with South Africa; ambassadors were exchanged and military policy discussed. Four years after the United Nations declared, "Zionism is racism," in 1975, Andrew Young, Jimmy Carter's appointee as U.S. ambassador to the UN, was forced to resign after meeting with a Palestine Liberation Organization (PLO) observer. Many in the Black community saw the forced resignation as Jewish muscle-flexing; many Jews saw Young's meeting as the merging of African American "Third Worldism" and anti-Semitism. The next year, Jesse Jackson, probably the most prominent Black in America at the time, shook hands with and embraced the leader of the PLO, Yassir Arafat (before the Oslo accords and Israel's recognition of the PLO). In 1996, Farrakhan along with Reverend Al Sharpton and Illinois representative to Congress, Gus Savage, among others, led a World Friendship Tour that visited Iraq, Iran, Sudan, and

Libya, visits sure to raise the sensitivities and scrutiny of the Jewish American community.

The official U.S. boycott of the Durban conference in 2001, which condemned Zionism as racism, was especially galling to many African Americans, since an African American, Colin Powell, gave the order. In March 2009, a review conference (Durban II) was held in Geneva under UN auspices. Strenuous efforts were made to keep Zionism off the agenda and there was no resolution on Israel, a fact bemoaned by Jeremiah Wright, once Obama's pastor. To the cleric, Obama was ethically bankrupt on the major questions in the Middle East. To Wright, it was clearly "the Jewish vote, the AIPAC [American Israel Public Affairs Committee] vote that's controlling him [Obama]."[67] At the opposite end of the political spectrum, Norman Podhoretz remained suspicious: "Even though Obama either distanced himself from or repudiated the ideas [of anti-Zionists], he got around to doing so only when the political exigencies of his campaign left him with no prudential alternative."[68]

Obama was aware of the amount of opposition his supposedly pro-Third World stance provoked. Wisely, he did not answer his more bizarre accusers head on, but did readily acknowledge the heritage of the Black–Jewish alliance: "Jewish Americans like Andrew Goodman and Michael Schwerner were willing to die alongside a Black man—James Chaney—on behalf of freedom and equality."[69] At the same time, he strenuously tried to emphasize his comprehension of the various sufferings in the Middle East. In 2006, while still a senator, mixing poesy and politics, Obama wrote of the Middle East, "I spent a week traveling through Israel and the West Bank, meeting with officials from both sides, mapping in my own mind the site of so much strife. I talked to Jews who'd lost parents in the Holocaust and brothers in suicide bombings; I heard Palestinians talk of the indignities of checkpoints and reminisce about the land they had lost."[70] Obama had already moved in that direction of contextualizing Black suffering, when, in the summer of 2009, he visited Ghana in West Africa. He spoke of the Atlantic slave trade and its horrors, and then commended two Ghanaians for their present-day work against continuing slavery. Breaking with narratives of the exclusivity of suffering, he proclaimed, "I think the way it has to be thought about, the reason it's relevant is because whether it's what's happening in Darfur or what's happening in the Congo or what's happening in too many places around the world—you know, the capacity for cruelty still exists."[71] In 2009, Obama also visited Buchenwald concentration camp, where he spoke to varied constituencies in terms of universal norms. The president noted, "These sites have not lost their horror with the passage of time.... We have to guard against cruelty in ourselves."

The theme of fighting a hydra-headed cruelty is one to which Obama has frequently returned. Accompanying him to Germany was Elie Wiesel, who remarked, "[E]very war is absurd and meaningless.... The world hasn't learned.... Had the world learned, there would have been no Cambodia and no Rwanda and no Darfur and no Bosnia."[72] Visits to a Nazi concentration camp and to a European slave fort are symbolic and significant. They suggest a return to both the solidarity of the oppressed and an acknowledgement of peculiaristic narratives of suffering. Obama attempts to bridge Jewish and Black narratives of suffering by noting the continuing universality of pain and cruelty. There is no need to trump 6 million with 60 million, he claims in the "More Perfect Union" speech. He aims to transcend narrow claims of ethnic pain: "Those stories [in the African American narrative]—of survival, and freedom, and hope—became our story, my story; the blood that spilled was our blood, the tears our tears.... Our trials and triumphs became at once unique and universal, Black and more than Black."[73] Obama, the son of an African sojourner, does not have the luxury of saying that political roils in Kenya are the results of the machinations of the West or amorphous White men. He cannot reduce the problems of the twenty-first-century world to the color line. This will not explain the struggles in places like the Congo, Côte d'Ivoire, Libya, or Somalia.

Obviously, the Obama administration does not mark the end of Black–Jewish relations in the United States. Compared to the late 1990s, relations now seem to be in a lull. They are fragmented and range from warm to tepid. The Middle East remains a contested area, both on the ground and in the halls of academe. For example, in 2007 a row burst out at Harvard on disinvestment in Israel and the institution's openness to pro-Palestinian speakers. An African American faculty member was most prominent in both causes. He was opposed by some very ardent Zionists, among others. The conflict failed to gain traction; what might have ignited a firestorm of interethnic wrangling in the 1990s failed to find combustible material.[74] In addition, debates about the past are bound to shift. The majority of Africans in the Atlantic slave trade were not taken to North America. Immigrants today from the Caribbean and Africa have their own stories, many of which do not grow out of the American slave experience. It is doubtful if peculiaristic stories of Old Dixie will fully resonate with incoming Nigerian or Dominican strivers. The Black narrative in America will shift, and with it relations with other communities, including those of Jews and Latinos.

Some African Americans and Jews are now focused on the commonalities of suffering that stretch across time and ethnic groups. Of course, we must avoid the tendency to blend all sufferings into one universal tale of woe. In a criticism of the use of the Holocaust as an example of generalized intolerance, Edward Rothstein observes, "[T]he homiletic approach to the Holocaust has broken down almost all inhibitions in using the Holocaust as an analogy." He adds, "[J]udging from recent history, the analogies that have already been established, far from making genocide unthinkable, have helped make it seem as commonplace a possibility as schoolyard bullying."[75] This is indeed important to remember. Groups have a right to mourn their own, but we must strive to do two things: avoid a narrow insistence on the universal centrality of *any* past horror, and avoid a bland homogenization of what must still be horrific lived or remembered experience.

Notes

1. Quoted in Pauline Dubkin, "Obama and the Jews," *Chicago Jewish News*, October 24, 2008.
2. Quoted in ibid.
3. Norman Podhoretz, *Why are Are Jews Liberals* (New York: Vintage, 2010), 255.
4. Andrea Stone, "Jewish Vote Goes 69 Percent for Barack Obama: Exit Polls," *Huffington Post*, http://www.huffingtonpost.com/mobileweb/2012/11/07/jewish-voter-exit-polls_n_2084008:html
5. For a discussion of the psychodynamics of Black-Jewish relations, see Alan Helmreich and Paul Marcus, eds., *Blacks and Jews on the Couch: Psychoanalyitic Reflections on Black–Jewish Conflict* (Westport, CT: Praeger, 1998).
6. Budick, *Blacks and Jews*, 23, citing Ralph Ellison.
7. Henry Louis Gates Jr., "Black Demagogues and Pseudo-Scholars," *New York Times*, Op-Ed, July 20, 1992.
8. Henry Louis Gates Jr., "Ending the Slavery Blame-Game," *New York Times*, April 22, 2010.
9. Yaacov Shavit, *History in Black: African-Americans in Search of an Ancient Past* (London: Frank Cass, 2001), 4.
10. Charles Johnson, "The End of the Black American Narrative," *The American Scholar* (Summer 2008 http://theamericansholar.org/the-end-of-the-black-american-narrative/ reprinted in Gerarld Early and Randall Kennedy, eds., *Best African American Essays* (New York: One World/Ballantine, 2010), 116.
11. Toni Morrison, *Beloved* (New York: Everyman's Library, 2006).
12. Stanley Crouch, *Notes of a Hanging Judge: Essays and Reviews, 1979–1989* (New York: Oxford University Press, 1990), 205. See chapter 2 this volume on Crouch and the politics of reading.
13. Anna Deavere Smith, *Fires in the Mirror: Crown Heights, Brooklyn and Other Identities* (New York: Anchor Books/Doubleday, 1993).

14. See *The Final Call,* July 1, 2010, http://www.finalcall.com/artman/publish/National_News_2/article_7137.shtml. See chapter 7 in this volume for another perspective on Farraqhan.
15. Sophia Tareen, "Farrakhan Charges Jews with 'Anti-Black' Behavior,'" *Boston Globe,* June 29, 2010.
16. Ibid.
17. The Nation of Islam Research Department, *The Secret Relationship between Blacks and Jews of the Secret,* Volume 1 (Chicago, IL: The Nation of Islam, 1991).
18. Tony Martin, *The Jewish Onslaught at Wellesley: Despatches from the Wellesley Battlefront* (Dover, MA: Majority Press, 1993).
19. Replies include Harold Brackman, *Jew on the Brain: A Public Refutation of the Nation of Islam's The Secret Relationship between Blacks and Jews* (New York: self-published, 1992), later renamed and republished by the Simon Wiesenthal Center as *Farrakhan's Reign of Historical Error: The Truth behind The Secret Relationship;* expanded and published as *Ministry of Lies: the Truth Behind the Nation of Islam's* The Secret Relationship Between Blacks and Jews (New York: Four Walls, Eight Windows Press, 1994); Marc Caplan, *Jew-Hatred As History: An Analysis of the Nation of Islam's "The Secret Relationship"* (New York: The Anti-Defamation League, 1993); and David Brion Davis, "Jews in the Slave Trade," in *Culturefront* (Fall 1992): 42–45. Ralph A. Austen, "The Uncomfortable Relationship: African Enslavement in the Common History of Blacks and Jews," *Tikkun Magazine*, 9, no. 2 (1994): 65–68, 86. Thomas Sowell's view of the topic is contained in his collection of essays, *Black Rednecks and White Liberals* (San Francisco: Encounter Books, 2005).
20. Marc Caplan, *Jew Hatred as History: An Analysis of "The Secret Relationship."* (New York: The Anti Defamation League, 1993), http://www.adl.org/main_Nation_of_Islam/jew_hatred_as_history.htm
21. Nat Hentoff, "Slavery and the Million Man March," *Washington Post,* November 28, 1995.
22. Jeff Jacoby, "Slavery in Our Time," *Boston Globe,* April 2, 1996.
23. Charles Jacobs, "Where Are the Liberals," *Boston Globe,* April 2, 1997, xxxi.
24. Abdul Cader Asmal, "Chairman of Communication, Islamic Council of New England," *Boston Globe,* September 25, 1998.
25. Farrakhan cited in Askia Muhammad, "Slavery in Sudan?" *Final Call,* July 23, 1996.
26. Farrakhan cited in ibid.
27. Kaubab Siddique, "A Critical Look at 'Slavery in Sudan,'" *Final Call,* July 16, 1996.
28. Ronald Segal, *Islam's Black Slaves*: The *Other Black Diaspora* (New York: Farrar, Straus and Giroux, 2001), 35.
29. Alex Haley, *Roots, the Saga of an American Family* (New York: Doubleday, 1976).
30. Jim Sleeper, *Liberal Racism* (New York: Viking, 1997), 112.
31. Henry Louis Gates cited in Alex Beam, "The Prize Fight Over Alex Haley's Tangled 'Roots,'" *Boston Globe,* October 30, 1998.
32. Oscar Handlin cited in Philip Nobile, "Uncovering Roots," *Village Voice,* February 23, 1993, 32.

33. Alvin Poussaint cited in Don Aucoin, "Digging up Roots," *The Boston Globe,* January 17, 2002, http://www.racematters.org/digginguproots.htm
34. Askia Muhammad, "'Roots' Author Haley an Inspiration—Not a Liar," New America Media, http://news.newamericamedia.org/news/view_article.html?article_id=6d1b3e3281b02eeb38f8ee5ecc8e9d30
35. Murray Friedman, *The Creation and Collapse of the Black–Jewish Alliance* (New York: Free Press, 1995), 39.
36. Ibid.
37. Maurianne Adams and John Bracey, *Strangers and Neighbors: Relations between Black and Jews in the United States* (Amherst: University of Massachusetts Press, 2000), 240, citing *Springfield Republican,* June 28, 1903. See also *New York Age,* July 16, 1905.
38. Adams and Bracey, 240, citing Eric Foner, "Black-Jewish Relations in the Opening Years of the Twentieth Century," *Phylon,* 36, no 4 (1975): 359–67, quoting *The Freeman,* July 25, 1903.
39. Adams and Bracey, *Strangers and Neighbors,* 240, citing Foner, *Black–Jewish Relations,* quoting *Springfield Republican,* June 28, 1903. See also *New York Age,* July 16, 1905.
40. See Isabel Wilkerson, *The Warmth of Other Suns, The Epic Story of America's Great Migration* (New York: Random House, 2010).
41. Bertram Wallace Korn, "The Rabbis and the Slavery Question," from *American Jewry and The Civil War* (New York: Atheneum, 1970), 15–31, cited in Adams and Bracey, *Strangers and Neighbors,* 205**,** citing *The Jewish Record,* January 9, 1863.
42. Ibid., 209, citing Korn, "The Rabbis and the Slavery Question," *American Jewry and the Civil War* (New York: Atheneum, 1970), 15–31, citing the *Jewish Record,* January 23, 1863, 2.
43. Adams and Bracey, *Strangers and Neighbors,* 240, citing Foner, *Black–Jewish Relations,* quoting *The Public,* August 22, 1903.
44. Cheryl Greenberg, "Negotiating Coalition, Black and Jewish Civil Rights Agencies in the Twentieth Century," in *Struggles in the Promised Land: Toward a History of Black-Jewish Relations in the United States,* ed. Jack Salzman and Cornel West (New York: Oxford University Press, 1997), 253–276.
45. *The Marcus Garvey Papers* (Los Angeles: University of California Press, 1997), Vol. 7, 918.
46. W.E.B. Du Bois to Joseph Proskauer, November 14, 1944, *Correspondence of W. E. B. Du Bois,* ed. Herbert Aptheker (Amherst: University of Massachusetts Press, 1997), 24.
47. Abraham Joshua Heschel quoted in United States Holocaust Memorial Museum, "National Days of Remembrance, Selected Readings for a Day of Remembrance Commemoration" http://www.ushmm.org/remembrance/dor/organize/pdf/selected-readings.pdf
48. Lawrence Fuchs, *The Political Behavior of American Jews* (Glencoe, IL: Free Press, 1956).
49. Podhoretz, *Why Are Jews Liberal?,* 279.
50. Ibid., 288.
51. Friedman, *The Creation and Collapse,* 82.
52. David Levering Lewis, "Parallels and Divergences–Assimilationist Strategies of Afro-American and Jewish Elites from 1910 to the Early 1930s," from the *Jour-*

nal of American History 71, no 3 (1984), 543–64, cited in Adams and Bracey, *Strangers and Neighbors,* 331.

53. Ibid.
54. Sundquist, *Strangers in the Land,* 38–39, citing Louis Marshall quoted in Hasia Diner, *In the Almost Promised Land: American Jews and Blacks, 1915–1935* (Baltimore: Johns Hopkins University Press, 1995), 151–152.
55. Julius Rosenwald cited in David Levering Lewis, *When Harlem Was in Vogue* (New York: Knopf, 1981) 102.
56. Podhoretz, *Why Are Jew Liberals?,* 71.
57. Fred Ferretti, "New York's Black Anti-Semitism Scare," *Columbia Journalism Review* 8, no 3 (Fall 1969), 18–29, cited in Adams and Bracey, *Strangers and Neighbors,* 657.
58. *Time,* January 31, 1969.
59. There were different versions of this incident circulating; its media coverage and the finer ethnic tensions involved will be discussed in more detail in chapter 7 of this volume.
60. "ADL Survey: More Blacks Found To Be Anti-Semitic," Jewish Virtual Library, http://www.jewishvirtuallibrary.org/jsource/anti-semitism/black98.html
61. Bernard Avishai, "Obama's Jews," *Harper's Magazine,* October 2008, http://harpers.org/archive/2008/10/obamas-jews/
62. Podhoretz, *Why Are Jews Liberals?,* 263.
63. Andrea Stone, "Jewish Vote Goes 69 Percent for Barack Obama: Exit Polls," *Huffington Post,* http://www.huffingtonpost.com/ mobileweb/ /2012/11/07/jewish-voter-exit-polls_n_2084008.html
64. Transcript of Obama's Speech at the American Israel Public Affairs Committee (AIPAC), "Les Dessous de l'Information Mondiale—Downside World," http://middleeast.about.com/od/usmideastpolicy/a/me080605.htm
65. Pauline Dubkin Yeawood, "Obama and the Jews," *Chicago Jewish News Online,* October 24, 2008, http://www.chicagojewishnews.com/story.htm?id=252218&sid=212226
66. Bishop E. W. Jackson Sr., "The Source of Obama's Anti-Israel Policy," June 29, 2009, http://www.israpundit.com/2008/?p=15789=more15789
67. Jeremiah Wright, *Virginia Daily Press,* June 10, 2009.
68. Podhoretz, *Why Are Jews Liberals?,* 255.
69. Transcript of Obama's Speech at the American Israel Public Affairs Committee (AIPAC), June 4, 2008, http://middleeast.about.com/od/usmideastpolicy/a/me080605.htm
70. Barack Obama, *The Audacity of Hope, Thoughts on Reclaiming the American Dream* (New York, Crown, 2006), 381.
71. "Obama on Slavery: 'Capacity for Cruelty Still Exists,'" July 17, 2009, http://www.cnn.com/2009/US/07/17/obama.slavery/index.html}}
72. "Visiting Buchenwald, Obama Speaks of the Lessons of Evil," CNN.com, http://www.cnn.com/2009/POLITICS/06/05/obama.germany/index.html
73. Obama cited in Bakari Kitwana, "Between Expediency and Conviction," in *The Speech, Race and Obama's 'A More Perfect Union,'* ed. T. Denean Sharpley-Whiting (New York: Bloomsbury, 2009), 98.
74. See J. Lorand Matory, "Israel and Censorship at Harvard," *Harvard Crimson,* September 14, 2007; Alan Dershowitz, "Motto of Anti-Israel Academics: 'Free

Speech for Me, but Not for Thee!,'" http://www.huffingtonpost.com/alan-dershowitz/motto-of-antiisrael-acade_b_74414.html; "J. Lorand Matory Leaving Harvard for Duke," http://www.solomonia.com/blog/archive/2008/09/j-lorand-matory-leaving-harvard-for-duke/index.shtml

75. Edward Rothstein, "Making the Holocaust the Lesson on All Evils," *New York Times*, April 30, 2011, C5.

CHAPTER 3

Stains, Plots, and the Neighbor Thing

Jews, Blacks, and Philip Roth's Readers

Adam Zachary Newton

Loudmouths

"Inappropriateness is the Jewish style," says a character named Smilesburger toward the end of Philip Roth's 1993 novel, *Operation Shylock*. "We talk too much, we say too much, and we do not know when to stop. Part of the Jewish problem is that they never know what voice to speak in. Refined? Rabbinical? Hysterical? Ironical? Part of the Jewish problem is that the voice is too loud. Too insistent. Too aggressive. No matter what he says or how he says it, it's inappropriate."[1] The characterization is echoed in Roth's *The Plot Against America* (2004), where New York mayor Fiorello LaGuardia eulogizes syndicated columnist Walter Winchell this way: "Walter is too loud, Walter talks too fast, Walter says too much"—the second of two Jews in the novel to be branded a loudmouth.[2]

Philip Roth, let it be said, is not our most genteel novelist, either. In a review of *The Human Stain* (2000), critic James Wood describes his late narrative voice as "bludgeoningly explicit, crudely emphatic ... determined to illuminate what might better be crepuscular ... to haul into speakability the wordless." Yet Wood is just as quick to add that what offsets Roth's sensationalism is his intelligence, "the sun that burns off his impurities. If there is such a mode as highly intelligent sensationalism, then Philip Roth is now practicing it."[3]

This essay, in part, will be about the loudmouthed, intelligently sensationalist fiction of Philip Roth—peculiarly suited as an audio equalizer for the ethnic volume and tone of American Jewishness. But the angle I want to pursue chiefly is prompted by a different sort of loud-mouthedness from beyond the fence of Jewish particularity. I refer to a controversy precipitated in 2004 by the critic and novelist Stanley Crouch upon the publication of *The Plot Against America,* a novel Crouch felt was seriously undermined even as a work of counterfactuality by its inattention to a persecuted African American presence in the midst of homegrown—albeit fictive—state discrimination. I will adduce two discussions of Roth in light of that controversy that anticipate or echo Crouch. I will pause to look at two earlier moments of agitating Black–Jewish collaboration from the 1930s and 1940s. Finally, I will revisit some of Roth's fiction, early and late.

As the essay modulates, fugue-like, from the reception of *The Plot Against American* by Jewish audiences in the United States to the reception of *The Human Stain* by Stanley Crouch, to the reception of Roth's short story "Eli, the Fanatic" (1958) in twenty-first-century Tel Aviv, its *cantus firmus* is the capacity of a literary text to call out, summon, or "ex-cite" other voices. Such torque can be ideological in the case of Crouch and a subset of Roth's readers—willful but perhaps not entirely self-conscious. It can also be a more deliberate critical strategy, an altered, contrapuntal reading of texts. My name for the latter is "the neighbor thing," a formulation I explain in my conclusion.

Here, however, let it *not* be confused with the discourse known as "Black-Jewish relations." In the 1980s and 1990s, the critical literature in humanities and social sciences was fairly saturated with alliterative or symbolic locutions that figured relations between American Jews and Blacks as "secret sharers," "ambivalent allies," "ancestors and relatives," who meet in "bittersweet encounter" or "cooperation and conflict" or "literary conversation" in order to reckon with "arguments and alliances" or establish "bridges and boundaries." Such was the rhetorical capital, much of it nostalgic, that, at its heyday, underwrote a cottage industry of books preoccupied with what *Tikkun* magazine called "that Black-Jewish thing."[4] The thrust of my meditations here, by contrast, is antinostalgic.

And so I begin four years after the publication of *The Human Stain,* at the moment when reviews for *The Plot Against America* are just beginning to appear. One of these belonged to Stanley Crouch, African American essayist, poet-novelist, jazz critic, public intellectual, professional contrarian, and amateur pugilist. Published in *Salon* magazine, it sounded a note of compunctious outrage and began with a gruesome account of a lynching in 1937 Mississippi. Entitled "Roth's Historical Sin," the article went on to accuse the writer of committing in his latest novel an offense no less than "taking on the mantle of Alzheimer's when addressing major periods in American history" and thus even worse than the "great sins of monstrous allegiance, of bigotry, of individual cruelty."[5]

In an earlier essay on Roth, Crouch extolled the virtues of *The Human Stain* (2000), was unstinting in his acclaim for its achievement, and placed its author in the company of Hawthorne, Twain, Faulkner, and Ellison, asserting, "No, Philip Roth will not be held into a simply defined position, and that is why his example has a particular importance to the motion on the contemporary frontier of American fiction. … [He] rises to challenges … that take him beyond the territory his genius usually explores."[6] Waxing (w)roth instead, Crouch reckoned with *The Plot Against America* (2004) in very different terms: "How could this book pass everyone at Roth's publisher without the unmentioned smell of burning flesh filling room after room until someone raised a question about the stench for which the novel had cut off its nose in order to avoid acknowledging? In *The Human Stain,* Philip Roth hit one out of the park. In this new one, he took to an old American tradition, the segregated baseball team, and became Casey at the Bat."[7]

What Crouch most admired about the earlier novel was that "[Roth] finally broke out of this ongoing segregation of American fiction. You know—Black people writing about Black people over and over again, Jews writing about Jews. Brother Roth decided to climb the fence. It's a good sign not only for him but for American fiction."[8] Not so for *The Plot Against America,* "this ethnically self-absorbed book."[9]

As told through the author's seven- to nine-year-old eyes, that novel narrates an alternative mid-century U.S. history in which Charles Lindbergh defeats Franklin Delano Roosevelt in the 1940 election, America signs a nonaggression pact with Nazi Germany, and the nation flirts with fascism on a government-sanctioned scale, as thinly veiled resettlement programs with benign tags like Just Folks and Homestead 42 are put into effect for test communities of East Coast American Jews sent to the South and Midwest, under the Office of American Absorption. At the end of the plot, there are riots, the worst being a pogrom in Detroit, which in 1942 was home to three of the most famous Jew-baiters in the American heartland: "Radio Priest" Father Coughlin, Reverend Gerald L. K. Smith, and automobile magnate Henry Ford.

One is left to wonder what steps the nefarious Lindbergh administration and its nativist sons might have taken against American Blacks. But this is not a question the plot of *The Plot Against America* even remotely considers—unless, that is, one wants to read the novel allegorically, as many reviewers preferred.[10] Crouch did not, however, and his resistance proves instructive. Roth's sin in the book was not novelistic, a failure of art. It was *historical,* a failure to deepen the quality of national memory. Crouch echoed James Baldwin from 1964: "What happened to the Negro in this country is not simply a matter of my memory or my history; it's a matter of *American* history and *American* memory."[11] That its author had not bothered to include any evidence of institutionalized racism and systematic violence directed toward African Americans points, Crouch argued, to an unpardonable blind spot at that novel's core. Now Roth certainly has his blind spots. However, racial insensitivity is a different sort of accusation.

Part of Crouch's critique is literary historical: not only should Roth have been a closer reader of, say, Ralph Ellison (a frictional reader of Irving Howe), but he also should have been a closer reader of himself, that is, the author of *The Human Stain*. But the more significant part of Crouch's critique is historical in the plain sense, rebuking a culpable simplemindedness on Roth's part that translates into avoidance of what Crouch calls "the heat and weight of a time in the past where [a writer] chooses to put his story," and lends itself perhaps directly to the allegorical readings of the novel that were its majority reception.[12]

How could a novel that portrays a home-grown pogrom in 1942 Detroit, a large-scale version of the fate of Leo Frank, *not* allude in some way at the very least to pogroms in all but name such as the New York City Draft Riots of 1863, the race riots in East St. Louis in 1917, in Washington, DC, and Chicago in 1919, and, closest to Roth's own environs, in Carteret, New Jersey in 1926?[13] How could a novelist who has forged so much of his work of late in the crucible of history have blithely ignored that decisive shadow, even if it was only penumbral to the plot of *The Plot Against America*?

Conscientiously (if somewhat crudely) reframing the novel's horizon of reception, Crouch's polemic's precipitated a small firestorm of countercriticism on blogs for several weeks and months afterward. The most common resentment was directed at its "cheap shot" of criticizing an author for the book he didn't write. One riposte, for example, suggested that it was "a little bit like damning *Native Son* for its failure to investigate the de facto anti-Semitism of the Hoover administration."[14] Another cited evidence that rabble-rousing against Jews in the early 1940s was a matter of historical record.[15] For Crouch, however, the tight focus in the novel on Jewish families and the growing specter of persecution resulted in an unwitting swerve toward literary segregation. His complaint in *Salon Magazine* targeted Jewish particularism as a failure of Jewish universalist nerve. "The most important movement in American fiction, regardless of style," wrote Crouch, "is about moving beyond ethnic provincialism in order to summon a more real and more complex world."[16]

Why particularism of Roth's knowing sort should fall short of either the reality or complexity principle is a question worth posing here. And why Roth, who has pushed the American literary frontier into strange and enlivening contexts, including Central Europe and Israel, should be held hostage to a nativism that his own complex plots about America would seem to have robustly critiqued is curious, to say the least. Yet for Crouch, what appears to be tribal loyalty pure and simple doesn't read as retroactive postmodernism, but rather as retrograde Jewish nostalgia. Crouch wanted to know why.

So does theorist Walter Benn Michaels. "Why should we be outraged by what didn't happen rather than outraged by what did?" he asks, against the grain of allegorical readings of Roth's novel, in an essay from 2006. "[T]he fact that it could have happened here and the fact that it didn't—are given additional power by a third fact, the fact that, of course, it did happen here, only not to the Jews. It has surely occurred to every reader of this novel that its distinctive set pieces—above all, the scene in which the Roths are denied rooms at the hotel—were a standard feature of American life at least from 1896 (when Plessy legalized segregation) until the early 1960s."[17]

It certainly occurred to Crouch, who, conjecturing on a possible "animus in our intellectual community," wondered aloud about whether it was therefore "preferable to forget the savage racial history of our nation." Roth certainly had access to important recuperative historiography like the New York Historical Society's 2001 exhibit of lynching photographs entitled "Without Sanctuary," or David Levering Lewis's assessment of recent lynching studies for the *New York Review of Books* in 2002. "So there was plenty of fresh information about that time period," Crouch smoldered, "information that it is hard to believe everyone so easily forgot when reading *The Plot Against America.*"[18]

Michaels marshals his own facts about lynching—but with the specific object of deflating the kind of self-satisfied Jewish paranoia that many Jewish readers took to be the very point of Roth's novel, its paradoxical believability. For Crouch and Michaels alike, this paradox conceals the novel's blind spot (an occlusion perhaps more determinative for, and revealing of, its readership rather than its author). At any rate, Michaels says,

> what undoes the paradox, what makes the book believable is that we think of anti-Semitism as a significant factor in American history and

> we think of the success of Jews in American life as a tribute to the ways in which Jews and America itself overcame that anti-Semitism. But this is false. Anti-Semitism was never a very significant factor in American life—the fact that Jews were White was almost always more important than the fact that they were Jewish, and Jewish success in America today is less an effect of the triumph over racism than it is an effect of the triumph of racism.[19]

While Michaels shares Crouch's dismay at the novel's avoidance of race prejudice in America as a predominantly Black rather than Jewish experience, he differs by attributing it to a logic of substitution that chooses cultural categories over distinctions of class for predicates of social identity. According to this argument, where American Jews have always been in a material sense the beneficiaries of racism because their Jewishness was contained or deferred by their whiteness, "the point of a novel like *The Plot Against America*—the point of calling it the plot against America—is that it's not just Jews but the very idea of America that's the target of anti-Semites, that anti-Semitism is a kind of anti-Americanism."[20]

Americanism, to condense Michaels's argument, represents the social agreement not to discriminate or to tolerate discrimination for all Americans whose identity is defined by cultural or ethno-racial difference.[21] The problem, he says, is that this leaves the inequalities of class untouched. When class difference is flattened into a set of value-neutral differences between races, cultures, and genders, then it suffices simply to be sensitive or even appreciative rather than to seek meliorative justice through political or legislative repair.

In its fuller elaboration, Michaels's critique echoes Crouch's in exposing a deep vein of nostalgia—but a nostalgia, strange to say, for racism, or for its perhaps unwitting surrogate in the case of Roth's novel, anti-Semitism. "What we like about racism is precisely the fact that its victims are the victims of discrimination rather than exploitation, of intolerance rather than oppression, or of oppression in the form of intolerance."[22] Put another way, "The House I Live In," the song made famous by Frank Sinatra in 1945 and written to oppose both racism *and* anti-Semitism, does not offer free room and board.

As it happens, Michaels's reframing of Roth's *The Plot Against America* also allows us to discern a certain nostalgia at play for Stanley Crouch, too. Where Michaels analyzes Roth's blind spot as the self-satisfied equation of Americanism with neoliberalism, Crouch laments it as a case of authorial regression or cowardice—preferring, one suspects, the brand of authorial power to legislate meaning that Marxist critic György Lukács ascribed to the realist goal of an "objective totality of social relations."[23] For both its critics, however, *nostalgia* blunts the novel's critical edge; either its Jewish readers are pandered to (Crouch), or all others fall under the spell of its generalized antiracist plot *for* rather than against America (Michaels).

Nostalgia

It may seem counterintuitive to see *The Plot Against America* as nostalgic. And certainly for the average Jewish American reader, the novel confirmed basic ontological insecurities (however blinkered in the American context) that prefer fears of anti-Semitism to recognizing an historical victimization in the novel's substitution of Jews for Blacks as distinctly *American* victims of persecution—in Crouch's words, "as though that bestial level of social bigotry was not a highly visible *fact* of American life at the time that *The Plot Against America* is imagined to have taken place, between 1940 and 1942" [emphasis added].[24]

For Jewish indignation and antinostalgia equal to such hard social facts (or Crouch's ideological rectitude), the poem "Salut" written not quite a decade before the imagined plot in *The Plot Against America* by the Yiddish American poet Moyshe-Leyb Halpern would seem to have been made to order. An unflinching and gruesome elegy for a young Black American burnt and lynched, in its final stanza the poet implicates himself as fellow citizen *and* culpable bystander, the very stance Crouch demanded from Roth.[25]

> But not only did they loop a rope
> Around this piece of cattle,
> The flag of the republic too
> Was raised on high
> And the sky was blue—it didn't care
> And the wind rejoiced with the flag in the air,
> And I—a beaten dog—said not a word.
> Took no part—a partner to murder.[26]

Halpern was born in Galician Zlochow (now Ukraine) in 1886, emigrating to New York City in 1908. The height of this savage American pastime coincided with his own lifetime, continuing sporadically even past his death in 1932. According to figures at the Tuskegee Institute, between 1889 and 1930, a Black man, woman, or child was murdered nearly once a week, every week, in the American South.[27]

If this poem or its poet are not immediately familiar, readers will recognize a more celebrated poeticizing of American barbarism surely known to Stanley Crouch: the 1938 song "Strange Fruit," lyrics and music by Abel Meeropol, Jewish schoolteacher, union activist, future adoptive parent of Julius and Ethel Rosenberg's sons, and also, coincidentally, author of "The House I Live In." It was sung first and most famously by Billie Holiday and begins as follows:

> Southern trees bear strange fruit,
> Blood on the leaves and blood at the root,
> Black bodies swinging in the southern breeze,
> Strange fruit hanging from the poplar trees.[28]

In Halpern's poem, the ironical speaker calls himself a "partner in crime"; the crime is ghastly, the self-implicated voice does its politically incorrect work, but the subject of the salute, a martyred Black American, is brought before us only as a defiled body—no voice of his own, ironical or otherwise, to speak in. "Strange Fruit" is different. A collaborative exercise, it welded Black voice to Jewish empathy for a truly plangent moment in the entangled history of American Blacks and Jews.

There were only three recorded lynchings in 1939, the year Billie Holiday first sang "Strange Fruit." This was the same year that Germany invaded Poland and the Nazi plot against the Jews was exported outside German borders to all of Europe, and the year that precedes the storyline narrated in Philip Roth's *The Plot Against America*—at a time when the United States maintained neutrality and closed its doors to thousands of Jewish refugees. For more than two decades prior to the song's debut, the Yiddish and English-language Jewish press devoted considerable attention to exposing anti-Black racism. After the East St. Louis Race Riot of 1917, for example, which still holds the record for more lives lost than any single interracial conflict in twentieth-century America, the *Forverts* editorialized as follows: "Everywhere the same world. Kishinev and St. Louis: the same soil, the same people. It is a distance of four and a half thousand miles between these two cities, and yet they are so close and similar. Actually twin sisters which could easily be mistaken for each other."[29]

As Halpern's poem and "Strange Fruit" thus remind us, the correlation of Black and Jewish American experiences need not be solely an exercise in scar rivalry or an invidious turn of the intergroup relational screw. But in place of the subversive spirit in Halpern and Meeropol, what *The Plot Against America* appears to serve up is either a blind spot where racial consciousness should have been (Stanley Crouch's critique) or nostalgia for racism as a convenient blind for class consciousness (Walter Benn Michaels's critique).

Race in Roth

Race is not entirely occluded in Roth's novel, and where it isn't proves instructive. Consider the following vignette. Early in the book, Roth's brother Sandy designs an Arbor Day poster that includes a boy and a girl planting a tree, and, at their mother's suggestion, the image of a third child, who is Black; in other words, an early-1940s image of multicultural American precisely along the lines of the "The House I Live In." What encouraged his mother to suggest the Black figure, the narrator says, was not merely the desire to instill in her children the civic virtue of tolerance, but a new issue in Philip's stamp-collection of "educator stamps," a ten-center that featured Booker T. Washington. "'Do you think there'll ever be a Jew on a stamp?' Philip asks his mother. 'Probably—someday, yes. I hope so, anyway.'" And the narrator—the grown-up Roth—comments, "In fact another twenty-six years had to pass, and it took Einstein to do it."[30]

The flat and iconic images of the master of Tuskegee and of literal poster children for America the beautiful and racially tolerant do not necessarily bode well for rounder portraits of African American characters in the novel. And indeed such portraits don't ever appear. In point of fact, there is no substantive Black persona visible in *The Plot Against America,* even on the small stage of seven-year old Philip Roth's family life on the home front of Weequaic, New Jersey—and this is Crouch's very complaint. Instead, there is this: after his brother Sandy has returned from a sojourn on Kentucky farm, through the Just Folks Resettlement Program, Philip queries him about the laborers he has seen there:

> Can you understand when the Negroes talk?
>
> Sure.
>
> Can you imitate one?
>
> They say "baca" for tobacco. They say "I 'clare." I 'clare this and I 'clare that. But they don't talk much. Mostly they work. At hog-killing time, Mrs. Mawhinney has Clete and Old Henry who gut the hogs. They're Negroes, they're brothers, and they take the intestines home and eat 'em fried. Chitterlings.
>
> Would you eat that?
>
> Do I look like a Negro? Mrs. Mawhinney says Negroes are starting to move away from the farm because they think they can earn more money in the city. Sometimes old Henry got arrested on Saturday nights. For drinking. Mr. Mawhinney pays the fine to get him out because he needs him on Monday.[31]

And amazingly, just a few lines down, Philip asks, "Anybody say anything about anti Semitism?" "They don't even think about it, Philip," Sandy replies. "I was the first Jew they ever met."[32] Precisely here, one imagines, lay an opportunity to draw a subtle connection between two Jewish brothers in Newark and two African American brothers on a farm in Kentucky, not least because spectral anti-Semitism seems to coincide with the concrete legacy of Jim Crow. But Roth does not seize the opportunity, presumably on purely technical grounds, since the mimetic dictates of the brothers' conversation ensure that reality could not have impressed itself in more than restrictively Jewish terms.[33] If the closest *The Plot* comes to a multicultural America is the Roths' downstairs neighbors, the Cucuzzas, an Italian American family who shelters them during the riots that ensue at the end of the novel, then that lower-case plot device merely reflects the true demographics and sociopolitical realities of the 1940s Newark in which Roth actually grew up.

And yet it is very much those demographics that constitute a plot of their own about the material facts of difference, behind or above the novel's immediate purposes—a lower-case plot that many of Roth's Jewish readers simply failed to register in possible collusion with another strain of nostalgia that would rhapsodize Roth's Newark cityscape as if it were the Jewish American counterpart to Joyce's Dublin or Faulkner's Yoknapatawpha. In Lawrence Schwartz's words, "In short, when imagining the racial politics of Newark, Roth the hard-edged, thoughtful, and ironical realist, becomes a conservative 'utopian'—too much caught up in the interplay between his liberal, civil rights conscience and his sentimentalizing of Weequahic ... a 'romanticizing of the world that Roth usually dismisses as naïve.'"[34]

But such nostalgia comes with a cost. When we see an older Roth returning to the Newark of his youth and playing off the stereotype of burned-out, slum-ridden, now wholly Black neighborhoods, not only does it idealize the counterlife of edenic Jewish Newark (supporting Crouch's Ellisonian point about willed invisibility), but it also conveniently sidesteps the fact that this same cycle had already occurred in the 1920s when Roth's parents' generation had vacated for the residential neighborhoods of Weequahic and Clinton Hill the poorer Third and Central Ward neighborhoods into which Southern Blacks poured during the Great Migration, followed by a second wave to do the war work of the 1940s. As Schwartz explains,

> For the few short years of Roth's adolescence (1945 to 1950), Newark's almost two decades of industrial decline was held in check. Roth and

> his generation were the inheritors of an efflorescence that was the culmination of Newark's "golden" era, but one that was built on long-term, cynical exploitation of racism and deep, pervasive political corruption. What undermined many northern cities was deindustrialization, which in Newark had started in the 1920s (despite the economic boom), accelerated by the Depression, briefly reversed during World War II, and then resumed with breath-taking speed shortly after the War.[35]

Unique in Roth's oeuvre, *The Plot Against America* ends with a thirty-page appendix of bibliographies, documents, and factual biographies. Roth even wrote an ancillary essay in *The New York Times Book Review* entitled "The Story Behind *The Plot Against America*."[36] But no such demographic facts about 1940s Newark as Schwartz enlists appear anywhere in the novel. Does the blind spot Crouch assign to the novel have an even longer genealogy in Roth's career, then? If we were to imagine a book called *Philip Roth and the Blacks* on the model of critic Alan Cooper's *Philip Roth and the Jews,* an inventory for the latter category would take predictable form: cameos, stand-alone figures, totems—like the stamp and poster in *The Plot Against America*—precisely *not,* in other words, what *The Human Stain*'s narrator Nathan Zuckerman on behalf of his friend Coleman Silk (and in unintended echo of *Tikkun* magazine) calls "the whole *ramified* Negro thing" [my italics].[37]

The Plot in The Stain

By sheer contrast, Roth's millennial novel *The Human Stain* came as a revelation, as did its protagonist, perhaps Roth's most ambitious fictive Jew, Coleman Silk, "the greatest of the great pioneers of the I."[38] Recall that Crouch saw the novel as triumphantly "climbing the fence" of segregation in American fiction and ethnic provincialism. As far as the Black–Jewish dynamic is concerned, what we see in *The Human Stain* is not the familiar Jewish cathexis onto Black popular culture that Ishmael Reed wittily dubbed "cultural tanning," but rather African American hero of high culture Silky Silk, going along for the ride of Jewish self-infatuation, or as the novel puts it, "*ramifying*" as a Jew.[39]

The novel's plot involves a light-skinned Black who discovers he can pass as Jewish and therefore gain entry to academe, becomes a classics professor and dean at a small liberal arts college, and is outed for, first, what is taken to be a racist remark, and later, a sexual indiscretion, whereupon his racial subterfuge is discovered. As the epigraph to the novel from Sophocles' *Oedipus the King* anticipates, he is banished and made the victim of "expiation, of blood by blood."[40] True to form, Roth plaits an allusive skein for the text whose several strands include Greek and Roman mythology, Hawthorne and Hemingway, Ralph Ellison and Saul Bellow.

Yet, in the inventory of Black figures from Roth's fiction, there is actually one that beckons at Coleman Silk from a long way away off, almost forty years removed. He is a "small colored boy," so described by the character Neil Klugman working the desk of the Newark library in the 1959 novella *Goodbye, Columbus*.[41] The boy, roughly the same age as the boy Roth in *The Plot Against America*, makes repeated trips to the library, favoring a book containing reproductions of paintings by Paul Gauguin. He refers to it as "That Mr. Go-Again's Book"—a malapropism we can borrow to describe *The Human Stain* itself as its own kind of "go-again" text for Roth's racial imaginary in *Goodbye, Columbus*.

Neil at one point dreams that he and the boy are captain and mate on a sailing ship, anchored in the harbor of an island in the South Seas. On the beach are "beautiful bare-skinned Negresses," who, as the ship moves away from shore, throw leis, and croon, "Goodbye, Columbus, goodbye."[42] (The actual referent for "Columbus" in the text is the city in Ohio, which Neil's dream transposes accordingly.) The boy shouts at Neil that it is his fault they are drifting away and Neil shouts at the boy that it is his fault for not having a library card, but the island recedes and the women disappear.[43] There are certainly Black–Jewish resonances to the figure of Columbus in the book's title—not just immigrant arrival in America (a famous Yiddish American saying is "a klog oyf Kolumbus" (a curse on Columbus), that is, blame him for fooling us into coming to America), but also the discovery of America in 1492 marks the fate of Spanish Jews and West Africans alike. In Roth's novella, it functions as a trope of escapism for Neil Klugman as well as the boy, both of them, as Alan Cooper puts it, thus "intertwined in their Columbus-like venturings."[44]

Coleman Silk has his own Columbus-like venturings, and certainly one way of understanding *The Human Stain* in the context of *Goodbye, Columbus* and its escapist sensibilities is the urge to be elsewhere as the impulse to be otherwise: Jewish author finally inhabits Black character from the inside; Black character, as if in recompense, reinvents himself as Jew. Notwithstanding the fact Roth's fictional Jews no longer live "in overcrowded ghettos," as the Israeli novelist and close friend of Roth's, Aharon Appelfeld, notes, they are "nevertheless ... immersed in the ghetto existence," thus explaining "the manner in which they relate to strangers by being attracted to as well as alienated from them. Philip

Roth has observed the stranger closely; in fact, the stranger brings out the Jew in Roth."[45]

Roth, crucially I think, makes Coleman Silk an academic, and even more crucially, a professor of classics. In a passing nod to Lionel Trilling perhaps, he writes, "Coleman was one of a handful of Jews on the Athena faculty when he was hired and perhaps among the first of the Jews permitted to teach in a classics department anywhere in America."[46] In an open letter to Wikipedia that takes its administrators to task for the "misstatement" of alleging that the character of Coleman Silk is based on the life or experiences of Anatole Broyard, Roth emphasizes the fact that Silk is a teacher-scholar not a "cosmopolitan literary figure."[47] After an opening meditation on the summer of 1998 and the Lewinsky affair, the novel segues to Coleman's lecture on the *Iliad*: "You know how European Literature begins? ... With a quarrel. All of European Literature springs from a fight."[48] The novel ends, however, with the back-story behind a family quarrel, Coleman's family, as narrated by Silk's sister Ernestine who relates the cultural history of Lawnside, New Jersey, that runaway slaves in 1850 had called Free Haven, one of the truly magnificent pieces of ventriloquism in a Rothian oeuvre where so many characters sound too much like Philip Roth. And yet this is precisely the history that Coleman Silk has disowned in the story, although it proves to be inescapable. And thus the thing the novel takes for granted is Silk's pretend-Jewishness, not his authentic blackness, and the serviceability of a cultural escalator over and above an ethnoracial fence.

What the novel seems to say to us in Coleman Silk's decision to reinvent himself is that one path to cultural legitimacy in postwar America is "the equivocal form of whiteness that is postwar American Jewishness," and in particular its variant form of the anti-parochial and comfortably secular Jewish academic who speaks for Western Culture—falling on the spectrum somewhere between Allan Bloom (or Ravelstein) and Harold Bloom.[49] It is because the link between being Jewish and being a certain kind of intellectual culture hero becomes a given that Coleman Silk can use Jewishness as a strategy to his cultural advantage. This is the kind of Jew that Roth selects for Coleman's impersonation because, implicitly, this is the kind of Jew with whom Roth's narrators can be quasi–blood brothers, the wish-fulfillment Jewishness at the heart of wish-fulfillment blackness. The "go-again" boy in *Goodbye, Columbus* may be a double for Neil Klugman in that novella, but as a neighbor-figure for Coleman Silk on the broader terrain of Roth's fiction, he supplies the sort of ironic counterpoint Stanley Crouch had been straining for but did not quite find.

On a parallel track, potentially more intriguing than Roth's own putative blind spots rests the question about the fence-climbing skills of his books' *readers*—like the various critical responses to *The Plot Against America* too easily persuaded by allegory, too easily animated by tribal loyalties, more willing to trust that good fences make good neighbors than that they beckon to be climbed, even to get snagged upon. For a fence may also be an opening to "the neighbor thing," a text's material capacity to summon and "ex-cite".

Consider the short story, "Eli, the Fanatic" (1959). If we were to look for other exemplars of transformative agency to rival Coleman's shift from Black to Jew, the only character in Roth's work who comes close (if, that is, we bracket his Kafkaesque tale of English professor Alan Kepesh who morphs into a breast) is Eli Peck, in the same collection of short fiction that includes the "Go-Again" boy. When Eli compulsively dons the costume of an Orthodox refugee from postwar Europe, he feels "those black clothes as if they were the skin of his skin.… For the first time in his life, he smelled the color of blackness."[50] The story ends on this note: "The drug calmed his soul, but did not touch it down where the blackness had reached."[51] Yet all this blackness is the blackness of Jewish orthodoxy, or else something altogether allegorical, something to do with the price paid for suburban Jewish assimilation.

It was the glaring *absence* of blackness in *The Plot Against America,* let us recall—Roth as a bad neighbor, by Crouch's lights—that served as a prompt for the "go-again" effect, whereby we discover avatars for the late fiction in the early. How might textual neighboring serve us differently, however? When does a text's internal resistances trump our own, external ones?

The Stain in the Plot

In her essay, "Resisting Allegory, or Reading 'Eli, the Fanatic' in Tel Aviv," Hana Wirth-Nesher explains how different that story became for her, with its tropes of blackness, assimilated suburban Jewish Americans, and post-Holocaust Orthodox Jews, after she made aliyah and taught it, crossculturally, to her students at Tel Aviv University.[52] What had originally been read as an allegory of assimilationist trade-off, Roth's satire of suburban self-enclosure and complacency was now revealed to be something quite different. The 1950s displaced persons and Hasidic Jewish survivor figures who are identified in the story by the blackness of their attire are displaced once again to an Israeli milieu forty years later. As Wirth-Nesher puts it, "The Haredi survivor can be read allegorically only if he is universalized out of the sphere of Israeli politics, and out of Jewishness altogether."[53]

Blackness, in other words, is existential blackness, not Holocaust or Orthodox blackness. For Wirth-Nesher, such transposition teaches a lesson in how books can be read differently in different places—the "go-again" effect in inverted counterpoint, so to speak. As lives generate counterlives in Roth, so plots generate counterplots—or at least, the variable syntax *of* plot—something Sigmund Freud unpacked long before Roth in his 1919 paper, "A Child Is Being Beaten," where he showed how, through repression, a storyline can mystify, convolute, and replot itself.[54] Reading such a plot, consequently, would mean more than simply decoding it; it would mean opening to its torsions, letting its gaps or inversions instruct us in uncanniness generally. In an earlier text from 1895, "Project for a Scientific Psychology," Freud provides a peculiarly Rothian account of the *neighbor:* "And so the complex of the neighbor [*Nebenmensch*] divides into two constituent parts the first of which impresses through the constancy of its composition its persistence as a Thing [*Ding*], while the other is understood by means of memory-work."[55] This is a formulation richly mined by Eric Santner, whose recent work investigates the materially dense quality another person presents to me in everyday social relations, which is the effective plot of so many of Roth's own fictions: for Eli the fanatic, for Coleman Silk, for 1940s counterfactual non-Jewish America.[56] But the "neighbor thing" also captures the peculiarly uncanny scenes of *reading* Roth: like Crouch's response to *The Plot Against America,* it reveals the applied heat and weight unbinding a literary work from within through its proximity to neighbor-strangers outside its bounds—both readers and other texts.

The Neighbor Thing

While it may sound a little like the Just Folks program in *The Plot Against America,* the neighbor thing is actually far removed from it. What it denotes is the fact that human individuals and groups are troubled in *the midst of life,* in their aliveness to the world, not because of some deficiency in character or through some twist of fate, but simply because their neighbor is *uncanny*—nearer perhaps than we wish, but also distant from us and thus strange—opaque, enigmatic, unassimilable in a way that makes us consequently strange to ourselves.

In Santner's very serious pun, human subjectivity is as much *ibidinal* as libidinal. The human subject is ex-cited, literally "called out," as well as psychically charged, by being placed in largely unconscious citational relationship to the authorities (especially those that are symbolic and intangible) that legitimate the symbolic predicates of identity.[57] But through a potentially redemptive transference, every self also answers directly to neighbors who attract or demand its attention. In my adaptation of Santner's analysis here, the neighbor-thing just is the materiality of the text, or the scene of reading, in all its ex-cited transference. It both calls to us and calls us to be alive to its alterities. This is why Dostoyevsky called *Don Quixote,* at its end, "the saddest book of them all."[58] If Don Quixote himself becomes a victim of "the nostalgia for realism," we draw near to the book's allegorizing power even as we resist it.

Alongside both its special penchant for nostalgia and its latent critique of such penchant, Philip Roth's *The Plot Against America* is supercharged by a set of imagined historical coefficients and by its own textual and political unconscious. What the neighbor thing opens up for staging such a work in the company of other voices, it ex-cites—Crouch's on one frequency or vector, *Goodbye, Columbus* and "Eli, the Fanatic," on another—is a set of new *ibidinal* possibilities. "There's going to be no pogroms in Woodenton, 'cause there's no fanatics, no crazy people," says Ted Heller to his neighbor, Eli Peck in "Eli, the Fanatic,"—a sentiment to be revised with a vengeance half a century later by *The Plot Against America.*[59] What the neighbor thing offers us finally, is the *staining* of a text that is any reader's responsibility, the maculation that *The Human Stain* says "is there before its mark ... is so intrinsic it doesn't require a mark."[60] This is the anti-utopianism that leaves a literary work, with all its ex-cited surplus meaning, in our staining human hands. *The Plot Against America* ends when its author-narrator, referring to another character victimized by that plot whom he has been obliged to take care of, announces somewhat ruefully, "I was the prosthesis."[61] This is, properly speaking, any reader's burden, too.

Acknowledgments

I am grateful to Miriam Udel for playing the role of "go-again" reader.

Notes

1. Philip Roth, *Operation Shylock: A Confession* (New York: Simon and Schuster, 1993), 332.
2. Ibid., 304.

3. James Wood, "The Cost of Clarity," *New Republic* 222, no. 16–17 (April 17–24, 2000), 71.
4. Bob Blauner, "That Black–Jewish Thing: What's Going On?" *Tikkun* 9, no. 5 (September–October 1994): 27–32. See also, e.g., Budick, *Blacks and Jews*; Melnick, *A Right to Sing the Blues*; Newton, *Facing Black and Jew*; and Sundquist, *Strangers in the Land.*
5. Stanley Crouch, "Roth's Historical Sin," *Salon Magazine,* October 11, 2004, http://www.salon.com/2004/10/11/crouch_9/.
6. Stanley Crouch, "Segregated Fiction Blues," in *The Artificial White Man: Essays on Authenticity* (New York: Basic Books, 2004), 40.
7. Crouch, "Roth's Historical Sin."
8. Quoted in Jennifer Senior's profile, "Philip Roth Blows Up," *New York Magazine,* May 1, 2000, 42. On the Fence metaphor, see also Sanford Pinsker, "Climbing over the Ethnic Fence: Reflections on Stanley Crouch and Philip Roth," *Virginia Quarterly Review* 78, no. 3 (Summer 2002): 472–480.
9. Crouch, "Roth's Historical Sin."
10. Examples are: Ruth Wisse, "In Nazi Newark." *Commentary* 118.5 (December 2004): 64–69; Robert Kuttner,"What Would Jefferson Do? An Essay on Faith, Reason, Terror, and Democracy," *American Prospect* 15, no. 11 (November 2, 2004): 31–39; and Frederic Raphael, "Pastoral of an Urban Kind," *Spectator,* October 30, 2004, 57–58. As an instance of resisting allegory, Clive James, "Fatherland," *Atlantic Monthly* (November, 2004): 143–149 is exceptional for introducing something akin to Crouch's standing objection, albeit in less inflammatory tones.
11. From a roundtable discussion, "Liberalism and the Negro," *Commentary* (March 1964): 25–42, featuring Baldwin, Sidney Hook, Nathan Glazer, Gunnar Myrdal, Kenneth Clark, and Shlomo Katz. See also Baldwin, "The American Dream and the American Negro," *Collected Essays* (New York: Library of America, 2002), 717.
12. Crouch, "Roth's Historical Sin."
13. See Leonard Dinnerstein, *The Leo Frank Case* (New York: Columbia University Press, 1968); and Jeffrey Melnick, *Black–Jewish Relations on Trial: Leo Frank and Jim Conley in the New South* (Jackson: University of Mississippi Press, 2000).
14. Sean Nelson, "Get With the Pogrom: Roth Is Still the Laureate of Jewish Mischief," *The Stranger* (October 28–November 3, 2004), http://www.thestranger.com/seattle/get-with-the-pogrom/Content?oid=19726
15. http://fagistan.blogspot.com/2004/10/take-that-stanley-crouch.html (October 13, 2004), citing historian David Greenberg's review, "The Facts", in *Slate* Magazine: http://www.slate.com/articles/news_and_politics/book_blitz/2004/10/the_facts.single.html
16. Crouch, "Roth's Historical Sin."
17. Walter Benn Michaels, "Plots Against America: Neoliberalism and Antiracism," *American Literary History* 18, no. 2 (Summer 2006): 289.
18. Crouch, "Roth's Historical Sin."
19. Michaels, "Plots Against America," 290. See also Goldstein, *Price of Whiteness,* Michael Rothberg's response to Michaels ("Against Zero-Sum Logic: A Response to Walter Benn Michaels," *American Literary History* 18, no. 2 (2006):

311); and Ginevra Geraci, "The Sense of an Ending: Alternative History in Philip Roth's *The Plot Against America*," *Philip Roth Studies* 7: 2 (Fall 2011), 187–204.

20. Michaels, "Plots Against America," 298.
21. But see Theodor Adorno's trenchant analysis of this development in *Minima Moralia: Reflections of a Damaged Life* (London: *Verso*, 2006).
22. Michaels, "Plots Against America," 297.
23. I thank my colleague David Lavinsky for turning me back to Lukács, especially the 1938 essay, "Realism in the Balance," *Aesthetics and Politics* (London: Verso, 2007), 28–59.
24. Crouch, "Roth's Historical Sin."
25. Ruth Wisse discusses the poem briefly in her study of Halpern and a fellow Yiddish poet in New York, Mani Leib, in *A Little Love in Big Manhattan* (Cambridge, MA: Harvard University Press, 1988), 182–183. For studies on literary depictions of lynching by African American writers, see Trudier Harris, *Exorcising Blackness: Historical and Literary Lynching and Burning Rituals* (Bloomington: Indiana University Press, 1984); and Sandra Gunning, *Race, Rape, and Lynching: The Red Record of American Literature, 1890–1912* (New York: Oxford University Press, 1996).
26. Benjamin Harshav and Barbara Harshav, eds., *American Yiddish Poetry: A Bilingual Anthology* (Berkeley: University of California Press, 1986), 431.
27. See http://law2.umkc.edu/faculty/projects/ftrials/shipp/lynchingyear.html at The University of Missouri at Kansas City School of Law.
28. The performance took place at Café Society, a racially integrated nightclub on Sheridan Square in Greenwich Village. See David Margolick's account of the song in *Strange Fruit: Billie Holiday, Café Society, and an Early Cry for Civil Rights* (Philadelphia: Burning Press, 2000).
29. Hasia Diner, *In the Almost Promised Land: American Jews and Blacks 1915–1935* (Westport: Greenwood Press, 1977), 75. The Yiddish American press took a particular interest in the African American presence, expressing solidarity both when it demanded outcry and when it prompted admiration.
30. Philip Roth, *The Plot Against America* (New York: Random House, 2005), 23.
31. Ibid., 99.
32. Ibid., 99.
33. On Blacks and Jews in the military, see Deborah Dash Moore, *GI Jews: How World War II Changed a Nation* (Cambridge, MA: Harvard/Belknap Press, 2004); and Nat Brandt, *Harlem at War: The Black Experience in WWII* (Syracuse, NY: Syracuse University Press, 1997).
34. Larry Schwartz, "Roth, Race, and Newark," *Cultural Logic* 7 (2005): 26 pars. 1 (August 2005), http://clogic.eserver.org/2005/schwartz.html
35. Schwartz, "Roth, Race, and Newark."
36. Philip Roth, "The Story Behind 'The Plot Against America'," *The New York Times Book Review*, September 19, 2004, 10–12.
37. Philip Roth, *The Human Stain*, 342.
38. Ibid., 108.
39. On cultural tanning, see Ishmael Reed, "Boxing on Paper," quoted in Budick, *Blacks and Jews*, 144. On "ramifying" as a Jew, see Roth, *The Human Stain*, 131.

40. Epigraph to *The Human Stain.*
41. Philip Roth, *Goodbye, Columbus: And Five Short Stories* (New York: Vintage, 1993), 29.
42. Ibid., 29.
43. See the analysis of this passage in Budick, *Blacks and Jews,* 145.
44. Alan Cooper, *Philip Roth and the Jews* (Albany: State University of New York Press, 1996), 49.
45. Aharon Appelfeld, *Beyond Despair: Three Lectures and a Conversation with Philip Roth* (New York: Fromm International, 1994), 15.
46. Roth, *The Human Stain,* 5.
47. http://www.newyorker.com/online/blogs/books/2012/09/an-open-letter-to-wikipedia.html
48. Ibid., 4.
49. On the equivocal form of whiteness: see Ross Posnock's essay on *The Human Stain,* "Purity and Danger: On Philip Roth," *Raritan* 21, no. 2 (Fall 2001): 85–101. On Allan Bloom and Harold Bloom: see Martin Tucker, "Ravelstein / The Human Stain," *Confrontation,* 72/73(Fall 2000/Winter 2001): 260–264. See also Crouch, *The Artificial White Man,* 38.
50. Philip Roth, "Eli, the Fanatic" in *Goodbye Columbus,* 284.
51. Ibid., 296.
52. Hana Wirth-Nesher, "Resisting Allegory, or Reading 'Eli, the Fanatic' in Tel Aviv," *Prooftexts* 21, no. 1 (Winter, 2001): 103–120.
53. Ibid., 110.
54. Sigmund Freud, "A Child Is Being Beaten" [1919], in J *The Standard Edition of the Complete Psychological Works of Sigmund Freud,* ed. James Strachey, vol. XVII (1917–1919): *An Infantile Neurosis and Other Works* (London: The Hogarth Press and the Institute of Psychoanalysis, London, 1955), 179–204.
55. Sigmund Freud, "Project for a Scientific Psychology" [1895] in *Standard Edition of the Complete Psychological Works of Sigmund Freud,* ed. James Strachey vol. I (1886–1899): *Pre-Psycho-Analytic Publications and Unpublished Drafts* (London: The Hogarth Press and the Institute of Psychoanalysis, London, 1955), 28–391.
56. Quoted in Eric L. Santner, *On The Psychotheology of Everyday Life: Reflections on Freud and Rosenzweig* (Chicago: University of Chicago Press, 2004), 80.
57. Santner, *On the Psychotheology,* 50.
58. Fyodor Dostoevsky, *A Writer's Diary.* Kenneth Lantz (Trans). (Evanston: Northwestern University Press, 2009), 449.
59. Roth, "Eli the Fanatic" in *Goodbye Columbus: And Five Short Stories,* 277.
60. Roth, *The Human Stain,* 242.
61. Roth, *The Plot Against America,* 362.

CHAPTER 4

Urban Space and the Racial–Ethnic Difference

Jews Without Money *and* Home to Harlem

Catherine Rottenberg

In the past two decades, scholars have become increasingly interested in tracing the genealogy of the category of ethnicity in the United States. Indeed, recent scholarship has convincingly argued that the construction of race and the construction of ethnicity have had very different historical trajectories in the United States, and that ethnicity as a category of identity evolved out of a discourse of race, which itself revolved around the poles of whiteness and blackness.[1] Eric Goldstein and others have demonstrated that ethnicity as a concept only gained widespread currency in mid-twentieth-century America when minority groups, such as the Jews, began to self-define in ways that deemphasized the importance of biology while highlighting the importance of social conditions.[2]

Goldstein and other scholars most often date the emergence of the category of ethnicity in the United States to the late 1930s or the post–World War II period, and, yet, while it may indeed be true that the morphing of race into ethnicity for certain minority groups was not complete until mid-century, I propose that the 1920s were absolutely crucial for the beginning of an articulation and representation of an *American* Jewishness, as well as for the already widely documented "new Negro." In this chapter, I argue that Jazz Age African American and Jewish American literature gives us insight into the hows and whys of the emergence and widespread currency of the slippery category of ethnicity. Juxtaposing two noncanonical novels that explore the possibility of mobilizing blackness and Jewishness for counterhegemonic purposes, I suggest that these texts gesture toward a more general cultural process in which Jewishness was being deracialized and disarticulated from race as the Black–White divide was being strengthened and reinscribed. This subcultural literature can therefore be read as dramatizing with particular force questions of racialization and the still ambiguous or in-between status of Jews in early-twentieth-century America.

Jews Without Money and *Home to Harlem*

Published just two years apart, Michael Gold's *Jews Without Money* (1930) and Claude McKay's *Home to Harlem* (1928) each depict, in vivid detail, the underbelly of New York City's two most famous neighborhoods.[3] While Gold's portrayal of the gangs, prostitutes, and criminals of the Lower East Side, and McKay's depiction of the saloons, sweetmen, and violence of Harlem have fascinated readers ever since they first appeared, they have also provoked controversy and scathing critique. Over the years, both novels have been accused of sensationalism, primitivism, and, most recently, of idealizing a certain type of hypermasculinity. Neither has ever managed to enter the mainstream of the Jewish American or African American literary canons, and yet both texts continue to be read and analyzed.

The two novels share a focus on low-class life, a lack of an organized plot structure, and a history of ambivalent literary reception. They are both set in New York City during the early part of the twentieth century, and they both dwell on the significance of their specific urban contexts. Through their extensive descriptions of the poor, the downtrodden, and the working class, the two novels paint vivid pictures of Blacks and Jews who have not made it in U.S. society. Moreover, the texts present complex male protagonists who are resistant to and often contemptuous of dominant U.S. culture. These protagonists inhabit the marginal spaces of the already marginalized Harlem and the Lower East Side and are not portrayed as aspiring to integrate into mainstream middle-class U.S. society. *Home to Harlem* and *Jews Without Money* can, I suggest, be considered particularly useful sites for exploring questions of African American and Jewish American subculturality during the late Progressive Era and Jazz Age. By subculture I mean a liminal space in which a group of marginalized subjects produce and circulate a set of practices and norms that are at variance with and sometimes even in active opposition to the dominant White culture that surrounds them.

In what follows, I juxtapose *Home to Harlem* with *Jews Without Money,* concentrating on the representation of the physical spaces of Harlem and the Lower East Side. These neighborhoods, I argue, come to signify the make-up and the boundaries of the Jewish and Black subcultural worlds in the novels. Such a comparative analysis reveals that, despite the many similarities between McKay and Gold's narratives, these city spaces are described in strikingly different ways. Whereas Harlem is construed as a positive all-Black space whose very blackness seems to have a certain radical potential to counter dominant White society and even engender some kind of political renewal, the Jewishness of the Lower East Side is depicted as unable to mobilize such radical potential.

Because they dramatize the different ways certain countercultural sections within the African American and Jewish American communities were attempting to create alternative norms and inscribe themselves as oppositional subjects in the U.S. landscape, these texts can be read as revealing something about the markedly dissimilar positionality of these two minority groups during the Jazz Age. McKay's narrative underscores the definitional power of the Black–White divide and points to the ways in which blackness as a signifier was sutured to relatively stable and legible signifieds; this suturing, in turn, made the strategic deployment of an essentialist blackness possible, while endowing such a deployment with a subversive and empowering potential. Gold's text, I argue, points toward a process by which "Jewishness"—which, it is crucial to remember, was still inscribed within a racialized discourse—was already being unhinged from more stable and traditional significations during this period, making the strategic mobilization of an essentialist Jewishness for counterhegemonic purposes virtually impossible.

McKay's Harlem

Home to Harlem tells the story of Jake Brown, an African American who deserts the U.S. Army during World War I after suffering intense racial discrimination in its ranks. Jake finds his way back to his native Harlem, and, on his first night in the city, spends the last of his savings to procure the services of a prostitute. Felice, it turns out, has enjoyed the pleasures of the returning soldier so much that she refuses to accept Jake's money and leaves before Jake wakes up. For the rest of the narrative, Jake is searching for Felice.

McKay's novel appears to glorify a certain kind of African American working-class existence, where blackness is essentialized. Throughout the novel, blackness is linked to passion, while Black blood is connected to the primitive, the rhythmic, and even the barbaric. These linkages of blackness to certain stereotypical characteristics led many early critics to dismiss the novel as an example of Black pandering to White racist stereotypes.[4] However, scholars have recently reinterpreted McKay's use of primitivism, arguing that it is not simply an appropriation of "the White cult of the primitive" or a straightforward lionization of a new urban Black masculinity, but rather a way of presenting working-class Black protagonists who are unfettered by middle-class White moral norms.[5]

In fact, *Home to Harlem*'s primitivism can be read as oppositional. McKay's protagonists are fully aware that they can never and will never become part of mainstream White U.S. society, yet rather than dwell on their marginality or strive for a higher status, McKay depicts many of the characters as reveling in the life available to them. This can be read as a rejection of dominant White society and an attempt to carve out an alternative way of being in the world. Jake is described throughout the novel as simply loving life, which he takes as it is and as it comes. The space of Harlem, described as a uniquely Black space filled with places of entertainment and houses of pleasure, signifies and seems to make possible—to a large degree—the good life.

It is on the ship taking Jake back to America that Harlem as a physical space is evoked for the first time. Jake is "crazy" to see the streets of his neighborhood again: "It was two years since he had left Harlem. Fifth Avenue, Lenox Avenue, and One hundred and Thirty-fifth Street with their chocolate-brown and walnut-brown girls, were calling him" (*HH* 8). Before he actually reexperiences his old neighborhood, Jake dreams about it. There are at least two aspects of this initial description that are worth noting. First, the streets are remembered as extremely desirable places, and Jake cannot wait to walk their lengths. Second, the streets are populated in Jake's imagination and fantasy with "brown" women and their "tantalizing brown legs" (*HH* 8). There is what might be termed a sexualized racialization of these city blocks. The streets are color coded and fleshed out with brown bodies; in addition, the bodies inhabiting these streets are feminized and exude sexuality, as well as sexual availability.

Upon returning to his old neighborhood, Jake is thrilling to Harlem: "Harlem! Harlem! Little thicker, little darker and noisier and smellier, but Harlem just the same" (*HH* 26). The world that Jake reenters is crowded, perhaps a little too crowded, with dark bodies and full of strident noises and pungent smells. Yet this world also very clearly has its own texture and richness. After he manages to pick up Felice, the two find a place to sleep for the night. Jake is overjoyed at his luck, and he asks himself where else but "Chocolate Harlem" could he have "all this life?" (*HH* 14). Harlem's charm is intimately linked to pleasure—gaiety, sex and sexuality, drink, syncopated movement, and music.

While some contemporary scholars have underscored McKay's portrayal of Harlem as a vibrant if seedy and masculinized urban center of working-class Black life, not enough has been said about McKay's specific use of and emphasis on color to depict this racial enclave.[6] There are very few descriptions of Harlem—its streets, its buildings, and the people inhabiting and traversing them—where the blackness of this space is not stressed. Blackness, in all of its various manifestations and shades, forms the background and frames all that pertains to Harlem; color, perhaps more than anything else, is the defining feature of this neighborhood and the subculture it has generated. Black America, the text intimates, came to Manhattan's northern tip and created this alternative world, a world with little use for Whites.

In this sense, McKay's portrayal of Harlem is similar to the depictions found in the contemporaneous genteel novels of Nella Larsen and Jessie Fauset. The descriptions of Harlem in Larsen's *Quicksand* (1928) and Fauset's *Plum Bun* (1928) also emphasize the color and the racial make-up of these city streets.[7] The difference between McKay's portrayal and these genteel novels can be seen in their extremely ambivalent description of Black Harlem. Helga Crane, the protagonist of *Quicksand,* for instance, fluctuates dramatically between a certain admiration of the Black neighborhood, since it seems to represent racial solidarity and pride, and a strong abhorrence to being yoked to the thousands of Black bodies inhabiting Harlem's streets.[8] Given that Fauset and Larsen's protagonists are depicted as actively negotiating between minority and mainstream norms, it is perhaps not surprising that most of the depictions of this space in these genteel novels fall into a mode of ambivalence. No matter how positive the initial description of Harlem, there is almost always a qualification or some conflicted affectivity that seeps into or follows the affirmative depictions.

By contrast, the descriptions of Harlem in McKay's text are almost always positive; when ambivalence does emerge, as it occasionally does, the pattern in *Home to Harlem* is inverted. Rather than beginning with a more positive description and then falling into some qualification or negativity, the negative pole emerges first, and then the depiction usually ends with a recuperation of the positive. Even Ray, the displaced

Haitian intellectual, articulates the allure of this unique space: "Black Harlem! Its brutality, gang rowdyism, promiscuous thickness. Its hot desires. But, ho, the warm accent of its composite voice, the fruitiness of its laughter, the railing rhythm of its 'blues' and the improvised surprises of its jazz" (*HH* 267). Recognizing all of its vices, violence, and brutality, McKay still has Ray underscore the positive aspects of this urban space and emphasize what seems to define it as uniquely Black.

Harlem's Oppositional Force

Alain Locke famously stated that Harlem, as the largest Black urban enclave in the US, if not the world, initially emerged through prejudice.[9] Blacks from dissimilar backgrounds and with dissimilar aspirations were thrown together into a common area of contact and interaction. Indeed, the Black settlement of Harlem was part of the Great Migration during which approximately half a million African Americans left the South for northern cities between 1916 and 1920. Hoping for better economic conditions, an escape from the violence of Jim Crow racism, and more social and cultural freedom, many of these migrants settled in New York City. By the mid-1920s, some 200,000 African Americans were living cheek-by-jowl in the increasingly segregated neighborhood of Harlem.[10] However, Locke continues, "what began in terms of segregation is becoming more and more, as its elements mix and react, the laboratory of a great race-welding."[11] In a sense, McKay's descriptions of Harlem can be seen to parallel this assertion, but with a certain crucial twist. In *Home to Harlem,* the positive aspects of this distinctively Black world do not emanate from the so-called talented tenth, or the middle class, but rather from the common working person who endeavors to shun as completely as possible the racist and capitalist norms of the dominant society. Harlem, as the largest all-Black community and as a common meeting ground for African Americans from all over the country as well as from the West Indies, is portrayed as having created its own vibrant positive *Black* culture. The negative aspects of Harlem, while undeniably present, tend to fade in comparison—at least for most of the narrative—or are depicted as having helped to make possible the welding of a rich urban subculture that endeavors to produce, circulate, and live by counterhegemonic norms.

Even though there is a certain lingering ambivalence expressed in the descriptions of Black Manhattan in the novel, there is also a very pronounced attempt to explore the possibility of creating a subculture full of race pride, pleasure, and value not based on the standard of

White imperialism, exploitative capitalism, or the compromised (because complicit) ideals of the Black middle class. Thus, the most important alternative norm emphasized in McKay's novel is the one that reevaluates blackness as worthy in and of itself. As the early critics of *Home to Harlem* noted and mostly decried, the traits that were historically linked to blackness in the United States, such as a primitive passion, a love of pleasure, music, and movement, remain linked to blackness—and, it is important to note, in the novel these traits are linked to a perhaps amorphous general blackness and not just to Black masculinity or to the Black working class.[12] However, the valence of these traits is turned on its head and affirmed as positive. These are exactly the characteristics, as the novel intimates, that can be used to oppose racist and capitalist oppression in the United States. McKay's early version of "Black is beautiful" can be read as a move that is meant to challenge White America and empower African Americans, and in this sense the space he depicts through the tropes of primitivism is oppositional, since it serves as a site where standards of industrial capitalism are criticized through the elevation of alternative norms like bodily pleasure and the occasional work ethic—the latter best represented in the railroad sections of the novel (especially Jake's stint as third cook; see *HH* 125–126). McKay's emphasis of blackness in all its various manifestations and its particular presentation should be understood as a strategic move that aims both to uncover and to advance a possible counterhegemonic option. The Harlem sections in McKay's novel, then, can be read as an experiment—but not an uncritical or completely successful one—in creating an alternative and desirable Black world. Consequently, this world becomes a positive alternative both to the White mainstream and to the ideals of the Black middle class.

Gold's Lower East Side

Michael Gold's *Jews Without Money* is a meandering pseudo-autobiographical novel, narrated in the first person, that strings together a variety of impressionistic vignettes from the fictional Mikey's childhood and transition to adolescence. It is, in many ways, the story of Mikey's ultimate conversion to communism. The text describes Mikey's impoverished childhood on the Lower East Side, and his family's struggle to maintain a modicum of self-respect amidst the neighborhood's violence and poverty. It is a novel strewn with images of prostitution, gangsterism, and corruption.

It is important to note that the area in lower Manhattan that would later be called the Lower East Side had a Jewish presence long before the turn of the twentieth century. However, it was only following the tidal wave of Jewish Eastern European immigration, that commenced in the early 1880s, that a certain swath of lower Manhattan—south of 14th Street and north of Fulton, nestled between Broadway and the East River—began to be perceived as a specifically "Jewish" place. At the peak of Jewish residence in 1910, there were more than half a million Jews living in the Lower East Side.[13]

The majority of literary critics who have attempted to reclaim *Jews Without Money* as part of the Jewish American literary tradition have—while praising its sincerity—ultimately judged the novel to be devoid of any literary merit or to be a relatively transparent vehicle for communist propaganda.[14] More recent scholarship, though, has begun to offer increasingly complex analyses of *Jews Without Money*. Lee Bernstein, for instance, asserts that Gold mobilizes Black and Native American racial stereotypes as a kind of racial masquerade. These masquerades, problematic as they are, serve in the novel as the conduit for a *White* Jewish working-class performance of opposition.[15]

Bernstein convincingly stresses the significance of a kind of Jewish opposition (albeit channeled through racial masquerade) in Gold's text as well as the protagonist's resistance to "middle class respectability."[16] Indeed, unlike the protagonists of the more canonical Jewish novels written in this period, Mikey is not portrayed as desiring to become part of dominant culture, but rather as constantly searching for an alternative. Toward the end of the novel, for example, Mikey refuses to go to high school like the other so-called smart boys and chooses instead to go to work even though he knows that high school and college are perhaps his only ticket to upward mobility. But in contrast to Bernstein, I propose that the novel is concerned with the question of whether Jewishness itself can serve as oppositional, and the text registers a certain equivocation in relation to this question. This ambivalence is articulated not only in the ways in which the Lower East Side is described, but also in the narrative trajectory. The novel begins with an ethnically neutral description of the Lower East Side. The text then goes on to mark the neighborhood as Jewish, while exploring three Jewish subcultural spaces as possible oppositional sites to the American Dream—the working-class Jewish world of Mikey's father, the Jewish gangster, and, finally, the Jewish religious world of Hasidism.

On the very first page of *Jews Without Money,* Gold describes the East Side street where Mikey, the narrator, lived as a boy. The street, the reader is told, "never slept. It roared like a sea.… People pushed and wrangled in the street. Women screamed, dogs barked. Babies cried."[17] Similar to McKay's portrayal of Harlem, the Lower East Side is depicted as vibrating with life: "Pimps, gamblers and red-nosed bums. ... Excitement, dirt, fighting, chaos!" (*JWM* 13–14). While it would be difficult to read these descriptions as an attempt to paint a glowing picture of the neighborhood, the portrayal evinces a pulsating expectation and contagious energy. Yet the race or "ethnicity" of the people inhabiting the streets is not immediately noted.

As the novel progresses, however, and as the narrator begins to recount his early years on the East Side, the Jewishness of the city streets does in fact become more pronounced. The initial and "ethnically-neutral" picture of Mikey's streets is soon followed by a description of how, with the advent of spring weather, the parades of Jews suddenly emerge from their winter seclusion to sniff at the crisp, fragrant air (*JWM* 16). In subsequent descriptions, Mikey reminds the reader that the space he is describing is Jewish by inserting reference to the "race" of its inhabitants or pedestrians: For instance, Gold has Mikey emphasize the Jewishness of the space by describing how it has been invaded by foreigners: "Germans, Poles, Russians, Armenians, Irish, Chinese; there were always a *few* of these *aliens* living among our Jews" (*JWM* 174; emphasis added). The very title, *Jews Without Money,* frames the way in which the reader understands the space. Thus, not unlike his African American counterpart, Gold does mark the "ethnic" character of the space while commenting on its animation and vibrancy.

Although Jewishness is not foregrounded to nearly the same degree as Harlem's blackness is in McKay's novel, *Jews Without Money* nonetheless limns the Lower East Side as an ethnically specific space to a much greater degree than the canonical Jewish texts of this period. In novels such as Anzia Yezierska's *Arrogant Beggar* (1927) and *Salome of the Tenements* (1923), the protagonists describe and emphasize the dirt, the sordidness, and the poverty of the Lower East Side, but not its Jewishness.[18] Moreover, these novels depict their characters' deep ambivalence toward the neighborhood through class-inflected rather than ethnically inflected language, and the positive pole of the ambivalence is rarely evidenced in the physical descriptions of the space. For these Jewish protagonists—who are negotiating their position in relation to mainstream middle-class society—the most pressing problem is presented as poverty and not being defined or defining oneself as Jewish. This, I believe, points to the concern in more canonical novels with inscribing a positive Jewish American identity, one in which there is compatibility between the two aspects of this identity.[19] *Jews Without Money*, by contrast, raises and thematizes the problem of Jewish difference in a much more overt and arguably sophisticated way.

The Lower East Side's Oppositional Force

I maintain that Gold's ambivalence toward the Jewishness of the neighborhood is informed by Mikey's search for an oppositional space. Although the narrator initially hopes to find what he would consider a countercultural and oppositional *Jewish* subculture, he ends up disappointed with the Jewish subcultural spaces on the Lower East Side because he finds that most of the people who occupy these spaces are ultimately willing to negotiate with mainstream society and therefore are ultimately unwilling to challenge the status quo. There are three places in which the possibility of an alternative and positive Jewish subculture seems to arise in Gold's text. One such space emerges in the informal get-togethers of Mikey's father and his working-class friends. The novel describes how every night at Mikey's house "there was a convention of ... Jews struggling in the promised land" (*JWM* 82). These Jews are Mikey's father's friends: housepainters, peddlers, and clothing workers, who gather to play poker, while philosophizing, singing, and telling stories. These conventions constitute a world unto themselves—a Jewish world on the Lower East Side in which these men (and occasionally women) congregate to tell stories, debate, and drink tea or wine. While the narrator is described as being captivated by this all-Jewish working-class space, filled with "Jewish talk," which is at great odds with the demand for efficiency in the workplace, Mikey concludes this is a place where "magic mountains and wishing lamps ... were as real as the sweatshops and garbage cans" (*JWM* 84). From the point of view of the retrospective narrative, there is also another critical problem with this all-Jewish subculture: it does not shun the values of the dominant White society.

This is perhaps best represented in the scene in which Mikey's father and his friends decide to convene their nightly meeting in one of the Jewish wine cellars. On the wall of this very popular Jewish joint there is a "big American flag ... showing Roosevelt charging up San Juan Hill. At the other end hung a Jewish Zionist flag ... and star of David" (*JWM* 115). The juxtaposition of Roosevelt on an imperialist mission and the Zionist flag appears to gesture toward the increasing compatibility of these two nationalisms. Even in this cavernous and literally subterranean alternative Jewish space, where "people talked, laughed, drank wine, listened to music" (*JWM* 114) in a so-called Jewish rather than Christian manner, the novel underscores how Jewishness—even a kind of subcultural Jewishness—was already enmeshed in dominant images of Americanness. To punctuate this imbrication, Mikey, who has been invited to join the men, is asked by his father to stand on the table and recite a poem he has learned at school. Mikey dutifully complies, declaiming the lines, "I love the name of Washington, I love my country, too, I love the flag, the dear old flag, the red, white and blue" (*JWM* 120). It is the red, white, and blue flag and not the white and blue flag that is being saluted here. Walking home that evening, Mikey's father tells his son, "All is lost unless I can borrow three hundred dollars somewhere" (*JWM* 122). These mythical $300 are what Mikey's father believes will allow him to open his own business and make good on the American Dream. Unlike Jake and his fellow working-class Black Harlemites, Mikey's father and the other Jewish working-class men on the Lower East Side are not described as reveling in the world available to them; rather they constantly rail against their marginality, which points to their desire to move out of the margins and into the mainstream.

The second possible Jewish subcultural alternative to dominant society is the Jewish gangster, whose reign is both enabled and circumscribed by the Lower East Side. While the future gangster named Nigger is presented as the positive embodiment of Jewish gangsterism, Louis One Eye, the other prominent gangster, is portrayed as a brutal despot. Louis One Eye is certainly defiant of society's norms and even defends old frightened Jews who are harassed by neighboring Gentiles, yet he is also ruthless and cruel. Mikey eventually comes to hate Louis after the gangster attempts to rape his beloved aunt Lena. Following this traumatic incident, Mikey realizes that the Jewish gangster is actually a mercenary, "a bad egg hatched by the bad world hen" (*JWM* 125). In other words, not only does the narrator understand that there is nothing essentially Jewish about the gangster, but also that the Lower East Side gangsters are complicit in the very structures of domination that they are supposed to counter as outlaws. The "Jewish" gangster, it turns out, is a creation of the state, "useful to bosses in strikes, and to politicians on election day" (*JWM* 140).

The third and last Jewish space that Mikey explores as a possible haven and alternative to both oppressive mainstream U.S. culture and the violence of his own working-class environment is the strain of traditional Judaism embodied in the Hasidic Reb Samuel (*JWM* 191). Mikey finds refuge in his friendship with the older man as the young narrator searches for Jewish religious answers to existential questions. Simultaneously mesmerized and disturbed by the notion of the Messiah, Mikey at one points asks his spiritual mentor whether the Messiah will look like Buffalo Bill—a very American and hypermasculine incarnation. Reb Samuel rejoins by insisting that he would be more like the ideal Jewish *yeshiva bokher* (religious seminary student), "pale, young and peaceful" (*JWM* 190). While the answer initially disappoints the young Mikey, it also seems to soothe him, for he continues to prompt the Reb to speak about the Messiah, even though Reb Samuel gives Mikey a similar response every time. This, I suggest, speaks to the young protagonist's desire to find a Jewish solution to his existential angst. Reb Samuel and his Hasidic community, with their practice of spiritual abandon and ecstasy, seem at first to symbolize something completely at odds with the land of "hurry up and all-rightniks." Ultimately, though, Mikey recounts how America manages to infiltrate even the alternative religious Jewish world that Reb Samuel has tried to create. First, a member of his sect shaves his beard because in the United States "beards are laughed at" (*JWM* 196). Soon after, other members of the congregation appear shorn of facial hair. The situation deteriorates to such a degree that Reb Samuel and the other Hasidim decide that they need a synagogue and a rabbi, something they had not thought necessary before. The newly acquired rabbi—ordered and delivered from Eastern Europe—however, turns out to be a fraud, and a year following the rabbi's arrival in America, and after Reb Samuel has spent all of his time raising funds to keep the congregation head in relative luxury, the rabbi deserts the community. When Reb Samuel hears the news of the rabbi's abandonment, he suffers a stroke from which he never recovers. Mikey realizes, "[i]t finally defeated him, this America" (*JWM* 191).

Mikey's youthful odyssey on the Lower East Side takes him through various Jewish Lower East Side subcultural spaces, and yet none of these seem to provide him with a strong enough foundation for countering what he perceives to be the United States' structures of domination. The marking of the Lower East Side as Jewish alongside the ambivalence evinced in the portrayal of this space can thus be read as linked to the narrative's ideological trajectory. In other words, Gold's text traces Mikey's attempt to find a solution to the structures of oppression and domination that he finds in his world. Initially, as I have argued, Mikey believes that Jewish subcultural space can provide an oppositional space. But, as the narrative progresses, it becomes clearer and clearer to the young protagonist that Jewishness—at least as it manifests itself on the Lower East Side—cannot serve as a basis for opposing hegemonic norms. Unlike blackness in McKay's text, which serves as a relatively stable signifier that can be deployed to empower African Americans, Jewishness in Gold's narrative becomes, in many ways, a floating signifier whose meaning is constantly being renegotiated. For the narrator, who is looking for absolutes, the shifting signification of Jewishness presents a real obstacle to political action and renewal. Thus, it is not until Mikey encounters the possibility of communism that he sees the possibility of a truly oppositional position.

Leaving the Urban Spaces Behind

Both protagonists of *Home to Harlem* and *Jews Without Money* ultimately leave their racially or "ethnically" specific subcultural spaces behind at the end of the novels. Mikey aligns himself with a movement and worldview that eschews the particularity of "ethnicity," and thus, in a sense, abandons what he perceives to be the already Americanized Jewishness of the Lower East Side. By contrast, Jake's abandonment is literal, since he takes up and actually leaves Harlem for Chicago. While the ending of *Jews Without Money* is predictable given the narrative trajectory, Jake's departure from Harlem needs explanation.

The fact that *Home to Harlem* ends with Jake's decision to leave New York suggests that McKay's glorification of "blackness," which is exemplified and literally embodied in the descriptions of Harlem, is indeed strategic and not without a certain internal criticism. What is so interesting about this narrative twist is that Jake's decision to leave New York for Chicago is not—as might be expected—ascribed to Harlem's spatialized racialization but rather to Black Manhattan's sexual politics. Jake departs, unwillingly as it were, to avoid a conflict with his friend Zeddy. Jake and Felice end up together, but there is a certain triangulation and a threat of violence that compel Jake to start anew in the Midwest instead of fighting Zeddy for Felice. He is, we are told, fed up with "[t]hese miserable cock-fights. They had always sickened, unmanned him.... Love should be joy lifting out of the humdrum ways of life" (*HH* 328). So if Jake's odyssey began with the feminized sexualization of Harlem's streets and a predatory pursuit, his odyssey ends with a celebration of mutual love (masculinist as it still might be) and a rejection of the sexualized violence that characterizes most of the heterosexual unions in McKay's Harlem. While it would be difficult to read the novel as feminist, there is a certain thematized and critical reassessment of normative Black urban masculinity.

Such an internal critique problematizes or at least unsettles the text's celebratory essentialist racial tendencies, since the novel reveals that while the lionization of certain racial traits can potentially lead to a unique and rich Black subcultural space, such a glorification can also potentially generate destructive effects, such as Black-on-Black and sexualized violence. McKay's text then can be read as strategically complex—attempting, as it were, to empower African American readers through a reevaluation of racial difference and to challenge White racist capitalism, while simultaneously destabilizing some of its own essentialist and masculinist tendencies by creating narrative contradictions and tensions.

As we have seen (and in contrast to McKay's depiction of Harlem), in Gold's novel the space of the Lower East Side does not come to signify or make possible the good life. The description of this Jewish space is much more overtly ambivalent. On the one hand, the narrative does maintain a certain appreciation of and even admiration for the Jewish Lower East Side—the text's descriptions of the neighborhood are laced with adjectives connoting excitement and vibrancy. Moreover, it is on an East Side soap box that Mikey first hears about the Revolution and his experiences in the neighborhood help render Mikey's ideological conversion possible (*JWM* 309). On the other hand, the economically depressed but also specifically Jewish space must be eradicated in order to provide an alternative to the structures of domination. The book ends with the famous lines, "O workers' Revolution, you brought hope to me.... You are the true Messiah. You will destroy the East Side when you come, and build there a garden for the human spirit" (*JWM* 309). The Lower East Side must become a garden—stripped of its urban element—for the *human* spirit—without a trace of "ethnic" difference. While the novel is unequivocal with respect to the Jewish Lower East Side's lack of countercultural potential, there does remain a lingering ambivalence—evidenced in the invocation of the Messiah to describe the revolution—which registers Gold's ultimate inability to completely erase or settle on the question of what exactly constitutes Jewish difference.

Conclusion

While McKay glorifies a racial identity in his novel, mobilizing blackness to imagine an alternative space and to critique U.S. society, Gold's protagonist becomes disillusioned with the various manifestations of Jewishness on the Lower East Side and therefore can neither exult in a "Jewish" identity nor mobilize Jewishness for radical political purposes. This last begs the crucial question: Why could McKay conceive of a fictional Harlem that not only embodies the good life, but also functions as oppositional and countercultural, while Gold's Jewish Lower East Side neither signifies the good life nor serves as a true alternative space?

Gold's narrative can be read as gesturing both toward the way many Jews were attempting to inscribe themselves as normative American subjects and thus whiten themselves (not always very successfully), and toward the more particular ways Jewishness as a category of identification was being refashioned during this period. Even though being

Jewish is still articulated in racial terms in the text, what actually occurs in the narrative is a destabilization of this racialization. So while the narrator speaks on the one hand about Jewish understanding and smartness, he also insists that there is no Jewish racial type (*JWM* 81). Even the conceived bookishness of the Jews is ultimately attributed to social conditions rather than an inherent tendency (*JWM* 87). Moreover, as we have seen, Gold identifies and links Jewishness more to a set of diverse *practices*—a certain kind of stylized talk, religious rituals, or performances of loyalty and defense.

By contrast, as a category of identity, "blackness" was still very much defined in terms of racial traits in the popular U.S. imagination during the 1920s.[20] This is one of the main reasons that Harlem could be imagined as a racialized space with a rich alternative culture. The stubbornness with which blackness remained linked to a series of identifiable characteristics produced a set of powerful effects. One effect was, of course, the reinscription and reinforcement of the Black–White divide, which, in turn, enabled Jews to jockey for a position as normative and White Americans.

Thus, *Jews Without Money* raises the question of Jewish difference in a complex if provocative way, whereas *Home to Harlem* mobilizes blackness to imagine an alternative to dominant U.S. society and to critique existing norms as well as its own strategic and narrative maneuvers. In their representation of rich and multifaceted subcultural spaces, both texts meditate on questions of otherness and opposition in the United States—questions that gain even more urgency in the twenty-first century.

Acknowledgments

An earlier version of a portion of this chapter originally appeared in my essay "Writing on the Margins of the Margins: *Michael Gold's Jews Without Money* and Claude McKay's *Home to Harlem*," *MELUS*, Vol. 35. no. 1 (2010): 119–140.

Notes

1. See, e.g., Catherine Rottenberg, *Performing Americanness: Gender, Race, and Class in Modern African and Jewish American Literature* (Hanover, NH: University of New England Press, 2008), 70–92.
2. See Goldstein, *Price of Whiteness*, 165–208.
3. Michael Gold, *Jews Without Money* [1930] (New York: Carroll & Graf, 1996); and Claude McKay, *Home to Harlem* [1928] (Boston: Northeastern University Press, 1987).

4. See, e.g., Wayne Cooper, "Foreword," in McKay, *Home to Harlem* (Boston, 1987), ix–xxvi. In his foreword, Cooper discusses the way early critics responded to *Home to Harlem.* All subsequent references to the novel will be to this edition and will be cited parenthetically in the text as *HH.*
5. See, e.g., Michael Maiwald, "Race, Capitalism, and the Third-Sex Ideal: Claude McKay's *Home to Harlem* and the Legacy of Edward Carpenter," *Modern Fiction Studies* 48, no. 4 (2002): 825–857. Maiwald concentrates on McKay's depiction of sexuality and gender as sites of opposition. While my argument is indebted to his insights, I focus on the way in which Harlem comes to represent an alternative to White America as well as the way the more general category of blackness is deployed as countercultural in McKay's text.
6. See, e.g., Sidney Bremer, "Home in Harlem, New York: Lessons from the Harlem Renaissance Writers," *PMLA* 105, no. 1 (1990): 47–56. Bremer claims that McKay is typical in his use of "sensory images to present Harlem as home place.... It is fleshy—embodied in lively colors, tastes, and sounds" (49).
7. Nella Larsen, *Quicksand and Passing* [1928,1929] (New Brunswick, NJ: Rutgers University Press, 1986); and Jessie Fauset, *Plum Bun* [1928] (Boston: Beacon Press, 1990).
8. See Larsen, *Quicksand and Passing,* 55.
9. See Alain Locke, "The New Negro," in *The New Negro: Voices of the Harlem Renaissance* (New York: Simon & Schuster, 1997), 7.
10. See Wallace Thurman, "Negro Life in New York's Harlem," in *The Collected Writings of Wallace Thurman* (Brunswick, NJ: Rutgers University Press, 2003), 42.
11. Alain Locke, "The New Negro," 7.
12. See Cooper, "Foreword," ix–xxvi.
13. For a short history of the Lower East Side prior to the 1880s, see Hasia Diner, *Lower East Memories* (Princeton, NJ: Princeton University Press, 2000), 46–47.
14. See Alfred Kazin, "Introduction," in Gold, *Jews Without Money,* 1–9.
15. Lee Bernstein, "The Avengers of Christie Street: Racism and Jewish Working Class Rebellion," in *The Novel and the American Left: Critical Essays on Depression-Era Fiction,* ed. Janet Galligani Gasey (Iowa City: University of Iowa Press, 2004), 118–130.
16. Bernstein, "Avengers of Christie Street," 125
17. Gold, *Jews Without Money,* 13. All subsequent references to the novel will be cited parenthetically in the text as *JWM.*
18. Anzia Yezierska, *Arrogant Beggar* [1927] (Durham: Duke University Press, 1996) and *Salome of the Tenements* [1923] (Urbana: University of Illinois Press, 1995).
19. See Rottenberg, *Performing Americanness,* 92–108.
20. See Shane and Graham White, *Stylin': African American Expressive Culture from Its Beginnings to the Zoot Suit* (Ithaca, NY: Cornell University Press, 1998), where they argue that in the 1920s the features that had historically been linked to blackness in the United States were being revaluated by African Americans themselves.

CHAPTER 5

African American Culture, Anthropological Practices, and the Jewish Race in Zora Neale Hurston's *Mules and Men*

Dalit Alperovich

This chapter examines the ways in which Zora Neale Hurston's collection of African American folklore in *Mules and Men* (1935) identifies strategic and self-serving dimensions to Jewish anthropologists' engagement with African American culture and sheds light on the role Boasian anthropological practices played in consolidating negotiated definitions of whiteness in the 1920s and 1930s. *Mules and Men* portrays African American oral cultural productions from the rural South. The work presents oral folktales about the time when slavery was common, mythic creation stories, songs and sermons, and is part of the modern anthropological tradition. The ethnography was written under the guidance of the renowned Jewish American anthropologist of German origin, Franz Boas, the father of American anthropology. Deviating from Boasian ethnographic writing norms, however, the book is an autoethnography, and includes its author's adventures as an anthropologist doing fieldwork, dialogues among storytellers, and informants' responses to Hurston's endeavor.

Shortly before the book's publication, Hurston contacted Boas, and asked him to write a preface to *Mules and Men,* despite the work's awkward, unscientific, nature. She wrote apologetically to Boas,

> I have inserted the between-story conversation and business because when I offered it without it, every publisher said it was too monotonous. Now

> three houses want to publish it. So I hope that the unscientific matter that must be there for the sake of the average reader will not keep you from writing the introduction. It so happens that the conversations and incidents are true. But of course I never would have set them down for scientists to read. I know that the learned societies are interested in the story in many ways that would never interest the average mind. He needs no stimulation. But the man in the street is different.[1]

Rejecting former evolutionist anthropological conceptions via the Boasian principle of cultural relativism, the new participant-observation methodology of modern anthropology required the scientist to study each culture on its own terms rather than according to any Western precepts. The written product, the ethnography, was to objectively relate solely to that culture, describing the ethnographer's initiation into the field of study as the only moment of the author's presence in the text. Yet Hurston's position as an ethnographer was different: using "the spy-glass of anthropology," as she put it in the introduction to *Mules and Men,* she was to investigate her own community, complicating the Boasian call for objectivity.[2] Moreover, depicting her experiences and including informants' reactions to the ethnographic enterprise went against Boasian rules of writing. Critics have claimed that the autoethnographer's threshold position generates a critique on modern anthropology's doctrine and methodology. Pointing to Hurston's resistance to the empowering White male gaze over objectified, powerless Blacks, they have constructed *Mules and Men* in terms of colonization and power relations. Yet, since both Boas and at least half of his students at Columbia University were not White, but Jewish, the critical tendency to construct the book in Black and White terms is surprising.[3] The beginning of the twentieth century witnessed a fascinating shift in America's definition of whiteness, from hierarchically ordered plural White races in the 1840s to a consolidated White Caucasian race in the 1920s.[4] By investigating various, unexplored, aspects of Hurston's critique of Boasian tenets, this chapter presents the author's resistance to the role anthropological practices played in such redefinitions of whiteness in the 1920s and 1930s, and traces Hurston's representation of the empowering anthropological gaze as predominantly Jewish. Moreover, *Mules and Men* has been read as a striking prefiguration of postmodern anthropology, with its polyvocal quality, the author's presence in the text, and its emphasis on subjectivity.[5] Yet some scholars warn against postmodern readings of the text, and claim that such analyses ignore the context of the work's production, its reception, and the context of the traditions in which it was produced.[6] Reading *Mules and Men* using the spyglass of postmodern anthropology, I wish to recontextualize the text in the sociopolitical circumstances of its production and publication in order to reveal the impact of anthropologists and of the discipline itself on the ways in which the color line is redrawn in this period.

As Hurston's letter to Boas shows, the African American ethnographer comes to realize that in order for her book to be published, she has to objectify herself. Her White readership is interested not only in the group under investigation, but also in its Black investigator. Hurston presents her work as split between the scientific matter that the average reader is reluctant to consume, and the between-story conversation, supposedly redundant for the intelligent scholar. Rather than rejecting *Mules and Men* as unscientific, Boas qualifies Hurston's work as more authentic than former research conducted by White anthropologists. In contrast to Hurston's claim in the letter to Boas, her racial visibility is equally important to both the scientist and the average reader, since it is the "between-story conversation and business" that marks her in the text as an African American insider-ethnographer, a position Boas clearly finds advantageous.

Autoethnography, then, both is appealing to the general public as exotic and provides a sense of authority and authenticity to the anthropological enterprise. However, for Hurston it is a double-edged sword, facilitating her own cultural dispossession and anthropological marginalization. The scene portraying Hurston's moment of initiation into the field of study offers a revealing example. Returning to her hometown at Eatonville, Florida, as a well-educated woman, driving a car from New York to the rural South, Hurston is considered an outsider. Nevertheless, she is admitted into Eatonville's community when she participates in a toe party. Standing behind a curtain concealing everything but toes, the young women at the party 'sell' their toes to the men, and then each 'buyer' treats the lady whose toes he has just 'purchased.' As this scene exemplifies, racial visibility and ethnographic invisibility are presented as advantageous because they allow Hurston to gain access to the community under investigation. The curtain enables Hurston to truly become a participant observer, but it also exposes, if only through the toes, her black body to both the Black Southern men and to the readers.

The toe party raises the issue of blackness as possession. Benigno Sánchez-Eppler points out that the custom is reminiscent of slave auctions—the ultimate embodiment of the Black body as commodity.[7] The scholar reads Hurston's boast of being sold five times as proof of her self-possession—she 'sells' her toes for the sake of accessing ethnographic knowledge, but she always owns herself enough to sell herself once more.[8] Yet Hurston's resold black toes turn into a commodity not only for the Black buyer, but also for both the book's publisher and the anthropological community. Requiring Hurston to avoid the objective, scientific, dry style of ethnography, the publishing houses are interested in objectifying a Black ethnographer in order to increase the book's market value. At the same time, using such unconventional style keeps Hurston at the margins of anthropology at the moment of the discipline's institutionalization and professionalization as scientific and objective.[9]

Hurston's marginal position in the anthropological field is not merely a matter of writing style. The basic premise of the Boasian anthropologist's work is that he or she is to investigate the culture of the Other, and Boas has a clear sense of the identity of that Other. Although in his book *The Mind of Primitive Man* (1938) Boas insists on examining culture and resists biological definitions of race, his own research and that of his most prominent students of American groups focuses mainly on Native Americans and, to a lesser degree, African Americans.[10] To Boas, who presents in his preface his wish to reveal the "true inner life" of the Negro, the Black rural South is perceived as an unknown primitive culture worthy of investigation and of understanding. When he declares that Hurston's identity as a Black woman from the rural South enables her to "penetrate through that affected demeanour by which the Negro excludes the White observer effectively from participating in his own true inner life," Boas clearly identifies two racial groups: a White anthropologist and a Black object of study.[11] Matthew Frye Jacobson warns against a simplistic view, which sees Boas and others as creators of the social division between Black and White. "Nonetheless," writes Jacobson, "in defining certain social relations as the proper object of study and in absolutely neglecting others, the disciplines devoted to 'race relations' did generate their own 'races.' And inasmuch as there was a broad consensus on which relations were most important, for good or bad the populace became racialized along certain lines and not others."[12] Moreover, defining certain groups as worthy of anthropological investigation both racialized these groups and identified the anthropological community as nonracial. Scott Michaelsen contends, "exclusion is anthropology's very possibility, even though anthropology's project, its goal, is to attend to the other according to its own terms—that is, to make a space for the other in the world, to record and account for its differences."[13] The anthropological project draws a clear color line between the supposedly White observer and the racially defined Other. And the black toes, which enhance Hurston's penetration into the Black community, limit her ability to become a member in the supposedly White anthropological community.

Boasian anthropology called for the separation of race from culture. Boas rejected the assumption that races were hierarchically ordered, and claimed that the civilization of certain groups was a random historical process.[14] Hurston's research was to serve as another proof of Boas's claim regarding the equal value of all cultures. In the name of cultural relativism, both Boas and Hurston saw her mission as a valuable documentation of African American cultural productions, and the folktales as underlying ethnocultural identity. Yet, as Hurston's black toes exemplify, anthropological practices underlying her research rely heavily on race, and the racial identity of the autoethnographer posits her in a subordinate position within the discipline, thereby reproducing a racial hierarchy.

Profit is another question raised in reading the toe party scene. According to Hurston's biographer, Robert Hemenway, the book was not the property of its author. Funding the research, the ethnography was legally owned by Hurston's White benefactor, Mrs. Rufus Osgood Mason, who held its copyright and was entitled to edit the work and make changes as she saw fit. Hurston did not have a formal education, and even though Boas urged her to convince Mason to financially support her doctoral studies, Mason objected, determined to keep Hurston as a collector, not a professional.[15] Holding neither a doctoral degree nor an academic position, Hurston could not enjoy any of the benefits related to having a professional book published. Ironically, then, the 'sale' of Hurston's toes undermines rather than guarantees her access to cultural and economic capital granted to professional anthropologists.

Investigating the text by applying the tenets of postmodern anthropology, it is possible to explore *Mules and Men* within the historical and political contexts of its production. Ethnographic penetration into the field of study, a major concern in postmodern anthropology, is described in the toe party scene. Through the scene Hurston introduces race and possession as important terms in the context of anthropological practices and points at their convergence. The author discusses the autoethnographer's limited access to anthropological translation of cultural products into cultural capital and economic value. Last but not least, Hurston implicitly presents anthropological practices as a means to draw a color line, separating the visibly racial observed Other from the supposedly White anthropologist.

Hurston's private letters, dealing with problems of initiation into the field of study, further explore the concerns raised in the toe party scene. In a letter to Ruth Benedict, a Boasian teacher and mentor, Hurston reveals,

> My task is harder at times than I had anticipated. You see there are Negroes with "Race Consciousness" and "Race pride" drilled into them and they resent anything that looks like harking back to slavery. I am getting along splendidly in a group—everybody digging their heads to tell me things when some "race man" or woman shows up with something like this: "Whuts all this fur, nohow? Some White folks is trying tuh get something so they kin poke fun at us. They want us back in slavery. Why don't they write something bout our school principal—*Professah* Smith? [emphasis in original] Now they wants tuh drag us down an y'all sittin here like a pack uh dunces pewking yo' guts." Reproachful glances at me. Of course I never let things rest there. That person must be won over, and I haven't failed so far, but sometimes it sets the spirit back a few days and delays me.[16]

In sharp contrast to the Boasian call for objectivity, the letter portrays scientific investigation as political and ideological, operating in an arena in which both the investigator and the investigated strive to empower themselves. Hurston introduces in the letter politically conscious people, who manipulate the anthropological texts written about them to promote their own agenda.[17] Instead of the featherbed resistance, which Hurston depicts in the introduction to *Mules and Men,* whereby the anthropological "probe gets smothered under a lot of laughter and pleasantries," collaborating with folklore collectors is viewed here as a form of performing the role of the laughing darky, and informants refuse to turn back to the minstrel stereotype.[18] They see the project of salvage anthropology as an extreme form of dispossession, even enslavement, a move meant to distance them from socioeconomic privileged positions in America. Instead, they wish to present themselves as civilized, educated, and capable of fully participating in contemporary America.

The letters reveal that, in contrast to Boas's belief, being an autoethnographer does not guarantee penetration. Instead of objectively collecting folklore, Hurston's letters to Langston Hughes present her endeavor as a form of cultural exchange: "In every town I hold 1 or 2 story-telling contests, and at each I begin by telling them who you are and all, then I read poems from *Fine Clothes to the Jew.*"[19] Hurston describes such poetry readings as an answer to the ethnographic resistance presented in a different letter to Hughes : "When I have to meet people in group & am asked to tell about myself—which I don't want to do for fear of saying that which I don't wish—I say I can't talk, but I'll read some verses from a Negro poet. You know these self-conscious

Negroes are dynamite. Some are likely to object to my work so I can keep from explaining myself & still satisfy by talking about poets."[20] By reading an educated Black writer's poetry, Hurston both satisfies the call for a favorable representation of African Americans and relates to the value of Black Southern culture and life, reflected in the poems.

Cultural exchange ensures penetration into the field of study. Hurston does much more than reading a few poems out loud: she holds public readings, sells copies of Hughes's poetry collections, places copies in public libraries in Eatonville, even loans books.[21] By so doing she turns the ethnographic experience into a highly subjective and reciprocal process. Moreover, the poems Hurston introduces to her objects of study have an impact on the very cultural products she aims to collect, and are incorporated by the investigated group as part of the folkloristic tradition. Thus, in contrast to the anthropological conception of culture as static, Hurston emphasizes in her letters fluidity and change and undermines the notion of scientific objectivity.

Hurston's choice to read from Hughes' second poetry collection *Fine Clothes to the Jew* (1927) is hardly accidental.[22] Indeed, it sheds light on the author's preoccupation with Black–Jewish relations in general and with the empowered position of Jewish anthropologists in particular, and this is important for an understanding of positionality in *Mules and Men*. In a letter to Hughes, Hurston describes a card game, a scene elaborately portrayed in the ninth chapter of *Mules and Men*. Although in both the private and the public texts Hurston refers to the same social practice, even in the same locale, the chants of the published text accompanying the card game bear no resemblance to the poem quoted in the letter. Paraphrasing Hughes's poem, "Hard Luck," the dealer teasingly chants it when he notices that his opponent is about to lose the game:

> "When hard luck overtakes you
> Nothin for you to do
> Grab up yo' fine clothes
> An' sell em to-ooo-de Jew Hah!!"
> (slaps the card down on the table)
>
> The other fellow was visibly cast down when the dealer picked up his money.
>
> Dealer gloating continued:
>
> "If you wuz a mule
> I'd git you a waggin to haul—
> But youse *so* low down-hown
> You aint even got uh stall."[23]

Besides the extraordinary way in which a written text is transformed into an oral tradition, Hurston presents in the letter a complex connection between culture, race, and possession. The poem is performed in the immediate context of money lost at a card game, but is also a metaphor for Black art and culture sold in markets imagined to be controlled by Jews. Daniel McGee suggests that the clothes sold to the Jew are a metaphor for Black art, corrupted through its sale in a market system imagined to be specifically Jewish.[24] That the clothes are bought second-hand presents the Jew as incapable of producing his own art and as consequently stripping African Americans of their culture. Moreover, as Hurston recites poems from *Fine Clothes to the Jew,* lamenting the fact that the book has a large audience and a small market in the poor South, she already knows the book's sales are low. Arnold Rampersad notices that, in his autobiography, *The Big Sea* (1940), Hughes attributes the book's failure to the unfortunate title choice, which upset potential Jewish readers.[25] While the poor Black Southerners depict economic exploitation as specifically Jewish, and Hurston calls attention to the empowering position of the Jewish anthropologist for whom she collects data, Hughes imagines Jewish control over the book market and Jewish possession of Black art.

Hurston's letters promote an understanding of the disturbing first tale in *Mules and Men.* The tale explores anthropological negotiations of racial definitions in the United States, resists the way in which anthropological practices homogenize the anthropological community as racially White, and relates to Jewish appropriation of African American culture. Unconventionally, Hurston narrates the story herself in Black dialect at the end of her introduction. Hurston tells us that when God created the human soul he decided to postpone its distribution, saying, "if Ah give it out it would tear them shackly bodies to pieces. Bimeby, Ah give it out." God covered the soul with a cloth, and whenever the wind was blowing people could see the soul shining and hear its music. The White man took a look, but did not come near. The Indian and the Negro came closer, but did not touch it. "De Jew come past and heard de song from de soul-piece then he kept on passin' and all of a sudden he grabbed up de soul-piece and hid it under his clothes, and run off down de road." The soul burnt him and tore him, and he tried to break loose, but could not. He called for help, but the others hid, and only when he passed them did they come out of their hiding and pick up the little pieces that had fallen on the ground. "So God mixed it up wid feelings and give it out to 'em. 'Way after while when He ketch dat Jew, He's goin' to 'vide things up more ekal.'"[26] Even though the tale is strikingly different from any other tale in the book in terms of its racial categorization into White, Black, Indian, and Jewish, it has received little critical attention.[27]

The soul stolen by the Jew in this tale brings to mind the African American cultural marker—soul music.[28] Hurston fiercely objected to Jewish blackfaced performances of soul music, and the Jew stealing the soul is part of the criticism directed at "the current mammy-song-Jolson conception of the Southern Negro," as she put it.[29] Jewish appropriation of Black music is an accusation apparent in her private letters. In one incident, for example, while collecting folklore in South Carolina, Hurston comes across music she wishes to record and incorporate into a play dramatizing Black American folklore, cowritten with Paul Green, but is preceded by "two very enthusiastic Jews who want to take the spirituals for commercial purposes!."[30] Hurston emphasizes in this letter to Paul Green cultural dispossession and economic gain as specifically Jewish actions. Michael North asserts that Hurston's folklore research was meant to serve as the means by which she would correct the distorted image of Black culture, created by non-Black impersonations of Black cultural production. Such performances were particularly beneficial for those considered non-White, since, as North claims, "the grotesque exaggeration of blackface makeup had always been meant at least in part to emphasize the fact that the wearer was not black."[31] Thus, Hurston expresses her objection to Jewish control of Black culture and to Jewish use of blackface performances as a whitecover.

Soul music is only one instance of Jewish cultural appropriation of African American art and culture and its incorporation into the performative arts. Hurston's letters reveal her objection to theatrical productions that, in her view, distort African American representations. In a letter to the Broadway actress, writer, radio broadcaster, and editor, Katherine Tracy L'Engle, Hurston maintains that such plays are "neither true to the facts of Negro life, nor to the psychology." Suggesting "[t]he money is put up by Jews for the Negro to carry the ball for them," the letter presents the notion of Jewish strategic and self-serving appropriation and manipulation of African American culture. In addition, reminiscent of her letters to Hughes on *Fine Clothes to the Jew,* Hurston raises the issue of Jewish control over what can and cannot be published: "I could say a whole lot and tell a lot of truths that would not look pretty, and I have considered writing something about it right out loud, but I doubt if I could get it published in the present state of things."[32]

Hurston views Jewish appropriation of African American culture as both a means to achieve economic gain and a mask to conceal racial identity. By analogy, anthropological practices serve as a way for Jews to accumulate cultural capital by dispossessing Blacks of their culture, and of Jewish whitewashing. Soul music, as well as other cultural products, makes up the anthropological subject matter. In the tale, by emphasizing the Jew's non-White identity and presenting him in a stereotypical way, Hurston draws attention to Jewish anthropologists' concealment of their racial identity behind the mask of scientific investigation. According to Gelya Frank, the fact that Boas himself and half or more of his students were Jewish was hushed. Frank speculates that this was either due to Boas's insistence on liberal humanism and cosmopolitanism or out of fear that anti-Semitic reactions would discredit the discipline of anthropology and individual anthropologists, either because Jews were considered dangerous due to their presumed racial differences or because they were associated with radical causes.[33] Nevertheless, ethnographic practices, requiring objectivity, emancipated the ethnographer from both ethnic culture and racial categorization. Clifford and Marcus suggest that Boasian ethnography provides the ethnographer with "a standpoint from which to see without being seen."[34] As has already been noted, Hurston is deprived of this advantage, yet the practice is particularly beneficial for another group of Boasian anthropologists, including the master himself—namely those of the Semitic race. In using the curtain of the toe party as a metaphor for the discipline itself, Hurston shows anthropology was a curtain behind which Jewish identity could be concealed. Since Hurston's authority as an anthropologist relied on her position as an insider, she did not enjoy the same privilege and was forced to expose her black toes.

The tale brings to the fore the two groups in American history—African Americans and Native Americans—that are devoid of self-possession and that are dispossessed of homelands, respectively. In the context of Boasian anthropological practices, these are also the two most investigated and studied groups, dispossessed of their cultural assets, since copyrights to all ethnic folktales belong to the anthropologists transcribing them. Through the opening tale Hurston comments on anthropological practices that generate the African American and the Native American as the cultural and ethnic Other, help Jews escape racial categorization, and are financially profitable for Jewish anthropologists.

The stereotypical "Jew" in the tale also refers to the position of superiority taken up by Jews who served as patrons of Black artists and scientists. Scholars of race have examined instances in which Jewish Americans fought for the Black cause in the first half of the twentieth century, taking up the role of the benefactor patron helping disadvantageous African Americans strategically to allow Jews to assume a position of superiority and seem to be White.[35] Hurston's own career was directed by Jewish benefactors, whose motives were probably mixed. The Jewish writer Fannie Hurst gave Hurston a job as a secretary when she first arrived in New York, and helped her make a living while Hurston studied. While Hurst's altruism is not to be disregarded, Hemenway discloses the fact that, privately, Hurston told at least one friend that Hurst was probably interested in their appearing in public together because Hurston's dark skin highlighted her own lily-white complexion. The novelist and one of the founders of Barnard College, Annie Nathan Meyer, arranged a Barnard scholarship for Hurston.[36] And, of course, Franz Boas served as her teacher and mentor. Through the tale, Hurston points at a self-serving dimension to Boas's altruism, which makes it possible to conceal a Jewish identity behind both his role as an anthropologist and his position as mentor to the Black Hurston.

In *Mules and Men,* the Jewish anthropologist 'thief' is redrawing the color line by robbing the Black and the Indian of their souls as a means of whitewashing. The soul is deprived of both the Black man, the Indian, and the White man, and the consequence of stealing is harsh—the soul burns the Jew's body, and he is left suffering and helpless. This detail might serve as a comment on Jewish assimilation, which Boas advocated to the point of literal disappearance for Jews. Whereas Boas saw Native Americans as on the verge of extinction, and believed that African Americans would, in the course of history, eventually assimilate, his relation to Jews was completely different. Rather than celebrating their culture in the name of pluralism, he perceived assimilation as the immediate answer to the Jewish problem of anti-Semitism, and saw Jews as already deeply and rapidly assimilated.[37] Leonard Glick identifies the relation between Boas's call for cultural relativism and pluralism, on the one hand, and Jewish assimilation on the other, as paradoxical.[38] Yet the paradox is illusory, for the anthropological practices that define ethnic Others in the name of cultural pluralism, empower, by so doing, the anthropological investigator, conceal the anthropologist's racial identity, and facilitate the Jewish anthropologist's assimilation. At the same time, suggests Hurston, this strategy has a cost, as Jewish effacement and assimilation result in loss of the Jewish soul.

In sharp contrast to Boas's notion of cultural relativism, the tale presents a set categorization of people into races arranged in a hierarchical order. Hurston draws an analogy between this hierarchical order and the anthropological order. "I was glad when somebody told me,

'You may go and collect Negro Folklore,'" says the author at the opening lines of her introduction.[39] The initiative to collect folklore is not her own, but belongs to an ominous authoritative voice, namely that of Franz Boas. A similar reference to Boasian paternalizing is found in Hurston's autobiography, *Dust Tracks on the Road* (1942). Hurston strategically refers to Boas in this text as Papa Franz, emphasizing her subordinate position with relation to the anthropological patriarch. However, just as she does in the opening tale, Hurston simultaneously sabotages this position by, once again, implicitly calling attention to Boas's Jewish identity. Hurston portrays an incident in which she calls Boas Papa Franz at a social gathering of the department of anthropology at his house. "'Of course, Zora is my daughter. Certainly!' he said with a smile. 'Just one of my missteps, that's all.' The sabre cut on his cheek, which it is said he got in a duel at Heidelberg, lifted in a smile."[40] According to Julia Liss, the scar was indeed the result of dueling. Boas joined a students' association, the Allemannen, at Bonn University, differentiating himself from the Jewish society, but, as he wrote to his mother, atypical of his fraternity, the duels were occasioned "because with the damned Jew Baiters this winter one could not survive without quarrel and fighting."[41] Although scars were perceived at the time as signs of manliness and successful assimilation, Boas later preferred to attribute the scar to polar bear clawing in one of his scientific investigations.[42]

Boas was a nonpracticing Jew who saw himself as a German American, not as Jewish, but he suffered from anti-Semitism both in Germany and in the United States. In 1887, at the early stages of his career, he felt compelled to immigrate to the United States when he realized his career in Germany could not take off due to his Jewish identity. America did not provide the expected haven, and Boas suffered setbacks in his attempts to secure employment. Jews of German origin witnessed a decline in their status due to anti-Semitism and to the immigration of many Eastern European Jews since the 1880s.[43] In 1912 Boas conducted large-scale research for the U.S. Immigration Commission in physical anthropology, mainly on the shape of the heads of Jewish immigrants from southern and eastern Europe. He showed that even the immigrant's bodily and mental make-up changes the longer the residence in the United States.[44] In response, Lothrop Stoddard dismissed his views as "the desperate attempt of a Jew to pass himself off as 'White.'"[45] As these biographical details suggest, the anthropological mask conceals not only Boas's Judaism, but also the very facial marks of anti-Semitism. Hurston, though, hints at Boas's true colors by implicitly referring to the real circumstances of Boas's facial scar.

As her writings indicate, Hurston identified strategic and self-serving dimensions to Jewish anthropologists' and artists' engagement with African American culture. The tale opening *Mules and Men* seems disturbingly anti-Semitic. Yet in the context of Hurston's private letters, it becomes clear that her criticism is focused and specific. Hurston was not an anti-Semite. In a letter written only one day prior to the one addressed to Paul Green, for instance, Hurston encourages her colleague and friend, Jane Belo, to marry a Jew, Frank Tannenbaum, in spite of Belo's family's objection.[46] In a similar way, in 1935 Hurston asks Meyer to add a German artist, Jacob Annot, to a list of guests invited to the Writer's Tea, an annual affair of which Hurston is the guest of honor. According to Hurston, Annot had a large art school in Germany, and was almost sent to a concentration camp for refusing to exclude Jewish students from her classes.[47] In another letter, she describes the fate of the man who tried to spread a rumor about her lover's allegedly Jewish ancestry: "I knew that the bastard had race prejudice that must include Negroes as well as Jews, so I booted his hips right off my boat. I am colored, and so I cannot be a regular member of the Halifax River Yacht Club, but I have lots of friends in there and am invited to the Club House, so I got that guy black-balled when he tried to join in."[48] Finally, Hurston's comment on her last unpublished manuscript, *Herod the Great,* sheds new light on the Jewish thief described in *Mules and Men.* As Hurston wrote in a letter to Carl van Vechten, in that work she planned to show, "instead of the Jewish people being a peculiarly evil and hard-headed race of people, doomed by God to suffer and be hated, that they were just people, fighting for all those things which other people hold sacred and conducing to the rights and dignity of man."[49]

Boasian anthropology participated in redrawing the color line in binary racial terms of Black and White in the 1920s and 1930s. At the same time, these practices provided Others, particularly Jews, various means of social mobility. Jacobson believes that anthropologists, Boasian among them, played an important role in courts of law, establishing whiteness, and thereby determining citizenship rights and economic distribution.[50] As Boas's own study for the U.S. Immigration Commission indicates, anthropologists participated in American political culture in more pronounced ways, directly influencing the process of policy decision-making, as governmental policy increasingly relied on the work of race scientists. Yet Hurston's *Mules and Men* explores both the extent of that power and its limits. As its opening tale suggests, if one wishes to uncover "that which the soul lives by" in order to use it as a cover to one's own race, one will find that it calls attention to that same concealed race.[51] And just as Hurston knows she cannot escape being viewed as an African American woman rather than simply as an ethnographer, Boas may invent cultural relativism, but can never escape the troubling stereotype of the selfish, ambitious, greedy, God-defying "Jewish" thief.

Notes

1. Zora Neale Hurston to Franz Boas, August 20, 1934, cited in Carla Kaplan, ed., *Zora Neale Hurston: A Life in Letters* (New York, 2003), 308–309.
2. Zora Neale Hurston, *Mules and Men* (New York, [1935] 1990), 1.
3. Gelya Frank, "Jews, Multiculturalism, and Boasian Anthropology," American Anthropology 99.4 (1997): 731–732.
4. Jacobson, *Whiteness of a Different Color,* 7–8, 13–14. Eric Goldstein claims in *Price of Whiteness* that "the period was characterized more by tension and uncertainty than by the ability to craft a neat synthesis between Jewish and American identity" (166), and asserts that Jews did not become White until the 1940s (189). Yet he singles Boas and wealthy Jewish patrons out as exceptions to the rule. Whereas Goldstein attributes Boas's whitewashing to his distinguished academic position and his affiliation with German Americans rather than Jewish Americans (147), I see modern anthropology as a new arena in which whitewashing could occur.
5. Beth Harrison reads Hurston's dramatization of the encounter between the ethnographer and her informants as a hint that to become a participant observer, the ethnographer must renounce her objectivity, and objectivity is one of the building blocks of Boasian methodology ("Zora Neale Hurston and Mary Austin: A Case Study in Ethnography, Literature, Modernism and Contemporary Ethnic Fiction," *MELUS* 21, no. 2 [1996]: 89–90). Following Harrison, Lori Jirousek believes that Hurston produces a "genre-crossing ethnographic text designed to reveal a more complete picture of the studied community, ethnographic techniques, and herself as an ethnic ethnographer" ("Ethnics and Ethnographers: Zora Neale Hurston and Anzia Yezierska," *Journal of Modern Literature* 29, no. 2 [2006]: 21). D. A. Boxwell points at the ways in which the text deals with problematic aspects of writing ethnography ("'Sis' Cat as Ethnographer: Self-Presentation and Self- Inscription in Zora Neale Hurston's *Mules and Men,*" *African American Review* 26, no. 4 [1992]: 609–611). Lynda Heep claims ("Creating Ethnography: Zora Neale Hurston and Lydia Cabrera," *African American Review* 39, no. 3 [2005]: 346), that *Mules and Men* is an experimental feminist ethnography—allowing Others to become subjects by speaking for themselves.
6. See, e.g., Keith Walters, "'He Can Read My Writing but He Sho' Can't Read My Mind': Zora Neale Hurston's Revenge in *Mules and Men,*" *Journal of American Folklore* 112 (1999): 365.
7. Goldstein describes contemporary urban slave markets in the Depression years, in which Jewish housewives bid for cheap Black domestics (Goldstein, *Price of Whiteness,* 161).

8. Benigno Sánchez-Eppler, "Telling Anthropology: Zora Neale Hurston and Gilberto Freyre Disciplined in Their Field-Home Work," *American Literary History* 4, no. 3 (1992): 479–480.
9. In the opening decades of the twentieth century, anthropology was institutionalized in the academy and professionalized. If before amateur anthropologists needed no former education or knowledge to conduct their studies, now culture was the primary object of professionals. See Susan Hegeman, *Patterns for America: Modernism and the Concept of Culture* (Princeton, NJ: Princeton University Press, 1999), 44–45.
10. Franz Boas, *The Mind of Primitive Man* (New York: Macmillan, 1938), 13. For an interesting analysis of the excluding power of anthropology see Scott Michaelsen, *Limits of Multiculturalism: Interrogating the Origins of American Anthropology* (Minneapolis: University of Minnesota Press, 1999), xvii. According to Robert F. Murphy, whereas the anthropology department in Chicago followed the British tradition by investigating colonized groups abroad, Boas' department at Columbia University examined internally colonized groups ("Anthropology at Columbia: A Reminiscence," *Dialectical Anthropology* 16, no. 1 [1991]: 66).
11. Hurston, *Mules and Men*, xiii.
12. Jacobson, *Whiteness of a Different Color*, 106.
13. Michaelsen, *Limits of Multiculturalism*, xxvii.
14. Boas, *Mind of Primitive Man*, 3–18. Also see Franz Boas, *Anthropology and Modern Life* (New York: Norton, 1962), e.g., chap. 3.
15. Robert E. Hemenway, *Zora Neale Hurston: A Literary Biography* (Urbana and Chicago, 1980), 109–110, 132–133.
16. Zora Neale Hurston to Ruth Benedict, Spring 1929, cited in Kaplan, *Zora Neale Hurston*, 140–141.
17. For more on the ways in which *Mules and Men* presents a split and diverse investigated group, in contrast to the homogenized way in which the ethnographer imagines that group, see Alice Gambrell, *Women Intellectuals, Modernism and Difference: Transatlantic Culture 1919–1945* (Cambridge: Cambridge University Press, 1997), 121.
18. Hurston, *Mules and Men*, 2–3.
19. Zora Neale Hurston to Langston Hughes, July 10, 1928, in Kaplan, *Zora Neale Hurston*, 120.
20. Zora Neale Hurston to Langston Hughes, August 16, 1928, in Kaplan, *Zora Neale Hurston*, 125.
21. Kaplan, *Zora Neale Hurston*, 113, 124, 125, 127, 130.
22. Langston Hughes, *Fine Clothes to the Jew*, Alfred A. Knopf, 1927.
23. Zora Neale Hurston to Langston Hughes, July 10, 1928, cited in Kaplan, *Zora Neale Hurston*, 120–121.
24. Daniel J. McGee, "Dada Da Da: Sounding the Jew in Modernism," *ELH* 68, no. 2 (2001): 512–513.
25. Arnold Rampersad, "Langston Hughes's *Fine Clothes to the Jew*," *Callaloo*: *A Journal of African American and African Arts and Letters* 9, no. 1 (1986): 148. According to Goldstein, in this period many Jews worked as editors, artists, performers, creators of mass media productions, especially the radio and motion pictures, and although they were not dominant, were very visible (*Price of Whiteness*, 121–122).

26. Hurston, *Mules and Men,* 3–4.
27. Keith Walters suggests that through the tale Hurston comments on the patronizing behavior she endures at the hands of her patrons (Walters, "'He Can Read My Writing,'" 361).
28. Michael North, *Dialect of Modernism: Race, Language and Twentieth Century Literature* (New York: Oxford University Press, 1994), 176. I am indebted to Hana Wirth-Nesher for pointing out the connection between the stolen soul and soul music.
29. Hemenway, *Zora Neale Hurston,* 205. On Al Jolson's career as a Jew in blackface, see Rogin, *Blackface, White Noise,* 200–201; Michael Alexander, *Jazz Age Jews* (Princeton, NJ: Princeton University Press, 2000), 135–137.
30. Zora Neale Hurston to Paul Green, May 3, 1940, in Kaplan, *Zora Neale Hurston,* 458–459.
31. North, *Dialect of Modernism,* 7.
32. Zora Neale Hurston to Katherine Tracy L'Engle, December 11, 1945, cited in Kaplan, *Zora Neale Hurston,* 538.
33. Frank, "Jews, Multiculturalism": 731–732.
34. James Clifford, "Introduction: Partial Truths," in *Writing Culture: The Poetics and Politics of Ethnography,* ed. James Clifford and George E. Marcus (Berkeley: University of California Press, 1986), 12.
35. See, e.g., Goldstein, *Price of Whiteness,* 147, 157–158; and Frank, "Jews, Multiculturalism," 735.
36. Hemenway, *Zora Neale Hurston,* 21. For a thorough discussion of Hurston's personal relationships with Jewish benefactors see Lori Harrison-Kahan, *The White Negress: Literature, Minstrelsy and the Black-Jewish Imaginary* (New Brunswick, NJ: Rutgers University Press, 2011).
37. Amos Morris-Reich, *The Quest for Jewish Assimilation in Modern Social Science* (New York: Routledge, 2008), 49–50.
38. Leonard B. Glick, "Types Distinct from Our Own: Franz Boas on Jewish Identity and Assimilation," *American Anthropologist* 84, no. 3 (1982): 546.
39. Hurston, *Mules and Men,* 1.
40. Zora Neale Hurston, *Dust Tracks on the Road* (New York: Harper Perennial, [1942] 1996), 140.
41. Julia E. Liss, "German Culture and German Science in the Bildung of Franz Boas," in *Volksgeist as Method and Ethic: Essays on Boasian Ethnography and the German Anthropological Tradition,* ed. George W. Stocking Jr. (WI: University of Wisconsin Press, 1996), 167–169.
42. Frank, "Jews, Multiculturalism," 732–733.
43. Vernon Williams Jr., "Franz Boas's Paradox and the African American Intelligentsia," in *African Americans and Jews in the Twentieth Century: Studies in Convergence and Conflict,* ed. V. P. Franklin (Columbia: University of Missouri Press, 1998), 58.
44. Glick, "Types Distinct from Our Own," 557–558.
45. Quoted in Rogin, *Blackface, White Noise,* 89.
46. Zora Neale Hurston to Jane Belo, May 2, 1940, cited in Kaplan, *Zora Neale Hurston,* 457.
47. Zora Neale Hurston to Annie Nathan Meyer, April 25, 1935, cited in Kaplan, *Zora Neale Hurston,* 349.

48. Zora Neale Hurston to Carl Van Vechten, July 24, 1945, cited in Kaplan, *Zora Neale Hurston,* 526.
49. Zora Neale Hurston to Carl Van Vechten, September 12, 1945, cited in Kaplan, *Zora Neale Hurston,* 530–531.
50. Jacobson, *Whiteness of a Different Color,* 224–225.
51. Hurston, *Mules and Men,* 2.

CHAPTER 6

Jewish Characters in *Weeds*

Reinserting Race into the Postmodern Discourse on American Jews

Shlomi Deloia and Hannah Adelman Komy Ofir

While identifiably Jewish characters have featured on popular American television for decades, only recently have scholars given them their attention.[1] In his study *Something Ain't Kosher Here: The Rise of the "Jewish" Sitcom,* Vincent Brook argues that the prevalence of Jewish protagonists in sitcoms from the early 1990s can be "explained partly as a response to changing industrial conditions in American television, partly as a complex negotiation of assimilationist and multiculturalist pressures specific to the Jewish American experience."[2] His study supports the often-reiterated claim that "stereotyping has been seminal to the formation of Jewish identity."[3] As Brook and others demonstrate, from the 1990s onward, Jews and Jewishness have been presented in prime-time television in terms of inside or outside the mainstream vis-à-vis intermarriage, Jews' relationship to Israel, and religious renewal. Yet, although cultural stereotypes such as the Jewish American princess, the Jewish mother, and the shlemiel have been present in a wide variety of shows, race has only rarely been part of this conversation.

This chapter looks at how the American television series *Weeds* (2005–2012) subverts pervasive representations of contemporary post-ethnic Jewish identity in prime-time television by reinserting the issue of race into the discourse.[4] In its depiction of Jewish characters, *Weeds* exhibits a pointed engagement with the idea of Jewish whitening in postwar American culture—a notion that has underpinned representations of Jews in popular culture for more than half a century. The series probes and humorously challenges assumptions regarding Jewish assimilation and secularization that accompanied the post–World War II historic transformation of Jewishness in the United States from race to ethnicity.[5] By focusing on the old–new racial perspective in *Weeds,* this chapter examines the ways in which the series unearths anxieties about the indeterminacy of contemporary Jewish identity within the ethnoracial tapestry of American culture.

Created by the Jewish television writer, producer, and director Jenji Kohan, *Weeds* is a darkly comic satire set in the fictional California suburb of Agrestic (later Majestic). The action centers on the misadventures of the non-Jewish Nancy Botwin, a newly widowed housewife who turns to dealing marijuana in order to maintain her bourgeois lifestyle after the sudden death of her Jewish husband, Judah, of a heart attack while jogging with their ten-year-old son, Shane. The cast of characters includes various neighbors, business associates and customers, Nancy's lovers and husbands, her two sons, her brother-in-law Andy, her father-in-law Lennie, and his mother, known as Bubby, among others.

The series offers a caustic critique of suburbia, subverts preconceptions about nearly everything it portrays, and treats sensitive subjects controversially. The ethnics in the series are, at least on the surface, largely stereotyped; the cast of characters includes, for example, a Black matriarch who controls her family with an iron hand; a young, unmarried Black mother; a Hispanic housekeeper; and Mexican drug dealers. The Jewish characters and themes are no exception to this approach. "There are no boundaries," Kohan has said of her portrayal of Jewish characters.[6] After decades in which it has been virtually taboo in American television to openly view Jews in terms of race, the show presents an array of Jewish characters whose Jewishness is often reflected in racial characteristics, whether physical, behavioral, or both. However, as this essay demonstrates, Kohan's tongue-in-cheek employment of stereotypes such as the effeminate, parasitic, or chameleonic Jew should not be read as self-deprecating, but rather as an attempt to carve out a space for the subversion of ethnic self-censorship in prime-time television. "Why should a Jew be portrayed in some special light, as opposed to anyone else?" she asks.[7] Kohan's complex engagement with the vicissitudes of Jewish whitening in American culture, of which prime-time television is a part, can only be understood in relation to the possibilities, or lack thereof, mapped out for her by the small screen from the post-Holocaust period to the present.

Jewish characters in American television first appeared in the prime-time series *The Goldbergs,* which revolved around the daily lives of a Jewish family in the Bronx. The series began on radio and aired on television from 1949 to 1956. The members of the Goldberg family were universalized figures—as Daniel Itzkovitz puts it, "quintessential and fundamentally American 'other[s]'"—portraying the American dream of rags to riches, complete with the obligatory move to the suburbs in the final season.[8] While they were blatantly Jewish—the parents even spoke English with Yiddish accents—they were otherwise largely whitewashed: neither physical attributes nor religious practices suggested their Jewishness.

Henry Popkin, in his 1952 essay in *Commentary,* described what he called "the vanishing Jew of our popular culture"—a de-Semitization stemming from an effort to hedge anti-Semitism and to sanitize or neutralize depictions of Jews.[9] The effort to normalize Jewish difference and to claim that Jews were "just like everyone else" was not, however, entirely successful.[10] "For every Molly Goldberg invited into 'America's living room' there was an Ethel or Julius Rosenberg or a Hollywood blacklist chock full of Jewish names reminding Americans just how un-American the Jews really were."[11] Real events challenged the television script. As a result, the Jewish presence receded in popular culture. The cancellation of *The Goldbergs* in 1956 reflected this trend, and marked the beginning of a fundamental change in the way Jews were portrayed on American television.

During the late 1950s and the 1960s, Jewish television characters were largely invisible, their Jewishness "predominantly emerg[ing] as subtext."[12] This phenomenon may be connected to a kind of self-censorship of Jews in the television industry, who, despite their "fame and material success ... sensed that they were not quite as White as the Joneses" and were ambivalent about both their Jewish and American identities, and were sensitive to what was perceived by many as Jewish control of the media. The next Jewish sitcom appeared in 1972, in the form of *Bridget Loves Bernie,* a short-lived series about an intermarried couple, which was cancelled in 1973 amid much protest from the American Jewish community over the intermarriage issue.[13] Several more series in which characters acknowledged their Jewishness to varying extents appeared in the 1970s and early 1980s.[14] During much of the 1980s, there was a hiatus in the appearance of Jewish characters. All this changed radically in the 1990s with the culmination of the process that led to widespread acceptance of Jews as part of the White American mainstream in the 1980s and 1990s—a moment when multiculturalist ideology was gaining momentum in academic, political, and popular debates.

In the past two decades, whiteness scholarship has been preoccupied with tracing the complex ways in which Jews transcended their racial status as an off-White race and moved, after World War II, into the privileged sociocultural position implied by whiteness.[15] Jewish whiteness, however, still remains a disputed and unresolved category. Since the rise of multiculturalism in the 1960s, as David Biale observes, Jews have found themselves in a "doubly marginal" position: "marginal to the majority culture, but also marginal among minorities."[16] Indeed, the place of Jews on the American multicultural map constitutes a kind of no-man's land. Jews are positioned neither among the White majority nor among people of color; moreover, Jewish religious practices, diverse national origins, and the ancient–new Jewish homeland in the Middle East all mark Jews as different from Americans of European origin as well. Although Jews have been discursively excluded from the multicultural agenda as too White, questions about their status continue to resurface in the American multicultural context. Are Jews simply mainstream Americans, a distinct diasporic group, supposedly genetically pure, or mixed by way of intermarriage?

The explosion of prime-time Jewish sitcoms at the turn of the 1990s provides an example of how Jews, perhaps feeling a need to define themselves as other than White, became increasingly obsessed with expressing, if not celebrating, their Jewishness before a largely non-Jewish mainstream audience. Compared with the de-Semitized characters of early American television, the representation of Jews in series such as *Seinfeld, Will and Grace, Mad About You,* and *Dharma and Greg* mark a major shift. However, as Brook points out, the "commercial and cultural constraints of American television [i.e., public television] necessarily muted the particularist aspects of the Jewish TV revival."[17] While these sitcoms feature explicitly Jewish characters, their ethnic particularity is only rarely essential to the narrative, and is often downplayed in a context in which intermarriage, Gentile and Jewish cross-cultural or cross-sexual interaction (as in the gay–straight pairing in *Will and Grace*) are the prevailing norm. In the Jewish sitcom of the 1990s, representations of Jews have just enough performative cultural markers to suggest ethnic distinction, but not enough to render them racially distinct. The distinction between ethnic and racial deserves further consideration in this context.

The editing of race out of the representation of Jewish characters can be understood in relation to the complex historical factors that correlated with post–World War II whitening of the Jews. As Matthew Frye Jacobson points out, under the impact of events in Nazi Germany and the mid-twentieth-century civil rights protests against racial discrimination, race was deliberately relegated to the background of the ongoing cultural debate on European immigrants. The racial characteristics of Jews were, as Jacobson writes, "emphatically revised away as a matter of sober, war-chastened 'tolerance,'" while the culture-based notion of ethnicity became increasingly dominant.[18]

The shift from race to ethnicity is very clear in the post–World War II Jewish discourse of self-identification, especially in the ethnic revival years of the 1960s and 1970s.[19] The rise of the civil rights movement and its attack on White privilege placed Jews, as well as other White ethnics, on the advantaged side of the color line. Eager to underline their double consciousness as both Americans *and* Jews, to disassociate themselves from the WASP majority, but also to avoid the entanglements of race, Jews found a useful interpretation of their own distinctiveness in the culture-based notion of ethnicity. The discourse of ethnicity offered Jews a sense of particularity that, now, unlike in their prewar racial past, was self-ascribed as well as socially imposed—a sense of distinctiveness as neither Black nor thoroughly White, but ethnic. Yet, with the burgeoning of multiculturalism as an ideological and political concern in the United States, other minority groups have come to consider Jews as too White or not ethnic enough to be included in what David Hollinger calls "the ethnoracial pentagon"—a color-coded project that emphasizes racial and interracial identification by choice.[20] The ambivalently and ambiguously portrayed Jew of the 1990s clearly demonstrates how Jewish prime-time television was having difficulty defining its characters' ethnic identities, and the distinction between Jewish whiteness and mainstream whiteness became thoroughly blurred.

A notable exception to this trend is Fran Drescher's series *The Nanny* (1993–1999). Refusing to follow her sponsors' recommendation to change her Jewish character, Fran Fine, into an Italian American (as had been done earlier with Seinfeld's George Costanza character), Drescher resurrected the 1920s image of the loud, flashy, and flirtatious Jewish ghetto girl to comically subvert the stereotype of the self-centered, manipulative, spoiled, and frigid Jewish American princess.[21] The series paved the way for other blatantly Jewish representations in prime-time television, such as *The Big Bang Theory*'s nerdy Howard Wolowitz and his invisible, but vocally present, shrieking mother, and Larry David's nebbishy, neurotic, and money-obsessed Jew. By flirting with the racial, these series mark a departure from the 1990s attempts to reethnicize the Jew within a safe, highly assimilated, often white-washed cultural environment. *Weeds*, daring to enter territory hitherto uncharted on prime-time television, explores the ethnoracial ambiguity of Jewish whiteness within an explicitly multicultural American milieu.

The first few episodes of *Weeds* seem to present a conventional upper-middle-class suburban setting in which, as character Celia Hodes puts it, "the people are White and [even] the help is brown, not Black."[22] Black experience—represented by Nancy's drug suppliers Heylia and Conrad as well as other dealers, such as the African American gangster U-Turn—is relegated to the inner city, away from the privileged suburban community. Color-line difference is clearly marked in an early incident in the series where a plane full of Coca-Cola bottles crashes into Celia's house; Nancy recounts the event to Heylia moments before bullets start flying through Heylia's window. The event is neatly summed up by Heylia: "White folks get soda pop, Niggas get bullets."

However, the discrepancies between White and Black experiences only serve as background for series creator Kohan's fascination with what she calls the "gray areas" between "Black and White," demonstrated by her cynical take on the ideal of the multicultural project.[23] As Nancy and Conrad establish their own marijuana grow-house later in the first season, their drug organization brings together a multicultural rainbow of partners in crime. The White Nancy and Doug, the African American Conrad, the Jewish Andy, the Indian Sanjay, and the Mexican Guillermo all join together to cultivate their own genetically unique strain of marijuana. Their project is soon threatened by a rival organization led by the Armenian mafia. This multicultural salad bowl, however, does not offer an environment in which difference is tolerated and valued; instead, it is characterized by fleeting comic references to the "weird" dishes served in ethnic restaurants, the Armenian genocide, and African American dietary practices. Kohan's critique of the multicultural enterprise becomes even more overt as Jewish racial difference resurfaces in a scene of bodily disfigurement involving Andy's foot.

Andy—Nancy's "freeloading brother-in-law," as Celia characterizes him—is required to report for military duty years after signing up for the United States Army reserves under the dual influence of alcohol and a woman he was trying to impress at the time. Andy schemes to avoid service by registering as a full-time rabbinical student. "Once you go rabbi," Andy tells Nancy, "you never go bye-bye." Yet, before he manages to fulfill his highly dubious Jewish calling, a foot injury renders him, or at least so he thinks, unfit for military conscription. In the grow-house, Andy and the rest of the company are joined by Doug and a Rottweiler he has found in the street. A debate ensues over whether the dog belongs to the Armenian drug lords, but before a consensus can be reached, Andy accidentally spills some cheeseburger sauce on his bare foot, resulting in a dog attack that leaves him with two missing toes. Moments before the attack, Sanjay recalls Jewish dietary laws that forbid mixing milk and meat, and comments to Andy: "I thought your people didn't eat cheeseburgers," Andy responds, "I feel it's my destiny to induce positive change in my tribe ... beginning with the cheeseburger and progressing to extreme sports and police work." Just at the moment when Andy is trying to "induce changes in the tribe" that would make Jews more normatively American, as well as more masculine, the very cheeseburger with which he proposes to do so leads to his being rendered not only physically unfit, but also sexually perverse, a point to which we will soon return.

Andy's desire to avoid military service is so intense that in an earlier episode he asks Nancy to cut off his toe in order to avoid duty, but, despite Nancy's willingness to comply, he turns out to be too cowardly to implement his plan. Andy's antimilitary stance clearly marks him as a stereotypical, unpatriotic Jewish slacker—a figure that was the subject of alarm and contention from the American Revolution and throughout World War I.[24] But Andy's particular physical disfigurement harks back even farther, to an earlier conception of Jewish difference. One of the tropes of Jewish inferiority that Sander Gilman explores in *The Jew's Body* is the notion of the Jew's foot as a "hidden sign of difference."[25] In an ongoing debate that originated in the European religious discourse of the Middle Ages and persisted in scientific and popular debates well into the twentieth century, the deformed foot marked the Jew as inherently different. The Jew, as Gilman notes, was thus seen as "unable and, therefore, unworthy of being completely integrated into the social fabric of the modern state," including "social institutions such as the armed forces, which determined the quality of social acceptance."[26]

Kohan uses this stereotypical image of the Jew's foot to signify Jewish racial difference within a staged multicultural setting in which the Jew is neither a full-blooded White American, like Nancy or Doug, nor one of the so-called new ethnics like Sanjay or Guillermo. Yet this employment of the foot image should not be simply read as the internalization of an anti-Semitic construction of the Jewish body. The internalization of stereotypes such as the Jew's deformed foot, according to Gilman, "can lead to self-destructive behavior ('self-hatred'), but it can also lead to productive and successful means of resistance."[27] Indeed, later in the series, Andy uses his deformed foot as a springboard to porn stardom. Functioning as a phallic symbol, Andy's foot is featured in a series of wild, hilarious scenes that add a tongue-in-cheek twist to his already discernible Jewishness. His appearances as a White UPS driver, a Mexican gardener, or a brown-faced bell-hop illustrate the idea of Jewish shape-shifting across ethnoracial divides. Much like Kohan's employment of the Jewish foot, the image of Andy as a shape-shifter harkens back to the Jew's troubled racial past. As Daniel Itzkovitz demonstrates, images of racial indeterminacy marked Jews at the early twentieth century as a "chameleonic race" whose "fluid instability" paradoxically constitutes the most essential, "embodied stability of Jewish racial distinctiveness."[28] Against a multicultural backdrop, therefore, Kohan's Jew is light enough to perform whiteness, on the one hand, yet, on the other, poses a challenge to a simple model based on color differentiation.

In the Western sexual and gender construction of Jewish difference, Jewish men are often presented as blatantly effeminate, or in some way not completely masculine. Constructions of the male Jew's body have frequently included some degree of gender ambiguity. Arguments for Jewish racial difference, whether in popular or so-called scientific discourse, have traditionally been informed by notions of sexual difference (in male Jews) that included female characteristics, diminished sexual potency, sexual deviance, and homosexual tendencies. At the other end of the spectrum, the Jewish male was perceived, by virtue of his circumcision, as prone to hypersexuality.[29]

In *Weeds,* there are two live central male Jewish characters, the above-mentioned Andy, and Dean Hodes, a conniving Jewish lawyer and neighbor. Nancy's deceased husband, Judah, also appears—in home movies that Nancy and her young son, Shane, view, as well as in Nancy's dreams. Judah is what we might call a 1990s television Jew—that is, not ethnically identifiable. But unlike Seinfeld or Paul Buchman, he is masculine, very handsome, and sexy. "Did he pass?" an Evangelical camp counselor asks Nancy, referring to Judah's death. Nancy assumes that the question refers not to death, but rather to Judah's passing as a non-Jew. But the question and Nancy's interpretation of the word passing in this conversation reflects a tension surrounding the issue of race, as opposed to ethnicity or culture. Judah is a kind of Jewish imago—successful, smart, funny, but also masculine, assimilated, and married to an all-American girl—in other words, he is a Jewish Superman, or a version of that Shuster and Siegel figure. In the context of Kohan's attack on the tendency to whitewash Jewishness, it is not at all surprising that Judah is dead. And yet his occasional presence in other characters' memories, imaginations, and on film sets him up as a model against which other Jews in the series, particularly his brother, Andy, are held up and measured.

Andy is the self-described black sheep of the Botwin family, perpetually unemployed (in accordance with the traditional conception of the nonproductive, parasitic Jew), and with a pronounced propensity for becoming involved with bizarre women. In the first season he has recently arrived from Alaska, where he has been living with a girlfriend, ostensibly to help out in Nancy's household in the wake of his brother's demise, but actually more to take advantage of the free room and board. Andy sees his own Jewishness in purely physical, even explicitly racial and genetic, terms. "Being a Jew means I have no foreskin and may be a Tay-Sachs carrier," he quips at one point.

Andy epitomizes numerous aspects of traditional racial or sexual constructions of the male "Jew" and the "Jewish" body. He is good looking but not in a particularly macho way. His facial features are soft and his body is hairless, not very muscular, and somewhat childlike. His relationship with Yael, the Israeli administrative director of the yeshiva he attends in his attempt to avoid the draft, serves to highlight his feminization. The beautiful Yael is configured as the stereotypically tough but womanly Sabra. Her representation as a former Israel Defense Forces (IDF) soldier who lost her commanding officer and boyfriend to terrorists and bears the scar of a gunshot wound on her shoulder both disassociates her from American Jewish women and places her within the male fantasy of the masculine woman. She rejects Andy's attempts to woo her on the grounds that he is "not what [she's] looking for in a man." "I like a man," she clarifies, "[s]omeone big and strong. Someone who can grow a beard. You're pretty and I could flip you like a pancake ... but we can still be friends." When she eventually decides to take control of the situation and seduce Andy, it happens on her own terms. She explains that Andy just does not have the qualities that attract her as a man. Andy's reply is, "Now what exactly are those qualities? Cause I can get them. I know a guy who ... knows a guy." Of course, this response brings to mind stereotypes of the Jewish wheeler-dealer in the tradition of *I Can Get it for You Wholesale,* as well as the aforementioned stereotype of the chameleonic Jew, who can change his shape according to his needs. At the moment when Andy is about to resign himself to continuing his platonic relationship with Yael, she admits that he does have just what she is looking for in a woman, including "sad eyes and soft skin," and proceeds to sodomize him with a large, black sexual aid. Like Alexander in Philip Roth's *Portnoy's Complaint,* Andy is emasculated by an Israeli woman soldier, who possesses the sexual potency that the American Jewish man seems to lack. Andy, like Alexander Portnoy, is doomed to remain emasculated in this sexual equation. The representation of Yael as a phallic character resonates strongly with the story of the biblical Yael and her piercing, emasculating tent-peg. "Does it have to be black?,"

Andy asks. Later in the series, we learn that Yael's equipment was modeled on the sexual organ of a certain Black porn star known for his impressive size, which further complicates the racialization of the gender issue by juxtaposing the feminized Jewish male with the stereotypical hypermasculinity and sexual prowess of the African American. Andy is cast, particularly in juxtaposition with the highly eroticized Yael in red lingerie and with her black phallus, as overly effeminate, indeed desirable only for his sad eyes, soft skin, pretty face, and sexual passivity.

Andy's racially determined Jewish sexuality is not only feminized, but is also presented as perverse, as we have noted in connection with his foot, and possibly queer. On the run from the United States Army, Andy dons a blonde woman's wig in a lame attempt to disguise himself. Sanjay takes him in this disguise to his non-English-speaking parents' home for dinner, where he acts as interpreter as Andy raves on about his army experience. Sanjay's father suspects Andy is gay and demands he leave the house. In other episodes throughout the series, Andy is presented as obsessed with sex and indiscriminately hypersexual, which shows his sexual abnormality, so familiar from anti-Semitic stereotypes.

The character of Dean Hodes, the other central Jewish character in *Weeds,* is, like Andy, configured as feminized and somewhat perverse. He is, as Judah was, assimilated and married to a non-Jew. But, in contrast to Judah, he is not really passing. He does not come across as attractive or sexy, and, throughout the series, he is emasculated in numerous ways. As his WASP mother-in-law puts it, Dean is just "not man enough." His affair with his Asian tennis coach reveals the racially determined sexual perversion of the Jewish man when it is strongly hinted that his lover wields the racket in their relationship, and not only on the tennis court. His wife's discovery of the affair leads to his further emasculation at her hands, when, Delilah-like, she shaves his head with an electric razor while he sleeps. In her anger and disappointment at his infidelity, Celia mentions that she married Dean because she thought he would be "rich, powerful, and faithful"—that is, what one might expect of the traditional Jewish family man. Dean's own internalization of racial stereotypes becomes clear when Celia's one-night stand with Conrad, Nancy's Black business partner, puts Dean into an obsessive panic over who is better endowed (although in a later episode, we learn that Dean has nothing to be ashamed about in terms of his own anatomical proportions). After being shorn, Dean is further emasculated by losing his job and having his adolescent daughter replace him as the family breadwinner. Depressed and frustrated, he buys himself a large motorcycle and attempts to play the role of the hypermasculine biker, but this strategy backfires when he is run off the road by a gang of Hell's Angels types and seriously injured, indeed injured so badly that for a long time he is diapered and cared for like an infant, abused and mocked by Celia, by now his ex-wife. Clearly, there is no way for him to escape his racial destiny and be man enough.

We can see that Kohan's treatment of Jewish men is rich with racial implications, but Jewish women are conspicuously absent from the suburban world of *Weeds*. Interestingly, women have often been virtually invisible in the racial discourse on Jews, subsumed by the effeminate Jewish male. In this context, it is fascinating to note that there are only two Jewish women in the entire series; one of these is Yael, the ideal Israeli Sabra; the other is Bubby, Judah and Andy's grandmother and a survivor of Auschwitz, who we only see unconscious on her death bed. There are no normative American Jewish women in the series—the intermarried families are both headed by Jewish men married to non-Jewish women, a conventional pattern in American television. Nancy claims that her father-in-law sees her as "a terrible shiksa monster." He, in turn, calls her "not-Francie," Francie being the girl Judah was supposed to marry, a typical nice Jewish girl who has become a doctor and married a cantor. The absence of American Jewish wives and mothers among the series' characters implies that Jewish identity, for Kohan, might hinge on something other than matrilineal descent and traditional endogamy. The fact that both Judah and Dean marry non-Jewish women strongly implies their desire to disappear into whiteness and Americanness, but, as it turns out, this strategy fails miserably when it comes to each couple's youngest offspring, Shane and Isabelle.

While her elder sister, Quinn, resembles her non-Jewish mother, Isabelle has inherited many of her father's "Jewish" features, including his curly "Jew-hair" and what Celia laments as his "unfortunate," "pear-shaped" body build. In order to tame the "Jew-hair from your father's side," Isabelle's maternal grandmother tells her, "tie it back until you're old enough to straighten it." Isabelle provides perhaps the most dramatically blatant example in the series of essentialized racial Jewishness; blood or genetic determinants will tell. Isabelle's outsider position is further emphasized by her marginalized status as a young lesbian in the largely heterosexual world of *Weeds*. Yet, despite her alleged drawbacks, she becomes a famous large-size child clothing model for Huskeroos, and takes over as provider for the family when Dean loses his job. Like Andy the porn star, Isabelle makes a virtue of her so-called weaknesses, using stereotype, as Gilman suggests, to resist rather than to self-hate. In the face of her mother's constant abusive commentary on her "Jewish" physical features as well as her lesbianism (deemed by Celia as an "excuse for not losing weight"), Isabelle actively resists interpellation, seeking a more fluid identity than the mirage of herself generated by her Gentile mother and grandmother.

Throughout the series, Kohan juxtaposes Isabelle's Jewish queerness with Shane's affinity with cultural hybridity to explore the complex multiple identifications that may affect children of Jewish–Gentile intermarriage. Like Isabelle, Shane is characterized as not quite Jewish, nor White; a "weird" kid who is often excluded at Agrestic's local school by the ruling, normative clique. His indeterminate ethnoracial identity is a recurring point of contention in the series. Physically, he is said to resemble the Botwin side of the family, while his older brother, Silas, is called a *"goyishe punim"* (Gentile face) by his great-grandmother at their father's funeral. Nancy is shocked to hear Shane shout *"Sh'ma Yisrael"* when he bites an opponent's foot in a karate competition. Yet, despite this awkward and perhaps misplaced proclamation of Jewish faith, Shane does not see himself as Jewish, perhaps because he lacks the required matrilineal descent. In fact, as he tells Andy, he wishes to be cremated and have his ashes enclosed in a particular cigar box he has found at the home of his great-grandmother, a Holocaust survivor. Shane is surprised when Andy tells him that his wish will not be honored, for he *is* Jewish in accordance with the Reform movement's recognition of patrilineal descent: "You are in the Reform movement," Andy says, "and those are the cool Jews."

Shane's complex relationship to Jewishness and its confusedly divergent definitions are further complicated by his sense of his own marginality vis-à-vis whiteness. He writes gangster rap lyrics to distinguish himself from other "bitch-ass White boys" at school, as he calls them. Yet his vanilla rap performance is immediately detected and demasked as fake by the school guidance counselor, who tells him, "I hate to break this to you, but you are also a bitch-ass White boy." Later in the series, Shane's attempts at crossidentification include an obsession with a biography of Sammy Davis Jr. (in which the African American entertainer recounts his conversion to Judaism) and a fascination with Spanish gangster lingo that he learns to mimic from a Mexican drug dealer. Shane Botwin's attempts to find his place in the multicultural salad bowl leave him dazed and confused about his own identity.

Whether represented as an interpellative force that marks the body or one that puts fantasies of escape into whiteness into question, Jewishness resurfaces in Kohan's vision of the present-day multicultural

United States in a most subversive way. Determined, as she says in a recent interview, to "make [her] own way" in American television, Kohan departs from what she calls the "patronizing" trend of whitewashing Jewish characters to the point they represent everybody."[30] Unlike conventional portrayals of Jews in the media, Kohan contends, "I don't look to improve the image." Instead, she suggests, "I look to create complicated, complex, interesting [Jewish] characters with flaws, warts and all. I don't necessarily concern myself with the question, 'is it good for the Jews?'" The question of whether or not "everything is," as she says, "available for laughs" is an ethical question that tests the limits of Jewish representation, which Kohan, unlike many other Jewish directors and producers, dismisses as irrelevant.[31]

Time will tell if Kohan's project of reinserting Jewish difference into the postethnic multicultural context has been successful. Numerous viewer responses posted on Internet blogs and magazines suggest otherwise. In a later *Weeds* episode, Doug and Dean scheme to reclaim a bag of weed Celia has stolen from them by tricking her into believing that a Black police officer is chasing her. The Black cop is, as it turns out, the Jewish Dean in blackface. *Slate Magazine*—a relatively intellectual, liberal-leaning publication—comments on this episode: "[A] White character actually tried to pass for Black."[32] The writer of one Internet blog angrily asks, "Why is that necessary? Why couldn't [Kohan] pay a Black [rather than White] man to impersonate an officer and trail Celia? … I can see how all of this was possibly an attempt by the writers to be edgy and subversive but that line is thin and dangerous to tread. There could have been much better and less offensive ways to do that because the fact is that people who do not know about the history of minstrelsy or Blackface do not have the tools to decode that type of humor."[33]

This seemingly unanimous reading of Dean as White, rather than as a Jew in blackface, and the cultural amnesia (or ignorance) that these commentators demonstrate regarding the central role Jews played in the history of blackface raises questions about Kohan's audience's ability to, indeed, "decode [her] type of humor." Yet Kohan's unrecognized intertextual reference to Al Jolson's performance in *The Jazz Singer* (emphasized by Dean's mention of the part-Jewish, practicing Catholic jazz singer Harry Connick, Jr.) raises an even more pressing question for Kohan and other Jewish makers of popular culture, indeed for all American Jews and scholars of ethnicity: Have Jews in multicultural America indeed been irreversibly relegated to the pale of whiteness or can they be incorporated into multiculturalism?

Notes

1. See Vincent Brook, *Something Ain't Kosher Here: The Rise of the 'Jewish' Sitcom* (New Brunswick, NJ: Rutgers University Press, 2003); Joyce Antler, "'Yesterday's Woman,' Today's Moral Guide: Molly Goldberg as Jewish Mother," in *Key Texts in American Jewish Culture,* ed. Jack Kugelmass (New Brunswick: Rutgers University Press, 2003), 129–146; Jack Kugelmass, "First as Farce, Then as Tragedy: The Unlamented Demise of Bridget Loves Bernie," in *Key Texts in American Jewish Culture,* 147–160; Michele Byers and Rosalin Krieger, "Something Old Is New Again? Postmodern Jewishness in *Curb Your Enthusiasm, Arrested Development,* and *The O.C.,*" in *You Should See Yourself: Jewish Identity in Postmodern American Culture,* ed. Vincent Brook (New Brunswick, NJ: Rutgers University Press, 2006), 277–297; Tamara Olson, *Popular Representations of Jewish Identity on Primetime Television: The Case of The O.C.,* master's thesis, Macalester College, St. Paul, Minnesota, 2006.
2. Brook, *Something Ain't Kosher,* 2.
3. Ibid., 12.
4. Jenji Kohan (dir.), *Weeds,* Lionsgate Television, Showtime, eight seasons, August 7, 2005–September 16, 2012. This essay relates to the first five seasons.
5. On this transition from race to ethnicity, see Brodkin, *How Jews Became White Folks.*
6. Danielle Berrin, "Smoking the Stereotypes," *JewishJournal.com,* http://www.jewishjournal.com/summer_sneaks/article/smoking_the_stereotypes_20090520/
7. Ibid.
8. Daniel Itzkovitz, "They All Are Jews," in *You Should See Yourself: Jewish Identity in Postmodern American Culture,* ed. Vincent Brook (New Brunswick, NJ: *Rutgers* University Press, 2006), 232.
9. Henry Popkin, "The Vanishing Jew of Our Popular Culture," *Commentary* 13 (July 1952): 47.
10. Itzkovitz, "They All Are Jews," 232.
11. Ibid.
12. Byers and Krieger, "Something Old is New Again?," 278.
13. Ibid.
14. E.g., *Rhoda* (1974–1979), *Welcome Back, Kotter* (1975–1979), *Barney Miller* (1975–1983), and *Taxi* (1979–1983).
15. See Brodkin, *How Jews Became White Folks;* Jacobson, *Whiteness of a Different Color;* Roediger, *Working toward Whiteness;* and Goldstein, *Price of Whiteness.*
16. David Biale, "The Melting Pot and Beyond: Jews and the Politics of American Identity," in *Insider/Outsider: American Jews and Multiculturalism,* ed. David Biale, Michael Galchinsky, and Susannah Heschel (Berkeley: University of California Press, 1998), 27.
17. Vincent Brook, "American Jews and Television," in *Encyclopedia of American Jewish History,* vol. 1, ed. Stephen H. Norwood and Eunice G. Pollack (Santa Barbara, CA: ABC-Clio, 2008), 477.
18. Jacobson, *Whiteness of a Different Color,* 96.
19. See Matthew Frye Jacobson, *Roots Too: White Ethnic Revival in Post–Civil Rights America* (Cambridge, MA: Harvard University Press), 2006.

20. As Hollinger argues, "[t]he key point about multiculturalism is that there has been almost no place in it for Jews. Multiculturalism has been organized largely on the basis of the ethnoracial pentagon, our mythical, five-part structure with cultures ascribed to color-coded communities of descent, often in recent years labeled African American, Asian American, European American, Hispanic or Latino, and Indian or Native American"; David A. Hollinger, "Communalist and Dispersionist Approaches to American Jewish History in an Increasingly Post-Jewish Era," *American Jewish History* 95, no. 1 (March 2009):17.
21. For a discussion of the Jewish ghetto girl stereotype, see Riv-Ellen Prell, *Fighting to Become American* (Boston: Beacon, 1999).
22. All quotations from *Weeds* are transcribed by the authors from copies of the televised episodes.
23. Julie Wolfson, "LAist Interview: Jenji Kohan, Creator of *Weeds*," *LAist*, http://laist.com/2008/06/12/laist_interview_jenji_kohan_creator.php
24. On anti-Jewish prejudice in the U.S. Army, see Jacob Radar Marcus, *United States Jewry 1776–1985, Volume 3: The Germanic Period, Part 2* (Detroit, MI: Wayne State University Press, 1993), 162–163.
25. Sander L. Gilman, *The Jew's Body* (New York: Routledge, 1991), 39.
26. Ibid., 40, 44.
27. Ibid., 240.
28. Daniel Itzkovitz, "Passing Like Me," *South Atlantic Quarterly* 98 (1999): 38.
29. See Daniel Boyarin, *Unheroic Conduct* (Berkeley: University of California Press, 1997); Joshua Trachtenberg, *The Devil and the Jew* (New Haven, CT: Yale University Press, 1943); and Sander L. Gilman, *Freud, Race, and Gender* (Princeton, NJ: Princeton University Press, 1996).
30. Danielle Berrin, "Smoking the Stereotypes."
31. Ibid.
32. June Thomas, "More Cable TV Blackface," *Brow Beat: Slate's Culture Blog*, http://www.slate.com/blogs/blogs/browbeat/archive/2009/09/02/more-cable-tv-blackface.aspx
33. "Weeds, Women, and Blackface," *Candice Uncompromised* (blog), http://candigram.blogspot.com/2009/08/weeds-women-and-blackface.html

PART II

JEWS AS BLACKS / BLACK JEWS

CHAPTER 7

A Member of the Club?

How Black Jews Negotiate Black Anti-Semitism and Jewish Racism

Bruce D. Haynes

A Strained Alliance

This chapter uses a sociological lens to evaluate how American Black Jews, that is, individuals with one Black parent and one Jewish parent, negotiate the realities of Jewish racism and Black anti-Semitism in their various communities. In particular I examine how their sense of belonging, that is, the extent to which their claims to both a Black and Jewish identity are accepted within their respective reference groups, impacts their responses to incidents of racism or anti-Semitism. The analysis is based on a series of in-depth interviews conducted between 1998 and 2001, following a period when tensions between Black and Jewish Americans had reached a boiling point.

Charges of rising Black anti-Semitism and Jewish racism go back to at least the 1930s, when Black Harlemites first picketed Blumstein's Department Store for discriminatory hiring practices. Still, studies during the 1930s and 1940s concluded that prejudice toward Jews was less widespread among Blacks than it was among Whites.[1] Surveys conducted in 1964, 1981, and 1992 suggested a steady rise in Black anti-Semitism, yet the vast methodological differences among the surveys made it impossible to establish any trend with certainty.[2] In addition, survey results have yet to disentangle the degree to which anti-Semitism among Blacks reflects a distinct form of anti-Jewish feeling that does not conform to traditional Western anti-Semitism.

Recent data gathered in three American cities reveal that Black church-goers do not share in the vilification of Jews as Christ killers, and in fact have more favorable views of Jews than of other White Americans.[3] The fact that many Blacks identify with the story of the Jews' captivity in Egypt and their exodus into freedom has long been recognized by scholars such as Lawrence W. Levine.[4] Yet if the antipathy toward Jews among at least some Black Americans is not classic anti-Semitism, what is it and how widespread is it? Is there something unique about anti-Jewish sentiment among Blacks that sets it apart from the commonplace variety?

Many have claimed that negative Black attitudes toward Jews have emerged out of a particular set of economic relationships—as tenants of Jewish landlords, domestics in Jewish households, employees in Jewish businesses, or customers in Jewish stores.[5] This is partly true, but in the 1960s and 1970s much of the anti-Jewish rhetoric among Blacks coalesced around the Israeli–Arab conflict, the 1968 New York City Teacher's Strike, and the Andrew Young affair. It is clear that the media has had much influence in shaping public perceptions of Jews, Blacks, and their relationship, but by far the single most controversial moment of Black/Jewish conflict came in 1984, when in an off-the-record remark the Reverend Jesse Jackson, who was then running for president, referred to New York City as "Hymietown."[6] While Jackson first denied having made the remark, he soon recanted and apologized, hoping to put the unfortunate blunder behind him. But the next month Minister Louis Farrakhan of the Nation of Islam catapulted the incident back to national attention when, in a radio broadcast, he compared himself to Adolph Hitler—while criticizing Jews for making the same comparison—and made veiled threats of retaliation toward Milton Coleman, the *Washington Post* reporter who broke the original Hymietown story.[7] By early April, New York City mayor Ed Koch, along with other prominent Jews, was calling for Jackson to distance himself from Farrakhan and his anti-Semitic invectives.[8]

In August 1991, City College of New York (CCNY) professor Leonard Jeffries delivered an address at the Empire State Black Arts and Cultural Festival in which he unleashed his extremist and fantastical theories about rich Jews, the slave trade, and a "Jewish" conspiracy. In the end, Jeffries' vitriol did nothing more than spark a new media frenzy and heighten scrutiny of CCNY. During that same month, seven-year-old Gavin Cato was killed and his young cousin severely injured during a Hasidic motorcade under police escort through the predominantly West Indian and Hasidic community of Crown Heights, Brooklyn. Both were children of Guyanese immigrants. While witnesses differed over what happened next, it seems that groups composed largely of Black Caribbean people—enraged by both the failure of the police to arrest the driver and the delayed response of medical workers—began a peaceful protest that soon escalated into a three-day riot and random attacks by youths on local Hasidic Jews, culminating in the tragic stabbing death of Yankel Rosenbaum, a 29-year-old Australian yeshiva student. The media characterized the riots as a Jewish pogrom, and Jews expressed outrage when false reports spread that Mayor Dinkins and Police Commissioner Lee P. Brown (both Black men) had initially withheld police protection from the Hasidim so that Blacks could "vent their rage."[9] The city's largest African American newspaper, the *Amsterdam News,* ran the headline "Many Blacks, No Jews Arrested." Little attention was given to the fact that the conflict was largely between West Indians and Hasidic Jews.

Two years later, in 1993, Wellesley history professor Tony Martin drew outcries from Jewish students for teaching from *The Secret Relationship between Blacks and Jews* (a notorious publication of the Nation of Islam) in his course on African American history. Later that year, Martin published his account of the campus controversy in a provocatively entitled paperback, *The Jewish Onslaught: Dispatches from the Wellesley Battlefront.*[10] Later the same year Nation of Islam spokesperson Khalid Abdul Muhammad made national headlines for denouncing Jews as "bloodsuckers of the Black nation" and the Pope as a "no-good cracker." Although he was subsequently dismissed from the Nation of Islam, his vitriol landed him a public platform on NBC's Donahue talk show.[11] Ironically, by the summer of 1993, when Cornel West published his book *Race Matters,* much of American society had declared itself color blind, and Jewish neo-cons were leading efforts to repeal affirmative action policies that had benefited Blacks in California, Michigan, and Washington.[12] The ability of Jews to wield economic and political power like other Whites in America further stoked Black resentment and helped pave the way for Farrakhan's Holy Day of Atonement, Reconciliation and Responsibility, touted as the Million Man March, that took place in Washington, DC, on October 16, 1995.

Polls from the Anti-Defamation League, the American Jewish Committee, and Harris were offered as evidence of a disquieting trend toward anti-Jewish thought, especially among African Americans, yet the data actually showed that the percentages of the most anti-Semitic among both Blacks and Whites had declined from levels recorded in the 1960s.[13] While some surveys revealed elevated levels of anti-Jewish feelings among younger, more-educated African American respondents compared to their White counterparts, the variances likely reflected the rising numbers of Caribbean immigrants. Furthermore, Anti-Defamation League surveys have repeatedly failed to distinguish between foreign-born and native-born Blacks, despite evidence of elevated anti-Semitism among new immigrant populations. Indeed, Gary Rubin later concluded from the 1992 Anti-Defamation League and Marttila and Kiley survey, "African Americans, like everyone else, became less prone to anti-Semitism as their incomes and education rise."[14] In addition, Anti-Defamation League surveys since 1992 may have tapped into rising Black resentment or envy of Jewish claims to White privilege, expressed as early as 1948 in James Baldwin's *Commentary* essay "The Harlem Ghetto."[15] Moreover, the Anti-Defamation League scale lumps both positive and negative feelings toward Jews into a single index. For example, subjects were typically asked to state the degree to which they agreed with the statement "Jews stick together more than other Americans." But a strong agreement with this statement may actually indicate an admiration for Jews rather than resentment toward them. Sociologist Lee Sigelman concluded, "[S]imultaneous acceptance of positive and negative images of Jews sounds a warning against any tendency to treat Blacks' views of Jews as an undifferentiated Gestalt," and draws attention to "a mixture of positive and negative attitudes more indicative of ambivalence than of anti-Semitism per se."[16]

Biracial Jews Weigh In

The presence of both racism and anti-Semitism in the United States makes the process of opting for an identity even more challenging for biracial Black Jews. In the postwar United States, Ashkenazic cultural hegemony placed Yiddish culture and the Holocaust as cornerstones of postwar Jewish identity. Some scholars have gone so far as to define Yiddishkeit as Jewishness.[17] Embedded within the prevailing postwar Jewish identity, which emphasizes its European roots and defines itself more in opposition to being Christian than on religious observance, is the acceptance by most Americans that Jews of European descent are White. While gaining the privileges afforded to middle-class White America, they have fashioned a specifically Jewish form of White identity rooted in a unique blend of religious and secular institutions, history of survival in Gentile-dominated societies, as well as an often intense commitment to Israel.[18]

Scholars have used Du Bois' concept of double consciousness—whereby one looks at one's self through the eyes of the majority—as a metaphor for Jewish identity in America.[19] In fact, Jews have been seen as both insiders and outsiders in American society.[20] While the notion of the Jew as the Other might have become a part of the legacy of American anti-Semitism, Jews were supplanted by Africans and their descendants as the quintessential Other in America. Still, a challenge of defining Jewishness arises because it is nearly impossible to distinguish between Jews as a people and Judaism as a faith. And while the diversity of American Jews in beliefs, practices, region, custom, and national background is often noted, Jewish racial diversity is seldom recognized. Yet previous sociological research does indicate that contemporary Jewishness in the United States is grounded in two principal ways. First, most Jews today regard being Jewish as including ethnic, cultural, and national dimensions.[21] Second, American Jewry defines itself in religious terms through the varied institutional frameworks and their rules of membership. While American Jews who identified as Reform and Conservative were evenly split by the 1990's, at 35 percent and 33 percent respectively, some 7 percent remained Orthodox and 26 percent held "none or other" religious identification.[22] Still, Jewishness in America can provide a basis for a stable identity while other bases of a group's social identity are in flux.[23] While scholars have explored the identity formation of biracial people with one Black and one White parent, few have examined those whose White parent is also Jewish.[24] The identities of Black Jews in general might well be understood as a wrestling with two forms of double consciousness, one created by the veil of blackness, the other through a Jewish Other.[25] Still, although Du Bois provides insights into the reciprocal nature of group boundaries and identity, the application of a strict Du Boisian model of double consciousness to understanding the self-conceptions of contemporary biracial Black Jews proves limited. Rather than defining themselves through the eyes of the majority, it was acceptance as the Other by "the Other" that our subjects often groped with. In fact many chose not to identify with either host society—Christians or Whites—but rather embraced two stigmatized social statuses, as Jews and Blacks.

I take an inductive comparative approach to establishing the boundaries of Jewish identity, beginning with the premise that there is no prototypical Jewish identity but only individuals situated, as Goldberg and Krausz write, "in positions contingently and perhaps contentiously identifiable as Jewish."[26] I conducted in-depth, semistructured interviews to gather data on racial and ethnic identity, religious practice and affiliation, and experiences with Jewish racism and Black anti-Semitism. Of my eleven biracial (Black–Jewish) participants, only two claim their Jewish identity through patrilineal descent. Consistent with other studies of Black–White biracial Jews constructed through snowball samples, my sample is biased toward matrilineal-descent Jews.[27] Some scholars suggest that what is central to Jewishness is a sense of group history, as distinct from Judaism (religion), which is rooted in a set of law-defined practices.[28] In fact our interviews show that to be Jewish by halakhic law (i.e., through matrilineal descent) is distinct from assuming and affirming a Jewish identity through patrilineal descent. And in America, affirming one's Jewish identity for people who do not look White requires adjusting the public image that Jews are White.[29]

Interviews were conducted between 1998 and 2001, a period—as we have seen—of heightened tension between Blacks and Jews. Their voices bring to light some key differences in how biracial individuals with Black and Jewish heritage respond to racism and anti-Semitism on the ground, while reframing how we think about the forces shaping the identity options of American biracials. Those who had a weaker sense of place within the Black community expressed more heightened and visceral responses to anti-Jewish rhetoric from Blacks, while those whose Jewish credentials were regularly challenged by mainstream Jews were far more preoccupied with racism from Jews—which they framed, interestingly, by their own personal experiences and struggles for legitimacy.

With the exception of one Arab-descent Black Jew, subjects—regardless of their status along the continuum of Jewish belonging—adopted the language and framework of mainstream Judaism to discuss both Jewish racism and Black anti-Semitism. Legalistic terms such as "halakha" (religious law) or "matrilineal and patrilineal descent" were central to discussions of legitimate claims to Judaism. When discussing anti-Jewish feelings among Blacks, many framed the discussion around the Jewish community's preoccupation with Farrakhan and other provocateurs (although subjects took great pains not to paint either community with broad strokes). Subjects who felt alienated or rebuffed from other Blacks expressed greater anger and outrage with Black anti-Semitism than did those who felt validated by other Blacks. In the end, it was not the strength of their sense of identity as Black or Jewish but their sense of belonging within the respective communities that shaped their interpretations of Jewish racism and Black anti-Semitism. Secure status was correlated with greater objectivity.

Our first subject, Dana, a matrilineal-descent Jew and original member of the Alliance of Black Jews, was born and raised on the South Side of Chicago, just around the block from Minister Farrakhan's home and the Nation of Islam headquarters.[30] She expressed frustration with the attention she often drew in Jewish circles: "You know, getting questions like, 'Are you Jewish? Why are you here? How did you become Jewish? There's a whole little like, every time you encounter Jewish people—White Jewish people they feel entitled to, you know, sort of ask about your Jewish identity if you're darker." Having grown up Black in a poor neighborhood, Dana was also very conscious of the role that class played in defining her identity and sense of belonging within her Jewish community: "There were class issues that led to not belonging that I think trumped my emotional analysis of the racial issues that were going on in my congregation.... Oh, I'm sure they were there, but I was not feeling them the same way. I think they were buffered by these class issues."

When directly questioned about incidents of racism among Jews, Dana gave an emotionally charged response:

> It does not shock my Black self, it shocks my Jewish self, and it's the only moment I bifurcate.... I get enraged as a Jew. And my Black self goes, 'Oh, yeah of course. I've seen this before.' It's like the only moment I can trace where I do the split. But it's more like the split ... when ... you're watching White folks react to you and you're watching you react to their reaction. I don't know if you ever do this, but you sort of, you know that kind of Duboisian second sight thing.

Her views on the public attention to the Holocaust, which had reached a new high in the 1990s, reflected those voiced by many young African Americans of the period: "But, the Holocaust ... is a lot more complicated for me because a lot of other feelings sort of seep in about, why this holocaust, why only this holocaust? Why don't we get to mark the other holocausts? And what does that mean about the way we value populations and communities." She attributed Jews' success in gaining recognition for the Holocaust to their whiteness:

> The way that cultural memory has been instituted successfully by Jews is both one of our greatest achievements and one of our most serious moments of myopic blindness ... the way that Jewish whiteness has been able to enact this ... the fact that these kids who perished were White, you know, these women who died were White.... So, and it angers me every time I hear it. Every time I hear people being moved by Holocaust experiences. Every time I hear people going back and reading off a hundred names, there is a moment where my heart just goes shhhhhh.

In contrast to the indignation she expressed over incidents of racism among Jews, she offered a fairly analytical critique of Black anti-Semitism:

> And this is what I don't understand about the way that Black anti-Jewishness is analyzed. It's analyzed as if it is separate and apart from broader anti-Jewish sentiment. And Black folks don't have the power to translate that and we don't have a history of translating that. It seems to me there are exceptional moments where, you know, you have conflagrations of anti-Jewish feeling, which, in New York, is largely immigrant based, not traditional African-American community based anyway, so there's that. But to me it's how it can become a catalyst for wider anti-Jewish sentiment.... Looking at the dynamic interrelationship between the Nation's [Nation of Islam's] anti Jewishness and how it affirms, confirms, and legitimizes larger anti-Semitic sentiment in the United States. That's the danger. The danger isn't coming from the Black community.

Dana placed Farrakhan's anti-Jewish rhetoric within a broader political context of race in America:

> I think there are lots of things that Farrakhan and the Nation [of Islam] are doing that are, you know, that are wonderful for our community in relationship to an increasing prison population which needs positive intervention, you know.... I have problems with his gender politics. I have problems with his sexuality politics. ... I have problems with his heterosexism, I have problems with his African politics ..., and I have problems with his anti-Jewishness ... but I would not elevate my problems with Farrakhan's anti-Jewishness above the other problems I have with him. And it annoys me to no end that White Jews insist that we do ... particularly, because it affects the African American community, and I don't think his anti-Jewishness affects the Jewish community much, which is not to say that we shouldn't be upset by anti-Jewishness wherever it appears ... but ... I think Jews have much more serious problems.

Seymour is a matrilineal descent Black Jew who grew up in New York in the mixed neighborhood of Morningside Heights, near Columbia University. Seymour was visibly Black and recognized as such by both Whites and Blacks, making him privy to uncensored talk about Jews from non-Jewish friends and acquaintances in his cosmopolitan Upper West Side neighborhood. He was raised not unlike other Manhattan Jews. Between the ages of nine and fourteen he attended the left-Zionist Hashomer Hatsa'ir youth camp in the Bronx. Seymour attended Hebrew school downtown at a Reconstructionist Synagogue on 86th Street and was bar mitzvahed there as well. At the same time, he had grown an Afro and become involved in Harlem's graffiti subculture. He seemed secure in his dual identities as Black and Jewish, and was at home in either community.

As we spoke at his midtown Manhattan office more than thirty years later, Seymour explained how he had negotiated his allegiances to both groups. He was skilled at contextualizing the debate, providing a calm and rational perspective to the conflict. At the same time, he did not hesitate to defend his Black brothers to fellow Jews or to make his Jewishness known to Blacks who expressed anti-Jewish sentiment:

> Being thrown between Black anti-Semitism and Jewish racism colliding on the streets of the city during the sixties wasn't pleasant.… I read a really, really good book, about anti-Semitism and the Holocaust, you may know about it, *Vessels of Evil,* Lawrence Thomas, and it sort of reminds me of just that, "who suffered the most?" There was that clear, you know, 'Look, this is not your time it's my time.' … I would sort of defend my Black brothers from any sort of attack that might be based purely on the color of their skin, or the way they chose to wear afros, or the way that they chose to dress a certain way.… And to Jews in the face of Blacks who would be anti-Semitic, you know, my perspective was that, "Do you like me? I'm Jewish, so what do you really know?"

Still, looking Black often trumped looking Jewish, even in Israel: "They [Israelis] saw me to a large degree as either Sephardic, Ethiopian or Falashan, or some of them would call me "Cushi" which I didn't take too well. Because I'd rather be called a Falashan, you know, than a Cushi." Today Seymour, an observant Conservative Jew, is married to an American Jew of European descent, and is active in the New York Jewish community.

Pnina, born to a Jewish mother and an African father, grew up in Los Angeles. She was raised there by her grandmother and a large extended family. Her parents sent her away to Catholic boarding school (an odd choice, given her family's embrace of Judaism) to escape a household in turmoil. Although she was visibly Black, Pnina had not been exposed much to Black American culture and was often rejected by other Black children at Catholic school: "The Black kids didn't accept me because I wasn't Black. That was in the days of, you know, Stokely and H. Rap. And, you know, you had to only listen to Motown. I didn't know how to dance!"

She was now in her forties and married to a foreign-born Sephardic Jew. They maintain a Jewish household and participate in Jewish community life. Throughout our discussion, Pnina made very few comments on Jewish racism but had a highly intense and visceral reaction to Black anti-Semitism and to Farrakhan in particular:

> I think he is a master manipulator. I think he's a charlatan. I think he is a murderer.… When we, when we were in Chicago and we were having this little conference, Gabriele said, "Oh let's go look at Farrakhan's house." So we drove around. And I have to tell you, I have been to Sach-

senhausen, I have been to Dachau, I have been to Bergen-Belsen. I have been to horrible places. I have been to, you know, prisoner of war camps during the Iraq/Iran War.… I have dealt with evil, right? And I felt as I was driving around his house at night the way I felt when I was driving around Evin Prison in Tehran. That there is an open hole in the earth boiling with gas and sulfur and it's in his living room. And the evil in the core of the earth is just bubbling up.

Pnina's remarks contrast sharply with the more tempered assessment of our next subject, Rebecca, who was also a matrilineal Jew but who grew up with strong Black and Jewish identities. Rebecca viewed Farrakhan as more of a media hound than an anti-Semite: "Look, if I was in the media and trying to get attention I would attack the Jews faster than anybody. I mean if you're trying to get attention you know what to do. And, you know, Farrakhan was nowhere in the Jewish press until the Jesse Jackson thing and he stepped in front of Jesse and said, 'If you're going to attack Jesse you're going to have to deal with me,' and then kind of attacked the Jews to, I think, to divert attention and get attention for himself."

Josh was a very light-skinned Black born to a White Jewish mother and an African American father. They had divorced when he was very young, and he was raised by his mother and Jewish stepfather in a secular yet culturally Jewish household on the North Shore of Long Island. He had weak ties to both the Black and Jewish communities—but for very different reasons. While he was fully accepted within the Jewish community, the acceptance he sought—and which seemed to elude him—was from other Blacks. His tenuous status among Blacks sometimes led him to overcompensate, even passing as a non-Jew in the presence of other Blacks: "Often kind of, I mean, I'm not as proud of my Judaism.… A lot of times, especially if I'm among, you know … Black groups, I just don't say anything about it. I figure that it's something I'm happier to have go unnoticed.… In a weird way, it's probably similar to the whole idea of passing … it's just easier." He described his feelings of inadequacy during college, when Professor Leonard Jeffries had been invited to the campus to speak:

They certainly had a whole bunch of, you know, nationalists in that group. You know, there were a couple of Nation of Islam members that didn't really welcome me.… And my whole kind of thinking then was trying to figure out who I am. I didn't really want to associate with the Jewish community very much. You know, couldn't really join their protesting in front of Jeffries, even though I kind of sympathized with their protests. I just didn't want to be a part of it, I guess, in my own personal insecurities in both communities. Not so like I was vocal enough in ei-

> ther one of them kind of, you know, and not feeling entitled to kind of claim membership firmly enough in either of them.

When speaking about Farrakhan, Josh expressed shame, disappointment, and anger: "He doesn't raise in me the anger and rage that he [does] in … the majority of Jews. He actually raises in me … just more shame and disappointment. I guess I'm pissed off at him. You know, it's like, 'Lou you make it harder for me.'" His frustration extended to the Million Man March, which he saw as a once-in-a-lifetime opportunity he had been robbed of: "I did think of the Million Man March.… And again, because I would have wanted to if it wasn't Farrakhan.… It's kind of a once in a generation kind of thing. But I couldn't really associate myself with him. I wouldn't have had any self-respect. And again, that's part of the disappointment, you know, you deprived me of my chance to actually be part of something that I'm entitled to partly because you're embarrassing."

Michael, a New York–born Jew with an Ashkenazic mother and West Indian father, was a journalist for a leading news outlet. Although he felt welcomed in both communities, he had a stronger Black identity. When we spoke in his office in June 1999, he gave his own analysis of Farrakhan's effect on his identity: "It's only Black people that are responsible for every other Black person. I mean but in our situation, you know, that's the only place where people want to know what an entertainer is doing to repudiate a politician.… He's speaking for himself or his group, but no one goes to Jerry Seinfeld and says well you you're going to repudiate whoever. It's just not an issue."

When our conversation turned to the Million Man March, he echoed the sentiments of Josh, noting that while the event "turned out nice," he—along with some of his non-Jewish Black friends—could not give support to someone so "wrong-headed." He also expressed disappointment that Farrakhan had failed to capitalize on the political momentum he had built. "And the interesting thing was really how little has … really come out of it. I mean, anyone else who put together, whatever it was—six-hundred-thousand—anyone else who had done that there would have been more to come out of it in terms of real goals, within that community."

Hannah, another matrilineal Jew, was born in New York City and grew up on the Upper West Side, near Columbia University. Her maternal grandmother had emigrated from Russia, and her mother had grown up in Manhattan. Her father came from a family of Black Episcopalians. Her parents had divorced when she was young, although her father still lived in their apartment building. While Hannah's family never attended synagogue when she was growing up, her mother was adamant about instilling in her a strong sense of who she was. "She always was like, 'You're a Jew, you know, this is what we do.' But it was very home based … they always had Passover. They always had Yom Kippur. They always celebrated Rosh Hashana. They always lit, you know, the candles though they didn't have Sabbath every weekend."

Her father had a more aggressive style of cultural indoctrination. Afraid she would grow up without a strong Black identity, he would "push stuff on me," which had the effect of pushing her away from it. The family was well-off by New York standards, and Hannah had attended a progressive private school in Manhattan and went on to earn a bachelor's degree in art from Yale University. Now in her mid-twenties, Hannah expressed curiosity about Judaism but was somewhat reluctant to pursue it in concrete ways or become involved in organized Judaism. She was drawn more to the mysticism of Judaism and found the Kabbalah fascinating.

Hannah lamented the broken alliance between Jews and Blacks and attributed much of the damage to Farrakhan:

> Yeah, I remember when I was younger. When he said all that stuff. And I was really angry and really upset.… I'm very liberal.… I feel like people should be allowed to feel what they feel. If he feels that way about Jews he's welcome to it. I think he's wrong, you know. I think he should educate himself about the reality of Jews and the reality of the history of Jews and Blacks. Which is there's always been a strong alliance. I'm angry that he said things because I think he was instrumental in making the situation between Jews and Blacks worse. When Jews and Blacks really had had a history together. You know, the Civil Rights Movements was Jews and Blacks working together. And I think, I think at that time yeah, Blacks needed the Jews' whiteness but I think the Jews because of their history needed to help Blacks in order to help themselves as well.

Jonathan and his brother Andrew are patrilineal Jews who grew up in the Philadelphia suburb of Mount Airy—a "refuge for aging hippies, and folkies and civil rights workers." Their Black mother held a master's degree in art and had studied in Israel for a year because, according to Jonathan, she was "attracted to the culture and the religion. … I know that her closest friends have been consistently Jewish. Her best friend now is Jewish. And she takes great pride that her sons are Jewish, although I'm not sure really what that means to her." Their father was an atheist—a "Jewish-influenced secular humanist" who had been raised in an upper-middle-class household. Their grandfather had come from Galizia, an area between Hungary and Poland, the grandmother "from an old established German-Jewish Philadelphia family, which included artists and printers."

Despite attending a Unitarian nursery school, having a Christmas tree during the winter holidays, and growing up with an atheist father, Jonathan had developed a strong spiritual connection to his Jewish roots by the time he had reached adolescence:

> I guess I always had a Jewish consciousness which was strange. I mean I could tell you one strange story. And I'm not really … I'm religious but I don't believe in formal religion as much as I'm attached to Judaism on a tribal level in terms of organizing.… It organizes my week, my schedule. Which is not inconsistent with Judaism as a legal code.… But I did always have this kind of feeling of faith and of connection. And then when I was 12, I realized that I wanted to express that in real knowledge about Judaism. So I learned it.

As a biracial Jew growing up in suburban Mount Airy, Jonathan had felt disconnected from the Black world, an experience he described as jarring: "I had grown up in a fairly rough school but I didn't realize it. I didn't realize how much every day there was a threat of basically getting my ass kicked. And I always talked my way out of it. I never got beat up. But when I went to the all-Jewish day school I kind of like had post-traumatic, like I became very, very fearful of, of going outside. And I became very, very fearful of Black people."

While his sense of Black belonging evolved as he grew older, he also continued to develop a strong Jewish identity, which was grounded more in spirituality than in community. In fact as a patrilineal-descent Jew, he often felt rejected from mainstream Judaism. The events leading up to Jonathan's bar mitzvah had been particularly painful and alienating: "The rabbi said, 'In order to have a bar mitzvah you have to convert.' I was like, 'Convert to what?' I mean because you couldn't have told me that I was not Jewish.… And even now, I met with some Orthodox rabbis that wanted me to reconvert to make sure my conversion's good. … Because the rabbis that converted, one of them was not observant of the Sabbath which technically nullifies the conversion. But, you know, my feeling is the rabbis can really kiss my ass."

Still, these difficult experiences in fact left him defiantly, triumphantly Jewish: "You don't have to count me for your minyan. You can bury me with Goyim, as if the rabbis can separate dust, you know. You can exclude me however you want. I know what I am. Actually one of the real comforting things I've ever heard anyone say was this, the rabbi in New York, in Utica, or in Brooklyn. 'The Pope can decide who's Catholic or not, but he can't decide who's Christian.'"

Jonathan's failure to become fully recognized as a Jew may have led him to emphasize the spiritual over the legalistic interpretation of the boundaries of the Jewish community: "I believe in Halacha [*sic*]. I do believe. It's like citizenship. You know, you have to have rules. But I'm not a legalist. I believe in the spirit which is one of the reasons I'm attracted to Hasidism. It's because I believe in the letter of the law is important but without the spiritual interpretation it's nothing. It's empty. And I refuse to submit to that kind of legal, I mean for me it was always legal, it was always legalism. My conversion was always legal, legalistic. Like I'm already Jewish."

Jonathan believed that Judaism's emphasis on distinctions led to racial exclusion: "The problem with Judaism is that … it's a religion of purity. And it's a problem. I mean, Judaism is a religion of distinctions between the week and the Sabbath, between culture and trade, Jew and non-Jew. And so when you have ethnic nuances or cultural nuances it's sometimes hard for people to reconcile. The fact is though, the Jews have been, have always been a diverse people, nationally, culturally, ethnically, racially.… And in fact you can even say that Judaism is the perfect balance between a continuous culture and a diverse population.

Dark skin often signifies outsider status in America, and many Jews reinforce a normative Black/White binary in which Jews are defined as White and Blacks are defined in opposition, that is, as not Jewish. Katya Gibel Azoulay has observed that the union of Black and Jewish identities has been neglected and negated largely due to conflating Jewishness with whiteness.[31] And, as Melanie Kaye/Kantrowitz has noted in her *The Colors of Jews: Racial Politics and Racial Diasporism,* this binary frame makes it nearly impossible to imagine Black Jews as real social beings.[32] Thus one's claims to Jewish identity and community membership can be challenged in both secular and religious settings simply for not looking Jewish.

Jonathan's responses make a striking contrast to those of his brother Andrew—two years his senior—and underscore the key finding of this analysis: that the ways in which biracial Jews interpret Jewish racism and Black anti-Semitism are determined by their perceived status (that is, the strength of their sense of belonging) within the Jewish or Black communities.

Andrew was a staunch defender of Jewish legalism and believed that it placed Judaism outside the boundaries of racism. In fact, despite the fact that he was an agnostic, he held the Orthodox community in high esteem:

> One of the interesting things of the Orthodox Jewish community is that they actually have clear rules which determine who is Jewish and who

> is not, which takes race out of it.... I mean, to be honest it is not a community that I could be part of but on the other hand they are as close to race blind as you can find in the Jewish community, so it is easy to kind of, you know, they do have a lot of irrational beliefs, you know, whatever, but, um, if you are looking for a community where nobody is going to say I am not Black, or nobody is going to question your Jewishness, it is about the only community I can think of.

While he described himself as multicultural, his responses to Black anti-Semitism and his comments on Jewish racism reflected his stronger links to the Jewish community. "There is a history of, there are a lot of Jewish communities where people will embrace you because people don't like the racism. In America, they see a parallel between anti-Semitism and racism, and to be very supportive. If I am honest about my Jewish experience I don't feel that welcome in a number of African American circles, I don't feel like a full member." His divisions were even sharper when contrasting life in the States and Israel: "In African American circles, there is a lot of, real anti-Semitism, a feeling like, you know the Jews are this, there are certain things like we aren't in the same boat," while in Israel, "I mean there are different traditions, but um, yet Israel is a place where being brown, I mean people are brown. The de facto color is brown."

Nadine, a twenty-year-old dark-skinned college student born to an Arab Jewish mother and African-American father, was raised on Manhattan's Upper West Side. Nadine was aware that people consider her authentically Jewish, but, with no Jewish identity or cultural grounding, she was largely oblivious to the debates on Black-Jewish relations and, as a result, contributed little insight for this forum.

In contrast, Olga, a 27-year-old matrilineal Jew who also grew up on the Upper West Side of Manhattan in a secular environment, had found herself developing a Jewish identity in high school after the family relocated to Beverly Hills. She explained how dealing with race and fitting in as a teenager was different in California. She explained, "I think I felt a little, slightly stigmatized by my father being Black. I really, really loved my mom and wanted to, you know, wanted to be like my mom and I wanted to be like my, you know, my friends at school who had houses and, you know, parents [who] drove Mercedes and it turned out they were White and they were Jewish and I wanted that ... There was something I felt comfortable around ... I don't know if they physically were able to identify that I was Black, or I mean that I had something in me other than Black. I don't know if they saw me as the dark-skinned Jewish person, but once they found out I was Jewish it was, like, I was in." Until college, she identified as White and Jewish, which she saw as the markers of success. Then she began to deal with her issues around race and develop a wholly integrated self, arriving at "an equilibrium," as she put it, – proud and secure in her blackness and Jewishness. When I asked her how she felt about Farrakhan she explained her mixed feelings, "When things like that actually come out of Louis Farrakhan's mouth, that's unacceptable, for anyone's mouth. Any form of prejudice or hatred is unacceptable! But ... being someone who is in both those communities, the Black community and the Jewish community, you know, every side accuses the other side of, you know, of not really listening and of ... hating the other. And, and stereotyping, and scapegoating and all that stuff. And I try not to do that. I mean, I'm a human being, we're all human beings, ... it's hard to be immune to society's racism, you know, we all are socialized in America and so it's hard. We learn racism, we can unlearn it and we're responsible to, responsible for that, each and every one of us. Not everyone takes that on. I take it on."

Conclusion

In this chapter, I introduced a paradigm to explain the nature and intensity of responses articulated by biracial Jews on Black anti-Semitism and Jewish racism. Scholars have relied on survey research to emphasize how biracial individuals choose their identities. However, interviews reveal that identity is not simply a matter of choosing, but requires a reciprocal relationship with the reference group of choice.[33] The extent to which their claims to a Black and Jewish identity were accepted within their respective reference groups shaped how the interviewees personally experienced and responded to incidents of Black anti-Semitism or Jewish racism. Strong status within either community was correlated with more neutral, open stances, while weaker links to the community correlated with more emotionally charged responses. The data also revealed that possessing a religious, cultural, or racial identity is not synonymous with feelings of group belonging. Dana, who had both strong Black and Jewish identities, sometimes felt like an outsider among Jews. Her remarks about Black anti-Semitism were considerably more guarded and measured than her remarks on Jewish racism. Seymour, who also had strong identities as both a Black and a Jew, felt secure in both communities and took a more detached stance when analyzing tensions between Blacks and Jews.

Pnina, who had felt rebuffed by other Blacks as a child, had a stronger sense of Jewish identity and belonging. Her comments on Black anti-Semitism, and on Farrakhan in particular, were highly charged and personalized. Rebecca, on the other hand, expressed strong ties to both communities and offered a more tempered, objective assessment of Farrakhan. Josh had a weak sense of identity as both a Black and a Jew and felt marginalized within both communities. While his status as a Jew was secure and unchallenged, the acceptance he sought was from Blacks. Like Dina, he had a more emotive response to questions on Black anti-Semitism.

While Michael had a strong Black identity and weak Jewish identity, he still had been brought up in a more culturally Jewish environment and felt a strong sense of belonging to both communities. When asked about Farrakhan, he questioned why Blacks were made to feel responsible for the actions and words of another Black person. Hannah, on the other hand, had a strong sense of her Judaism, yet had weak ties to a Jewish community, although this seemed to be more a matter of personal choice than of rejection by other Jews. Her Black identity was somewhat weaker than others and she had indeed experienced rejection from other Blacks when she was growing up. Her comments on Farrakhan were more emotional and personalized than those of Michael.

Finally, brothers Jonathan and Andrew, both patrilineal-descent biracial Jews, had distinct views on Black anti-Semitism and Jewish racism. These views were shaped by their own expectations, experiences, and needs within the Jewish community. Jonathan had a strong spiritual identity as a Jew, but his claims to Jewish membership had been rejected by many religious Jews. He in turn rejected the requirements of Jewish religious law, but never his Jewish soul. His Black identity had evolved since childhood. He now felt fairly secure in his belonging, and his comments on Black anti-Semitism can be described as analytical. His brother Andrew, on the other hand, who had both a strong cultural Jewish identity and sense of belonging as a Jew, was defensive of Jewish legalism and embraced a strict definition of who was a Jew. He had a weak Black identity and no strong ties to the Black community. Predictably, he characterized Black anti-Semitism as much more intense and problematic than Jewish racism.

In sum, scholars have often treated identity choices as synonymous with group membership, yet our data reveal that distinct processes are at work in shaping both identity and one's response to anti-Semitism and racism. While today identity for White Americans may be what sociologist Mary Waters calls a simple matter of choosing options, group membership for biracial individuals entails both making claims and having those claims legitimated by the group.[34] The individual may indeed choose but might not necessarily be chosen in return. Acceptance is critical to belonging, and the sense of belonging is critical to the framework through which individuals experience, perceive, and evaluate the rhetoric articulated by or attributed to the group. Acceptance creates reciprocity, which is required for individuals to establish moral obligations or a sense of affinity and feel the bonds of loyalty to the group. Finally, we found that rejection by the group does not necessarily undermine the strength of one's personal identity. Jonathan, whose patrilineal ties to Judaism often barred him from full participation in Orthodox Jewish worship, repeatedly asserted his Jewishness: "Who the hell is going to tell me I'm not Jewish?" Rather than forsaking his claims, he held fast to them, almost in defiance, as if his conviction were being tested. Andrew, who had no religious stirrings, but had developed a strong cultural identity as a Jew, defended the very bars that kept his brother out.

The acceptance–reciprocity dynamic is akin to belonging to a club and has an impact on the willingness to defend the members of the club. For example, Andrew, who reported not feeling like a full member in African American circles, confirmed s view generally held by American Jews: "In African American circles, there is a lot of real anti-Semitism." Yet not all subjects in this study sought membership in both clubs nor report experience of anti-Semitism and racism the same way. Josh, for example, viewed Judaism as an exclusive club that he did not want to belong to: "I'm part of the club but I don't like the club."

Nevertheless, subjects did not evince anguish or anger when discussing alleged discrimination from the group that they had rejected. Likewise, those who felt secure in their membership were more likely to defend the group, rationalize its behavior, or minimize the importance of racism or anti-Semitism. The most indicting comments came from subjects who had both sought membership in either group and experienced rejection. The more the subject felt excluded, the greater the frequency and importance of these charges, as if the very validation of Black anti-Semitism or Jewish racism validated the legitimacy of their own claims as Blacks and Jews.

Notes

1. Arnold Forster, *A Measure of Freedom: An Anti-Defamation League Report* (Garden City, NY: Doubleday, 1950).
2. Lee Sigelman, "Blacks, Whites, and Anti-Semitism," *Sociological Quarterly* 36, no. 4 (Autumn 1995): 649–656. Also see Tom W. Smith, "Actual Trends or Measurement Artifacts? A Review of Three Studies of Anti-Semitism," *Public Opinion Quarterly* 57 (1993): 380–393.

3. Hubert G. Locke, *The Black Anti-Semitism Controversy* (Selinsgrove, PA: Susquehanna University Press, 1994).
4. Lawrence W. Levine, *Black Culture and Black Consciousness: Afro-American Folk Thought From Slavery to Freedom* (Oxford, England: Oxford University Press, 2007).
5. Locke, *The Black Anti-Semitism Controversy,* 59.
6. Philip Kasinitz and Bruce Haynes, "The Fire at Freddy's," *Common Quest: The Magazine of Black Jewish Relations* 1 (1996): 24–34; Kaye/Kantrowitz, *Colors of Jews.*
7. The full text of Farrakhan's radio broadcasts is reprinted in *New York Times,* April 17, 1984, A15.
8. Sydney H. Schanberg, "New York: Jackson as Polarizer," (Op-Ed) *New York Times,* April 10, 1984.
9. Joseph P. Fried, "Cuomo Testifies on Crown Heights Rioting," *New York Times,* January 19, 1995.
10. Tony Martin, *The Jewish Onslaught: Dispatches from the Wellesley Battlefront* (Dover, MA: Majority Press, 1993).
11. Robert Gearty, "Khalid Quits: The 'burbs Farrakhan Pal Moving to Harlem," *Daily News,* May 31, 1995.
12. Cornel West, *Race Matters* (Boston: Beacon Press, 1993).
13. Gary E. Rubin, "How Should We Think About Black Antisemitism?" in *Antisemitism in America Today: Outspoken Experts Explode the Myths,* ed. Jerome Chanes (New York: Birch Lane Press, 1995), 156.
14. Ibid., 166.
15. James Baldwin, "From the American Scene: The Harlem Ghetto Winter 1948," *Commentary,* February 1948. This essay was also published in his *Notes of a Native Son* (New York: Beacon Press 1955).
16. Sigelman, "Blacks, Whites, and Anti-Semitism," 651.
17. Irving Howe, *World of Our Fathers: The Journey of the East European Jews to America and the Life They Found and Made* [1976] (New York: New York University Press, 2005), 30.
18. Karen Brodkin, *How Jews Became White Folks: And What That Says About. Race in America* (Brunswick NJ: Rutgers University Press, 1998), 139; Richard D. Alba, *Ethnic Identity: The Transformation of White America* (New Haven, CT: Yale University Press, 1990), 310.
19. W.E.B. Du Bois, *The Souls of Black Folk* [1903] (London: Penguin, 1996).
20. Biale, Galchinsky, and Heschel, eds., *Insider/Outsider.*
21. Roberta Rosenberg Farber and Chaim I. Waxman, "Assimilation of the American Jewish Population," in *Jews in America: A Contemporary Reader,* ed. Roberta Rosenberg Farber and Chaim I. Waxman (Hanover, NH: University Press of New England, 1999), 91; Biale, Galchinsky, and Heschel, eds., *Insider/Outsider,* 9.
22. On American Jews who identified as Reform, see Jack Wertheimer, "Religious Movements in Collision: A Jewish Culture War?" *Jews in America: A Contemporary Reader,* 377–391. On "none or other" religious identification, see Carmel Ullman Chiswick, "Economic Adjustment of Immigrants: Jewish Adaptation to the United States," in Farber and Waxman, eds., *Jews in America: A Contemporary Reader,* 16–27.

23. Bruce D. Haynes, "People of God, Children of Ham: Making Black(s) Jews," *Journal of Modern Jewish Studies* 8, no. 2 (2009): 237–254; Philip Kasinitz et al., *Inheriting the City: The Children of Immigrants Come of Age* (New York: Russell Sage, 2012), 80.
24. Dorcas D. Bowle, "Bi-Racial Identity: Children Born to African American and White Couples," *Clinical Social Work Journal* 21, no. 4 (1993): 417–428; Kerry Ann Rockquemore and David L. Brunsma, "Socially Embedded Identities: Theories, Typologies, and Processes of Racial Identity among Black/White Biracials," *Sociological Quarterly* 43, no. 3 (June 2002): 335–356.
25. See Biale, Galchinsky, and Heschel, eds., *Insider/Outsider,* 17.
26. Goldberg and Krausz, "The Culture of Identity," 9.
27. Azoulay, *Black Jewish and Interracial; It's Not the Color of Your Skin but the Race of Your Kin, and Other Myths of Identity* (Durham, NC: Duke University Press, 1997); Josylyn C. Segal, "Shades of Community and Conflict: Biracial Adults of African-American and Jewish-American Heritages," doctoral dissertation, Wright Institute Graduate School of Psychology, Berkeley, CA, 1998.
28. Azoulay, *Black Jewish and Interracial,* 8.
29. Goldberg and Krausz, "The Culture of Identity," 1–12.
30. All subjects' names have been changed.
31. Azoulay, "Jewishness After Mount Sinai," *Bridges* 9, no. 1 (2001) quoted in Kaye/Kantrowitz, *Colors of Jews,* 36, note 20.
32. Kaye/Kantrowitz, *Colors of Jews.*
33. Wendy D. Roth, "The End of the One-Drop Rule? Labeling of Multiracial Children in Black Intermarriages," *Sociological Forum,* 20, no. 1 (March 2005): 35–67.
34. Mary C. Waters, *Ethnic Options: Choosing Identities in America* (Los Angeles, CA: University of California Press, 1990).

CHAPTER 8

Ethiopian Immigrants in Israel

The Discourses of Intrinsic and Extrinsic Racism

Steven Kaplan

The arrival in Israel of more than eighty thousand Ethiopian immigrants has implications for the study of discourses about race that extend well beyond the borders of a single state. The immigration of a Black African group to a country perceived as predominantly White, with virtually no previous experience of such a population is rare, if not unique, in the late-twentieth and early-twenty-first centuries.[1] When it is also noted that these Ethiopians came to Israel neither for short-term educational programs nor to serve as guest workers, but to take their place as part of the dominant Jewish majority in the country, their experiences and the manner in which they are discussed become all the more riveting.

Not surprisingly, a vast literature (both scholarly and popular) has emerged that examines in considerable detail these Ethiopian Israelis and their absorption into Israeli society. Books, articles, and dissertations have documented their experience in the military and school system, and have chronicled their encounters with modern medicine, Hebrew instruction, and the immigration bureaucracy.[2] Moreover, several writers have examined their encounter with Israeli society through the exploration of racial concepts.[3]

In this chapter, I shall explore the case of Ethiopian Israelis through the lens of Kwame Anthony Appiah's distinction between intrinsic and extrinsic racism. I shall demonstrate that although extrinsic racist claims are rarely voiced openly in public discourse about Ethiopian immigrants to Israel, they are the explanation of first choice in almost any incident or with regard to any policy that is viewed as being anti-Ethiopian. In contrast, intrinsic racist claims can be found in many discussions of Ethiopian immigrants that seek to promote their *inclusion* into the larger Jewish Israeli society. Although rarely if ever labeled as racism, intrinsic racism lies behind many statements on behalf of Ethiopian Jews. Indeed, it is precisely because supporters of Ethiopian Israelis and Ethiopian Israelis themselves are so ready to brand their opponents as extrinsic racists that their own intrinsic racist positions—however well intended—warrant further analysis.

Ethiopian Israelis: A Background

Historically, the group who in Ethiopia referred to themselves as Beta Israel was mainly known to their neighbors and other outsiders as Falasha. In the 1980s, this latter term faded from usage and was replaced by the term "Ethiopian Jews," or most frequently in Israel, simply "Ethiopians." This terminological change obscures the fact that many of those who immigrated were not been recognized as Jews until after undergoing certain religious ceremonies. The term "Ethiopian immigrants" is often used rather carelessly to refer to the entire population, both immigrants and those born in Israel (second-generation immigrants).

Although the migration of Ethiopians to Israel has been punctuated by two dramatic episodes, it can most effectively be viewed as a series of waves. While a handful of Ethiopians had settled in Israel prior to the 1970s, it was only in 1977 that a significant number were taken to Israel at the initiative of the Israeli government. Beginning in 1980, however, Ethiopian Jews from the relatively isolated northern regions of Tigre and Walqayit began to migrate to refugee camps in the Sudan. Although some waited there for as long as two or three years, by the end of 1983 virtually the entire Beta Israel population of these regions (more than four thousand people) had been taken to Israel.

As word spread of this Sudanese route, Jews from the Gondar region began to migrate as well. Under cover of secrecy and Israeli military censorship, as well as with the silent agreement of the Sudanese government, they were slowly taken out of Sudanese camps by Israeli agents and taken to Israel. In the middle of 1984, confronted by deteriorating conditions in the camps, the Israeli government abandoned its policy of gradual immigration. Between mid-November 1984 and early January 1985, 6,700 Ethiopians were taken to Israel in what came to be known as Operation Moses. A few months later, an additional 648 Jews were taken to Israel in Operation Joshua–Sheba.[4] Thus, by mid-1985 there were approximately 16,000 Ethiopian immigrants living in Israel.

From August 1985 until the end of 1989 only about 2,500 immigrants reached Israel, primarily under the rubric of family reunification. The restoration of diplomatic relations between Ethiopia and Israel in the autumn of 1989 cleared the way for emigration in a manner agreeable to both countries. It also raised expectations among the Beta Israel, and by the summer of 1990, assisted by American Jewish activists, twenty thousand Ethiopians had migrated from the Gondar region to Addis Ababa. Although conditions were better than those that had faced refugees in the Sudan, these internal refugees resided illegally in the Ethiopian capital and suffered initially from many of the same difficulties: disease, harassment, and poverty. Eventually a framework for them was organized by Israeli authorities, and with the agreement of the Ethiopian government they were gradually taken to Israel. However, when Ethiopian leader Mengistu Haile Mariam fled the country in advance of the victorious Ethiopian Peoples' Revolutionary Democratic Front forces in mid-May 1991, it was feared that the Beta Israel would fall victim to urban warfare. A dramatic airlift was executed in which during a period of thirty-six hours between May 24 and 25, more than fourteen thousand Ethiopians were taken to Israel in Operation Solomon.[5]

Although many expected this airlift to mark the end of Ethiopian migration to Israel, additional groups surfaced. These included not only the relatively isolated Jews living in the Qwara region, but thousands of descendants of Beta Israel and their relatives, often referred to as Feres or Falash Mura.[6] With regard to the latter, each had to be checked individually in order to determine their eligibility to come to Israel. As of the end of 2009, more than forty-five thousand additional Ethiopians had arrived, more than the total number who had arrived prior to 1992.

The Falash Mura are of particular interest to our discussion. Because, for the most part, they had not been living as part of the traditional Beta Israel community prior to the late 1980s or early 1990s, the decision to take them to Israel was controversial. Government committees, political mobilization and demonstrations, and ministerial decisions were all required to arrive at a solution in which Israel eventually would take in more or less all of the Falash Mura.

Intrinsic vs. Extrinsic Racism

Although race has been invoked repeatedly in discussions of Ethiopian immigrants to Israel, the term is frequently used in an essentialist sense and as an explanatory variable. Only in a handful of discussions do authors appear to be familiar with recent scholarship on race in particular with social constructionist approaches.[7] In a similar way, most authors have not attempted to distinguish between personal and institutional racism in their descriptions of the Ethiopian experience in Israel.

The limits of this essay make it impossible to fully explore the relevance of recent discussions of Ethiopian Israelis for racial discourse as a whole. However, by invoking a distinction made already in the early 1980s by one of the United States' most articulate commentators on race, I shall attempt to shed new light on this topic. As I argue, it is a case of, if not a case of the "pot calling the kettle," at least one of the opponents of one form of racist discourse falling all too easily into another.

Kwame Anthony Appiah, currently a professor of philosophy at Princeton University, has long been one of the Anglophone world's most articulate social theorists. Almost three decades ago, in his award-winning book, *In My Father's House,* he presented a discussion of racial discourse which has since become classic. Appiah begins by rejecting what he calls racialism—the claim "that there are heritable characteristics, possessed by members of our species, that allow us to divide them into a small set of races, in such a way that all the members of these races share certain traits and tendencies with each other that they do not share with members of any other race."[8] However, the originality of his argument lies not in this rejection of the existence of distinct races, but rather in his attempt to differentiate between two different types of racism.

On the one hand, he distinguishes extrinsic racism, which claims not only that there are races, but also that "members of different races differ in respects that *warrant* the differential treatment—respects, like honesty or courage or intelligence" [emphasis added].[9] In other words, in addition to whatever phenotypical, genealogical, or biological differences are alleged to exist between the different races, the extrinsic racist believes that they also differ with respect to morally relevant characteristics to such an extent that it justifies differences in the way they are treated. Appiah cites apartheid South Africa and the mid-twentieth-century American South as examples of this type of racism, but of course there are numerous other cases. According to Appiah, at least in theory, if an extrinsic racist could be convinced that the differences he or she perceives between the different races do not exist that person would abandon racism and any claims for differential treatment.

As we shall see below, much of the literature and rhetoric about Ethiopian Israelis, their opportunities for aliyah, and their treatment after arrival in Israel claims that they are the victims of extrinsic racism. While obviously unfamiliar with Appiah's term, members of the community and their supporters believe that their opponents' alleged mistreatment of Ethiopian Israelis is based on the belief that there are morally relevant differences between Ethiopians and other Jewish Israelis. Almost inevitably these accusations are summarized by the simple phrase that they are treated differently "because they are Blacks."

As opposed to extrinsic racism, intrinsic racism makes no claims of morally relevant differences between different races. Rather, intrinsic racists "are people who differentiate morally between members of different races because they believe that each race has a different moral status, quite independent of the moral characteristics entailed by its racial essence."[10] The intrinsic racist assumes that the fact that members of different races are biologically related is sufficient reason to treat them differently, much as one would treat a cousin or aunt differently from a non–family member. Moreover, "the assimilation of 'race feeling' to 'family feeling' ... makes intrinsic racism seem so much less objectionable than extrinsic racism."[11] It is, argues Appiah, precisely because intrinsic racism is usually used to express racial solidarity, whereas extrinsic racism is used for oppression and hatred, that the former is often expressed unabashedly while the latter suffers from widespread condemnation. Significantly, for what follows in this chapter, Appiah cites as the two most familiar examples of the use of race as a basis for moral solidarity Pan-Africanism and Zionism.

Being Black

Prior to the immigration of the Ethiopians, the total number of residents in Israel of Sub-Saharan African descent (including the Black Hebrews of Dimona,[12] Muslims of African origin,[13] and Ethiopian Christians[14]) probably did not exceed a thousand people. Even the influx of African guest workers from Ghana and Nigeria in the 1990s only slightly altered this situation.[15] However, Israelis were no strangers to Western discussions of race. Almost from the moment of the arrival of the first Ethiopians in Israel, their experience has been described in terms borrowed from discussions of other groups of people of African origin and descent in predominantly Western countries. Not surprisingly, the experience of African Americans in the United States is frequently invoked in such discussions. Thus, programs designed to increase the number of Ethiopians admitted to university studies or hired in senior government positions are routinely referred to as affirmative action or positive discrimination.[16] Almost any large concentration in a particular neighborhood or town raises the specter of ghettoization, while a high percentage of Ethiopian students in a classroom or school is quickly labeled by the media as segregation.[17] More generally, others caution against the danger that the Ethiopians will become an underclass.[18] The use of such borrowed terms is based on the assumption that Ethiopians are particularly at risk of falling victim to certain behaviors because they are Blacks.[19] Or, in other terms, that as Blacks they will almost inevitably be subject to the extrinsic racism of their White Israeli neighbors.[20] In this context, it should be noted that the connection between extrinsic racism and discrimination against Blacks is so deeply embedded in popular discourse and consciousness that there is no need to articulate the step-by-step process: in other words, because they are Blacks, they are viewed as being different and inferior, and hence they are treated differently.

Many sources can be cited that claim that Ethiopian immigrants have been discriminated against because as Blacks they have been viewed as different and inferior to other Israelis. Virtually any action that appears to negatively influence Ethiopian Israelis including the discarding of blood donations because of fear of HIV, the dispensing of a particular form of birth control to Ethiopian women, or the refusal of a school to accept additional Ethiopian students quickly and vocally is condemned as racism. This is familiar ground and the handful of examples just cited may be multiplied with additional citations taken from publications that have appeared over the past thirty years or more.

It is not my intention here to claim that Ethiopians do not suffer discrimination in Israeli society, nor that they have achieved the goal of being equal Jewish citizens with the same rights as other Jews. However, the narrative that reduces all of their difficulties to either personal or institutional prejudices against Blacks is flawed and simplistic. If this was the case, then how could Ethiopians denied entry to exclusive clubs as Ethiopians gain entry by pretending to be Black (African American) tourists? In a similar way, the opposition of Orthodox and ultra-Orthodox schools to the acceptance of Ethiopian immigrant children who have only limited background in rabbinic studies would seem to be based on a number of issues including their lack of relevant studies, rather than on race alone.

However, even if one were to concede that Ethiopian Israelis suffer frequently from extrinsic racism, this would not provide a complete picture of the uses of racial discourse in Israeli today. If the racial discourse concerning Ethiopians in Israel was limited to the phenomenon of borrowed models framing their experience in light of the extrinsic racism they experience it would be worthy of comparatively little scholarly comment. What has gone, till now, largely unquestioned is the fact that those advocating on behalf of Ethiopian immigrants, almost in the same breath as they have criticized their opponents' extrinsic racism, have relied on the language of intrinsic racism to justify their position. Indeed, much as Appiah predicted, their use of this language goes largely unnoticed and is often immune from criticism because it is viewed as pro-Ethiopian, pro-Jewish proracial solidarity.

In this context it should be noted that while the association of Ethiopian immigrants with the experience of other Black people of African descent may seem obvious and natural, Ethiopian Jews (like other northern Ethiopians), did not view themselves as Black (Amharic *tequr*) in Ethiopia. Rather, they described themselves (as do other northern Ethiopians) as "*qeyy*," a term best translated as reddish-brown. The term "Black" was reserved for low-status groups, most notably slaves. Thus, in a very real sense, the experience of Ethiopian immigrants to Israel has not been one of *being* Black, but one of *becoming* Black on their arrival in the country.

Given their Ethiopian background, one cannot be surprised but to note that they have themselves in recent years actively identified as Blacks and with other Black African communities. Thus, speaking several weeks after the 1992 riots in Los Angeles California that followed the verdict in the Rodney King case, an Ethiopian immigrant stated, "We will join forces and for a Black Power group, like the Blacks in Los Angeles."[21] An anonymous graffiti artist in a predominantly Ethiopian Israeli neighborhood scrawled the word "Harlem" on one of the building's walls.[22] In search of a comparison, another Ethiopian immigrant warned that mobile home parks used to house immigrants in the period after Operation Solomon would "soon look like Soweto in South Africa."[23]

The rhetoric of such Ethiopian youth is clearly that of early Pan-Africanism and its intrinsic racism. It is, however, far from obvious or natural that Ethiopians identify with this movement or the people of the African continent. When the Ethiopian emperor Menelik II was offered the leadership of the Pan-African movement, he replied, "I wish you the greatest possible success. But in coming to me to take the leadership [of the Pan-African Congress] you are knocking at the wrong door, so to speak. You know I am not a Negro at all. I am a Caucasian."[24] Moreover, even today Ethiopian Israelis frequently attempt to distance themselves from "Kushim" (the colloquial Hebrew term for Blacks taken from the Bible) from other parts of the African continent.

Indeed, the experience of Ethiopians in Israel is not so much that they share a common history with others of African descent, but rather that they betake of a common present in their encounters with racism and discrimination. Or to once again cite Appiah, "What Blacks in the West, like secularized Jews, have mostly in common is the fact that they are perceived—both by themselves and by others—as belonging together in the same race, and this common race is used by others as the basis for discriminating against them."[25] Indeed, Ethiopian Israelis depict themselves as sharing a natural affinity and shared racial heritage with Africans, African Americans, and African Caribbeans with whom their historical links are minimal. Nor is this limited to raising issues of alleged discrimination. Drawing on images derived not from first-hand familiarity with the cultures they emulate, but from television and film, they have adopted an idiom as foreign to the dominant Israeli culture as it is to the specific Ethiopian traditions of their elders. As one anthropologist describes it, "Boys tend to base their hairstyle on Black American crew cuts. Girls plait theirs in a variety of elegant styles. A growing section of teenagers adopt a 'Rasta' image. They wear Bob Marley T-shirts, and adorn their clothes and jewelry with the emblematic red-yellow-green stripes."[26]

While several authors have seen this primarily as a rejection of Israeli society as well as their parents' Ethiopian roots, for the purposes of this essay I prefer to emphasize a different aspect of this youth culture. It is an attempt to evoke a connection to other people of African descent around the world and in a cultural idiom based on the same intrinsic racial claims as their mentions of Harlem, Soweto, or other archetypal Black locations.

Jewish Roots

So far I have focused on the blackness of the Ethiopians either as part of an apparent discourse of extrinsic racism of exclusion or as part of the intrinsic racism of Pan-African Black solidarity. I now turn my attention to the Jewish part of this story. As was noted above, the claim that Ethiopian Jews are the victim of extrinsic racism is ubiquitous and has dominated discussions of them throughout the nineteenth and especially twentieth centuries. Generally unremarked in these debates, however, is the thread of racial discourse that is found in the writings of those who have sought not to separate Ethiopian Jews from other Jews, but rather to connect them racially to Jews elsewhere in the world. The missionary Henry Aaron Stern, himself a Jewish convert to Christianity, who worked to bring the Falasha to Protestant Christianity in the mid-nineteenth century claimed that

> in physiognomy, most of the Falashas bear striking traces of their Semitic origin. Among the first group we saw at Gondar, *there were some of whose Jewish features no one could have been mistaken, who had ever seen the descendants of Abraham either in London or Berlin.* Their complexion is a shade paler than that of the Abyssinians, and their eyes, although black and sparkling, are not so disproportionately large as those which characteristically mark the other occupants of the land [emphasis added].[27]

Several decades later, Ya'acov (Jacques) Faitlovitch, the Jewish ethnographer who worked tirelessly on behalf of the Falasha and who rarely agreed with Stern on anything, quoted this description with approval. Moreover, he himself testified to the clear racial ties between Western Jews such as himself and the Beta Israel he encountered. "We can be proud to count among our own us these noble children of Ethiopia. … The ardor with which they seek to regenerate themselves, to leave the African barbarianism which envelopes and suffocates them, proves that the *instinctive characteristic of* [*our*] *race persists* [emphasis added].[28]

As Abraham ben Meir, himself a member of the community, told the researcher Aharon Zeev Aescoly, while *he* could not distinguish the Falasha from other Ethiopians, generally, "a Falasha can identify *his brethren* by his face, that is to say by his nose which distinguishes him from other Abyssinians who are not Jews [emphasis added]."[29]

Although such statements distinguishing the Falasha racially from the rest of the Ethiopian population and hence linking them racially to their Jewish kin were more common in the first half of the twentieth century, they also appear in more recent discussions of Ethiopian Jews. Indeed, they have been evoked with surprising confidence by Jewish and Israeli figures seeking to promote close ties with, and assistance to, the Ethiopian Israeli community. For example, in 1988 Rabbi David Chelouche, who was for a time the Israeli chief rabbinate's registrar of Ethiopian marriages and who leaned toward leniency in halakhic decisions regarding the religious status of Ethiopian immigrants, wrote, "In the color of their skin and the shape of their faces there are clear differences between them and the Amhara."[30] This view was echoed by Yehuda Azrieli and Shaul Meizlish, who, when, chronicling the Jewish Agency's activities in Ethiopia and particularly its role in promoting aliyah, noted, "In their appearance [the Falasha] resemble other residents of Ethiopia, but there are differences between them in the tint of the skin and the shape of the face."[31] In 1985, the American Association for Ethiopian Jews, one of the most prominent groups lobbying on behalf of Ethiopian immigration to Israel, in a critical response to Tudor Parfitt's book, *Operation Moses,* disputed Parfitt's claim that Ethiopian Jews physically resembled other Ethiopians, boldly declaring, "[A] different degree of blackness of skin characterizes the Falasha from other Ethiopian tribes ... they are less African and more Mediterranean than the others—they have less frequency of African associated chromosomes."[32]

It is difficult to imagine that such clear statements claiming to distinguish Jews from the rest of the population could have been made as part of extrinsic racist claims for limiting Jewish rights to equality. However, as Appiah suggests, because the authors were seeking to strengthen ties between the Ethiopian Jewish community and the rest of world Jewry, their views were viewed as essentially benign. For, when race is invoked on behalf of racial solidarity, it is rarely condemned and often applauded.[33] "The racism here is the basis of acts of supererogation, the treatment of others better than we otherwise might, better than moral duty demands of us."[34]

The Falash Mura: Blood and Bones

No better example of the parallel uses of two different types of racial discourse can be found than the debates that have taken place in recent years regarding the rights of those who have become known as Falash Mura. Throughout their history, Ethiopian Jews, like other Jewish communities, have experienced defections as members abandoned their Judaism in an attempt to affiliate with the dominant Christian majority. The reasons for such conversions are numerous and are to this day the subject of controversy. There can be little question, however, that only in the period after 1980 and the beginning of large-scale immigration to Israel do significant numbers of converts and their descendants appear to have attempted to return to their ancestral communities. In the early 1990s as thousands of Ethiopian Jews migrated to Addis Ababa in the hope of being taken to Israel, they were joined by several thousand Ethiopians whose connection to the Beta Israel community was less clear. Although it was decided not to take those whose status was in doubt to Israel as part of the May 1991 airlift known as Operation Solomon, their right to come on aliyah (and the right of forty thousand additional Ethiopians who followed in their wake) has been the subject of controversy for more than two decades.

During the period since 1991, thousands of Ethiopians have been admitted to Israel despite the fact that the authorities acknowledge that they were not Jewish according to the criterion of Israel's Law of Return. Most of them have been required to undergo a conversion ceremony of some sort to normalize their status.[35] However, the arrival of these most recent immigrants has not been a smooth, seamless process. For twenty years, their immigration has proceeded with fits and starts. On several occasions the last group of immigrants has been taken to Israel only to be followed by the arrival of a subsequent cohort. Moreover, each step along the way has been accompanied by demonstrations, angry debate, and fierce accusations.

Advocates of Falash Mura immigration typically accuse their opponents of extrinsic racism. Thus, Avshalom Elizur, chair of the Committee for the Falash Mura, claimed in 2007, regarding the refusal to bring the rest of the Falash Mure to Israel, "This is a clear violation of human rights and constitutes outright racism. More than a million immigrants from the former Soviet Union arrived in Israel over the past 10 years, yet no one questions their Judaism. I believe this is down to skin colour," he added.[36] Addisu Massala, the first Ethiopian member of the Israeli Parliament echoed these sentiments. "If 23,000 French, American and British people were waiting to immigrate," he asked, "Do you even think we would be having this debate? No, but since we are talking about Black Ethiopian Jews, the situation is different."[37]

Although superficially similar to the earlier debates of the 1970s regarding the aliyah of the Beta Israel, a closer look reveals some subtle differences. Beta Israel immigrants were ultimately taken to Israel because of a series of rabbinical and legal rulings that they were entitled to come to Israel as Jews under the Law of Return. Significantly, in the Falash Mura case the crucial criterion has not been the religious allegiance of the petitioner during the years prior to his or her aliyah. Rather, those seeking to reach Israel have been required to prove either that they have family ties to those Ethiopians already in the country, or that their family was historically connected to the Beta Israel (Ethiopian Jewish) community.

It is precisely this rhetoric of an extension of family ties that, as Appiah has pointed out, makes intrinsic racism seem so innocent. While Avraham Negusie, chair of the Representatives of Ethiopian Immigrant Organizations in Israel has no hesitation in accusing his opponents of extrinsic racism, "The way he is expressing himself [against their aliyah] has a smell of racism about it because he would not say such statements to any other immigrants from America or Russia." However, his own claims on their behalf are formulated in classically intrinsic racist terms. "They are our blood, our flesh and our bones."[38] In a similar way, rabbinic support for the aliyah of the Falash Mura often makes reference to their identity as applies only to *"the seed of Israel'*.[39] The use of such explicitly racialized language would itself be worthy of comment. However, there are two other reasons for drawing attention to this rhetoric. First, as we have noted above, pro–Falash Mura activists almost without exception accuse their opponents of applying racial criteria in the arguments against Falash Mura aliyah. Given their avowed aversion to the application of race as a standard for government policy, at the very least they should be held to a high standard themselves. Second, we must never forget that every inclusion in the name of (intrinsic) racial solidarity is also an act of exclusion. In the case of the Falash Mura, this exclusion extends not only to much of the population of Ethiopia, but in recent years many Ethiopians and Eritreans who have reached Israel as refugees, but receive no special consideration. Israel is simultaneously bringing Ethiopian Falash Mura into the country and expelling Ethiopian and Eritrean migrants. Of particular interest is the position of the Sephardic religious Shas Party that strongly advocates for Ethiopian migrants while favoring the expulsion of Eritrean migrants on the grounds that these non-Jewish Africans pose both demographic and health threats.

Conclusion

The limits of this chapter do not permit us to fully explore the multilayered and often contradictory ways in which race is invoked in discussions of Ethiopian immigrants to Israel. There can, moreover, be little question that Ethiopian Israelis face real challenges as they attempt to find their place in Israeli society. However, as we have shown above, the indignities that they suffer from racial discrimination as Blacks in a predominantly White society are only part of this story. While supporters of the Ethiopian community and Ethiopian immigrants themselves have been quick to point out situations in which they are discriminated against, there has been little if any attention to the phenomenon of what Appiah refers to as intrinsic racism. Here at the crossroads between Pan-Africanism and Zionism we encounter a form of racial discourse that goes largely unnoticed. Whether employed to link the Ethiopians to other people of African descent or to make the case for their racial-familiar ties to other Jews, intrinsic racism is a fascinating chapter in the complex relations between Jews and Blacks, and in the politics of race.

Notes

1. For a discussion of the problematic nature of the terms "Black" and "White" in this context see Steven Kaplan, "Black and White, Blue and White, and Beyond the Pale: Ethiopian Immigrants and the Discourse of Colour in Israel," *Jewish History and Culture* 5, no. 1 (2002): 51–68.
2. See, e.g., Steven Kaplan and Shoshana Ben-Dor, *Ethiopian Jewry: An Annotated Bibliography* (Jerusalem: Ben-Zvi Institute, 1988); Hagar Salamon and Steven Kaplan, *Ethiopian Jewry: An Annotated Bibliography 1987–1997* (Jerusalem: Ben-Zvi Institute, 1998) Shalva Weil, *Bibliography on Ethiopian Jewry (1998–2001)* (Paris: SOSTEJE, 2001). For overviews of Ethiopian life in Israel, see Tanya Schwarz, *Ethiopian Jewish Immigrants: The Homeland Postponed* (London: Routledge/Curzon, 2001); and Lisa Anteby-Yemini, *Les Juifs Éthiopiens en Israël: Les Paradoxes du Paradis (Paris: CNRS, 2004)*; Steven Kaplan and Chaim Rosen, "Ethiopian Jews in Israel," *American Jewish Yearbook 1994*, 94 (1994), 59–109; Steven Kaplan and Hagar Solomon, *Ethiopian Immigrants in Israel: Experience and Prospect* (London: Institute for Jewish Policy Research, 1998).
3. Kaplan, "Black and White; Steven Kaplan, "Can the Ethiopian Change his Skin? The Beta Israel (Falasha) and Racial Discourse," *African Affairs* 98, no. 393 (1999): 535–550; Steven Kaplan, "If There Are No Races, How Can Jews be a 'Race'?" *Journal of Modern Jewish Studies* 3, no. 1 (2003): 79–96. See also Salamon, "Reflections of Ethiopian Cultural Patterns," 126–132; Hagar Salamon, "Blackness in Transition: Decoding Racial Constructs through Stories of Ethiopian Jews," *Journal of Folklore Research* 40, no. 1 (2003): 3–32.
4. On this period and particularly Operation Moses, see Tudor Parfitt, *Operation Moses: The Untold Story of the Secret Exodus of the Falasha from Ethiopia* (London: Weidenfeld and Nicolson, 1985); Louis Rappoport, *Redemption Song: The Story of Operation Moses* (New York: Harcourt Brace Javanovich, 1986).
5. Stephen Spector, *Operation Solomon: The Daring Rescue of the Ethiopian Jews* (New York: Oxford University Press, 2005).
6. Don Seeman, *One People, One Blood: Ethiopian-Israelis and the Return to Judaism* (New Brunswick, NJ.: Rutgers University Press, 2009). The terms "Faras," "Falas," and "Falash Mura" appear to be neologisms which refer not to a clearly defined population but to descendants and relatives of Beta Israel, and more broadly to almost anyone claiming the right to come on aliyah after 1991.
7. See for example, Michael McGiffert, "Editor's Preface," *William and Mary Quarterly* 54, no. 1 (1997): 3.
8. Kwame Anthony Appiah, *In My Father's House: Africa in the Philosophy of Culture* (New York, Oxford: Oxford University Press, 1992), 13; see also Appiah's essay, "Racisms," in *The Anatomy of Race*, ed. David Theo Goldberg (Minneapolis: University of Minnesota, 1990), 3–17.
9. Appiah, *In My Father's House*, 13.

10. Ibid.
11. Ibid., 17.
12. Fran Markowitz, Sarit Helman, and Dafna Shir-Vertesh, "Soul Citizenship: Black Hebrews and the State of Israel," *American Anthropologist* 105, no. 2 (2003): 302–12.
13. William F. Miles, "Black Muslim Africans in the Jewish State: Lessons of Colonial Nigeria for Contemporary Jerusalem," *Issues* 35, no. 1 (1997): 39–42.
14. Enrico Cerulli, *Etiopi in Palestina: storia della communita di Gerusalemme, 2 vols. (Roma: Libreria dello Stato,1943–1947);* and Kirsten Stoffregen Pedersen, *The History of Ethiopian Community in the Holy Land from the Time of Tewodros II till 1974* (Jerusalem: Tantur Institute, 1983).
15. Galia Sabar, "African Christianity in the Jewish State: Adaptation, Accommodation and Legitimization of Migrant Workers 1990–2003," *Journal of Religion in Africa* 34, no. 4 (2004): 407–437.
16. The Israeli Ministry of Immigrant Absorption, *The Absorption of Ethiopian Immigrants in Israel: The Present Situation and Future Objectives* (Jerusalem: The Israeli Ministry of Immigrant Absorption, 1996), 2.
17. On the specter of ghettoization: see "Ethiopian Ghettos," *Jerusalem Post,* March 3, 1993, 14. Regarding being labeled by the media as segregation, see Joshua Mitnick, "Why Jews see Racism in Israel" http://www.csmonitor.com/World/Middle-East/2009/0902/p06s01-wome.html
18. Israel Association for Ethiopian Jews, *The Making of an Underclass* (Jerusalem: IAEJ, 1995).
19. Jacques Faitlovitch, "The Black Jews of Ethiopia," *The American Hebrew* 2 (1915): 3–15; Yael Kahana, *Achim Shechorim* (Black brothers) (Tel Aviv: 'Am 'Oved 1997); Simon Messing, *The Story of the Falashas: Black Jews of Ethiopia* (Brooklyn, NY: Balshom, 1982); Durrenda N. Onolemhernhen and Kebbede Gessese, *The Black Jews of Ethiopia: The Last Exodus* (Lanham, MD: Scarecrow Press, 1998).
20. Ethiomedia.com, Ethiopian Israelis Love Their Country but Not the Racism http://www.ethiomedia.com/courier/beersheva.html; Middle East Online, "Ethiopian Jews Still Face Racism is Israel" http://www.middle-east-online.com/english/?id=35796
21. Batia Tsur, "Olim from Ethiopia Stage Protest," *Jerusalem Post,* June 15, 1992, 12.
22. Joseph Algazi, "Harlem is Here," *Ha-aretz,* September 11, 1998, B2. (Hebrew) photograph: Alex Levac.
23. Herbert Keinon, "Immigrants Decry State of Mobile Home Camps," *Jerusalem Post,* April 9, 1992, 14.
24. Hosea Jaffe, "The African Dimension of the Battle," in *Adwa,* ed. Abdusammed H. Ahmed and Richard Pankhurst (Addis Ababa: Institute of Ethiopian Studies, 1998).
25. Appiah, *In My Father's House,* 17.
26. Schwarz, *Ethiopian Jewish Immigrants,* 99.
27. Henry Aaron Stern, *Wanderings among the Falasha in Abyssinia* (London: Frank Cass 1968), 2nd ed., 197.
28. Jacques Faitlovitch, *Notes d'un Voyage chez les Falachas (Juifs d'Abyssinie)* (Paris: Leroux, 1905), 27.

29. Aharon Zeev Aescoly, *Sefer Hafalashim* [The book of the Falasha] (Jerusalem: Reuven Mass, 1973), 5 (Hebrew).
30. David Chelouche, *Nidkhai Yisrael Yechanes* [The exiled of Israel will be gathered in] (Jerusalem: Reuven Mass, 1988), 20 (Hebrew).
31. Yehuda Azrieli and Shaul Miezlish, *Mission Ethiopia* (Jerusalem: Elinor Press 1989), 6.
32. Letter from Nathan Shapiro, president of the American Association for Ethiopian Jewry, November 27, 1985, to editors and book review editors. See also Parfitt, *Operation Moses.*
33. Ephraim Isaac, "Jewish Solidarity and the Jews of Ethiopia," in *Organizing Rescue: National Jewish Solidarity in the Modern Period,* ed. Selwyn Ilan Troen and Benjamin Pinkus (London: Frank Cass, 1992), 403–420; Ephraim Isaac, "Hearing the Call: Solidarity with Ethiopian Jews," *The Narrow Bridge: Jewish Views on Multiculturalism,* ed. Marla Brettschneider (New Brunswick, NJ: Rutgers University Press, 1996), 219–232.
34. Appiah, *In My Father's House,* 17. On the oft-repeated claim that the aliyah of Ethiopian Jews in some way contradicted the claim, "Zionism is racism," see Isaac, "Jewish Solidarity," 417; Isaac, "Hearing the Call," 228.
35. "Q & A on the 'Falash Mura' November 2008," http://www.nacoej.org/pdf/Q&A%20-%20November%202008.pdf, p. 21
36. Quoted in Nazret.com, "Waiting Falash Mura Languish in Squalor," http://nazret.com/blog/index.php/2007/02/27/ethiopia_israel_waiting_falash_mura_lang
37. Matthew Gutman, "Israeli Cabinet Approves Mass Aliyah for 18,000 Falash Mura in Ethiopia," http://www.jewishfederations.org/page.aspx?id=39296
38. Tom Butcher, "Israeli Minister in Ethiopian Racism Row," *Daily Telegraph,* August 3, 2007.
39. Joseph Felt, "Are the Falas Mura Jews? A View from Tradition," *Sh'ma* http://www.shma.com/2000/04/are-the-falas-mura-jews-a-view-from-tradition/

CHAPTER 9

Black Jews in Academic and Institutional Discourse

Jonas Zianga

> From beyond the rivers of Ethiopia my suppliants, even the daughter of my dispersed, shall bring mine offering.
> Zeph. 3:10

This biblical passage from the book of Zephaniah 3:10 is one of the traditional Jewish sources for the existence of an African Jewish Diaspora, indicating a Jewish presence on the Sub-Saharan part of Black Africa from early times. In fact, the biblical narrative played a crucial role in the initial widespread belief in the continued existence of the lost tribes of Israel. Accounts by Jewish travelers, such as Eldad the Danite (ninth century), Benjamin of Tudela and Ovadiah of Bertinoro (twelfth century),[1] as well as reports by Arab travelers during the medieval period, such as Leo Africanus (1483–1554) and Ibn Khaldun (1332–1406), have had a significant influence on the growing Black Jewish communities throughout Africa.[2] Many of these accounts attest to the presence of a Jewish kingdom in Ethiopia (the land of Kush), as well as flourishing Jewish communities in eastern, western, central, and southern Africa. Consequently, that continent is home to several African Jewish or judaizing communities claiming a Jewish ancestry, including the Abayudaya of Uganda,[3] the Ibo of Nigeria,[4] the House of Israel of Ghana,[5] and the Lemba of South Africa.[6]

Today it is possible to encounter a number of groups that still self-identify as Jews. Regardless of whether this identification with the people of Israel is accepted by Jewish religious authorities, the point is that, for several reasons, a growing number of individuals or groups claim the right to define themselves as a Jew in terms of an ethnic identity; or a religious and cultural identity. The discovery of several African judaizing communities in Sub-Saharan Africa has provoked curiosity inside the Jewish world, as well as among academics. In general, this Black Jewish Diaspora (and we refer here only to organized groups and not to isolated individuals) has no legal recognition from rabbinic and institutional authorities (we all know that only the Beta Israel are recognized today as Jewish by Jewish law). The Black Jewish phenomenon has nevertheless given rise to a number of studies dealing with African Jewry. A significant issue is the way some scholars define Black Judaism, or more precisely, Black Jewish identity.

In his book, *Black Judaism: Story of an American Movement,* James Landing tries to explain the phenomenon of Black identification with Judaism in modern societies and in the New World.[7] Landing coins the term "Black Judaism," which he defines as an institutionalized religious expression in which individuals of black skin color identify themselves as Jews, Israelites, or Hebrews. However, this identification generally remains outside the accepted and traditional boundaries of Jewish religion because these communities do not conform to halakha. Consequently, these Black Jewish communities exist without institutional control by rabbinical authorities. Therefore, Landing makes a very clear distinction: individuals with black skin can be categorized as Jews only on the condition that they were born to a Jewish mother, or were converted to Judaism by a rabbinical Jewish authority; in all other cases, their Jewishness is inauthentic, since it is incompatible with the criteria laid out by Jewish Orthodoxy. Landing systematically divides here the Jewish world into two distinct groups: one composed of the Jewish communities of the Diaspora, and one composed of groups of Black people who identify with Judaism but do not belong to this same Jewish Diaspora.

The main purpose of this chapter is to explain the contentions about the possible existence of a Black Jewish identity as part of world Jewry. I propose to analyze the academic and institutional discourse engendered by this new social and religious phenomenon. Obviously, the complexity of Black Jewish identity cannot be underestimated in Western and globalized societies, where Jewishness is related to whiteness. Why do Blacks claim Jewishness? Is it a way to claim whiteness?[8] The most common response found among many scholars is that Black Africans see Jewishness as a valuable model for improvement of their social conditions. This is an attitude very common to Western scholars. For two or three decades, interest in the Jewish identity of Africans has grown increasingly among researchers in the field of the social sciences; most of these scholars are of European origin (though recently a number of African scholars have joined the field), with the result that their findings are often skewed to a Western perspective. Some of them defend a pseudo theory about African Jewry that leads to the phenomenological approach, an attempt to understand social or cultural phenomenon through an analysis of political, economic, and historical events. These scholars, for the most part specialists in Jewish studies, assert that the identification of Black groups with Judaism is the consequence of missionary influence or the result of colonization.[9] Several missionaries and colonial agents identified some of the African groups they encountered as the descendants of the ancient or biblical Hebrews, and introduced to them new ideas about the history of their origins. Influenced by this discourse, the judaizing African communities would consequently claim a foreign (non-African) identity, describing themselves instead as Semites, Hebrews, or Jews. Another related argument is that Blacks who identify with Judaism are seeking the improvement of their social or economic conditions. In fact, several authors have written extensively about the external influence of environmental (i.e., social, political, or cultural) factors on Black Jewish identity. But an aspect of this discourse that is often ignored is that scholars who studied these groups did so through the lens of their cultural background, in accordance with their social, cultural, or academic preconceptions. It is therefore not surprising that an ethnocentric attitude toward African Jewry in general has gradually emerged in the academic literature. Without entering into a polemical debate on the definition of Jewishness, one can assert that academic discourse is not substantially different from the institutional and religious discourse on the Jewish identity of Blacks; theories of African Jewry promoted by scholars have been seriously affected by those scholars' ideologies and environments (political, sociocultural, etc.). The background of this debate is the assumption that only Whites can be true Jews whereas the Jewishness of Black or other non-Caucasian people is questionable. Here again, experience has proven that academic discourse is influenced by the institutional discourse, since most of the scholars in this field do belong to the Jewish community.

A Judaizing Community in Africa: The Case of the Lemba

To illustrate those arguments, let us focus on the example of the Lemba in South Africa. The selection of the Lemba—estimated at eighty thousand members living today in South Africa among a population of about 37 million Blacks—is justified by the existence of characteristics that distinguish them from other African ethnic groups and from other Jewish communities. Despite their modest numbers, the Lemba have drawn much attention among scholars from the social sciences and religious studies, among others. The consensus is that the Lemba apparently became conscious of a "Jewish" ancestry between the nineteenth and twentieth centuries, but the Lemba believe that their ancestors were Jews who left Israel many centuries ago.[11] Today, they want to reclaim their lost identity and, if possible, return to what they call their homeland—Israel.

The South African society to which the Lemba belong was structured until the 1990s by a policy in which racial distinction was the principal determinant of people's lives. The country was socially stratified into various racial groups over which Whites were in every respect dominant. In his book *Community and Conscience,* Gideon Shimoni describes South African Jews' experience as part of a privileged White minority that dominated a society defined by legalized racial discrimination.[10] The formation of the Jewish community of South Africa was the result of emigration from West Europe, especially Great Britain and Germany, and later on from East Europe. A defining characteristic of the Jewish immigrants was that they progressively earned the status of being Whites. This status offered them civic freedom, economic mobility, and relative prosperity. Because relations with non-Europeans were limited to the employer–employee or domestic master–servant spheres in South Africa, for most Jews (as for most Whites) Blacks were almost invisible in social terms, and most Jewish immigrants soon grew accustomed to regarding Blacks as inferiors—fit solely to be servants and unskilled laborers.

Edith Bruder in her discussion of the Lemba experience of the colonial period in South Africa maintains that a combination of factors, such as the missionary and the colonial discourse, on the one hand, and the results of the genetic tests proving Semitic bonds, on the other hand, have contributed to the crystallization of the Jewish identity of this African people.[12] In this view, European discourse was instrumental in providing the Lemba with new symbols that could be organized into a cultural and ethnic identity. But since the Lemba are neither culturally nor ethnically very different from their African neighbors, their leaders drew attention to other marks of difference. The discourse of ethnic differentiation is appropriated today by most of the Lemba who consider themselves an elite group. A highly placed Lemba civil servant in the government said, "With the Venda we were an elite group ...

in those days we were light skinned—White men really—and the Venda treat us like a sort of upper class, almost like gods. We were the elite. Like the Chosen People."[13]

The anthropologist Gina Buijs analyzes the reasons for the attraction to the Lemba of a non-African identity and specifically a Jewish ancestry. She writes, "The underlying motivation was to advance the material welfare of the Lemba ethnic group within the context of what seemed to be irreversible South African reality of White domination together with the apartheid system's encouragement of Black ethnic differentiation.[14] Indeed, according to her, the Lemba Cultural Association—created in 1947 by Mutenda Bulengwa with the aim of defending the interests of the Lemba community and promoting their cultural heritage—aimed to foster the Lemba's distinct cultural identity among a multiethnic society in which racial division was legalized.[15]

An additional factor was crucial in the identification of this community with modern Judaism. Mutenda Bulengwa, founder of the Lemba Cultural Association, had worked for a time in the household of a Jewish family in the town of Louis Trichardt, in South Africa. There, according to Shimoni, he had the opportunity to observe Jewish rituals that seemed to reflect Lemba practice and encouraged identification with Judaism.[16] Gina Buijs defends this explanation: "The Lemba themselves do not seem at this time to have been conscious of specifically Jewish connections, not surprisingly since there were only two Jewish families living in Louis Trichardt. It was, however, in the household of one of these families, that of Dr. and Mrs. Cohen, that Mutenda Bulengwa spent some time working, prior to his founding of the Lemba Cultural Association. Here, in Mrs. Cohen's kosher kitchen, it is said, he had ample opportunity to observe Jewish dietary ritual and similarities to Lemba traditional customs."[17]

The Jewish community in South Africa have for some time been aware of the existence of the Lemba community, but have never taken seriously the community's claim of a Jewish identity. The possibility of the Lemba's Jewishness, based on their oral tradition and recent genetic research, has sparked a negative response within the local Jewish community. While some scholars admit that the DNA-based genetic evidence seems to scientifically confirm the Lemba's assertion of their Semitic origins, the rabbis maintain that genetic links prove nothing about Jewishness. This opinion is shared by rabbis from both the Orthodox and the Liberal movements.

Rabbi Hecht, an Orthodox rabbi from the Chabad community of Johannesburg, affirms that the results of the genetic testing did not change his opinion about the Jewishness of the Lemba, and he recommends conversion for the ratification of their Jewish identity. However, he adds that it would be irresponsible for a *beit din* (rabbinical court) to allow such a conversion, given that, following their conversion, Lemba Jews will return to their communities or villages, none of which provide the necessary religious infrastructure such as rabbis, synagogues, Jewish schools, kosher food, *shohatim* (ritual slaughterers), or *mohelim* (ritual circumcisors) for an authentic religious life. Moreover, in view of South Africa's long history of apartheid an individual seeking integration into the South African Jewish community was expected to have a European (i.e., White) appearance.[18] The Orthodox Jewish community in South Africa is very homogeneous and conservative, making a massive absorption of Black converts impossible. Rabbi Hecht suggests that, in another social context, such as in Israel or in the United States, where there is greater ethnocultural Jewish diversity, the Lemba convert would enjoy acceptance. Another rabbinical authority, the late Rabbi Cyril Harris (chief rabbi of South Africa from 1987 to 2004) noted that the problem of Lemba identity is embarrassing. He points out that the Lemba have also considered identifying as Christians and argues that it is not possible to claim simultaneously two religious identities. Like Rabbi Hecht, Rabbi Harris insisted that it is impossible to educate the Lemba in the customs of normative Judaism outside of an appropriate religious environment, and for him, too, the idea of a mass conversion is unreasonable. Rabbi Charles Wallach, leader of the Reform Emmanuel Temple, takes the same position: the genetic tests do not provide any evidence to support the Lembas' claim of Jewishness, thus necessitating conversion. However, given the present circumstances, it would be impossible to consider their absorption within the local Jewish community, which is composed primarily of Jews of Eastern European origins.

The attitude of the Israeli rabbinical authorities echoes this skepticism. The head of the very active organization, Amishav, which promotes aliyah of Jewish minorities considered to be descendants of the lost tribes of Israel, clearly expresses his stand against the claims of most of those Africans who profess to belong to the lost tribes. He begins by arguing that the tribes of Israel, according to the Jewish (Talmudic) tradition, were spread throughout the north and the northeast of Israel, but not toward the south. Consequently, there is no possibility that these tribes reached Africa; in other words, none of the ten lost tribes of Israel can be found on the sub-Saharan part of the continent. He acknowledges that Ethiopian Jewry (identified as the tribe of Dan) remains the unique example of Jewish settlement in Sub-Saharan Africa.[19] Amishav has been involved in procedures—in partnership with Israeli governmental and rabbinical authorities—to bring the lost tribes to Israel after a process of rejudaization for some of them and symbolic conversion for others.

According to Arieh Oded, Kulanu (a philanthropic Jewish American organization dedicated to the aliyah of Jewish minorities to Israel and one of Amishav's donors) has asked in the past for the expertise of this Israeli organization in dealing with the growing number of African communities identifying with Judaism. Since their claim to Jewishness did not accord with the principles of halakha, and since their bond to the Jewish people and to the tribes of Israel had not been historically proven, Amishav refused any involvement in these cases in order not to lose its credibility in the eyes of the Israeli rabbinical authorities.[20] In response to questions about the organization's methods for proving Jewishness, Rabbi Avikhail, who heads Amishav, turns to Rashi, in his commentary on Numbers 1:18: "And they assembled all the congregation together on the first day of the second month; and they recited their ancestry by families, by their fathers' house, according to the number of names, from twenty years old and above, each one individually." According to Rashi, this passage suggests two ways to prove a Jewish lineage: (1) a written document certifying ties with a Jewish family (such as a *ketubah,* or wedding certificate, belonging to the individual's parents and administered by a rabbinical authority), or certifying a conversion overseen by a religious Jewish institution; (2) testimony of a viable witness declaring that an individual was born to Jewish parents, or was converted and lives according to Jewish law. In the latter case, the determination of Jewish status requires a *khazakah* (evidence based on the testimony of witnesses, i.e., Jews without any family tie to the person in question). A *khazakah* not only establishes a connection to a family, but also to the Jewish people, whether by birth or conversion. When there is no written document, this process is the only option for the validation of Jewishness. If neither the condition of documentation nor witness are fulfilled, conversion is the only way to guarantee a recognized Jewish status.

The process of conversion must be individual, however, and not collective, because Judaism does not look favorably on proselytism, though it does accept the *ger* (convert). However, there have been infrequent cases of collective conversion to Judaism, including the Khazars mentioned by Judah Halevi (1075–1141); the Jews of San Nicandro in Italy whose community converted in 1946 and immigrated to Israel in the 1950s;[21] and the Abayudaya of Uganda.[22] According to Jewish authorities, each candidate for conversion must be examined in order to verify his or her sincerity: Is the conversion motivated by social concerns (marriage with a Jewish partner) or economic concerns (such as immigration to Israel)? The rabbinate is concerned as well with the convert's integration into a religious environment, since that is the only guarantee of an acceptable Jewish education. In Israel, the rabbinate is the unique and official authority with the power to validate not only the religious, but also the ethnic status of men and women as members of the people of Israel. The institutional discourse denies the Jewishness of the Lemba since their religious practices and their traditions do not conform to halakha, and questions whether the Lemba were ready to exchange their own ethnic-cultural identity for the rigors of full religious conversion and absorption into the exclusive ethnoreligious identity of contemporary Jewry.

Debates on the Construction Process of Black Jewish Identities

In seeking an ethnic bond with the Jewish people, are Black Jews really looking for social mobility? In answering this question, we have to recollect that social class is not tied to ethnic identity (even if they often overlap): one is not born an unskilled worker, a clerk, a professional. Consequently, social mobility cannot explain the exchange of one ethnic identity for another. Social mobility applies specifically to the phenomenon of social *class,* just as assimilation and acculturation apply to the phenomenon of *ethnicity.*[23] And yet some academic theories have linked African affiliation with Judaism to social or economic interests, while Jewish authorities see these groups' affiliation with Judaism as inauthentic and suspect, likely hiding undisclosed interests: Why do Africans want to change their identity? Are they not satisfied with their present identity? Why do they want to abandon Christianity or Islam to embrace a new religion? What do they hope to get out of Judaism?

An article published in 2007 in the Israeli mass circulation newspaper *Yedi'ot akhronot* explains the motivations of Africans to identify as Jews by insisting on the socioeconomic character of this association. The author claims, "From data published by the Israeli Ministry of the Interior, thousands of members of Jewish tribes throughout the world made a request to the immigration office for aliya in the last two years. The majority comes from the Third World countries. The requests increase. According to the Ministry, the number of those who claim to be

Jews or of Jewish descent grows according to the economic situation of their country."[24]

In other words, a correlation should exist between poor or developing country societies and the rate of adherence to Judaism. Many scholars assert that interest in Judaism among African groups has been triggered by recent events like the migration of the Beta Israel (Ethiopian Jews) from Ethiopia to Israel in the 1980s and the 1990s. The exodus and the official recognition of the Ethiopian Jews as the lost tribe of Dan, they argue, have encouraged the development of similar lost tribe identities in other parts of Africa.[25] This seems to be confirmed by the fact that most of the African groups in question did not identify themselves as Jews until recently—that is, not before the twentieth century. Buijs writes, "As Israel struggles to absorb about 15,000 Black Ethiopians into a modern, Western society, tens of thousands of Blacks in South Africa, Zimbabwe and Mozambique are claiming descent from the lost Biblical tribes."[26]

Referring to the American context, Lenora Berson claims that Blacks who convert to Judaism are in search of security or power. She interprets an affiliation with Judaism as a group's attempt to create an acceptable self-image.[27] Most scholars agree that Jews sometime serve as role models for Blacks looking to improve their social and economic circumstances. In fact, Black Jews—including Blacks in Western countries but also in Israel—are consistently described in social sciences as poor and working class. These social conditions ought to prove that their compulsion for Judaism is motivated by economic interest. Consequently, for several Western Jews the emergence of Black people claiming Jewishness was unsettling, and most often provoked laughter and dismissal. For example in South Africa, when a Black worshipper arrives to pray in a synagogue, people look at him and joke, "Hey, who has brought his gardener to *Shül* [synagogue]?"[28]

The rejection of Black Jews is usually explained as a religious or halakhic matter, but this exclusion must also be understood as a product of ethnocentrism, based in large part on preconceived ideas about ethnic and cultural origin. Since we know that under certain conditions Judaism does admit ethnic diversity (such as Jews of Russian, Tunisian, or German descent), cultural diversity (Ashkenazim and Sephardim), and a variety of religious movements (Orthodoxy, Reform, Hasidism), it is hard to explain why Judaism cannot also contain minorities of other ethnic origins, or why only certain groups must prove their biological bonds with the Jewish people. When it comes to individuals of African origins, a possible discrimination may be noticeable: legal (religious) criteria determining someone as Jew must be normally applied to every man or woman and not only to a category of persons distinguishable by their ethnic origin, or their cultural or physical features—otherwise such criteria are not universal. But, even if this discrimination does not appear in the halakhic laws, it may be expressed in the relationships between African and Jewish communities. That is why, in most cases, the rabbinical authorities require a halakhic conversion of all the African judaizing groups. Acceptance of this process is necessary if Black Jewish groups want to achieve legal and official recognition by Jewish institutions.

Modern researchers on the phenomenon of African Jewry suggest innovative approaches of this very polemical subject: scholars are asked, first, to legitimize the narrative (as the translation of people's memory, feelings or ideas) of these communities about their Jewish identity and not interpret it as myth; and second, to reconsider this process of identification with Judaism.[29] Indeed, when we are dealing with the question of the construction of Black Jewish identity, we have to be concerned about the nature of the bond of Black communities with Judaism. Is it about a symbolic utilization of Judaism, such as its history (analogy with the history of the Black people), its values (universalism), its ethics (concern about Otherness), its morals (respect for every single life), and so on, for specific goals? Is it about a religious identification? In this case, it refers to the prominent debate on institutional recognition of Jewish identity. The response to the Black Judaism phenomenon in the Jewish world can be divided into two distinct attitudes: denial of the Jewish origin of the African communities, and attempts to show that their affiliation to Judaism is based purely on myth; recognition, particularly among some Liberal Jews who are more open to multiculturalism, of the Jewish identity of these communities and readiness to absorb them within world Jewry. Promoters of both attitudes have developed arguments (historical or theological) to defend their position. These arguments constitute the core of the debate on African Judaism today. Therefore, the reactions from the Jewish world, expressed both by scholars and rabbinical authorities, can be viewed as a pure strategy of defense against non-Jewish groups considered as intruders and representing a threat for worldwide Judaism, or an effort to understand a new social phenomenon that matters for world Jewry.

The Lemba have adapted their discourse to suit their audience (rabbinical authorities belonging to the Orthodox or the Liberal movement; Jews or Gentiles). Among those for whom Jewishness requires ethnic membership (by descent or by blood tie), an ethnic and essentialist discourse argues for their bond with the Jewish people by providing historical and genetic proof of their Jewish descent (stories about their migration from Israel to Yemen and later on to Sub-Saharan Africa). Among those for whom Jewishness is primarily a religious status, they point to their ancestral religious practices (respect of the Jewish precepts or *mitzvoth*). Practice of the Jewish law represents in their eyes the authentic proof of their Jewish identity.

Judaism is characterized—in contrast to other religions like Christianity or Islam—by its ethnic kinship rules. God did not make a covenant with all the nations of the earth but only with Abraham and his descendants. The sons of Abraham were the Hebrews (descendants of Isaac), the Ishmaelites (descendants of Ishmael), and the Edomites (descendants of Esau). But Judaism was the inheritance of the sons of Jacob—in other words, maintained by the people of Israel through the covenant at Sinai. Later, foreigners (by proselytism, conversion, or marriage) and other nations could be integrated into the covenant. There was never a universalistic claim attached to membership of the Jewish people.

In many cases, Christian missionaries were the first to bring to light the existence of African Judaic or judaizing communities; it was through Christianity that those communities came to Judaism. Indeed, one common scholarly argument is that members of the African Judaic communities, after first reading the Bible, decided to align their religious practices with those of the Israelites. At the same time, they were looking for an appropriate definition of their religious denomination: Was it another Christian church, a cult, or a sect, or rather a new Jewish movement? Originally, their religious identity, although syncretic, drew strength from their ethnicity, as in the case of the Black separatist Churches such as the Zionist Church in South Africa for whom ethnicity helped distinguish it from other, mainly White, Christian churches. Gradually, after encountering Jews, they progressively identified with them. The intention at the beginning was not to be assimilated within the (White) Jewish community, but to find their place within worldwide Jewry while maintaining their own cultural and ethnic characteristics. Unfortunately, this aim was in conflict with the skepticism of the rabbinical authorities who have continued to deny the African claim to Jewishness. The official representatives of Judaism were not ready to absorb the members of those communities if they did not give up their former identity through conversion or assimilation.

According to Rabbi Bleich, some African Jewish communities are still reluctant to convert but, in reality, the majority seeking institutional recognition are ready to fulfill the halakhic conditions through a process of conversion.[30] Sometimes, however, conversion is not allowed for diverse reasons: on the one hand, some organized Black Jewish communities, like the Lemba, wish to maintain their traditional ties and distinct identities, and do not want to disappear within an all-White Jewish community; on the other hand, some very homogenous White Jewish communities are unwilling to absorb other ethnic groups, such as Blacks, and have discovered various means to maintain a distance between them and the groups.

Conclusion

Modern academic approaches have given rise to a discourse about African Jewry. A significant concern is the way some scholars define African Judaism not only as a religious movement, but also as a social phenomenon. The fundamental question is to know if this is a debate involving the Jewish world, or a problem that has to be limited to African societies.

Rabbinical Jewish authorities in Israel and the Diaspora are aware of the existence of African judaizing communities throughout the world (in Africa, Israel, and the United States), but many Jewish institutions involved in the absorption of new Jewish groups paid a very heavy price for their acceptance: their expectations (like the reliance on conversion as a means of regulating claims to Jewish identity) have been misunderstood or misinterpreted. Today, these institutions are reluctant to be involved in the debate over the authenticity of African Jews. When there are new cases of African Jewish groups seeking rabbinical recognition, the rabbinical authorities refer to scholars—usually members of the Jewish community—who have studied the groups in question. On the basis of their assessments, the authorities decide whether African groups can be considered Jews. Experience has proven that academic discourse is at once limited by and put into practice by Jewish institutions. Consequently, Judaism's claim to be a multiethnic religion is problematic, since its gates remain closed for a certain category of people with regard to their ethnic origin.

Notes

1. Nathan Adler, *Jewish Travelers: A Treasury of Travelogues from Nine Centuries* (London: Bloch Publishers, 1930).
2. Tudor Parfitt, *The Lost Tribes of Israel: The History of a Myth* (London: Phoenix, 2003).

3. Arieh Oded, *The Bayudaya: A Community of African Jews in Uganda* (Tel Aviv: Shiloah Center for Middle Eastern and African Studies, University of Tel Aviv, 1973).
4. Remy Ilona and Eliyah Ehav, *The Igbo: Jews in Africa? Research Findings, Historical Links, Commentaries, Narratives* (Abuja: Mega Press, 2004).
5. Karen Primack, *Jews in Places You Never Thought Of* (Hoboken, NJ: Ktav Publishing House, 1998).
6. Tudor Parfitt, *Journey to the Vanished City* (New York: Vintage Books, 2000); and Magdel Le Roux, *The Lemba: A Lost Tribe of Israel in Southern Africa* (Pretoria: UNISA, 2003).
7. James Landing, *Black Judaism: Story of an American Movement* (Durham, NC: Carolina Academic Press, 2002).
8. The word "whiteness" is used metaphorically in this sentence. The appropriate expression might be "White social identity" or "Western cultural way of life."
9. Tudor Parfitt and Emanuela Trevisan Semi, *Judaizing Movements* (London: Routledge Curzon, 2002); Edith Bruder, *The Black Jews of Africa: History, Religion, Identity* (New York: Oxford University Press, 2008).
10. Gideon Shimoni, *Community and Conscience: The Jews in Apartheid South Africa* (Hanover, NH: Brandeis University Press, 2003).
11. Bruder, *Black Jews of Africa.* See Henri Junod, "The Lemba of the Zoutpansberg (Transvaal)," *Folkore* 9, no. 3 (1908): 276–287; Le Roux, *The Lemba.*
12. Bruder, *Black Jews of Africa.* See Mark Thomas et al., "Y Chromosomes Travelling South: The Cohen Modal Haplotype and the Origins of the Lemba—the Black Jews of Southern Africa," *American Journal of Human Genetics* 66 (2000): 674–686.
13. Quoted in Gina Buijs, "Black Jews in the Northern Province: A Study of Ethnic Identity in South Africa," *Ethnic and Racial Studies* 21, no. 4 (1998): 665.
14. Buijs, "Black Jews in the Northern Province," 664.
15. Ibid.
16. Shimoni, *Community and Conscience,* 178–179.
17. Buijs, "Black Jews in the Northern Province," 673.
18. Tudor Parfitt and Julia Egorova, *Genetics, Mass Media and Identity: A Case Study of the Genetic Research on the Lemba and Bene Israel* (London: Routledge, 2006).
19. Eliyahu Avikhail, *Les tribus d'Israël perdues ou lointaines* (Jerusalem: Amishav, 2003).
20. Arye Oded, *Yehadut betokhkhei Afrika: Haabayudaya shel Uganda—hayehudim haafrikanim shel Uganda vekishreyhem 'im ha'olam hayehudi* (Judaism in Africa, The Abayudaya of Uganda: The African Jews of Uganda and their contacts with World Jewry) (Jerusalem: Association for Israel-Africa Friendship, 2003). In Hebrew.
21. Elena Cassin, *San Nicandro: Histoire d'une Conversion* (Paris, Plon, 1957).
22. Oded, *The Bayudaya.*
23. Nathan Glazer, *Ethnic Dilemmas: 1964–1982* (Cambridge, MA: Harvard University Press, 1983), 239.
24. Nurit Palter and Natasha Mozgobia, "Hayehudim hekhadashim: 'Aliya bemispar toshvim medinot ha'olam hashlishi hamevakshim la'alot leyisrael"

(The New Jews: Increase in Third World residents who wish to immigrate to Israel), *Yedi'ot Ahronot,* September 16, 2007, 8–9.

25. Bruder, *Black Jews of Africa,* 4.
26. Buijs, "Black Jews in the Northern Province," 661.
27. Lenora Berson, *The Negroes and the Jews* (New York: Random House, 1971), 210.
28. Parfitt and Egorova, *Genetics, Mass Media and Identity,* 81.
29. Such innovative approaches can be found in the research of French anthropologists like Maurice Dores (in his film *Black Israel,* 2002) and Lisa Anteby-Yemini, *Les Juifs éthiopiens en Israël: les paradoxes du paradis* (Paris: Edition du CNRS, 2004).
30. David Bleich, *Contemporary Halakhic Problems* (New York: Ktav, 1977).

CHAPTER 10

The Descendants of David of Madagascar

Crypto-Judaism in Twentieth-Century Africa

Edith Bruder

Throughout Africa, interpretations of the Hebrew Bible and analogies of the experiences of Blacks and Jews have provided models for Africans to identify themselves with the descendants of the lost tribes of Israel.[1] Starting in the early Middle Ages, legends disseminated among Jews as well as non-Jews supporting the existence of Jewish kingdoms in East and West Africa gained in popularity and influence. The genealogy unearthed by the travel accounts of Jewish travelers such as Eldad the Danite in the ninth century or Benjamin of Tudela in the twelfth century still have relevance and resonance for a surprising number of Africans in search of a new identity. The question of their origins—and particularly their links with Judaism—is fed by mythical accounts according to which their ancestors are the descendants of Abraham and Jacob. The remarkable persistence of some narrative patterns, such as the theme of the lost tribes of Israel, or the arrival of Jews in Egypt following Jeremiah after the destruction of the First Temple, represents a complex search for origins that takes on ethnic, religious, spatial, historical, social, mythical, linguistic, and, more recently, genetic forms. At the same time, these symbolic constructions prove to be capable of perpetual invention and development resulting from the circumstances faced by the groups I will discuss.

In Madagascar, scores of existing traditions (*lovan-tsofina* in the Malagasy language) tell sometimes openly, but often obliquely, of ancestral origins in Ancient Israel in the culture of innumerable Malagasy clans constituting what some of them consider to be the Malagasy secret. According to Katherine Quanbeck, who lived for thirty-five years among the Malagasy people and collected archives of oral testimonies, it seems that many important Malagasy authorities (i.e., kings, priests, clan elders, professionals, pastors, as well as some historians) do not want anything written or produced about their oral histories. At present, a Jewish identity within an institutional framework does not exist in Madagascar, but the belief clearly does exist among certain groups, movements, or individuals that many Malagasy have Hebrew blood.[2] A young Malagasy of the Sevohitse clan nicknamed Que de Neuf, after several meetings, cautiously mentioned the existence of a place from where he came, Foibe Jiosy, which means "the headquarters of the Jews," near Ambovombe, Madagascar. He commented, "We marry only within our clan. No one likes to come to our town. People do not like us. We have to hide the fact that we are Jewish."[3]

According to what appears to be the dominant tradition, those Malagasy who refer to themselves as Jews assert that their ancestors are Descendants of David who came from a place outside Madagascar, that is, Arabia or Africa. They were shipwrecked off the coast of Africa, and arrived in dhows on the shores of Madagascar wearing long, white robes, always accompanied by a red cow. Those who claim to be Descendants of David affirm that their ancestors believed in one god and never had idols. There are a number of variants of this myth of origin, for example, Mr. B. Faradofay's description of the origin of his clan, the Tavaratra from Sandravinany (located somewhere in the south of the city of Vagaindrano, on the southeast coast of Madagascar) who

> came from somewhere in the area of Medina, or somewhere on the sea coast of Saudi Arabia, in scores of botries [boats] full of families to the northern coast of Madagascar. Some of them, the Tantakara, stayed in the area of that northern coast, others continued southward along the eastern coast of Madagascar. The dhow of our family contained one red zebu and when the dhow reached the Vohipeno area, the zebu brayed, so they stopped here temporarily. But then they continued southward, past what is known as Fort Dauphin, and continued on around the southern coast, even going as far as Androka. At the mouth of that river, the zebu brayed again, two times; so they stopped there but eventually left again, and returned the way they had come. After travelling back eastward along Madagascar's southern coast, then northward along part of the eastern coast, at the Vohipeno area, the red zebu brayed three times. So they stopped there, and our family eventually moved as far south as Sandravinany, a region which was open totally, with no persons having settled it. We were the original Malagasy people in that area around what is now known as Sandravinany.[4]

The legend of the red zebu probably came from the biblical tradition of the red heifer (Numbers 19:1–22). The red heifer was part of the temple sacrifice performed by the priest to purify someone from ritual contamination arising from contact with the dead.

Colonial Discourse and Ethnogenesis

Within a process of dynamic reorganization of symbolic cultural codes, local indigenous mythographies appropriated symbols from the seventeenth century, considerably increased by nineteenth-century Christian missionaries, while also recasting older mythic themes. One can recognize confused references to events and struggles that marked the first centuries of the Hegira and sometimes teachings from the Quran.[5] Antemoro legends combine in unexpected ways the names of Islamic leaders and of biblical figures from the most ancient times in search of a kind of spiritual kinship. One of these legends contracts and synthesizes the origin of various races or ethnic groups, and recounts that Mahomet had five sons who all became kings in Arabia: Abraham, Noah, Joseph, Moses, and Jesus, the last four of them having fathered Tsimeto, Kazimambo, Anakara, and Raminia.[6] The free use or reuse of myths of origin seem to serve a wide array of ideological and spiritual needs, and many of the elements that Malagasy societies cast as *tradition* are in fact the product of ongoing processes of cultural innovation.

In Madagascar, myths of origins seem to be a consequence of certain European theories that appeared in the seventeenth century among French observers and that were largely taken up again and developed by missionaries in the nineteenth century. As elsewhere in Africa, borrowings from the myth of the lost tribes included in the interpretative movement of the colonial enterprise contributed to the construction of the origins of Africans by foreigners. Etienne de Flacourt, the French governor of Fort Dauphin, during his stay in Madagascar in 1652 reported the discovery of remnants of an ancient Jewish colony on the eastern coast of Madagascar, on the island of Sainte-Marie (also called Nosy Ibrahim) and in Fenerive,

> The peoples who, I think, were the earliest to come to Madagascar were the Zaffre-Ibrahim, or Abraham lineage, who lived on the island of Sainte-Marie and neighbouring lands; all the more so, since although they practise circumcision, they have no mark of Mohammedanism, know neither Mohammed nor his Caliphs and consider their followers as Caffres and men without law; they do not eat or conclude any alliance with them.

> They celebrate and do not work on Saturday, and not on Friday like the Moors and have no name similar to the ones they have; this leads me to think that their ancestors visited this island during the earliest migrations of the Jews, or that they descend from the most ancient Ishmaelite families, as early as before the captivity in Babylon, or from those who could have remained in Egypt after Israel left the country. They have maintained the names of Moses, Isaac, Joseph and Noah ... even if there are here women and children much whiter than the Matatanes and having hair as straight as them.[7]

Following Flacourt, and abundantly referring to his account, subsequent observers such as Captain de Valgny and François Martin who settled there during the time of Louis XIII identified an ancient background of ideas among some Malagasy populations—particularly the belief in only one God who cannot be represented by an image—that evokes a similarity with the Jewish pre-Solomonic civilization. Martin, who met natives at Analambolo in the province of Fenerive where he lived from 1665 to 1668, considered that they

> do not practise any exercise of religion; they, nevertheless admit that there is a God whom they acknowledge to be the author of all beings.... They respect Saturday, they do not work on that day in their plantations; the specific observance of that day, their circumcision and the loathing of some of them for eating pork, let us know that a few Jews or persons of this religion visited this region in the past, that they instructed the people and that some customs have remained.[8]

Another suggestion of a possible Jewish or Hebrew presence in southeast Africa comes from Alfred Grandidier, the most important and influential authority on Madagascar of all times. Grandidier dedicated his life to the fifty-two volumes of his encyclopaedic *Histoire Physique, Naturelle et Politique de Madagascar* (1901) and is considered the ultimate authority on this subject. About an ancient Semitic migration to Madagascar, Grandidier wrote, "The fleets sent by King Solomon towards the Southeast coast of Africa had probably some of their ships lost on the coasts of Madagascar and it is not unlikely that, in ancient times, some Jewish colonies had been founded, voluntarily or not, in this island known from the Comoros."[9] Grandidier listed thirty-five traits common to all Malagasy and ancient Jews and concluded that Malagasy peoples derive from a pre-Solomonic Jewish civilization.[10] The monumental work carried out by Grandidier may be taken as institutionalizing knowledge about Madagascar, and subsequently came to have an impact on the native populations. This seems to be attested to by a document recently written by Pastor F.S., an Andrevola descendant of a Sakalava king who describes the Jiosy (Jewish) origins of his clan and compares more than two dozen of the Andrevola traditional practices, referring specifically to Grandidier's listing.[11]

Grandidier was largely inspired by an Arab text, written in Mayotte, quoted by Alfred Gevrey, that relates the history of the Comoros Islands and reveals that their earliest inhabitants would have been Idumeans originating from the Red Sea or Arabs who settled there shortly after the reign of King Solomon.[12] Grandidier himself inspired numerous collaborators, and disciples such as Keane, who would write in *The Gold of Ophir* (1901) about the ancient links between the land of Israel and Madagascar, "that people who preserve many Israelitish rites, usages and traditions, cherish the memory of Abraham, but have no knowledge of any of the prophets after the time of David," which implies that the alleged Jewish immigrants left their home at a very remote date.[13] Documents are quoted to show that the Comoros, a stopping-point between Madagascar and present-day Zimbabwe, were peopled during the reign of Solomon "by Arabs or rather by Idumean Jews from the Red Sea."[14] Such views continued to be expressed throughout the twentieth century and the Reverend Father Briand, a French missionary, dedicated a strange book to the influence of Hebrew on the Malagasy language, asserting, "the Malagasy language is a peculiarity, and the source of this peculiarity is in the Hebrew language."[15]

Although Christian missionary outposts were established from the sixteenth century, their greatest impact on Malagasy culture and politics began during the early nineteenth century when missionaries were allowed to settle in the highland kingdom of Imerina. In the nineteenth centuries, missionaries of the London Missionary Society, who had arrived in 1795, had not only created a considerable network of schools, but also had completed the translation of the New Testament and substantial sections of the Hebrew Bible.[16] A number of studies show how inextricably Christianity and Christian values became interwoven with beliefs and practices concerning ancestors, especially in the Highlands. Some missionaries believed that all of the Malagasy religious antecedents derived from the Hebrew religion itself, and all Malagasy were supposed to be the descendants of "Jews who came to Madagascar in Phoenician ships."[17]

In 1870, the missionary James Sibree visited the group at Vohipeno who called themselves Zaffy Ibrahim and recorded that they said to him during a conversation: "We are altogether Jews." Sibree adds, "But I could not detect any difference in colour, features, or dialect between them and the other people of the eastern coast, while observing that they emphasised their Jewish origins." Sibree also recorded that in

1876 he met an Anakara who told him that he was a Zaffy-Ibrahim, descendant of Abraham, and he added "Jiosy *mihitsy*," which means "entirely Jewish." Jiosy is the Malagasy transcription of "Jew" in English, and it was certainly after having heard the preaching of English missionaries that this idea came to him; Abraham was included among Antemoro's ancestors, along with Noah and Moses. [18]

The identification of Levitical customs was an obsession of the missionaries and early European anthropologists. One of those anthropologists detected Levirate survivals among the Bara, a Malagasy group considered to be the Africans of Madagascar; he hinted at an Ethiopian connection: "The Levirate still exists among several peoples, but it is basically Hebraic and it still exists in Abyssinia. Its presence in Madagascar seems to me evidence of a much more ancient and deep influence than one could imagine, coming from Hebrews or Arabs who migrated there or from elements belonging to eastern Africa." [19]

Nowadays, the Malagasy construction of ethnohistory has fully absorbed the identification of local tribes with the lost tribes introduced by the Christian missionaries. Pastor S., a professor of Old Testament studies at Boeny, asserts, "I know that there are many, many Malagasy who must be Levite priests; there is a specified clan elder, in each of these families, who has the special knife for killing the sacrificial animal, thus there is also a specified elder in the clan who has the privilege of killing the animal that is sacrificed." [20]

Biblical characters and themes did not wait for the nineteenth century's missionary movement to penetrate Malagasy traditions. They have been known over a much longer period, through Muslim intermediaries. Numerous figures from biblical episodes are condensed into a syncretistic framework without any direct link to a specific passage in the Bible. The legend of Noah, in particular, whose Arabic name *Nûh* is Malagasized into Noho or Ranoho, was mentioned by Flacourt who had himself met scribes who held Arabic Malagasy documents.[21] In the very same Malagasy legend can be found figures that traveled through Muslim traditions, and others deriving from biblical sources that were transmitted by missionaries. The biblical account acts as an available model able to be reemployed for an imagined Semitic or Judaic identity.

Semitic and Jewish Lineages in Madagascar: Historical Approaches

Malagasy origins have been the subject of much academic dispute that is still only partially resolved. There is a consensus among modern scholars that navigators from Indonesia settled along the coast of East Africa, acquired some Bantu vocabulary, and then sailed to Madagascar already speaking a language that contains a mixture of Bantu words.[22] In fact, ancient accounts attest to the trading or migratory movements of Phoenicians, Chinese, Indians, Malays, Persians, Arabs, and Jews along the coasts of southern Arabia, eastern Africa, and the Indian subcontinent.[23] Any of these people could have reached Madagascar in outriggers, dhows, junks, or any other kind of seafaring craft, with the help of wind and currents. Maritime contacts do not allow for any automatic inference of any significant contribution to the peopling of Madagascar. However, it can be postulated that many migrations into Madagascar took place. Therefore, the presence of Idumean colonies or Arab Jews from Yemen in Madagascar may be considered.

We know that Arabs traded down the eastern coast of Africa and that their boats visited Sofala on the eastern coast of Africa and the Comoros archipelago. In this context the word "Arab" is a convenient name covering various groups affected to a greater or lesser extent by Islam, originating in most cases in Arabia but who could have spent several generations in East Africa or elsewhere, en route to Madagascar. Local chronicles from the main islands of the eastern coast of Africa, as well as accounts of the great sea travels undertaken by the Portuguese in the sixteenth century, enable us to follow the major Arab and Persian migrations that could have reached Eastern Africa, Comoros, and Madagascar.[24] Immigration of groups belonging to minority religious sects and suffering persecution after the expansion of Islam in Arabia, Persia, and Egypt probably included the members of the Azd tribe of Oman, at the end of the seventh century, or the Zeidites and Sunnites of El Hasa persecuted by Ismaelians in the eighth century. Grandidier considered that the earliest Arab colons in Madagascar could have been "Zeidites, some of them having left the Sawad of Kawfa after having failed in their revolt against Caliph Hischam in 737 and the others after having overthrown the Ommayyad Caliph Walid … had to leave Arabia according to Masudi's record and the accounts of Barros and Joao dos Santos."[25] The evidential value of these hypotheses is discussed adequately by Gabriel Ferrand, an important Arabist and student of Muslim communities in Asia, Africa and Madagascar, in *Les Migrations Musulmanes et Juives à Madagascar* (1905). The study of an undated manuscript that refers to a caliph who reigned in the thirteenth century leads Ferrand to consider that the Islamized Malagasy descended from Sunnite Muslims. Ferrand discovered in a *khotba,* a special Friday prayer that Islamized Malagasy recited in Madagascar, the mention of the ultimate Abbassid caliph of Bagdad, Al-Mostas'im, who reigned from 1242 to 1258.[26] Ferrand also cited a text whose author is thought to be a member of the orthodox Shiite sect, or Imamites, and he envisaged that the Persian Shiites could have migrated to the eastern coast of Madagascar between 800 and 818, while acknowledging that the discrepancy of information does not make it possible to clearly determine the date and origin of the earliest Arab arrivals on the island.[27]

A Portuguese record by the Jesuit priest Luis Marianno, who visited the southeastern coast of Madagascar in 1613, evoked the hypothesis of a Muslim migration prior to the thirteenth century. According to the words that Father Marianno recorded from King Andriantsiambani, the king himself, they "originated from Mangalor and Mekka where his ancestors were born. Those [who had embarked] on one or several ships, got lost, and from the coast of India, ran onto the coast of the north tip of Madagascar island. Little by little they multiplied and came as far as the south tip. This had happened many years [earlier]. In one branch there had been seventeen generations and in the other fourteen. Thus, on the eastern coast of Madagascar people of this family are scattered."[28]

Father Marianno observed that the customs they kept were a testimony of their origin, that they were Moors, and that they called themselves Solimas, a derivation in modern Malagasy from Silamu or Islam. While pointing out "they have the same colour as Indians, Arabs and Javanese," Father Marianno added that they have a Quran written in Arabic, they observe Ramadan, do not eat pork, and practice circumcision.

Ascertaining the specific boundaries between groups in Madagascar is problematic, since groups overlap and merge into one another.[29] Hence the boundaries between clans are nebulous and anyone can identify with more than one clan.[30] Despite regional differences, members of numerous clans, mainly originating from the south-east and south-west, claim to be descendants of royal dynasties whose traditions are clearly of Semitic origin, such as Antemoro and Zafiraminia, descendants of Raminia.[31]

The first Arab ancestors are generally known in Madagascar as Antalaotra (people from across the sea).[32] It is likely that the first Arabs to cross the Mozambique Channel were some of these pre-Islamic traders who had been pushed out of Arabia or Africa by orthodox Sunnite Moslems expanding from the north. Elsewhere on the island, particularly along the east coast, there are numerous traces of Arab or Islamic cultural influence but no knowledge of the central features of the Muslim religion, the name Allah, the mosque, prayers, or pilgrimage to Mecca. Where the name of Muhammad is distantly remembered, he represents one prophet among others rather than *the* Prophet. This would seem to indicate that the Arabs from whom the Antalaotra descended and came to the east coast of Madagascar were either pre-Islamic or members of one of the sects that broke away from the orthodox Muhammedan faith during the turbulent times of Muhammad and his immediate successors, or Jews who had converted to Islam. Sometime in the eighth or ninth century, their boats reached the Malagasy coast, probably from the Comoros, and they set up trading posts along the northwest coast from where they expanded.[33] The combined evidence from archaeology, oral traditions and written sixteenth-century Portuguese accounts reveal that early Muslim traders had two important settlements on the western coasts of Madagascar.[34] Archaeological excavations at the northeastern site of Vohemar, known by its ancient name of Ihàrana, have yielded an entire cultural complex based on external commerce and dominated by traders who had written in Arabic since at least the twelfth century.[35] Probably due to the importance of its foreign trade, Ihàrana appeared as a trading post and must have welcomed sailors and traders from the western Indian Ocean.

A subsequent group was the Zafiraminia (descendants of Ramini) who probably arrived early in the fourteenth century, and who, according to their traditions, came from Mecca or from Ramni, which was the medieval name for Sumatra, some time after Islam had established itself in Indonesia in the thirteenth century. Whatever their origin, they appear to have spent some time in Ihàrana before moving south to settle on the coast around Mananjary. Later arrivals of Antemoro caused some of them to move farther south to the southeast corner around Fort Dauphin. The ancestors of the Antemoro arrived some two centuries after the Zafiraminia, around the end of the fifteenth century. They are of major interest as possessors of important historical manuscripts the *Sorabé* (which translates as great writings or sacred books), probably originally written in Arabic but adapted at an early stage to the Malagasy language.[36] The *Sorabé* are concerned with astrology, geomancy, divination, and medicine, the knowledge of which gave the possessors great prestige throughout Madagascar.[37] If they are historical records of major interest, the reliability of the *Sorabé* is uncertain because most of them appear to have been written relatively recently and copied, with varying degrees of accuracy, from older documents. Even if the *Sorabé* do not really help us to be precise about the origins of the Antemoro, like the Zafiraminia, with whom their traditions are often confused, they claim noble descent from Mecca and mention sometime a stay in Africa on the way to Madagascar. Up until now, the Antemoro were thought to have come from Africa. Another hypothesis of the origin of the Antemoro was recently suggested by Brown: "It has been recently argued very plausibly that the origin of both the name and the people is to be found in the Somali country of south-eastern Ethiopia, where there was a tribe called *Temur* which disappeared from the area in the fifteenth century," which coincides with the date of the arrival of the Antemoro in Madagascar.[38] Such a trace has been found by Enrico Cerulli in Ethiopia's epic song, *Negus Yeshak,* which refers to a vanished people named Temur in connection with the Somali. Therefore it is not impossible to consider that the original ancestors of the Antemoro came from Arabia to the Somalia area, which was traditionally a home for heretics and dissenters who were subsequently driven out by the expansion of the Galla people.[39] The Islamic faith of the Antemoro, who practice both tribal and clan endogamy, seems to have declined rapidly and little trace remains, apart from a taboo on eating pork, funerary rituals, and sacrifices.[40] It was mainly through the Antemoro that words borrowed from Arabic were absorbed into the Malagasy language, notably the days of the week and terms associated with astrology, arithmetic, and divination. The Antemoro carried a priestly prestige deriving from their magical arts, which enabled them to provide priest doctors and diviners to the ruling clans in their own regions as well as to many other tribes.[41] One might surmise that the Antemoro immigrants, like the Antalaotra in general, were predominantly male and married local Malagasy women.

If the Antemoro genealogical traditions allow for some reasonable speculation with respect to an initial Arab settlement, the Portuguese chronicles are more precise. In 1507–1508, a Portuguese captain, Ruy Pereira, mentioned a possible colony of Moors at Matitana, a place inhabited by the Antemoro, and reported that the local inhabitants were no strangers to external trade, having taken silver and beeswax to his ship.[42] Tristao da Cunha, admiral of the Portuguese fleet in the western Indian Ocean, was able to find in Mozambique a Moor named Bogima who had previously been to Matitana. In 1513, Lisbon sent Luis Figuera to establish a small fort and ginger-processing factory in Matitana. Luis Figuera wrote, by that time "Matitana [was] a town densely inhabited by Moors."[43] It is therefore possible to say that Moors on the African mainland knew about the region of Matitana and traded occasionally with it before the Portuguese discovery of Madagascar in 1506.

Trans-African Connections

Specific links with Africa can be found on the tombs at Sokoambé, on the western coast, where bird carvings appear on rectangular tombstones. Only the tombs of Sokoambé in Madagascar have bird effigies that are remarkably similar to soapstone carvings of birds found in Great Zimbabwe.[44] According to Dos Santos (1609), the term "Sakoambé" (or "Sakuambé" or "Sakumbe") was related to the Kingdom of Sacumbe on the Zambezi River, at a point marked by a cataract that impeded navigation.[45] While this link with Great Zimbabwe could be questioned, it coincides with numerous local traditions of a Malagasy dynasty in this area, the Maroseràna or Volamena, which appeared in the mid-sixteenth century.[46] This dynasty is considered by several traditions as formed by the marriage of new immigrants, described as White men with the daughters of local chiefs. The Maroseràna later took over leadership of the Sakalava society and the first Sakalava conqueror was called Andriandahifotsy, which means Prince White Man.

Throughout Madagascar, Grandidier observed, "nearly all of the chiefs and rulers [were of an] origin different from the mass of people" as attested by words of their mother tongue.[47] But even more striking was the observable fact that the rulers were physically different from their subjects. It has been generally accepted that an Arab or Indonesian origin might explain the legend of early White chiefs, but recently it has been argued that the founder of the Maroseràna came from Black Africa, more specifically, the Zimbabwe Empire, around the Zambezi.[48] The notion that the Antemoro could be White Arabs is contradicted by Flacourt, who reported in 1651 that members of the ten royal Antemoro ruling clan are "darker than the other Whites but are nonetheless their masters."[49] An African origin has also been suggested for the names of other early Maroseràna kings, particularly Andriamandazaoàla, whose name translates as "crusher of trees," which was one of the titles of Mwene Mutapa, the great Zimbabwe king. One Sakalava tradition is that precursors of the Maroseràna landed on the southwest coast of the island with a shipload of gold, which they used to gain supremacy over the local people.[50] The alternative name of the Maroseràna, Volamena, means "golden" in Malagasy, whereas the name Maroseràna itself may be derived from *mari,* which was the word for gold in Zimbabwe. If it is difficult to believe that Africans from Zimbabwe could be described as White, there is a possible explanation that would attribute a Zimbabwe origin of the dynasties with the White men tradition. In the late Middle Ages, the Zimbabwe gold may have been taken over by the Arabs. Nineteenth-century travelers to Vendaland and Mashonaland cited the local tradition that White men had once inhabited the interior. In *Twenty-Five Years in a Wagon in the Gold Regions of Africa* (1887), Andrew Anderson wrote, "The natives state that the gold was worked and the forts built by the White men that once occupied this country whom they called Abberlomba."[51] It is therefore imaginable that the ancestors of the Maroseràna were Arabs who could have landed on the southwest coast with a shipload of gold and that they set up kingdoms of their own based on the model of the Zimbabwe Empire.[52]

This hypothesis coincides with Murdock's opinion, which considers that a Venda-Zimbabwe link can be postulated for the Antanosy society inhabiting the southeast part of the island and who claim an Islamic descent. Murdock suggests interesting parallels between the Antanosy and the Venda-incorporated Lemba who possess markedly Semitic physical features, as well as cultural traits "that distinguish them sharply from their neighbors."[53] It seems that the Zimbabwe complex accounts for much African influence in Madagascar. Kent suggests that the Shona-like pottery discovered in southeastern Madagascar, dated circa 1100 ACE, may be "the indication of a terminal human migration of people or peoples familiar with some features of the Zimbabwe culture. Much later, no doubt, links between old Rhodesia and Madagascar proved to be both familiar and useful to the gold–bearing proto-Maroseràna."[54]

One can establish a parallel between these hypotheses and the opinion of Wilmot, who states, "Moguedchou (Mozambique) was founded about 930 years after Christ, and there seems little doubt that the political establishment of Arabs at Sofala can be shown to have taken place about 1100," in fact during the supposed period of Ihàrana settlement.[55] Most of the evidence thus suggests that the origin of some of the Malagasy dynasty could be connected with the Arab world, through Africa, since ancient times.[56] The White king myth, as well as the notion that dynastic change in Madagascar was imposed by a foreign culture, can be explained by repeated waves of Moorish migrations to "the Great Island."[57]

While questionable, there are some interesting analogies between the Lemba of Venda and Zimbabwe who claim a Jewish origin and the Malagasy group descending from the Antalaotra, particularly with respect to the prestige conferred by divination and medicine, which differentiates them from their neighbors, and the tradition of their being White men. A small group of Onjàtsy, to the north of Vohemar, who claims an Arab origin, has a reputation as *ombiasy* (priest-doctors) and *mpisikidy* (diviners) that strikingly recalls the characteristic activities of the Lemba such as tradition and the earliest observers recorded them.[58] Tudor Parfitt, who recently studied the Hebrew or Jewish identity of the Lemba, suggested that the Arab traders of the Sofala hinterland known as Amwenye Vashava could probably be the ancestors of the Mwenye or the present-day Lemba.[59] There are various indications that the red-skinned Mwenye traders occupied the northern part of today's Zimbabwe around the fourteenth century. There is also substantial evidence that these Mwenye were present at the Court of Monomotapa and that they formed a political entity.[60] In advancing connections between Madagascar and Zimbabwe, it is possible to imagine that the original ancestors of the Antalaotra could be these Mwenye Arabs who could have come from Zimbabwe to Madagascar. This hypothesis suggests that the Antemoro and the Lemba, who both reveal substantial Arabian or Islamic influences, could share a common Semitic substratum. They both could have subsequently developed the basis of a characteristic identity and religious system, during which time they lost the instructions of the Quran, but maintained certain traditions. However this hypothesis, which suggests connections between some Malagasy ruling clans and the Lemba, calls for further research, and can nowhere substantiate any single-origin or monolithic theory of the Malagasy past.

Most of the evidence thus suggests that the past of such groups as the Lemba in southern Africa or the Antemoro descendants in Madagascar are connected with the Arab world. What of the impact of all this on the Malagasy themselves? The religious traditions that have shaped contemporary Malagasy cosmologies and social practice, Islamic culture, taken to that island by traders and immigrants since at least the tenth century, have had a profound impact throughout Madagascar. The influence is well documented in the case of theories and practices such as divination, destiny, temporal and spatial categories, and in the sacred manuscripts of the Antemoro of the southeast. Today, the Islamic elements have become local Malagasy cultural practice and Islam is overtly practiced as a religion only in some Islamized communities, mostly in the northwestern province.

But there are also suggestions that earlier immigrants from Yemen could have been associated with the afore-mentioned Muslim followers of Said ibn Ali, constituting altogether the Moorish people, a kind of Judaic Arabic people, described by historians and missionaries. These few hypotheses suggest that, since ancient times, there could have been links between southern Arabia and the southeast coast of Africa, including Madagascar. Since pre-Islamic time, Arab Hebrew or Judaized Arab merchants could have migrated to the shores of Africa for trade, then, after the arrival of the Prophet, for religious, political, or economic reasons.

Certain parts of this saga of origin do suggest a Semitic ancestry that could be rooted in historical experience. We know that the fertile oasis of Yathrib in Arabia had been settled by Jews organized in tribes who formed the majority of the population and who, under Muhammad, were forced to sell their properties and leave the area. Thereafter, the history of those Arab Jews, who felt constrained to leave their oases, was perhaps linked with the Islamization of the east coast of Africa and of the shores of Madagascar by the Arabs. The Descendants of David appropriated these historical elements that serve the particular vision of their origins, and they consider that they are the descendants of the Jewish tribes subjugated or expelled by Muhammad. Their explanations abundantly refer to this by establishing numerous connections with Medina and southern Yemen. Mr. B. stresses that a clue to the origins of his clan, the Tavaratra, must be the names of two lakes near Sandravanany, Lake Erian and Lake Esazalan, whose names are similar to the name of cities of the southern coast of Yemen, Ar Riyan and As Said Azzan. Thus a Sabean or Yemenite involvement and influence in southeast Africa might have been possible. This seems to be confirmed by the recent genetic investigations carried out on the Lemba that suggest an extra-African origin, without entirely allowing us to distinguish between Jewish and Arab Semitic ancestry. Is the selection of a Jewish ancestry by some Malagasy a mirror of a particular characteristic of some clans in precolonial times? Or is it the reflection of some Semitic influence from Arabia or Africa centuries before? Or is it the result of interventions by outsiders? The eminently malleable accounts of lineage developed by the myths of origins of some Malagasy individuals are anchored in the earliest historical hypotheses on the migrations of Semites and Jews in Africa.

Today there are only limited echoes of the Malagasy secret and those who claim to know it appear somehow as crypto-Jews. If these Malagasy take pride in their Jewish heritage, there is no leader among them, nor any institution dedicated to promoting this identity. Up to now, these Malagasy individuals do not seem to have connections with other African Jewish organizations and movements, whether in Africa or elsewhere in the world. Moreover, the Descendants of David have been widely ignored up to now, by Jews in general and by lost tribes' research associations. Nor have they been subjected to any ethnographic study about Judaism. What does the future hold? As seen for the other African Judaizing movements, missionary activity, Jewish or Christian, as well as the activities of researchers, may well encourage cultural innovation or development. With the exodus and recognition of the Ethiopian Jews and their departure to Israel, with the recent rise of Judaizing communities throughout Africa, and with the impact of globalization and the spread of the Internet, it will be interesting to see how this latent Jewish identity might evolve once outside forces make their impact felt.

Notes

1. See Bruder, *Black Jews of Africa.*
2. The primary material of this section was taken from private archives collected between 1970 and 2003 by Katherine Quanbeck, to whom I am grateful for access to these documents.
3. Quanbeck Archives, Individuals' Discourses No 28, Que de Neuf, Antananarivo, August 1999.
4. Quanbeck Archives, Individuals' Discourses No 46, Mr. B. Faradofay, 2000.
5. Alfred Grandidier, *Histoire physique, naturelle et politique de Madagascar* (Paris: Imprimerie Nationale, 1908), vol. 1, part 1, 127–128.
6. The best documented example of this kind of process is the way Protestantism came to be regarded as a truly Malagasy ancestral tradition in the Highlands in the nineteenth century. See Françoise Raison-Jourde, *Bible et pouvoir à Madagascar au XIX è siècle. Invention d'une identité chrétienne et construction de l'état (1780–1880)* (Paris: Kartahala, 1991).
7. Etienne de Flacourt, *Histoire de la grande île de Madagascar* (Paris: A. Lesselin,1658), 3-4.
8. François Martin, manuscript in the Archives Nationales, 1668, p. 311.
9. Grandidier, *Histoire,* vol. 4, part 1, 96–103, quotation on pp. 405–406.
10. Ibid.
11. Quanbeck's archives, Individuals discourse, Pastor F.S., n.d.
12. Alfred Gevrey, *Essai sur les îles Comores* (Pondichéry: A. Saligny, 1870), 79.
13. Augustus E. H. Keane, *The Gold of Ophir, Whence Brought and by Whom ?* (London: Stanford, 1901), 151.
14. Ibid.
15. Joseph Briand, *L'Hébreu à Madagascar* (Tananarive: Pitot de la Beaujardière, 1946), 13, 8–10. The analysis of language has been widely used in Madagascar to determine where the first Malagasy came from. See Augustus H. Keane, "The Himyarites in Rhodesia and in Madagascar," *The Atheneoeum,* April 5, 1902, 435; Etienne de Flacourt, *Dictionnaire de la langue de Madagascar* (Paris: G. Josse, 1658), Gabriel Ferrand, *L'Élément arabe et swahili en malgache ancien et moderne* (Paris: Imprimerie Nationale, 1904).
16. English contributions have been published in *Antananarivo Annual.* See also Bonar A. Gow, *Madagascar and the Protestant Impact: The Work of the British Missions 1815–1855* (London: Longman, 1979). The first Norwegian Protestant missionaries arrived in 1866, the North Americans followed in 1888 and have remained there since. The presence of French Catholic missionaries during the same period led to the establishment of Christian churches, generating

ethnographic knowledge through their regular reports on local customs. On Norwegian missionaries, see Finn Fuglestad, *Norwegian Missions in African History,* ed. Jarle Simensen (New York: Oxford University Press, 1986), vol. 2; among French missionaries, R. P. Callet is known for having written the royal traditions of the *"Tantaran'ny Andriana"* (History of the Kings), ed. G. S. Chapus and E. Ratsimba (Tananarive: Académie Malgache, 1958).

17. Rev. J. Cameron, "On the Early Inhabitants of Madagascar,"*Antananarivo Annual* 3 (1877): 257–265.
18. James Sibree, *The Great African Island: Chapters on Madagascar, A Popular Account of Recent Researches in the Physical Geography, Geology, and Explorations of the Country and Its Natural History* (London: Trübner, 1880), quotations p. 108 and p. 425.
19. S. Zaborowski, "A propos des Baras et des Malgaches à cheveux crépus," *Bulletins et Mémoires de la Société d'Anthropologie de Paris,* vol. 8, 4 (1907): 398–399.
20. Quanbeck Archives, Individual Discourses, Pastor S. no date.
21. Flacourt gives a Malagasy version of the history of the Deluge: Flacourt, *Histoire de la Grande Île,* 1661, 58 ff. See also the Malagasy version by Rajaonarimanana of the "Prophet Noah the Red." Narivelo Rajaonarimanana, *Savoirs Arabico-malgaches: La tradition des devins Antemoro, Anakara* (Paris: Inalco, 1990), 169 ff. See also the texts gathered and studied by Noël J. Gueunier, "La Genèse de l'Homme Blanc. Récits d'origine du Sud-Ouest de Madagascar," *Etudes Océan Indien* 15 (1992): 227–259.
22. To summarize a vast amount of anthropological and ethnographic data, one can say that the Malagasy people are a mixture of African and Indonesian stock, with the African element predominating. However they speak an essentially Indonesian language and possess a culture that probably owes more to Indonesia than to Africa, but that contains many elements common to both areas of origin. What is more surprising is that the first human occupation in Madagascar did not take place until some time after the beginning of the Common Era. The language clearly belongs to the family of Indonesian and Polynesian languages, as the grammar and structure are 100 percent and its vocabulary 80 percent identical, with the remainder being mainly Bantu, but also Arabic, French, English, and Sanskrit. See Mervyn Brown, *Madagascar Rediscovered* (London: D. Tunnaclife, 1978), chapter 2; on the various hypotheses and assertions about the origins of the Malagasy people see Hubert Deschamps, *Histoire de Madagascar* (Paris: Berger-Levrault, 1960), 24–30, 39–59.
23. On Phoenician migrations, see Antoine Court de Gebelin, *Le Monde Primitif* (1773–1782), vol. 1, 52, 583, 553 Also I. Guet, *Les origines de l'Ile Bourbon et de la colonisation française à Madagascar* (Paris: L. Baudoin, 1885), 34 ff. Grandidier sees in the Malagasy, apart from their Semitic origin, Papuans and eastern Blacks, mixed with Indonesians. See Grandidier, *Histoire,* vol. 4, part 1, 16–71. Malayo-Polynesian and Malagasy customs were frequently compared; see, e.g., Robert S. Codrington, "Resemblances between Malagasy Words and Customs and Those of Western Polynesia,"*Antananarivo Annual* 2 (1882): 122–127. Razafintsalama evoked Buddhist missionaries who came from a vanished island where a Malagasy language, based on Sanskrit, would have been formed; J. B. Razafintsalama, *Le bouddhisme malgache ou la civilisation*

malgache: Essai d'analyse et de reconstruction historique (Tananarive, 1939). Ferrand imagined arrivals of Bantus followed by Hinduized Indonesians who came from Sumatra, mixed with Arab and Persian migrations. See Gabriel Ferrand, *Essai des phonétiques comparées du malais et des dialectes malgaches* (Paris: Geuthner, 1909).

24. Grandidier, *Histoire,* vol. 4, part 1, 105, who quoted the chronicles of Mogadiscio, Baroua, and the islands of Oungouya (Zanzibar) and of the Great Comoro.
25. Ibid., 107–108.
26. Gabriel Ferrand, "Les migrations musulmanes et juives à Madagascar," *Revue de l'Histoire des Religions* 1, tome 52 (1905): 381–417.
27. Ibid., 401–402.
28. *Exploraçao Portugueza de Madagascar em 1613. Relaçao Inedita de Padre Luiz Mariano, in Boletim da Soc. de Geog. de Lisboa* (1887), 3, II, 6, trans. into French by Alfred and Guillaume Grandidier, *Collection des Ouvrages Anciens de Madagascar,* tome 2 (Paris: Comité de Madagascar1904).
29. Today some 45 percent of Malagasy are said to be Christians, divided more or less between Catholics and Protestants. The Christian influence is far from homogeneous throughout the island. See Gillian Feeley-Harnik, "Madagascar: Religious Systems," in *Encyclopaedia of Africa South of the Sahara,* ed. J. Middleton (New York: Scribner's, 1997), vol. 3, 88–89.
30. Consequently, in order to avoid generalizing data or taking them out of their context, I shall cite observations from an individual or from a fragment of society without attempting to extend them to an entire ethnic group.
31. The societies and communities of Madagascar appear to be extremely diversified among themselves between social orders and suborders, ancestral differences, and subtle divisions; see, e.g., Paul Ottino, *Les Champs de l'Ancestralité à Madagascar* (Paris: Karthala et Orstom, 1998). The Zafiraminia antedates the Antemoro in Madagasacar by at least two centuries. Flacourt observed that two parallel societies existed among the Antanosy, White and Black, the former being Zafiraminia and the latter known collectively as *marinh*. Flacourt; *Histoire de la Grande Île,* vol. 8, 25–27; Grandidier, *Histoire,* vol. 1, part 1, 130–131 and notes.
32. On the Antalaotra, see Grandidier, *Histoire,* vol. 4, part 1, 75–87, 157–165; Brown, *Madagascar,* 21–22; Raymond Kent, *Early Kingdoms in Madagascar,* 1500–1700 (New York: Holt, Rinehart and Winston, 1970), 92, 323; Deschamps, *Histoire de Madagascar,* 44; A. Jully, "Origine des Andriana ou nobles," *Notes, Reconnaissances et Explorations* 4 (1898): 890–898, who considers that all of the Malagasy royal dynasties derive from Arab families.
33. Brown, *Madagascar,* 23–24; Kent, *Early Kingdoms,* 110–111.
34. Charles Poirier, "Terre d'Islam en Mer Malgache," *Bulletin de l'Académie Malgache,* special issue (1954) : 71–116; Deschamps, *Histoire de Madagascar,* 55; J. Faublée, *L'Ethnologie de Madagascar* (Paris: Maison neuve, 1946).
35. Grandidier, *Histoire,* vol. 4, tome 1, 130–131, 139, 141–142; Kent, *Early Kingdoms,* 102–103; A. Mouren and R. Rouaix, " Industrie Ancienne des Objets en Pierre de Vohemar," *Bulletin de l'Académie Malgache* 12, no 2 (1913): 3–13 of reprinted edition; also P. Gaudebout and R. Vernier, "Notes sur une Campagne de Fouilles à Vohemar," *Bulletin de l'Académie Malgache* 24 (1941): 91–114.

36. On the Antemoro and the *Sorabé,* see Grandidier, *Histoire,* vol. 4, tome 1, 124–127, 143–157, 202–205; Kent, *Early Kingdoms,* chap. 3, "The Anteimoro". See also Gustave Mondain, *L'Histoire des Tribus de l'Imoro au XVII è siècle d'après un manuscrit arabico-malgache* (Paris: Leroux, 1910).
37. Kent, *Early Kingdoms,* 109.
38. Brown, *Madagascar,* 23–4; Kent, *Early Kingdoms,* 110–111.
39. Enrico Cerulli, *Somalia, scritti vari editi ed inediti,* vol. 1 (1957), 3.
40. Kent, *Early Kingdoms,* 109.
41. Deschamps, *Histoire de Madagascar,* 57–58.
42. *Commentarios de Afonso d'Albuquerque* (1576), in Grandidier, *Collection,* vol. 1, 18.
43. Barros, *Da Asia* (Decade II), in Grandidier, *Collection,* vol. 1, 24, and (Decade III), vol. 1, 53.
44. Brown, *Madagascar,* 26. About the Sakalava, the inhabitants of this region, see Kent, *Early Kingdoms,* 160–204.
45. Eric Axelson, *Portuguese in South-East Africa, 1600–1700* (Johannesburg: Witwatersrand University Press 1960), 5, 37.
46. On Maroseràna, see Raymond Kent, "The Sakalava, Maroserana, Dady and Tromba before 1700," *Journal of African History* 9, no. 4 (1963): 517–546.
47. Grandidier, *Histoire,* vol. 4, tome 1, 6–7, and note 2; Kent, *Early Kingdoms,* chap. 1.
48. Grandidier claimed that Antemoro were Arabs from Arabia but considered that they could have reached Madagascar by way of East Africa instead of a direct route. Grandidier, *Histoire,* vol. 1, tome 1, 143–157, notes; in the 1917 edition, vol. 4, 508. See also Ferrand, "Migrations Musulmanes," vol. 1, 114; and Kent, *Early Kingdoms,* 167.
49. Flacourt, *Histoire de la Grande Île,* vol. 8, 40.
50. Brown, *Madagascar,* 27.
51. Andrew Anderson, *Twenty-Five Years in a Wagon in the Gold Regions of Africa* (London, 1887), ii, 144, quoted in Parfitt, *Journey to the Vanished City,* 102.
52. Brown, *Madagascar,* 27; R. Oliver and G. Mathew, *A Short History of East Africa* (London: Oxford University Press, 1963), vol. 1, 110.
53. George P. Murdock, *Africa, Its People and Their Culture History* (New York: McGraw-Hill, 1959), 387; see also James G. Frazer, *The Native Races of Africa and Madagascar* (London: Lund, Humphries, 1938), 14–16.
54. Kent, *Early Kingdoms,* 254–255. Also, Roland Oliver, "Discernible Developments in the Interior ca. 1500–1840" in *History of East Africa,* vol. 1, 191–192.
55. Alexander Wilmot, *Monomotapa: Its monuments and Its History.* (London: Fisher Unwin, 1896), 110.
56. Linguistic, ethnographic and historical material cannot however be compressed into this preliminary work; parallels between Shona/Venda culture and the Antemoro should be the subject of further investigations.
57. Kent, *Early Kingdoms,* 12–18, 20–22.
58. Brown, *Madagascar,* 22; Kent, *Early Kingdoms,* 92–93.
59. Parfitt, *Journey to the Vanished City,* 241, 290–291, 314.
60. Ibid.

PART III

DISCOURSES OF RACIAL AND ETHNIC IDENTITIES

CHAPTER 11

After the Fact

"Jews" in Post-1945 German Physical Anthropology

Amos Morris-Reich

This chapter focuses on discourse about "Jews" in writings by German physical anthropologists between the collapse of Nazi Germany in 1945 and the beginning of the 1990s. Physical anthropology is arguably the discipline most strongly associated with the idea of race.[1] A basic tension can be discerned that pertains to two aspects of the wider history of German physical anthropology. First, physical anthropology was (and still is) a field not only intimately associated with scientific writing on race but is practically founded on the concept of race; and, second, the discussion of Jews as a racial group was integral to the science of physical anthropology before 1945 but taboo in Germany after that date. It is important, however, for comprehension of the bigger picture, to point out that after 1945 this scientific discipline no longer fed into public discourse in the political sphere, and particularly in the context of a discussion of discursive representations of "the Jew," that there was virtually a complete separation between the figure of the "Jew" and the individuals who identify themselves or who identify as Jewish.

To properly understand writing on Jews after 1945 in German anthropology, it is necessary to appreciate the changes that occurred in the scientific status of this discipline. It is also necessary to suspend the kind of ontological questions actually addressed by physical anthropologists themselves, such as the nature of race, types, or human diversity, and focus rather on describing the changes in the way Jews were addressed and represented. Put another way, in this chapter I am more interested in a practical-epistemic description of "Jews" in the discourse of German physical anthropologists than in criticism or judgment. The nature of these descriptions was tied to the changing status of physical anthropology from its inception to the present. In this sense, the changing status of the discipline itself is crucial. The status of the science was enhanced steadily between the last third of the nineteenth century, when physical anthropology was primarily a science practiced by societies of amateurs, and the beginning of the twentieth century, when the first professorships in German universities were established.[2] With the professionalization of the field and the standardization of its techniques and methods, physical anthropology reached the peak of its scientific prestige in the Weimar and Nazi periods before it was gradually but steadily succeeded by human genetics. In Germany, the differentiation process between physical anthropology and human genetics was long. Both physical anthropology and human genetics were intricately involved in Nazi ideology and Nazi members of the profession implicated in Nazi crimes. German human genetics differentiated itself gradually from physical anthropology in the second and third decades of the twentieth century, and today enjoys immense scientific prestige, while from today's standpoint many view physical anthropology as essentially flawed scientifically.

The history of the discipline of physical anthropology as a science, however, cannot be separated from the abrupt cultural developments that occurred after 1945. Academic fields of knowledge hitherto closely associated with race divided after 1945 and, gradually, came to be fixed culturally as either legitimate (genetics) or essentially flawed and illegitimate (*Rassenkunde,* or racial lore). This cultural-semiotic separation is essential for understanding post-1945 developments, but, as will become apparent, it is also essentially anachronistic. My analysis is fixed on the signifier "Jews" and several other closely associated signifiers such as "Near Eastern," "Armenoid," and "Semitic." It is important that the reader take my analysis as understood that the signifier can never be fully separated from the historical referent, and vice versa.

Since the present volume focuses on the unstable comparative context of Jews, race, and color across several national and historical contexts, I will emphasize two aspects of this wider context at the outset: color and the relationship between race and anti-Semitism. To begin, and to be fairly straightforward, color, the quintessential category in the North American context, is of far less importance in the German context in general and in the context of physical anthropology in particular. A more complex historical and methodological point, however, pertains to the relationship between the sciences of race (in particular physical anthropology) and anti-Semitism. A comprehensive discussion of the relationship between the two transcends the framework of this chapter. But for our purposes, it is necessary to point to the basic historical difficulty that underwrites the post-1945 period.

On the one hand, it is necessary to acknowledge that, before 1918 (at the earliest) there was no strong connection between physical anthropology and anti-Semitism. Between the second half of the nineteenth century and the end of World War I, Jews were indeed an integrative object of scientific study and as such garnered a significant amount of research, but scientific views on their racial nature differed greatly. Within the many positions that were held, central opinions include the early view that the Jews were a pure race, a belief supported by both Jewish and non-Jewish writers, and the later view that, similar to many other peoples, Jews were racially a heterogeneous population—also a view sustained by both Jewish and non-Jewish writers. Thus, although both the scientific objectives and the political outlooks of writers were different, before 1918 there is no way to reduce the anthropological discourse to either explicit or hidden anti-Semitic motivations. Up to the end of World War I, physical anthropological literature did not cite anti-Semitic works, and in discursive terms the physical anthropological and the anti-Semitic discourses were to a great extent separate. In fact, the most prominent physical anthropologists in Germany—from the founding giant of the field, Rudolf Virchow, through Rudolf Martin, who standardized the field's methods and techniques, to prominent Berlin anthropologist Felix von Luschan—were politically liberal and outspoken opponents of political anti-Semitism.

On the other hand, race forms the specific feature of modern anti-Semitism. From the first decades of the twentieth century, arguably every anti-Semitic statement or utterance was explicitly or implicitly founded on the notion of race. Because physical anthropology was practically identical with the study of race and was associated with race more than was any other scientific field, there is therefore a complex network of connections between physical anthropology and modern anti-Semitism. While they are not identical, it is impossible, nevertheless, to comprehensively differentiate between the racialization of Jews (in which anthropology and anthropological notions played a key role) and anti-Semitic views. In the German context, it is only after the German defeat in World War I that anthropology and anti-Semitism converged gradually, and even then not without significant exceptions. This convergence was further enhanced during the Nazi period. Somewhat ironically, therefore, after 1945 the field as a whole was politically identified with nationalist tendencies and recognized as closely associated with anti-Semitic strains.

With Germany's defeat, and a long time before the ramifications of the murder of the Jews of Europe sunk into German consciousness, a social taboo was placed on the public discussion of Jewish—and, in particular, Jewish biological—difference. But physical anthropology as a science pretty much immediately recommenced its scientific career. Because Jews disappeared almost entirely from the German physical anthropological discourse, it is necessary to resort to historical and sometimes almost literary strategies in order to study the clash between continuing racial discussions and new taboos. I will examine writers who tackled this situation by looking at practical decisions they had to make regarding the use of historically tainted anthropological materials, references from blatantly anti-Semitic authors, and the use of older statistical tables in which Jews were classified as a racial entity. As a rule, the taboo held most strongly on the discussion of the Jews of Europe (that is, of citizens of European states). But the clash in the post World War II years between continued anthropological writing on Jews, on the one hand, and the taboo on discussion of Jews on the other, led to the development of various strategies by means of which Jews were excluded from discussion, racialized representation of the state of Israel replaced discussion of as such, and discussion of Jewish racial difference continued only in veiled form.

The Two Contexts of Physical Anthropology

I will focus on an anthropological genealogy known as the Breslauer School, the most important physical anthropological paradigm in post-1945 Germany. But before turning to this school I will contextualize physical anthropology in two separate but interrelated contexts, the scientific-political and the inner-scientific. Conceptually, post–World War II German physical anthropology emerged from the war to a great extent unharmed. The crisis was less Kuhnian or epistemic than it was social and political. Indeed, one of my central arguments is that between 1945 and the early 1990s there was a growing divergence between physical anthropological writing on race and the social and political responses that such writing generated.

The social and political significance of physical anthropology changed dramatically after 1945. In order to clarify the nature of this change it is necessary to dwell briefly on the situation between 1918 and 1945, when physical anthropology was highly politicized. In the first half of the twentieth century, and in particular after Germany's defeat in World War I when its aggressive aspiration for domination in Europe and competition with the colonial powers remained intact, and until the total collapse of Nazi Germany, physical anthropology increasingly addressed questions that had social and political implications. This occurred in the wider context of scientific discussions of race that appeared to suggest scientific solutions to social and political questions. Between 1918 and 1945, major sectors in German society perceived race as a scientific category with explicit social-political implications. That is, in terms that were introduced by Austrian American historian of science Mitchell Ash, science served as a resource for politics.[3] The scientific study of race became linked to German political and military ambitions. Scientific descriptions of physical differences had implicit if not overt political ramifications. With the Nazi Party's ascendancy to power in 1933, these tendencies intensified. Race was the basic component of Nazi philosophy and ideology, and for this reason Nazi Germany has been described as "the racial state."[4] In this latter period, the scientific discourse on race became part and parcel of the political order and the political leadership drew legitimacy, in both its domestic and foreign policies, from the scientific category of race. Anthropologists were deeply involved in activities that had immediate political ramifications and lent the regime their direct scientific prestige.

Germany's total military defeat and occupation by foreign forces in 1945 crushed its colonial and hegemonic ambitions. During the occupation (1945–1949), every publication had to pass through the vigilant eyes of foreign censors. The relationship between the new government and the sciences that dealt with race was now reconfigured. Anthropology, as well as other fields that studied race, became politically marginal. Race was no longer considered as a key to hegemonic aspirations or national superiority because all political and military ambitions had been leveled. The result was that racist or anti-Semitic statements made by anthropologists now had different social and moral implications. But it is important to stress that this did not mean that scientific belief systems associated with race were necessarily undermined. The discontinuity in racial studies in postwar Germany has far more to do with the relationship between science and society or science and politics than it does with any epistemic dimension of the scientific study of race.

According to German historian of anthropology Uwe Hoßfeld, the continuity between pre-1945 and postwar anthropology was strong conceptually, personally, and institutionally.[5] Anthropologists and geneticists who had been active in the Nazi period (von Verschuer, Heberer, Gieseler, Lenz, and others) gained academic positions in West

Germany, albeit on occasion only after several years of unemployment. They continued to publish and receive academic recognition in both Germany and the international community. In retrospect, postwar racial writing on Jews has been closely related to Germany's coming to terms with its past. In the history of West Germany, 1968 is commonly perceived as the public beginning of the reexamination of the past. In science, however, this process commenced at different moments in the different disciplines. By its nature, the process of reexamination has inevitably been accompanied by internal conflicts between the scientists and their former teachers, a discord not immediately apparent in scientific texts unless one is aware of their social contexts. In Austria, in the field of physical anthropology, this point was reached when a public outcry forced the Natural History Museum to remove its permanent exhibition entitled "The Family of Man" in 1993.[6] Physical anthropology in Germany arrived at its day of reckoning when the Anthropological Institute at the Free University was closed down and its materials moved to the Center for the Study of Anti-Semitism—that is, when materials formerly classified as scientific were socially reclassified as belonging to the phenomenon of German anti-Semitism. Some disciplines, such as *Rassenkunde* and racial phenomenology, disappeared altogether. But tracing this process is a complicated business because social and institutional histories tend not to correspond to conceptual history. Although a general context is necessary for understanding the process, the reader should also keep in mind that racial writing on the Jews is not necessarily the same as coming to terms with the past.[7]

Certain constraints can be observed in this period, such as the incongruities in published works on race and Jews. Most prominent scientists who dealt with race in the Weimar and Nazi periods, such as Eickstedt, von Verschuer, and Fischer, continued to write, but no longer discussed the Jews. When Verschuer was accorded scientific recognition, for example, his anti-Semitic publications were omitted from his bibliography.[8] In private correspondence, however, Fischer, Wolfgang Abel, Eickstedt, or Verschuer made no bones as to their unchanged views on Jews.[9]

Anthropologists and biologists rewrote the history of their discipline and attempted to distance themselves from those whom they now viewed as Nazi ideologues. Most important in this context was the attempts of anthropologists and geneticists to distance themselves from the notion of the so-called master race (the *Herrenrasse*). But this should not be confused with the deconstruction of the scientific belief in validity of the notion of race, the existence of distinct races, or the scientific importance of racial difference. Wilhelm Mühlmann,

Karl Saller, Ilse Schwidetzky, and Peter Emil Becker produced apologetic histories. Mühlmann claimed that Hans F. K. Günther, the most prominent racial writer in Weimar and Nazi Germany, was not an anthropologist but a philologist.[10] Some of the postwar German authors appropriated the term "pseudoscience" from their opponents in the 1920s and 1930s.[11] By employing this term they hoped to distinguish their own purely scientific work from that of the pseudoscientific Nazi ideologues. Mühlmann's new history described the racial sciences as the first victim of the Nazi regime.[12] Becker's *Wege ins Dritte Reich* raised what would become a familiar trope in Germany, appearing well into the late 1990s, namely, that arguments relating to the "Jewish" difference (*Andersartigkeit*—literally, belonging to a different species or form) were scientific observations that did not necessarily contain political or anti-Semitic undertones.[13]

A West German line of demarcation separated the racial scientists from the Nazi ideologues. However, even writers whose involvement in Nazi policies and ideology was undeniable, and whom the Allies barred from teaching, continued writing and attempted to reposition themselves on the side of legitimate science. Although the cultural code now made taboo any discussion of Jews within the general discourse of race, such discussions nevertheless continued. The demarcation line is semiotically indispensable for understanding German society's confrontation with its postwar present.

The Breslau–Mainz school of Physical Anthropology and the Jews from Weimar to West Germany

After 1945, physical anthropology in Germany became politically marginalized but remained scientifically intact and intellectually unchanged. For this reason, physical anthropology provides us with a rich source for the discrepancy between the taboo in public (including scientific) discussion of Jews in terms of race and a discourse practically founded on race. Three generations of physical anthropologists, Egon Freiherr von Eickstedt (1892–1965), Ilse Schwidetzky (1907–1997), and Rainer Knußman belong to a single school of racial anthropology, which lasted from the 1910s to the 1990s. Eickstedt was the supervisor of Schwidetzky, his assistant and successor in Mainz. Knußman, one of Schwidetzky's leading disciples, became a professor of anthropology at the University of Hamburg.

According to a recent historical interpretation, Eickstedt's school in fact enjoyed more prominence after 1945 than it did during the Weimar or Nazi periods.[14] Whereas in the Weimar and Nazi periods Eickstedt held a professorship in a peripheral German university and did not number among the leaders of the field, after 1945 his centrality grew and his student and successor Schwidetzky became for many years the most prominent physical anthropologist in Germany and, as one of the most prominent female scientists in postwar Germany, somewhat of a cultural idol.

Eickstedt, the founder of the Breslau–Mainz school of racial anthropology, studied and worked with Felix von Luschan and Eugen Fischer in Vienna's Natural History Museum and Munich's Academy of Science before obtaining an academic post in Breslau in 1929, where he was awarded a habilitation degree in 1930 and a teaching post in 1933. His racial classification system relied heavily on Hans Günther's typology. Günther was the most influential racial writer in Weimar and Nazi Germany; after 1945 his name became the epitome in Germany for corrupt and politicized science. Eickstedt's request to join the Nazi Party was turned down, but he worked closely with the Nazi Party's political office, penning reviews for the *Reichssippenamt* (Reich kinship office), and in disputed cases determining whether individuals were full-fledged Jews, half-Jews, or quarter-Jews. He also lent scientific support to the official National Socialist view on the Jewish question.[15] In 1934, he published *Rassenkunde und Rassengeschichte der Menscheit* (racial lore and a racial history of humanity). Eickstedt borrowed from Günther the basic typology of European races and the methodological differentiation between *Volk* and *Rasse*, although he inverted their relationship. During the Third Reich, Eickstedt undertook a major anthropological study of the racial profile of the population in Upper Silesia, a region that had been politically contested by Germans and Poles for a long time.[16] Here Eickstedt tried to prove the presence of Nordic racial traits that would qualify the population for Germanization.[17]

In 1946 Eickstedt fled Breslau (East Germany) and obtained a position at the University of Mainz. The following year he exploited the rejection of his request for membership in the Nazi Party by claiming that he had never been close to the Party or its ideology. As with Otmar von Verschuer, his scientific rival in the Nazi period, Eickstedt warned of the Jewish threat in terms of *Überfremdung* (an anti-Semitic term that means the threatening penetration of foreign racial elements). But as was also the case with other academic racial authors who did not deny their views after the war, Eickstedt wrote in 1959, "[R]acial madness developed not out of racial studies or racial knowledge, but out of racial ignorance" (*Rassenunwissen*).[18] After 1945, his works make no mention of the Jews. Nevertheless, a direct line runs from Eickstedt to Schwidetzky and Knußman, with whom such statements resurface. This link allows us to consider the persistence of certain unstated beliefs.

One will search in vain for evidence that Eickstedt or Schwidetzky altered their racial beliefs after 1945. But certain semantic adaptations to the new political era are visible. The term "race" was replaced by *Völkerbiologie* (population biology) until the early 1960s. Eickstedt retitled the revised and enlarged edition of the (Racial study and racial history of humanity), *Forschung am Menschen* (Research on man). The *Journal of Racial Studies* was rechristened *Homo* in 1949 and became the official journal of the Deutsche Gesellschaft für Völkerkunde (German Anthropological Association).[19] Less than two decades after the end of World War II, however, Schwidetzky announced that the time was ripe to readdress the problem of human races with "a new racial studies" ("Neue Rassenkunde").[20]

Shortly after Eickstedt's appointment in Breslau, Schwidetzky became his assistant and close associate. Under his supervision, in 1934 Schwidetzky completed her dissertation on the Polish national movement in Upper Silesia between 1825 and 1914. She was granted a habilitation in 1937 for her racial treatise on ancient Slavs. Schwidetzky frequently contributed racist and anti-Semitic articles to Eickstedt's journal *Rassenkunde*.[21] When Eickstedt left for Mainz, he invited her to work with him. In 1961, she succeeded her mentor as head of the anthropological institute, gaining wide recognition in the following years. Schwidetzky published in the English-language journal *The Mankind Quarterly* and other journals considered racist. She became part of an international network of racist scientists. As one of the most prominent female academics in West Germany, she was seen as the matriarch of German physical anthropology. Only in 1980, on the eve of being granted an academic award in France, did controversy erupt into student protests over her affiliation with the Nazi Party.[22]

French historian of science Benoit Massin criticizes Schwidetzky's history of racial studies for its flagrant historical errors and blatant falsifications regarding the discipline's role in the Nazi period, especially concerning her own institute's legal-anthropological involvement in the racial evaluation of individuals. But more interesting even than this is Schwidetzky's discussion of Jews in her 1950 book *Grundzüge der Völkerbiologie*). Here she focuses on the analysis of wandering as *Wanderbiologie* (a biological phenomenon), mentioning Jews numerous times, for example, in discussion of the Babylonian Exile[23] and in her assessment that a number three or four times bigger than the current population size of the Jews had been assimilated by their *Wirtsvölkern* (the untranslatable term for host-peoples)[24]—a term with explicit anti-Semitic connotations.[25] She also discussed the extinction of peoples, claiming that the selection processes introduced with the Europeanization of the world brought about the extinction of some peoples but led to the increase in the number of others.[26] Hence, while including Jews within her account of wider biological tendencies, she was careful to avoid mention of their more recent historical fate.

Far more interesting for our purposes, however, are decisions made with regard to the representation of Jews in the series *Rassengeschichte der Menschheit* (The racial history of humanity), which she founded, edited, and to which she contributed. The title of the series indicates that the project is an extension of Eickstedt's theory. This strategy meant that the editors and writers of articles had to cope with the conflict between the old system of classification and the new taboo.

The multivolume series in German, English, and French was generally arranged geographically according to nation-states. In most of the countries covered, including those in West Europe and the Americas, Jews, despite their typological classification, were omitted from discussion and passed over as a distinct racial category. Nonetheless, in at least three cases they were mentioned as a separate subpopulation: Germany, Tunisia, and Ukraine.[27] In the case of Tunisia, the article notes that Jews arrived in 1492 and lived there until the establishment of the state of Israel. In the case of the Ukraine a practical decision had to be made, as the article was based on older statistics in which Jews were separately classified. The solution finally opted for was that Jews were not discussed in the article, but were kept in the statistical table. Hence, without being referred to in the text, they remained in a separate statistical category.

Schwidetzky briefly discussed the Jews in her essay on Germany.[28] Rather than referring to them directly, however, she noted their absence in the course of a single brief paragraph that dealt with the evolutionary tendencies of selection. Here she admitted that the impact of the Jewish people's annihilation on the German psyche was still unknown. In this way she alluded to Jewish racial difference while eschewing a full-fledged academic discussion of it.

The most comprehensive discussion on the Jews in this series is in the section dealing with the state of Israel, which appears in Wolfram Bernhard's 1993 volume on Southwest Asia.[29] This choice indicates that the taboo on the discussion of European Jewry did not include the Jews of Israel. The account begins after World War II and claims that, following the establishment of the state of Israel, many Jews "not only from Europe but also from Middle Eastern countries returned (*zurückgewandert*) to Israel, where today they make up the majority."[30] Bernhard emphasizes the difference between the majority of Jews in Israel, who arrived after 1948 from the various diasporas, and the minority, whose presence there has remained unbroken since biblical times.[31] Jews no longer appeared as a single metageographical category. If they were discussed, then it was either in terms of the state of Israel or as a subgroup dispersed among local populations. The discussion of Israel remained linked to historical records, and avoided anti-Semitic tropes or overtones. Descriptions of the Jewish people no longer followed the older characterizations of Eickstedt and Günther.

The effect of the taboo on the classification of the Jews may be appreciated negatively when compared to the case of the Gypsies. In his 1939 *Die Rassischen Grundlagen des Deutschen Volkes* (The racial foundations of the German people), Eickstedt ends his discussion of the German people with a quick look at *zwei Fremdvölker* (two alien peoples): Gypsies and Jews.[32] Under new constraints, but based on Eickstedt's identical classification system as well as the alleged presence of Indo-Afghanistan and Iran-Afghanistan admixtures, the discussion on Gypsies, a population predominantly found in Europe, was relegated to a non-European volume in the series, where they appeared as a separate class alongside Australian Aborigines and the Asiatic population of Indo-China.[33]

The anthropologist Rainer Knußman provides a particularly interesting case for the analysis of the tension between the post-1945 taboo and racial classification and, for want of a better formulation, what could be termed suspicion concerning the presence of certain now elusive non-stated themes, beliefs, or signifiers. Knußman's second edition (1986) of his 1980 textbook, *Vergleichende Biologie des Menschen. Ein Lehrbuch der Anthropologie und Humangenetik* (Comparative biology of humans: a textbook of anthropology and human genetics), included a short passage that sparked a public controversy that casts light not only on the relationship between the intrascientific continuity and the fissure in the sciences-politics dyad after 1945, but also on the way that certain unstated beliefs resurfaced after the appearance of the new taboo:

> Racial ideologues and racial politicians confuse race, people, and even the community of faith—as in the case of the Jews. These do not represent a worldwide race (*weltweit … einheitliche Rasse*), but some kind of specific type (*Bevölkerungstyp*) in the European context because over the centuries they lived in isolation or partial isolation, which was strengthened, inter alia, by state prohibition on marriage between Jews and non-

> Jews. Furthermore, Jews continuously suffered from persecution and legal discrimination, especially marriage limitations. Hence only certain hereditary lines (*Erblinien*) managed to persist and to assert themselves in our European societies (*unseren Europäischen Gesellschaften*). The lawgivers did not realize that it was against their interest to create a selection of optimal achievement, a Jewish elite. The predominance (*Überlegenheit*) of Jews naturally caused envy, and time and again fueled hatred of that minority.[34]

This short passage reiterates a number of anti-Semitic themes: the adverse biological selection of the Jews, which strengthens parasitical genetic strains; the fundamental racial difference separating Jews from Europeans; and the Jews' own responsibility for being hated. The passage illustrates ideas that became taboo in 1945 but could resurface forty years later, pointing to their silent persistence throughout the intervening period. Yet the scientific and political context had changed and such ideas now caused a scandal that was more social than political.[35]

A more subversive aspect of the book, however, is found in Knußman's use of photographs. At the end of all three editions of his book (1980, 1988, and 1996) is a series of photographs of racial types with titles. Knußman does not divulge the sources of the photographs, but many clearly stem from an existing repertoire. Tucked away within the series of photographs is one particular image, that of a bearded man, which is entitled "Armenider aus Kurdistan"[36] ("Armenian type from Kurdistan").[37] Only an extremely sensitive reader would discern that the photographed individual is not an Armenian but a Jew from Jerusalem. The photograph was taken by Ludwig Ferdinand Clauss and appeared as part of a series of the same individual in *Rasse und Seele* (race and soul).[38] Clauss describes the man as "Jüdischer Lastträger aus Kurdistan. Erlösungsmensch, vorderasiatische Rasse," a Jewish carrier from Kurdistan, Redemption type, Middle Eastern race.

Reclassification was, it would appear, the way to circumvent the taboo on Jews, unless Knußman made a genuine mistake or was unaware of the original context of the photograph. If indeed Knußman believed the individual was a Kurd of an Armenian type, then Jews were not represented in his gallery of racial types. In any case, this misclassified photograph exemplifies the clash between taboo and classification that characterizes German racial writing on Jews that generates a form of suspicion on behalf of the reader. As opposed to the pre-1945 period when scientific statements concerning the Jewish difference and anti-Semitic statements were publicly legitimate, in the face of new cultural and social constraints some beliefs could no longer be stated directly and could only be stated between the lines.

Conclusion

This chapter has traced post–World War II writing on Jews in the most important German paradigm of physical anthropology. The basic tension at the heart of this history is that, while conceptually physical anthropology did not undergo any significant change after 1945, a social taboo on expressly anti-Semitic statements in the public sphere emerged in West Germany, and scientific discussion of the Jewish racial difference which up until that moment had been integral and sometimes even central to the scientific discussion. The status of physical anthropology was transformed in this period, both within science and in the interface between science and society. Writing on race continued into the 1990s but the general taboo on the discussion of the Jewish body, on the one hand, and the fact that physical anthropology as a scientific discipline lost its legitimizing ground, on the other, meant that the negative stereotype of "the Jew" remained largely insignificant in public discourse. Within the scientific sphere, physical anthropology gradually lost its prestige to genetics. In a process that had already begun during the Nazi period, genetics came to be seen as the modern paradigm for the study of human diversity, and anthropology was thereby gradually reduced to the study of archeological remains.

I stated in the opening of this chapter that before 1918 the relationship between physical anthropology and anti-Semitism was complex. On the one hand, the leaders of physical anthropology in Germany were politically staunch liberals who argued against political anti-Semitism. But on the other hand, modern anti-Semitism is defined by the fact that it is founded on the idea of race. One of the ironies of the history of German physical anthropology after 1945 is that the field as a whole—as opposed to individual utterances, as had been the case previously—became associated with the reactionary right. Following the close relationship between physical anthropology and the Nazi regime, including its implication in the persecution and murder of the Jews, Sinti and Roma, and other populations, physical anthropology could only dissociate itself from anti-Semitism through direct and unequivocal confrontation with its own history—that is to say, by a systematic deconstruction of earlier anthropologies of "Jews" and a confrontation with the role of physical anthropology in legitimating the persecution and murder of millions of human beings. In the period studied in this article, this confrontation did not occur. As a result, physical anthropologists maneuvered between an unchanged conceptual framework on the one hand and a taboo on the discussion of Jews on the other.

In this chapter, I have shown how scientific authors have used several tactics to deal with this tension. Jews were either removed from discussion (Eickstedt); disappeared as a distinct category (Schwidetzky); discussion of them was channeled to the state of Israel (Schwidetzky); or they were reclassified to disguise their presence in discussion (Knußman). Only from the 1990s onwards, forty years after the end of World War II, did a new generation of anthropologists turn to a methodical historicization of their own discipline and finally separated physical anthropology from anti-Semitism, two threads that in the German context had for so long been closely intertwined. As the actual methods and techniques of physical anthropology had not undergone any significant change in the decades prior to this confrontation of anthropology with its own past, the process of historicization necessarily destabilized some of its core concepts and beliefs. Anthropologists increasingly faced what could be termed (not without some irony) a form of double consciousness—between their scientific practice and its destabilization by their own historicization.

Notes

1. The closest English term for *Anthropologie* is "physical anthropology." *Anthropologie* once covered a wide territory including prehistory and archeology, and at the end of the nineteenth century broke down into several separate subdisciplines. According to one of the standard definitions, *Anthropologie* dealt with the natural-physical aspects of the human body and circumscribed the species of man (*Homo*) in its temporal and spatial extension. For definitions of *Anthropologie, Völkerkunde, Ethnologie,* and *Volkskunde,* see Andre Gingrich, "From the Nationalist Birth of *Volkskunde* to the Establishment of Academic Diffusionism: Branching off from the International Mainstream," in *One Discipline, Four Ways: British, German, French and American Anthropology,* ed. Fredrik Barth et al. (Chicago: University of Chicago Press, 2005), 86, 90. See also H. Glenn Penny, "Traditions in the German Language," in *A New History of Anthropology,* ed. Henrika Kuklick (Oxford: Blackwell, 2008), 80.
2. For a social history of the development of physical anthropology in Germany, see Andrew D. Evans, *Anthropology at War: World War I and the Science of Race in Germany* (Chicago: University of Chicago Press, 2010), 21–55.
3. See Mitchell G. Ash, "Wissenschaft und Politik als Ressourcen füreinander," in *Wissenschaften und Wissenschaftspolitik. Bestandsaufnahme zu Formationen,*

Brüchen und Kontinuitäten im Deutschland des 20. Jahrhunderts, eds. Rüdiger vom Bruch and Brigitte Kaderas (Stuttgart: Franz Steiner, 2002), 32–51.

4. Michael Burleigh and Wolfgang Wippermann, *The Racial State: Germany, 1933–1945* (Cambridge: Cambridge University Press, 1991).
5. Uwe Hoßfeld, *Geschichte der Biologischen Anthropologie in Deutschland: Von den Anfängen bis in die Nachkriegszeit* (Stuttgart: Franz Steiner, 2005), 422–424.
6. Marek Kohn, *The Race Gallery: The Return of Racial Science* (London: Jonathan Cape, 1995), 9–16; Andreas Mayer, "Von der 'Rasse' zur 'Menschheit : Zur Inszenierung der Rassenanthropologie im Wiener Naturhistorischen Museum nach 1945," in *Politik der Präsentation: Museum und Ausstellung in Österreich 1918–1945,* ed. Herbert Posch and Gottfried Fliedl (Vienna: Turia & Kant, 1996), 212–237; and Klaus Taschwer, "'Lösung der Judenfrage: Zu einigen anthropologischen Ausstellungen im Naturhistorischen Museum Wien," in *Wie ein Monster ensteht: Zur Konstruktion des anderen in Rassismus und Antisemitismus,* ed. Kirstin Breitnfellner and Charlotte Kohn-Ley (Bodenheim: Philos, 1998), 165–176.
7. For example, the library of the natural history museum in Vienna still catalogues Jews under *Juden und Judenprobleme* (Jews and Jewish problems).
8. Eric Ehrenreich, "Otmar von Verschuer and the 'Scientific' Legitimization of Nazi Anti Jewish Policy," *Holocaust and Genocide Studies* 21, no. 1 (2007): 67.
9. Hans-Walter Schmuhl, private communication. In 1945 Verschuer wrote his scientific autobiography, *Mein Wissenschaftlicher Weg.* The manuscript, which remains unpublished, is crudely anti-Semitic. Hans-Walter Schmuhl, *Grenzüberschreitungen: Das Kaiser-Wilhelm-Institut fur Anthropologie, menschliche Erblehre und Eugenik 1927–1945* (Göttingen: Wallstein, 2005), 304.
10. Hoßfeld, *Geschichte der biologischen Anthropologie in Deutschland,* 367–368. Discussion of the history of the discipline in the Nazi period was generally avoided. Even the two exceptions, Gustav Blume in Dresden in 1948 (*Rasse oder Menschheit? Eine Auseinandersetzung mit der nationalsozialistischen Rassenlehre*) and Karl Saller's 1961 book (*Die Rassenlehre des Nationalsozialismus in Wissenschaft und Propaganda* [Darmstadt: Progress, 1961]) refrained from discussing the history of the discipline, preferring to deal with individual writers. Both books portray their authors as victims of the Nazi period. Schwidetzky devotes a page and a half to postwar anthropology and two and a half pages to anthropology in the Nazi period. Historians rather than anthropologists began critical historical work on the subject, and only in the 1980s. Benoit Massin, "Anthropologie und Humangenetik im Nationalsozialismus oder: Wie Schreiben Deutsche Wissenschaftler ihre Eigene Wissenschaftsgeschichte?," in *Wissenschaftlicher Rassismus. Analysen einer Kontinuität in den Human-Naturwissenschaften,* ed. Heidrun Kaupen-Haas and Christian Saller (Frankfurt am Main: Campus, 1999), 17. Wilhelm Mühlmann, *Geschichte der Anthropologie* (Frankfurt a. M.: Athenaeum, 1968). Peter Emil Becker, *Zur Geschichte der Rassenhygiene. Wege ins Dritte Reich* (Stuttgart: Thieme,1988). Ilse Schwidetzy and I. Spiegel-Rösing, *Maus und Schlange. Untersuchungen zur Lage der deutschen Anthropologie* (München: Oldenbourg, 1992).
11. Veronika Lipphardt et al., eds., *Pseudowissenschaft: Konzeptionen von Nichtwissenschaftlichkeit in der Wissenschaftsgeschichte* (Frankfurt am Main: Suhrkamp, 2008).

12. Massin, "Anthropologie und Humangenetik," 16.
13. Ibid., 53. Becker, *Zur Geschichte der Rassenhygiene;* and Becker, *Sozialdarwinismus, Rassismus, Antisemitismus und Völkischer Gedanke. Weg ins Dritte Reich. Bd 2.* (Stuttgart: Thieme, 1990).
14. See Dirk Preuß, "Egon Freiherr von Eickstedt (1892–1965): Anthrophologe und Forschungsreisender. Selbstbild und Entwicklung der deutschen Anthropologie im 200 Jahrhundert am Beispiel des Begründers der „Breslauer Schule," 2 vols. (doctoral dissertation, University of Jena, 2006). For Eickstedt's early career, during World War I and the Weimar period, see Evans, *Anthropology at War.*
15. Egon Freiherr von Eickstedt, *Ausgewählte Lichtbilder zur Rassenkunde des Deutschen Volkes,* Begleitheft, 2nd edition, 1933, 19.
16. Christopher M. Hutton, *Race and the Third Reich: Linguistics, Racial Anthropology and Genetics in the Dialectic of "Volk"* (Cambridge, England: Polity Press, 2005), 149f, 159f.
17. Egbert Kautke, "German 'Race Psychology' and its Implementation in Central Europe: Egon Freiherr von Eickstedt and Rudolf Hippius," in *Blood and Homeland: Eugenics and Racial Nationalism in Central and Southeast Europe 1900–1940,* ed. Marius Turda and Paul J. Weindling (Budapest and New York: Central European University Press, 2007), 23–40.
18. Quoted in Massin, "Anthropologie und Humangenetik," 14.
19. Ilse Schwidetzky, *Einführung in die Völkerbiologie* (Stuttgart: Gustav Fischer, 1950). Egon Freiherr von Eickstedt, *Die Forschung am Menschen,* 3vols. (Stuttgart: Enke, 1963).
20. See Hoßfeld, *Geschichte der biologischen Anthropologie,* 406.
21. Egon Freiherr von Eickstedt et al., eds., *Ausgewählte Lichtbilder zur Rassenkunde des Deutschen Volkes. Erläuterungen* (Stuttgart: Ausgabe für politische Redner, Lichtbilder Verlag Theodor Benzinger, 1933), 12, 15, 19–22.
22. Jakob Michelsen, "Ilse Schwidetzky," in *Handbuch der völkischen Wissenschaften,* ed. Ingo Haar and Michael Fahlbusch (Munich: K. G. Saur, 2008), 634–638.
23. Michelsen, "Ilse Schwidetzky," 68.
24. Michelsen, "Ilse Schwidetzky," 108.
25. Schwidetzky, *Grundzüge der Völkerbiologie* (Stuttgart: Ferdinand Enke, 1950).
26. Michelsen, "Ilse Schwidetzky," 276–282.
27. Viktor V. Bunak, "Rassengeschichte Osteuropas," in *Rassengeschichte der Menschheit: Europa II: Ost- und Nordeuropa,* ed. Ilse Schwidetzky (Munich and Vienna: R. Odenbourg, 1976), 50, 52. D. Ferembach, "Histoire Raciale du Sahara Septentrional," in *Rassengeschichte der Menscheit Afrika I: Nord-und Mittelafrika,* ed. Ilse Schwidetzky (Munich and Vienna: R.Oldenburg, 1975), 164. Ilse Schwidetzky,"Rassengeschichte von Deutschland," in *Rassengeschichte der Menschheit: Europa V: Schweiz, Deutschland, Belgien und Luxemburg, Niederlande,* ed. Ilse Schwidetzky (Munich and Vienna: R. Oldenburg, 1976), 92.
28. Schwidetzky,"Rassengeschichte von Deutschland."
29. Wolfram Bernhard, "Asien IV: Südwestasien", in *Rassengeschichte der Menschheit,* ed. Ilse Schwidetzky (Munich: R. Oldenburg, 1993), 147–177.

30. Unlike the term "*zurückgekehrt*", the term "*zurückgewandert*" does not have Zionist connotations but rather anti-Semitic connotations of the "the wandering Jew." Bernhard, "Asien IV: Südwestasien," 149.
31. Bernhard, "Asien IV: Südwestasien," 174.
32. Egon Freiherr von Eickstedt, *Die Rassischen Grundlagen des Deutschen Volkes* (Cologne: Hermann Schaffststein, 1939), 28–31. The Jews, according to Eicksted, arrived far earlier than the Gypsies, in fact before Germany was Germanized. But the two peoples are described as *beherbergt* (accommodated) by *Wirtsvölker* (host peoples). The Jews are characterized as *mitleidslos* (merciless) and *rachsüchtig* (vindictive) (30). Their *zersetzender Geistigkeit* (destructive spiritual form) and their *Andersartigekeit* (underlying alien form) create constant tensions and disharmonies. Eickstedt concludes this section by stating that it is only natural and healthy that all defensive measures against this threatening force should be taken and *mit aller Kraft* (with full force) (31).
33. See Jaroslav Suchy, "Die Zigeuner," in *Australien, Indochina-Indopakistan, Die Zigeuner,* ed. Karl Saller (Munich and Vienna: R. Oldenburg, 1968), 185–91. For a comparison of Gypsies and Jews in this context, see Margalit Gilad, *Germany and Its Gypsies: A Post-Auschwitz Ordeal* (Madison: University of Wisconsin Press, 2002), 143–159.
34. Rainer Knußman, *Vergleichende Biologie des Menschen. Ein Lehrbuch der Anthropologie und Humangenetik* (Frankfurt am Main: Fischer Verlag, 1986), 429. For mention of the protests, see ann., "Alte Lehre zementiert," *Der Spiegel,* no. 20 (1997): 218. Through the use of the word "we," Knußman excludes the Jews from European societies; see on such usage Eric L. Santner, *Stranded Objects: Mourning, Memory, and Film in Postwar Germany* (Ithaca, NY: Cornell University Press, 1990), 35, 43, 51, 52.
35. Knußman, *Vergleichende Biologie des Menschen,* 426.
36. Knußman, *Vergleichende Biologie des Menschen,* 433.
37. In *Die Rassischen Grundlagen des Deutschen Volkes* (1939) von Eickstedt characterizes the Jews as a racial mixture that is primarily of the Armenian type. On standard characterizations of the Armenian type see Taschwer, "'Lösung der Judenfrage,'" 170–171; as well as Niels C. Lösch, *Rasse als Konstrukt: Leben und Werk Eugen Fischers* (Frankfurt: Peter Lang, 1997), 280.
38. Ludwig Ferdinand Clauss, *Rasse und Seele: Eine Einführung in den Sinn der leiblichen Gestalt* (Munich: Lehmann, 1937), 78–81.

CHAPTER 12

Genes as Jewish History?

Human Population Genetics in the Service of Historians

Noa Sophie Kohler and Dan Mishmar

Genealogical records of Jews, which form, in a sense, a genetic history, may be found in the Pentateuch and therefore are an essential part of the Jewish religious heritage. In the book of Genesis, we learn of Adam and Eve, Cain and Abel, after which we are told of the "book of the generations of Adam" (or, according to the interpretation of Ben Azai, cited by Samson Raphael Hirsch, "the book of the generations of mankind").[1] Traditionally, mankind is seen as one large family that gave rise to a branch forming the dynasty founded on the offspring of Abraham, Sarah, and Isaac. Until today, Judaism has a strong notion of being a family business. Gentiles may join the Jewish people following conversion to the Jewish faith; however, at least since the Middle Ages Judaism has not engaged in missionary activities. This is why geneticists regard Jewish subgroups, for example Ashkenazic Jews, as genetic isolates, although the scope of isolation is still under debate.[2] Since Talmudic times Jewish identity has been passed on through the maternal lineage, while affiliation to the Jewish priest caste of the *kohanim* and to the Levites are passed from father to son, excluding converts.

The emergence of genetic anthropology and genetic history, which combine DNA analysis with cultural studies, paved the path for geneticists to search for evidence of transmission of cultural markers along with genetic markers of persons who define themselves as Jewish. By introducing the reader to a small but representative selection of articles that have been written by geneticists, published in scientific journals of natural science but that deal with questions regarding Jewish history, this essay not only will present examples of the latest findings in this particular field, but also will discuss the possible contribution of genetic studies to historical research.

Today, there are several groups who use genetic means for many different purposes, some of which may be of great interest to identity research; I will omit them from this discussion simply due to lack of space. For example, geneticists and physicians investigate the probability or frequency of hereditary diseases in ethnically determined population groups all over the world. The various subgroups of the Jewish people, subgroups that are believed to have been relatively isolated populations, form preferred research targets to identify specific mutations that are factors in inherited disorders and diseases. The question as to whether or how these studies help create a feeling of cultural solidarity will not be addressed here. Recently, private genetic genealogy has become widely popular and a lucrative field of income for various bodies and institutions. Companies offer DNA tests to complement individuals' genealogical research and promise to connect them to their distant past relatives. There are television series featuring celebrities that exploit the popularity of genealogical investigation.[3] But the ethical and cultural implications of these endeavors lie beyond our present concerns.

Some of the papers that I will introduce in the following paragraph sparked a heated debate. There is much uneasiness when it comes to introducing genetics into questions of identity, nationality, or history. This is mainly because of the perceived danger of a new stigmatization of population groups, particularly Jews, who not long ago suffered a genocide that was ideologically based on scientific racism. In 2005, the controversial study by anthropologists and population geneticists, "Natural History of Ashkenazic Intelligence," for example, maintains that in medieval times Ashkenazic Jews were selected for intelligence, and therefore have higher IQ rates. Their IQ is also associated with an increased frequency of certain genes that on the one hand are responsible for the elevated IQ and on the other for certain hereditary disorders.[4] The notion that Ashkenazic Jews are more intelligent than others is a form of labeling a population group and encourages prejudices.[5] From this point of view, the methodology of geneticists is inherently problematic, because it attempts to single out and determine the differences between ethnic groups and then trace the mutations that cause diseases for targeted medical practice. The differences of approach turn out to be insurmountable. However, one has to keep in mind that population genetics studies calculate values as averages and do not make statements about individual members of the discussed population group, so that the perceived danger in fact stems from misuse or misinterpretation of the research results. Nevertheless, as long as Jewish identity is based on two principles, namely birth and religion (a religion that virtually anyone can join by conversion), biology or genetics is not and never was the only determining factor of being Jewish.

Studies at the intersection of genetics and Jewish historiography serve the construction of an identity based on biological markers and have therefore drawn criticism. Raphael Falk, professor of genetics (emeritus) at the Hebrew University of Jerusalem, who studied the interrelation of genetic research and Zionism, came to the conclusion that "Genetic research has to free itself from trying to base Zionism on a common biological origin."[6] Nadia Abu El-Haj has tried to show how notions of Jewish identity feed into the way questions were asked and answered by geneticists in order to fit "the ideology of settler-nationhood".[7] In an attempt to go beyond ideological questions, it is our goal, in the combined research endeavor of a geneticist and a social historian, to explore the possibility of using genetic tools to obtain historical data that we would have not been able to find anywhere other than the biological archive within the human body. A brief outline of what has been published by population geneticists concerning Jewish history will help understand the rationale behind our research project.

Human Population Genetics and Jewish History

Geneticists trace back human ancestry by comparing mutations that have accumulated in the human genome. The nucleus of every cell in the bodies of human beings harbors two sets of twenty-three homologous chromosomes, inherited from both parents. These chromosomes are made of genetic material (DNA) that encodes hereditary information and traits. More than sixty years ago, Watson and Crick identified the structure of the DNA molecule as a double helix that resembles a twisted ladder. The sides of that ladder are the sugar-phosphate backbone, while the rungs consist of pairs of two out of four building blocks, A, T, C, and G (standing for adenine, thymine, cytosine, and guanine). Read along the sides of the ladder, these four letters—nucleotides—form a genetic code. Human DNA consists of approximately 3 billion nucleotides, which are more than 99.8 percent identical among all humans. But considering the great number of nucleotides, even a 0.2 percent variation translates into a great number of differences between individuals or groups. Different kinds of so-called genetic markers are used in order to differentiate individuals (or groups). Microsatellites, for example, are patterns of repeated units of two to five nucleotides on a certain stretch of DNA. The number of repeats of this type of genetic markers is highly variable among individuals. Another genetic marker widely used in order to compare the genetic landscapes of people is called SNP (single nucleotide polymorphism) and designates exactly that: a site within the genome where most individuals have a certain nucleotide. Due to mutations that have occurred and been transmitted during human evolution some people carry a different nucleotide. Individual combinations of certain markers linked on the same chromosome are called haplotypes and can be specific for an individual or shared by a group and therefore make it possible for geneticists to trace back ancestry. A group of haplotypes that share a common ancestor—in other words, having common combinations of DNA sequences—is called a haplogroup. Genetically related populations may share haplogroups. Haplogroups and haplotypes are retained in regions of the genome that are inherited only from one parent and therefore cannot exchange genetic material, which means they cannot recombine. Such are regions within the Y chromosome, hereby tracing the changes in the DNA that are being passed on from father to son; or in the mitochondrial DNA, which is passed on from mother to offspring and hereby only tracing the changes that accumulated solely in the maternal lineage. The smaller the genetic divergence, the shorter the genetic distance, and the closer the groups are related—enabling geneticists to create maps depicting human migration by comparing haplogroups frequencies among populations.

In 1971, the population geneticist Luigi L. Cavalli-Sforza, together with his colleague, Sir Walter Bodmer, published his first book on worldwide human populations, *Genetics of Human Populations*.[8] Cavalli-Sforza's books take an interdisciplinary approach, blending genetics with anthropology and linguistics, trying to shed light on both human evolution and the transmission of cultural traits.[9] Predictably, anthropologists and historians expressed concern about the attempt to introduce the transmission of culture into a debate on human evolution, and since then a scholarly discourse has evolved around the question of whether or how the use of genetics invokes the notion of race.[10] Historical and cultural events in Jewish history were of interest to geneticists, but it took the study on the *kohanim* to capture the public's interest and bring genetics into the forefront of identity shaping factors.[11] In 1997, a team of geneticists headed by the population geneticist and physician Karl Skorecki, who himself is an observant Jew and a Cohen, set out to genetically compare *kohanim* from Sephardic and Ashkenazic backgrounds.[12] In theory, all Jews with a family history of belonging to the priestly caste should be able to trace their ancestry back to Aaron the High Priest as a common ancestor, no matter what their ethnicity. For the study, which was published in the journal *Nature,* 188 unrelated Jewish men from Great Britain, Israel, and North America were chosen for Y chromosome DNA analysis, some of which had a family history of being of priestly descent and belonged to various Jewish ethnicities. The analysis of two specific markers, an insertion of a certain repeated DNA called Alu repeat and a microsatellite marker, revealed a significant difference in the composition of the Y chromosome of the priests compared to the nonpriests, or, in their own words, "Accordingly, we sought and found clear differences in the frequency of Y-chromosomes haplotypes between Jewish priests and their lay counterparts. Remarkably, the difference is observable in both Ashkenazic and Sephardic populations, despite the geographical separation of the two communities.… These Y-chromosome *haplotype* differences confirm a distinct paternal genealogy for Jewish priests."[13] A year later, the scientific correspondence section of the journal *Nature* printed the paper "Origins of Old Testament Priests," in which the authors presented the results of a more detailed study: they had not only increased the genetic markers to six microsatellites and six unique-event polymorphisms, but also increased the sample size from 188 to 306 Jewish men.[14] As a further addition, this study also included Levites, who, according to Jewish belief, paternally trace back to the tribe of Levi. The results of this study supported the findings of the previous study, in that a difference could be established between the priests and nonpriests; it was shown that one of the 112 haplotypes was more frequent among the Ashkenazic and Sephardic *kohanim* than among other Jews, and was termed the Cohen modal haplotype. Specifying the calculation path step by step, the article dates the founding of the priestly caste to the temple period or shortly before that (2100–3250 years ago).[15] While in fact this study states that more than half of the Ashkenazic and Sephardic *kohanim* share a certain genetic signature, it does not claim that there was one priestly forefather of all of today's *kohanim,* or that it would be possible to establish who is or is not a Cohen. In its quest for a sensational headline, "Jewish Line Traced Back to Moses," the British liberal daily newspaper *The Independent* oversimplified and thus distorted the scientific findings.[16] Other media coverage[17] misleadingly conveyed the impression that genetic studies claim clear and unambiguous results concerning questions of Jewish history.[18] But not only does careful reading of "Origins of Old Testament Priests" show that this is not the case, in the same essay the scientists tested another oral Jewish tradition and found that it was not possible to trace back the Levites to one shared ancestry: "Contemporary Levites, therefore, are not direct patrilineal descendants of a paternally related tribal group."[19]

In 2003, some of the authors of "Origins of Old Testament Priests" published another essay with the explicit intention of answering questions in Jewish history. They took issue with a theory proposed by linguist Paul Wexler, who claims that the Yiddish language was established by Judaized Sorbs and Khazars.[20] The theory according to which Ashkenazic Jewry descended from the Khazars was publicized by Arthur Koestler in his popular *The Thirteenth Tribe: The Khazar Empire and its Heritage* (1976), and has recently been taken up by the Israeli historian Shlomo Sand.[21] The team of geneticists led by Karl Skorecki and Doron Behar explained, "Given the importance of the paternally defined Levite caste in Jewish history and tradition, the multiple theories of the ethnogenesis of the Ashkenazic Jewish community, ... we undertook a detailed investigation of the paternal genetic history of the Ashkenazic Levites and compared the results with matching data from neighboring populations among which the Ashkenazic community lived during its formation and subsequent demographic expansion."[22] This time the DNA of 988 unrelated men, 236 of which were Ashkenazim and 163 of which were Sephardim, were analyzed. In order to enhance the exactitude of the study, the researchers increased the analysis to one *Alu* insertion and eleven SNPs as markers and extended the genotyping of the Ashkenazic Levites to twenty-five markers, which enabled researchers to make out ten haplogroups for the Ashkenazic Levites. The details of the genotyping are laid out meticulously in the article and need not be recounted here. The results showed that more than half of the Ashkenazic Levites share a haplogroup that is uncommon in Sephardic Levites, meaning that, unlike *kohanim,* the Levites do not share paternal ancestry. Furthermore, the clustering of haplotypes within that haplogroup indicates a recent single common ancestor for the Levites, but this particular haplogroup is very rare for people of what they call Near Eastern descent, though common in people of Eastern European origin. In other words, their results point to something impossible according to halakha, namely male non-Jewish ancestry for Ashkenazic Levites. In the subsequent discussion of their findings, the authors suggest that although theoretically fifty non-Jewish men could be the founding fathers of today's Ashkenazic Levites, it is more likely that only the line of one non-Jew turned Levite survived and multiplied until today, while all other lines gradually died out, a phenomenon called "the founder effect." The explanation given is purely historical. It is argued that rabbis safeguarding religious law would not have permitted converts to become Levites, which also has left no traces in historical records. Reflecting the intense scholarly debate, a different team of researchers pursued the quest for the impact of the Khazars on the formation of Ashkenazic Jewry further, coming to the conclusion that its share among the Ashkenazic Israelites must have been higher than proposed, and even older than the founder effect of the Ashkenazic Levites.[23]

In addition, the maternal line of Ashkenazic Jewry has been researched, and in 2006 a group of twenty scientists, who published their results in a paper titled "The Matrilineal Ancestry of Ashkenazic Jewry: Portrait of a Recent Founder Event," made an effort to decide between the positions stated so far, namely whether a strong founder effect can be detected in the establishment of Ashkenazic Jewry.[24] One of their conclusions was that only four mothers account for 40 percent of today's Ashkenazic Jewish women, and these women were likely of Near Eastern descent. A study from a different team of geneticists on mtDNA in Ashkenazic Jews that was published the year after brought to light differentiations in the Ashkenazic mtDNA landscape and reflects the continuing scholarly debate on refining data and methodology.[25]

A study in 2002 by geneticists from England and Italy indicated that in different areas of the world Jewish communities were founded by only a few women and that on the maternal line genetic diversity is lower than that found on the paternal line, meaning Jewish women must have married either within their own or into a different Jewish community, indicating female mobility.[26] In 2008, a different team of geneticists published the results of a more detailed analysis of mtDNA of 1,142 Jewish women representing fourteen different non-Ashkenazic Jewish communities.[27] The results reflect the different developments in the various locations of the Jewish Diaspora: whereas for North Africa there is less evidence of local women joining the Jewish people, for Ethiopian and Indian communities there is evidence of women joining the Jewish people; those communities seemed to have been more open. The authors' discussion of their results highlights not only the technical, but also the historical complexity of the research.

Recently, new technological developments have made a genome-wide comparison possible, and several geneticists have used this new tool in order to follow up their own previous research, this time comparing 226,839 autosomal SNPs of 121 Jews from fourteen Jewish Diaspora communities and 1,166 non-Jews belonging to sixty-nine populations, in addition to genotyped data from eight thousand Y chromosome and fourteen thousand mtDNA samples. The research team, which included Doron Behar and Karl Skorecki, found that most Jewish communities are genetically more similar to each other than they are to their Diaspora host populations. The fact that the closest non-Jewish relatives of most Jews are Druze or Cypriot indicates a common ancestry of the Jewish people in the Levant. Ethiopian and Indian Jews formed an exception in that they were genetically closer to their host population than they were to other Jewish communities.[28]

The other genome-wide study examined an even greater number of genetic markers in a larger sample size. For "Abraham's Children in the Genome Era: Major Jewish Diaspora Populations Comprise Distinct Genetic Clusters with Shared Middle Eastern Ancestry" in 2010, 362,566 SNPs from 237 unrelated Jews representing seven Diaspora communities were first compared with a dataset comprising 418 people from sixteen non-Jewish populations and then with another dataset comprising 383 non-Jewish Europeans from ten different populations.[29] As in the other genome-wide study, the geneticists came to the conclusion that Jews are more related to each other than they are to their host populations, and share Middle Eastern ancestry. The fact that Ashkenazic Jews are closely related to each other, on the one hand, and to the non-Jewish population of France, Northern Italy, and Sardinia, on the other, refutes, according to the authors the claim that Ashkenazic Jews directly trace back to Khazars or Slavs who converted to Judaism. Since then, new studies have been trying to shed light on the Jewish past, turning to a Sub-Saharan African ancestry of pre-Diaspora Jews approximately two thousand years ago.[30] Nevertheless, the theory of converts forming the Ashkenazic ancestry has not been abandoned.[31]

Conclusion

While there is no single gene common to Jews or Jewish subgroups, the published genetic research we have discussed shows that despite their genetic diversity, Jews are more closely related to each other than they are to other European populations: "This study [Abraham's Children] demonstrates that the studied Jewish populations represent a series of geographical isolates or clusters with genetic threads that weave them together.... Over the past 3000 years, both the flow of genes and the flow of religious and cultural ideas have contributed to Jewishness."[32] While Jews are regarded as a genetic isolate, there is nothing particularly Jewish about this feature. It applies to many population groups, including the Sorbs in Germany, the Finns, the Old Order Amish, and others.[33]

Have geneticists constructed a new form of Jewish identity in the above-mentioned papers? It can safely be said that geneticists understand Jewish identity as a prerequisite for their research endeavor—just as any historian who writes about Jewish history concentrates on people who define themselves as Jewish. Probably most of them share the opinion that Jews are a nation that is, among other factors, based on ancient kinship relations. Therefore one of the authors of the genome-wide study "Abraham's Children in the Genome Era" comments on his research results, "I would hope that these observations would put the idea that Jewishness is just a cultural construct to rest."[34] The fact that geneticists have a pronounced idea as to whether the Jewish people share a common ancestry should not induce the lay reader to think that results are not trustworthy. Not only are they published in peer-reviewed, highly regarded scientific journals, but also they follow further, more medically motivated aims:

> The Ashkenazi Jewish (AJ) population has long been viewed as a genetic isolate, kept separate from its European neighbors by religious and cultural practices of endogamy.... Population isolates are frequently used in genetic research, as such groups are presumed to have reduced genetic diversity, along with increased frequencies of recessive disorders, identity-by-descent (IBD), and linkage disequilibrium (LD) as the result of founder events and population bottlenecks.... Accordingly, the AJ population is often the subject of Mendelian and complex disease studies, although evidence that the AJ population carries all of the hallmarks of a genetic isolate has not been fully established.[35]

This also explains the ever-increasing number of markers and datasets used in the discussed studies. The above-mentioned article on Ashkenazic Levites can rather be considered a case in point for unbiased research and a good example of a traditional Jewish belief not being reinforced by genetic findings.[36] There is no place in Jewish legal rulings for a convert to become a Levi, nor has historic evidence been found. It is solely due to genetics that we have a support for this. Obviously, the new field of human population genetics opens up many questions, much more than can be asked here and certainly more than can be answered. One of them is the ethical implication of scientific research into myths and beliefs.[37] The result of the study does not seem to have unsettled Ashkenazic Levites, because their religious status is determined by family tradition and is not revised according to scientific research results.

However, one might ask whether by finding a supposed Jewish ancestry in individuals or population groups geneticists create a new notion of Jewish identity. Apparently, even though there is not one section of the genome shared by all Jews, it is by now possible to genetically determine who has Jewish ancestry.[38] Genetic evidence of a Jewish ancestry has been established, for example, for members of the African Lemba tribe or of the Indian Kuki-Chin-Mizo tribes.[39] The implications of this can become political in nature, because being recognized as Jewish by Israel's chief rabbinate makes one eligible for Israeli citizenship.[40]

The dismissal by geneticists of Sand's thesis that most of East European Jewry is descended from converted Khazars raises the question of whether human population genetics can be used as a tool for historians asking specific historical questions. The drawbacks are obvious: not only is it a difficult tool to handle and virtually impossible for nonspecialists, it seems that it is not accurate enough for historians in its predictions as to time and place. On the other hand, for studying concrete aspects of history whose point of focus is on human relations and networking, genetics might become a valuable and new means of research. That is why the authors of the present essay are currently investigating the network of Ashkenazic family relations in order to shed light on kinship networking within or among Ashkenazic communities in Europe. The fostering of family relations was one way in which Diaspora Jews helped each other in times of political or economic difficulties. It is our goal to find out whether we can detect family relations and networking dating up to ten generations back and covering all of Europe by comparing DNA samples of a number of unrelated Ashkenazic Jews that were collected in the United States. We might be able to detect clustering of certain DNA samples, thus indicating past family connections between the seemingly unrelated individuals. As we also have information of the place of origin of many of these families, we will be able to trace these connections on the map. The advantage of using the information hidden in the individual's DNA over the usual way we trace family networks in public and private archives is that through DNA analysis we know for sure who was once related, which is not the case when we try to trace networks by following fragmentary documentation through archives, in many languages, scattered all over Europe. But, more important, we might be able to prove that human population genetics is a useful tool even for social historians.

Notes

1. Sifra, Kedoshim 12. Samson R. Hirsch, *Pentateuch: Erster Theil: Die Genesis* (Frankfurt am Main: Verlag der J. Kauffmann'schen Buchhandlung, 1883), 111.

2. Bray et al., "Signatures of Founder Effects, Admixture, and Selection in the Ashkenazi Jewish Population," *PNAS* 107, no. 37 (2010): 16222–16227; advance publication August 26, 2010, doi:10.1073/pnas.1004381107.
3. For a discussion of the combination of human population genetics and genetic genealogy based on the example of the Genographic Project and the Family Tree DNA company, which offers genetic testing, see Catherine Nash, "Mapping Origins. Race and Relatedness in Population Genetics and Genetic Genealogy," in *New Genetics, New Identities,* ed. P. Atkinson, P.E. Glasner, and H. Greenslade (New York: Routledge, 2007), 77–101. On the impact of genetic genealogy on the understanding of race and ethnicity, see Alondra Nelson, "The Factness of Diaspora: The Social Sources of Genetic Genealogy," in *Rites of Return: Diaspora Poetics and the Politics of Memory,* ed. Marianne Hirsch and Nancy Miller (New York: Columbia University Press, 2011), 23–40. On the notion of a "Jewish" gene, see Kahn, "Are Genes Jewish?".
4. Cochran et al., "Natural History."
5. Not everyone shares this discomfort, of course. Publicist Jon Entine quite uncritically included findings of geneticists in his book *Abraham's Children: Race, Identity, and the DNA of the Chosen People* (New York: Warner Books, 2007), and medical anthropologist Melvin Konner adopted genetic theories in *The Jewish Body.*
6. Raphael Falk, *Tzionut vehabiologia shel hayehudim* (Zionism and the Biology of the Jews) (Tel Aviv: Resling 2006), 241 [Hebrew].
7. Nadia Abu El-Haj, *The Genealogical Science. The Search for Jewish Origins and the Politics of Epistemology* (Chicago: University of Chicago Press, 2012), 64–65.
8. Luigi L. Cavalli-Sforza and Walter F. Bodmer, *Genetics of Human Populations* (San Francisco: W.H. Freeman, 1971).
9. For a scientific biography of Cavalli-Sforza, see Linda Stone and Paul F. Lurquin, *A Genetic and Cultural Odyssey: The Life and Work of L. Luca Cavalli-Sforza* (New York: Columbia University Press, 2005).
10. Stone and Lurquin, *Genetic and Cultural Odyssey,* 85–114. See also S. Gilman, ed., *Race in Contemporary Medicine* (London: Routledge, 2008); and N. Abu El-Haj, "The Genetic Reinscription of Race," *Annual Review of Anthropology* 36 (2007): 283–300.
11. See Nurit Kirsh, "Genetic Research on Israel's Populations: Two Opposite Tendencies," in *Twentieth Century Ethics of Human Subjects Research: Historical Perspectives on Values, Practices, and Regulations,* ed. V. Roelke and G. Maio (Stuttgart: Franz Steiner Verlag, 2004), 309–319; and Kirsh, "Genetic Studies of Ethnic Communities in Israel: A Case of Values-Motivated Research Work," in *Jews and Sciences in German Contexts,* ed. U. Charpa and U. Deichmann (Tübingen: Mohr Siebeck, 2007), 181–195.
12. See David B. Goldstein, *Jacob's Legacy. A Genetic View on Jewish History* (New Haven, CT, and London, Yale University Press, 2008), 8–39; and Yaakov Kleiman, *DNA & Tradition: The Genetic Link to the Ancient Hebrews* (New York: Devora Publishing Company, 2004), 13–23.
13. K. Skorecki et al., "Y Chromosomes of Jewish Priests," *Nature* 385 (1997): 32.
14. Thomas et al., "Origins of Old Testament Priests," 138–140.

15. Ibid., 139. For criticism concerning the study's methodology, see Jits van Straten, *The Origin of Ashkenazi Jewry. The Controversy Unraveled* (Berlin and New York: De Gruyter, 2011), 115.
16. Steve Connor, "Jewish Line Traced Back to Moses," *The Independent,* July 9, 1998.
17. Edward Rothstein, "Ideas & Trends; DNA Teaches History a Few Lessons of Its Own," *New York Times,* May 24, 1998.
18. The CMH was made subject of further research, resulting among others in the publication of the paper "Extended Y Chromosome Haplotypes Resolve Multiple and Unique Lineages of the Jewish Priesthood," which analyzed 75 binary markers and twelve Y chromosome STRs of 215 *kohanim* from various Jewish communities, 1,575 Jewish men from all over the world, and 2,099 non-Jewish men from the Central Asia, Europe, India, and the Near East, and concluded that the hypothesis of a common origin of the CMH in the Near East predating the Jewish Diaspora can be upheld; see Hammer et al., "Extended Y Chromosome Haplotypes," 707–717. See also "Response," *Human Genetics* 126, no. 5 (2009): 725–726).
19. Thomas et al., "Origins of Old Testament Priests," 139.
20. See Paul Wexler, *The Ashkenazic Jews: A Slavo-Turkic People in Search of a Jewish Identity* (Columbus, OH: Slavica Publishers, 1993); Wexler, *Two-Tiered Relexification in Yiddish: Jews, Sorbs, Khazars, and the Kiev-Polessian Dialect* (Berlin, New York: De Gruyter, 2002).
21. Koestler, *The Thirteenth Tribe.* See also Sand, *The Invention of the Jewish People.* The Khazars were a Turkic-speaking people who founded an empire in the region of the northern Caucasus and whose ruling class is said to have converted to Judaism around the year 740.
22. D.M. Behar et al., "Multiple Origins of Ashkenazi Levites: Y Chromosome Evidence for Both Near Eastern and European Ancestries," *American Journal of Human Genetics* 73, no. 4 (2003): 768–779; quote is from p. 768. The methodology and research process is described for lay readers in Goldstein, *Jacob's Legacy,* 61–74.
23. A. Nebel et al., "Y Chromosome Evidence for a Founder Effect in Ashkenazi Jews," *European Journal of Human Genetics* 13 (2005): 388–391.
24. D.M. Behar et al., "The Matrilineal Ancestry of Ashkenazi Jewry: Portrait of a Recent Founder Event," *American Journal of Human Genetics* 78, no. 3 (2006): 487–497.
25. J. Feder et al., "Ashkenazi Jewish mtDNA Haplogroup Distribution Varies among Distinct Subpopulations: Lessons of Population Substructure in a Closed Group," *European Journal of Human Genetics* 15 (2007): 498–500.
26. M.G. Thomas, M.E. Weale, and A.L. Jones, "Founding Mothers of Jewish Communities: Geographically Separated Jewish Groups Were Independently Founded by Very Few Female Ancestors," *American Journal of Human Genetics* 70, no. 6 (2002): 1411–20.
27. D.M. Behar et al., "Counting the Founders: The Matrilineal Genetic Ancestry of the Jewish Diaspora," PLoS One 3, no. 4 (2008): e2062. doi:10.1371/journal.pone.0002062.
28. D.M. Behar et al., "The Genome-Wide Structure of the Jewish People," *Nature* 466, no. 7303 (2010): 238–242.

29. Atzmon et al., "Abraham's Children."
30. P. Moorjani et al., "The History of African Gene Flow into Southern Europeans, Levantines, and Jews," *PLoS Genetics* 7, no. 4 (2011): e1001373. doi:10.1371/journal.pgen.1001373.
31. See Jits van Straten, *The Origin of Ashkenazi Jewry: The Controversy Unraveled* (Berlin and New York, 2011). The geneticist Avshalom Zoossmann-Diskin uses selected markers for supporting his claim that the close proximity of Ashkenazic ("Eastern European") Jews and non-Jewish Italians points to a common ancestry of Romans who converted to Judaism; see A. Zoossmann-Diskin, "The Origin of Eastern European Jews Revealed by Autosomal, Sex Chromosomal and mtDNA Polymorphisms," *Biology Direct* 5 [2010]: 57. doi:10.1186/1745-6150-5-57).
32. Atzmon et al., "Abraham's Children," 859.
33. For Sorbs, see A. Gross et al, "Population-Genetic Comparison of the Sorbian Isolate Population in Germany with the German KORA Population Using Genome-Wide SNP Arrays," *BMC Genetics* 12 (2011): 67. More generally, see M. Arcos-Burgos and M. Muenke, "Genetics of Population Isolates," *Clinical Genetics* 61, no. 4 (2002): 233–247.
34. Quoted in M. Balter, "Who Are the Jews? Genetic Studies Spark Identity Debate," *Science* 328 (2010): 1342. See also Harry Ostrer, *Legacy: A Genetic History of the Jewish People* (Oxford, New York: Oxford University Press, 2012).
35. Bray et al., "Signatures of Founder Effects," 16222, see fn.2.
36. D.M. Behar et al., "Multiple Origins of Ashkenazi Levites: Y Chromosome Evidence for Both Near Eastern and European Ancestries," *American Journal of Human Genetics* 73, no. 4 (2003): 768–779.
37. For an insight into this topic, see the video, Henry Greely, "Ethical Issues in Human Population Genetics," in *Human Population Genetics: Evolution and Variation,* The Biomedical & Life Sciences Collection, Henry Stewart Talks, ed. L. L.Cavalli-Sforza and M. Feldman (London: Henry Stewart Talks, 2007), http://hstalks.com/main/view_talk.php?t=315&r=27&j=757&c=252.
38. A. C. Need et al., "A Genome-Wide Genetic Signature of Jewish Ancestry Perfectly Separates Individuals With and Without Full Jewish Ancestry in a Large Random Sample of European Americans," *Genome Biology* 10, no. 1 (2009): R7.
39. For the Lemba tribe, see Thomas et al., "Y Chromosomes Traveling South." See also Parfitt and Semi, *Judaising Movements,* 39–53; and Parfitt and Egorova, *Genetics, Mass Media and Identity.* See also chapter nine by Zianga in the present volume. On the Miso, see Goldstein, *Jacob's Legacy,* 89.
40. For a critical discourse on Israel's position in determining Jewishness, see Nadia Abu El-Haj, "Jews—Lost and Found: Genetic History and the Evidentary Terrain of Recognition," in *Rites of Return,* ed. Hirsch and Miller, 40–59. See also Gad Barzilai, "Who Is a Jew? Categories, Boundaries, Communities, and Citizenship Law in Israel," in *Boundaries of Jewish Identity,* ed. S. A. Glenn, N. B. Sokoloff (Seattle: University of Washington Press, 2010), 27–43.

CHAPTER 13

Sarrazin and the Myth of the Jewish Gene

Klaus Hödl

In fall 2009, the Berlin journal *Lettre International* conducted an interview with Thilo Sarrazin, a member of the German Social Democratic Party, former member of the executive board of the Deutsche Bank, and senator for finances in the Berlin local assembly. In a conversation about Berlin and its Muslim population, Sarrazin spoke derogatorily about Muslim immigrants and, among other things, criticized their inadequate efforts to acquire sufficiently good educational skills for social achievement. He also compared them with East European Jews who, in his opinion, had an IQ that was 15 percent above the average level of the (non-Jewish) German population—and, by implication, higher than that of Muslims.[1] Thus, Sarrazin placed Ashkenazic Jews at the top of the hierarchy and Muslims at the bottom.

Sarrazin's remarks on Jewish intelligence hardly caused any bewilderment among the readers of the journal. This may be due to the fact that the reference to a superior IQ among East European Jews has a history that dates back to the nineteenth century.[2] Recently, such assertions have acquired momentum as a result of new research in genetics.[3] A frequently cited study published in 2005 was undertaken by three anthropologists at the University of Utah. They discovered genetic defects among Ashkenazic Jews that apparently accounted for their high IQ. Usually, such genetic mutations are weeded out by evolution. In the case of Jews, however, they have been retained because they proved beneficial to their existence: in the past, anti-Jewish hostility restricted their occupational patterns to particular fields where intelligence was instrumental to their success. These circumstances, along with the religious restrictions on intermarriage, helped to preserve the high IQ among Jews.[4]

Even though the findings of genetic research are generally published in scientific journals and thus have remained within scholarly discourses, some have become popularized. Sarrazin's reference to a superior Jewish intelligence therefore did not provoke much dismay or wonderment because it already was a fairly well-known—and apparently accepted—concept. Consequently, the debates on the interview in *Lettre International* focused almost exclusively on the remarks on Muslims.

Viewed from a different angle, however, the lack of criticism of Sarrazin's statement concerning Jewish intelligence is quite astonishing for at least two reasons. First, it clearly represents a stereotype. Admittedly, it emphasizes a seemingly beneficial trait among Jews, but philo-Semitism is only the reverse of anti-Semitism.[5] They both fallaciously ascribe specific qualities to Jews that render them different from non-Jews. This should have been sufficient reason to remonstrate against Sarrazin's image of the smart Jew.

Second, some sixteen years before the interview in *Lettre International,* similar remarks on Jews had been made in *The Bell Curve* by two American scholars, Richard J. Herrnstein and Charles Murray.[6] Their goal was to link differences between social groups, such as their level of income or disposition to crime, to intelligence. Herrnstein and Murray tried to corroborate their thesis by drawing on Jews who allegedly possessed a comparatively high ratio of intelligence and were successful in their upward social mobility. Yet, in contrast to the interview in *Lettre International,* the authors' references to the Jews were swiftly contended by the public and their arguments refuted by fellow academics.[7] Sarrazin's image of the smart Jew seemed too much in consonance with widely held concepts of Jews to instigate a stand against it.

About one year after the interview, Sarrazin published a book in which he expanded on his theses on Muslims and Jews in Germany, *Deutschland schafft sich ab!* ("Germany is doing away with itself").[8] The book triggered a fierce debate strongly reminiscent of the controversy over Sarrazin's comments in *Lettre International:* it focused on the author's disparaging remarks about Muslims couched in a language highly redolent of the vocabulary used by Social Darwinists in the late nineteenth and early twentieth centuries.[9] Jews were not the topic of the dispute, at least not at the beginning. It did not take long, however, for the controversy to take a radical turn. In an interview conducted by the newspaper *Welt am Sonntag,* Sarrazin attempted to counter the accusation that he had used racist arguments by stressing that differentiating social groups on account of their genes is backed by scientific findings. Many groups, among them Jews and Basques, may be classified on the basis of their genes.[10] Thus, all of a sudden Jews found themselves in the middle of the debate. The common perception was that Sarrazin promoted Jewish racial differences, raising fears of the return of Germany's horrendous past.

My essay will first discuss Sarrazin's publication and his remarks on Jews. Second, I will relate these remarks to a larger context and to contemporary intellectual and scientific developments. I will argue that *Deutschland schafft sich ab!* is a text that matches a specific zeitgeist that may partly explain its strong resonance. Basically, Sarrazin's book is concerned with the future of Germany. The author maintains that the country is rich and is faring well. It has adequate human resources to safeguard its well-being. The prerequisites for its favorable economic status, a specific mentality and particular traditions, have started to change, however, due to demographic trends. They indicate that the proportion of young people in the population is declining precipitously. In principle, a low fertility rate can be offset by immigration, as is evident in Canada and several other countries. Germany, however, does not benefit from this strategy. Its immigrants overwhelmingly come from the Middle East, former Yugoslavia, Africa, and Turkey, and most of them are unwilling to integrate into the culture of the majority population, so they do not provide the preconditions for the country's economic progress. With the steep decrease in the birth rate of native Germans, fluid intelligence—the kind of intelligence that accounts for technical innovations and reaches its apex in people below forty-five—is dwindling as well.[11] The high fertility rate among immigrants can compensate for the decline in births among native-born Germans only numerically, not qualitatively, because (according to Sarrazin) immigrants show low levels of intelligence. With 50 to 80 percent of the IQ inherited and thus not susceptible to a rise by a supportive, fostering environment, Germany is in Sarrazin's view becoming increasingly stupid.[12] Not long from now, if we believe Sarrazin, it will have to forfeit its wealth and give up its high level of quality of life.

Deutschland schafft sich ab! may be understood as a wake up-call, meant to warn the German population and politicians of the eventual loss of economic competitiveness and, even worse, cease to exist as we know it. Sarrazin calculates that on the basis of extant birth rates, within three generations the share of native Germans among the country's population would amount to only 20 million people, whereas Turks would constitute around 35 million people.[13] It must be conceded that Sarrazin has pointed to essential problems that many highly industrialized societies with a well-developed social safety net and an increasingly tight budget are currently facing. For example, how can those parts of the larger population that have lived on welfare and shown little aspiration to improve their situation or to loosen their dependency on public support become part of the workforce? How can the transformation of an industrialized economy into an information- and knowledge-based society best be accomplished? How can immigrants be integrated into the larger society and the development of so-called parallel-societies be avoided, in other words, social milieus whose members abide by their own values and norms and live largely segregated from the rest of the society? The importance of such questions notwithstanding, Sarrazin does not come up with any new and conclusive answers. Much of what he is concerned with are familiar debates in the media and in the writings of various scholars. This especially holds true for many of his references to Muslim immigrants, which can be found in the books and articles of the German-Turkish sociologist Necla Kelec, the late judge Kirsten Heisig, or the German attorney of Turkish-Kurdish origin, Seyran Ates.[14]

In addition, the central premises of Sarrazin's inferences are, I would contend, factually incorrect. In arguing, for example, that 50 to 80 percent of an individual's intelligence is inherited, he reveals a simple-minded and fallacious understanding of the complex interrelations between cultural and biological factors in the shaping of IQ.[15] Sarrazin's inability to comprehend the issue properly makes him not only jump to wrong conclusions about the future of Germany, but also to succumb to various stereotypes. This comes paradigmatically to the fore when he connects social status or professional achievement with largely inherited intelligence. According to this notion, the ratio between men and women among the group with the highest level of intelligence (IQ of 145 and more) is eight to one.[16] Women, in other words, are rarely geniuses. Such a view is starkly reminiscent of the neurologist P.J. Möbius' misogynist pamphlet, *Über den Physiologischen Schwachsinn des Weibes* (1900).[17]

If much of what Sarrazin concerns himself with has already been touched upon and dealt with by other scholars, what makes his book so special and contentious is that he no longer views the difficulties Muslims face in their everyday lives in Germany or their problems with integration as resulting from social and cultural factors, but as something supposedly genetically determined. He thus approaches societal issues from a biological perspective.[18] In this way, he deviates from prevalent forms of discourses and argues in the context of a new paradigm.

Sarrazin and the Jews

The shift in paradigm and its consequences can best be exemplified by taking a look at Sarrazin's references to Jews. Actually, they play only a secondary role in the book. He touches upon the Jews merely to substantiate the thesis of an intimate link between a high ratio of intelligence and social achievement on the one hand, and of the inheritance of intelligence on the other. In this context, Sarrazin repeats his statements made in the interview in *Lettre International* that in the late nineteenth century East European Jews had an IQ surpassing that of non-Jewish Germans at the rate of 15 percent. This high level of intelligence, so he claims, accounted for their above-average share among Nobel Prize laureates, for their high ratio of students at German universities before World War II, their numerous artists, and so on. The preservation of the high intelligence among Jews was due to the pressure of *Selektionsdruck* (selection) in a Christian environment—the anti-Jewish hostility that restricted their occupations to commerce, banking, and intellectual professions; and to Jewish marriage patterns, which promoted the birth of children of intelligent parents.[19]

Sarrazin points to selection, procreative trends, and inheritance of intelligence in order to account for the high amount of Jewish students at German universities and Jewish social achievement. In so doing, he deliberately deviates from prevalent explanations. Many scholars claim that the high value granted to education in traditional Judaism prepared Jews for intellectual professions. Other approaches try to reveal correlations between the occupational structure of Jewish parents and the university attendance of their children.[20] Relevant here are the remarks reported on *Y-net*, an Israeli online news magazine, on May 12, 2011, by the South Korean ambassador to Israel, that many people in his country read the Talmud because they think that studying it will enhance their mental capacities. "We believe," so the ambassador said, "that if we teach our children Talmud we could also be geniuses."[21] This statement refers to a belief that learning, and not inherited intelligence, may have played a role in preparing Jews for succeeding in intellectual professions.[22]

Sarrazin, in contrast with the various explanations for Jewish intelligence, focuses narrowly on biological factors. His line of reasoning (which ignores the rich and varied literature on Jewish social achievement) indicates that he has a political agenda rather than a scholarly interest in tackling complex social issues: through his book, he is trying to stop Muslim immigration to Germany instead of easing their way into German society and removing stumbling blocks to their integration. This motif explains why Sarrazin presents overly simplistic, monolithic solutions to intricate societal problems, but it does not clarify why he is so obsessed with a biological—instead of a sociological or any other—approach, or why he did not choose a completely different but probably more effective strategy to scare Germans about immigrants by referring to them as criminals or people infected with contagious diseases, as populist politicians tend to do.

Sarrazin refrains from pure populism because he considers himself a member of the educated middle-class, which is adverse to any rabble-rousing.[23] He therefore has to pretend that his line of reasoning is predicated on scientific findings—which is basically correct, although he draws on selected data while using studies that have already been refuted.[24] His pursuit of a biological approach is intended to show that his arguments are solidly grounded in scientific research and bereft of any xenophobia. And he prefers this approach to a sociological or other so-called sophisticated approach because it fits best into a general trend in academic disciplines toward essentialization.

Generally speaking, the term "essentialization" designates a procedure that reduces the complexity of any phenomenon to a single determinant. In the social realm, essentialization is the ascription of a specific property to a particular group by which it can be identified; this characteristic is thought to be possessed by all members of the respective entity and tends to be quantifiable and measurable. Sarrazin's remarks about inherited intelligence as the major, sometimes even single cause for Muslims' problems with immigration may thus be considered an expression of this essentialized thinking.

Another question that must be answered in this context is, why Sarrazin refers to the Jewish gene although it apparently contributes nothing to the major thesis of his book, the alleged failure of Muslims to integrate? The answer is bound up with repressed discourses about the Jewish body in present-day Germany. By repressed discourses I mean, as I will explain below, the taboo on talking and writing about the Jewish body with exceptional public statements, that burst out despite efforts to counteract and silence them. In what follows I will first address the trend to essentialization in public discourse and then turn to the repressed discourses on the Jewish body.

Essentializing Trends

Essentialized, reductive thinking can paradigmatically be illustrated by the changing understanding of identity. So far it has convincingly been argued and agreed on by most scholars that Jewish identity is a process and therefore volatile, always changing and never static.[25] Because of its fluid and dynamic character, it has multiple forms and is nearly impossible to define. The notion of multiple identities in each Jewish person is intimately connected with the assumption that he or she is the outcome of the individual's interactions with other people and shaped by the (social, cultural, but also natural) environment. It is thus culture in the broader sense that is responsible for identity's multiple configuration. And this understanding of identity as multiple has come under attack recently. The most-often-cited rejection of the notion of multifarious identities comes from Mark Zuckerberg, the founder of Facebook, who claimed, "[T]he days of … having a different image for your work friends or coworkers and for the other people you know are probably coming to an end pretty quickly.… Having two identities for yourself is an example of a lack of identity."[26]

In the cybernetic world, personality seems to be determined and no longer to reflect a Jewish individual's changing performances in his or her everyday life. It is stored as a single image. Sarrazin's assertion that Jews can be distinguished from other ethnic groups by a solid, unchanging property—in other words, a specific gene—attests to the same simplistic (essentialized) reasoning. Jews are not seen as a fragmented group, differentiated among themselves due to their many-layered interactions with non-Jews, their differing interests, or the lives they lead, but, owing to their assumedly sharing of a specific gene, as representing a single, homogeneous entity.

The striving for objective definitions of cultural phenomena has increased lately and found expression in various academic fields. An exemplary discipline that adamantly endeavors to explain cultural articulations by biological or neural processes and thereby furthers the trend to essentialization is neuroscience. Therefore it comes as no surprise that neuroscientists formulate some of the central arguments Sarrazin uses in his book. For example, his suggestion of raising the fertility rate of gifted, talented people in order to elevate the level of intelligence in the population at large was made at a conference on brain doping in Oxford in summer 2009.[27] This is not to say that Sarrazin had cognizance of what the scientists attending the conference demanded or vice versa; but that their respective lines of reasoning are embedded in the same paradigm. Sarrazin thus merely proposes what other scholars express, although with much more sensational public response.

The central issue is not whether Sarrazin understands scientific work, whether he interpreted studies on the inheritance of intelligence adequately, or whether he cited research on the Jewish gene correctly. The prime question concerns the reason for his focusing on biological processes as the explanatory framework for cultural and social differences between collectives. The answer lies at least partially with the tendency to essentialization in science and the humanities. Sarrazin's reductionist thinking, which singles out largely biological properties to identify ethnic or religious groups and to determine their societal accomplishments, is very much in consonance with similar enunciations of various scientists. They also maintain that people are driven by inherited factors rather than by voluntary efforts. It is the body that determines social performances.

Repressed Discourses on the Jewish Body

Sarrazin's book appeared at a time when various discourses, which in part were influenced and derived from the same cultural and intellectual contexts as *Deutschland schafft sich ab!,* merged and generated a climate particularly responsive to his claims. References to Jewish genes were not novel in Germany. Just a few months before Sarrazin's work was released from the press, newspapers reported on the findings of Doron Behar, a geneticist at the Rambam Health Care Campus in Haifa who compared the DNA of Jews and non-Jews and found genetic congruence among the former.[28] Whereas Israelis apparently met these findings with much enthusiasm Germans did not respond in any particular way to it, neither critical nor approving.[29]

Along with other examples of rather sober media coverage on genetic studies on Jews, this instance seems to confirm the thesis that, apart from the far-rightist camp, there is no public discourse on the Jewish body in Germany today. Some indications may be discovered in specific academic fields (see chapter 11 by Amos Morris-Reich in this book), but they have no impact on the larger population. The physical difference of the Jew is referred to in Bernhard Schlink's short story "Die Beschneidung" (Circumcision) as a bodily difference between Jews and non-Jews in their circumcised penis, but it turns out that after the German gives up his foreskin to appease his American Jewish lover, who has been reminding him of Germany's guilty past, she does not notice and he leaves her.[30] But even these sporadic references to the Jewish body shed little light on public discourses. As Sander L. Gilman asserts in the foreword to this volume, "in twenty-first-century Germany, historically it is still the Jews who define a race." However this is not due to an overt or vocal preoccupation with Jews in racial terms or concerning their genetic make-up, but, as I argue, to the taboo on discussing it. The implicit admonishment not to touch the Jew is the very reason for the Jew's conspicuous position.

A taboo forces people to repress ostracized views but cannot prevent them from sporadically bursting out.[31] If this happens, they are reported on at length as if to compensate for the lack of unbiased discourses. This came to the fore when, in 2010, the current European commissioner for trade, Karel De Gucht, claimed that it made no sense to talk to Jews using rational arguments, because they think they are always right. And he warned against underestimating the influence of the "Jewish lobby" on the policy in the United States.[32] As German newspapers expatiated on this statement, it helped, along with Sarrazin's remarks, to solidify the image of the Jews as the Other.

De Gucht's assertion is reminiscent of the old stereotype of the Jews' perverse stubbornness against conversion to Christianity, but it is a mirror image of Sarrazin's claims. The Jews' purported imperviousness to rational arguments is the very opposite to the view according to which Jews possess a high IQ and therefore are at the forefront of new developments. Instead, it is seen as an indication of their premodern state of mind. And this characteristic had historically been linked to their physiognomy, to their facial features.[33] The Jews, so De Gucht's statement implicitly says, have a particular brain, they think differently—something that Sarrazin claimed, although he stresses their intelligence and rational personality.

The contemporary German indifference to genetic studies on Jews is in striking contrast to how Germans responded to Sarrazin's references to the Jewish gene. The difference between the overall reticence about, for example, the outcome of Doron Behar's study and the almost fierce reaction to Sarrazin's claims may be due to the fact that the Israeli research was considered a Jewish affair, unrelated to German interests. Once Sarrazin, a representative of Germany's political elite, articulated his opinion, it affected Germany's self-understanding and thus became a German discourse.

Not all parts of German society were equally unconcerned about genetic studies on Jews. Some political circles followed the publications with great curiosity and made ample use of them to further their own goals. The rightist camp, for example, profited from the findings of specific Jewish genes. In this social and political realm, a discourse on the Jewish body unfolded unabated by any discursive constraints that resulted from Germany's Nazi past. The pertinent statements and enunciations could be ignored if they were made only by radical right-wing activists whose activities are closely observed by German internal security authorities. Yet the discourse was published by media that straddle far-rightist and respectable conservative camps and cannot be ranked exclusively among the extremists.

The German weekly *Junge Freiheit,* which cites copious genetic research on Jews, picked up on the study on Jewish intelligence undertaken by three scientists from the University of Utah, and explicitly interpreted the linkage, purportedly scientifically confirmed, between Ashkenazic Jewish high levels of intelligence and their genetic makeup as proof of the existence of a Jewish race. The principle of equality of the generation of 1968, so the *Junge Freiheit* claims, and the concept that the social-cultural environment accounts for differences between peoples are no longer valid. Nowadays genetics provides explanations for societal differences and inequalities, and so, although it sounds politically incorrect, the usage of the notion of race has become legitimate again.[34]

Whereas in the original study the three scientists emphasized a connection between a genetic defect and cultural practices, the *Junge Freiheit* no longer includes the latter. For the weekly, it is only the Social Darwinian process of selection that accounts for the Jews' advantages. Jews are thus considered a race with highly favorable characteristics. Although more inclined to exaggerate and thus more radical, the weekly's line of argumentation is very similar to Sarrazin's reasoning, and so are the conclusions. Both attribute a genetically determined status of difference to Jews.

The Role of Islamophobia in Public Discourse

Not only those on the political right were inspired by widely cited references to a higher level of intelligence among Jews in comparison to non-Jews to transgress the taboo on the Jewish body in public discourse and on the linking of Jews and racist theories. The studies on Jewish intelligence had, as could be expected, other consequences as well. Anti-Semites and neo-Nazis used the research in order to emphasize the detrimental influence of Jewish intellectualism on society.[35] However, political activists on the extreme right do not reflect the mood and thinking of society at large.

In the final section of this chapter, I want to link the question of why Sarrazin mentioned the Jewish gene to wider political developments that point at a pervasive Islamophobia. As a consequence, anti-Semitism, at least for the time being, seems to be on the wane. The question as to whether anti-Semitism has been replaced by Islamophobia is currently hotly debated. The dispute, which was covered by German newspapers and gained international attention, was understood as a debate about Germany's attitude toward the Holocaust: holding anti-Semitism comparable with Islamophobia was interpreted as a denial of the singularity of the Shoah.[36]

This has paradigmatically come to the fore when rightist politicians from various European countries traveled to Israel in the spring of 2011. They had become aware that, due to Europe's history of anti-Semitism in the twentieth century and especially the Holocaust, collective memory forbade them to show anti-Semitic affinities. Their denial of any Judeophobic inclinations served as a credit card to be accepted by voters and compete with political mainstream parties in their own countries. And how could this be better achieved than by going to Israel and promising their support? A bridge between traditionally anti-Semitic rightist politicians and Jewish Israelis was their common goal to find allies in the fight against Islam, though not all Israeli Jews welcomed them. In this case, Jews were assigned the task of validating the democratic legitimacy of the rightwing activists.

A similar motive seems to have driven Sarrazin to talk about the Jewish gene, albeit only once and peripherally in an interview, in order to acquit himself of the potential accusation of being a racist and using racist language.[37] This can be explained by looking at how the possibility of a Jewish nation sharing a specific gene is dealt with in Germany. In Germany, one of the most important consequences of the Nazi past is the opposition to biological conceptualizations of social groups. This collective attitude, as I argue, accounted for the more-or-less unanimous rejection of Sarrazin's genetic classification of Muslims by the German population. When it comes to the Jews, the aversion to biological description becomes even more profound. Talking about Jewish genes is thus considered a serious and grave violation of the social consensus, which Sarrazin transgressed consciously and deliberately because he assumed that many Jews would concur in his assertion and thus make it a legitimate proposition in Germany.[38] A narrative of "Jewish genes"[39] is widespread in the Jewish world, both in Israel and the Diaspora, especially so-called population genetics research to prove that various Jewish groups, such as Ashkenazic and Sephardic populations, are genetically linked to each other.[40] In Germany, for example, the Jewish website *Ha-Galil* encourages people to find out if they are Jewish by an examination of their genes.[41] Many additional studies on Jewish genes may be mentioned in this context, which might have provided Sarrazin with a legitimization of his statement about the Jewish gene and allow him to talk about Muslims in biological categories as well.[42] However, Jews in Germany bluntly and vocally disapproved of his statement about the Jewish gene whereas Israelis paid hardly any attention to the controversy over Sarrazin.

Conclusion

By referring to the Jewish gene, Sarrazin sought to link his arguments in *Deutschland schafft sich ab!* to prevalent discourses on Jews and genetics within the Jewish world. Yet he ignored the fact that his line of reasoning unfolded in a German context which differs from that in Israel or among Jews in other parts of the world. Germany is still haunted by its Nazi past, and consequently the conceptualization of Jews as genetically distinct from other ethnic or religious collectives is understood differently than among Jews, not as proof of genealogical continuity of the Jewish people but as attesting to an essential difference of Jews from other societal groups. It was therefore impossible for Sarrazin to transplant part of the Jewish discourse on the Jewish gene to Germany in order to legitimate Social Darwinist reasoning about Muslim immigrants.

Acknowledgment

The research for this chapter was funded by the Austrian Science Fund (FWF), grant P23325-G18.

Notes

1. Thilo Sarrazin, "Klasse statt Masse," *Lettre International* 86 (2009): 199 (interview with Frank Berberich).
2. Gilman, *Smart Jews*, 64–65.
3. See, e.g., Allen Buchanan (et. al.), "From Chance to Choice: Genetic and Justice," a study carried out at Cambridge University. According to the findings, Ashkenazic Jews have an IQ 20 percent higher than the global average (N. Lalany, "Ashkenazi Jews Rank Smartest in World," http://www.ynetnews.com/articles/0,7340,L-4098351,00.html http://www.ynetnewscom/Ext/Comp/ArticlelayoutCdaArticlePrintPreview/1,2506,L
4. Cochran et al., "Natural History."
5. See Lawrence Grossman, "Love Me, Love Me Not: Is Philosemitism Good for the Jews?" (review of Jonathan Karp and Adam Sutcliffe, eds., *Philosemitism in History*), *Jewish Daily Forward*, July 20, 2011, http://www.forward.com/articles/140128

6. Richard J. Herrnstein and Charles Murray, *The Bell Curve: Intelligence and Class Structure in American Life* (New York: Free Press, 1994).
7. Russell Jacoby and Naomi Glaubermann, *The Bell Curve Debate. History, Documents, Opinions* (New York: Three Rivers Press, 1995).
8. Sarrazin, *Deutschland.*
9. Frank Schirrmacher, "Sarrazins drittes Buch," in Sarrazin, *Eine Deutsche Debatte,* ed. Deutschlandstiftung Integration (Munich: Piper, 2010), 50–52.
10. Seibel, Schumacher, and Fahrun, "Ich bin kein Rassist," 4f.
11. Sarrazin, *Deutschland,* 56.
12. Ibid., 100.
13. Ibid., 317.
14. See M. Kamann, "Nur als Provokateur aktuell," *Die Welt,* August 27, 2010, 3.
15. M. Hoffmann, "Nachdenken wäre der Intelligenzdebatte zuträglich," *Frankfurter Allgemeine Zeitung,* September 15, 2011, N3.
16. Sarrazin, *Deutschland,* 216.
17. Paul Julius Möbius, *Über den physiologischen Schwachsinn des Weibes* (Halle: Marhold 1900).
18. F. Schirrmacher, "Ein fataler Irrweg," *Frankfurter Allgemeine Zeitung,* August 29, 2011, 21.
19. Sarrazin, *Deutschland,* 93–96.
20. Steven Beller, *Wien und die Juden 1867–1938* (Vienna: Böhlau Verlag, 1993).
21. T. Hirschfeld, "Why Koreans Study Talmud," http://www.ynetnews.com/articles/0,7340,L-4065672,00.html
22. A. Rosen, "Why Are Jews So Smart?," http://www.jewishmag.com/156mag/smart_jews/smart_jews.htm
23. See the interview with Thilo Sarrazin in *Die Zeit* August 25, 2011, 6.
24. See F. Schirrmacher, "Eine Falle namens Thilo Sarrazin," *Frankfurter Allgemeine Zeitung* July 28, 2011, 37.
25. Laurence J. Silberstein, "Mapping, Not Tracing: Opening Reflection," in *Mapping Jewish Identities,* ed. Laurence J. Silberstein (New York: New York University Press, 2000), 13.
26. Eli Pariser, *The Filter Bubble. What the Internet Is Hiding from You* (London: Penguin Books, 2011), 106.
27. Thomas Thiel, "Wettrüsten im Kopf," *Frankfurter Allgemeine Zeitung* July 2, 2009, 34.
28. See, e.g., Hartmut Wewetzer, "Genetische Abstammung: Abrahams Kinder," http://www.tagesspiegel.de/wissen/abrahams-kinder/1860976.html
29. Genetische Ähnlichkeit der Juden: Erst bejubelt, dann bestritten, http://www.unzensuriert.at/001878-genetische-hnlichkeit-der-juden-erst-bejubelt-dann-bestritten
30. Bernhard Schlink, "Die Beschneidung," in *Liebesfluchten* [Flights of love] (Zürich: Diogenes, 2000).
31. On anti-Semitic statements in Germany that triggered fierce controversies, see Wolfgang Benz, *Was ist Antisemitismus?* (München: Beck, 2004).
32. Maram Stern, "Der Benutzte Jude," in *Sarrazin: Eine Deutsche Debatte,* ed. Deutschlandstiftung Integration (München: Piper, 2010), 142–145.
33. Gilman, *Smart Jews,* 36.

34. Anni Mursula, "Intelligenz in die Wiege gelegt" http://www.jungefreiheit.de/Single-News-Display-Archiv.52
35. This line of thinking has been put forward by *Alpen-Donau Info,* a website maintained by Austrian neo-Nazis, that links the allegedly higher IQ of Jews to their so-called practice of inbreeding.
36. An example of the acrimonious controversy is the attack on Wolfgang Benz, the former director of the Zentrum für Antisemitismusforschung in Berlin, who was castigated for his presumed blurring of distinctions between anti-Semitism and Islamophobia. The accusation originated from feelings of indignation at a conference on "Feindbild Muslim—Feindbild Jude" organized by the Zentrum in December 2008 (Britta Bürger, "Neue Feindschaft, alte Muster," http://www.dradio.de/dkultur/sendungen/thema/1114583/ See B. Weinthal, "German Scholar Takes on anti-Semitism Center's Policies," *Jerusalem Post,* March 7, 2010, 5.
37. Interview with Sarrazin, *Welt am Sonntag* 35, August 29, 2010, 4.
38. On the reaction in Israel, see Reuters, "Banker Says Nazi-Era Guilt Has Turned Germany into Hostage of Euro Zone," *Haaretz,* May 22, 2012, http://www.haaretz.com/misc/article-print-page/jewish-gene
39. On the false designation of genes as "Jewish," see Susan Martha Kahn, "Are Genes Jewish? Conceptual Ambiguities in the Genetic Age," in *Boundaries of Jewish Identity,* edited by Susan A. Glenn and Naomi Sokoloff (Seattle: Washington University Press, 2010), 21.
40. Nebel et al., "The Y Chromosome Pool of Jews as Part of the Genetic Landscape of the Middle East," *American Journal of Human Genetics* 69, no. 5 (2001): 1095–1112.
41. iGENEA.com, http://www.igenea.com/docs/hagalil/hagalil/htm
42. See, e.g., "Jewish HapMap Project," http://www.einstein.yu.edu/labs/harry-ostrer/projects/jewish-hapmap-project.aspx See also Sharon Begley, "The DNA of Abraham's Children," *Newsweek,* June 3, 2010, http://www.thedailybeast.com/newsweek/2010/06/03/the-dna-of-abraham-s-children.html

CHAPTER 14

Blood, Soul, Race, and Suffering

Full-Bodied Ethnography and Expressions of Jewish Belonging

Fran Markowitz

Full-Bodied Ethnography: Blood, Soul, Race, and Suffering

Seeking to destabilize static truths about the Jews as an unchanging and uncanny people, this essay advances a full-bodied ethnography that, with its double focus on the embodied subjects of research and the bodies of researchers, and the meanings conveyed by both, involves mutual participation in the social process: ethnographers and their hosts together enact and hence entrench cultural categories. Yet at the same time the unmediated sensual interactions of full-bodied ethnography also challenge, if not blow apart, the verity of these categories. A review of fieldwork that I conducted among Jews, non-Jews, and those precariously placed on the Jewish–non-Jewish divide—in New York among Soviet Jewish immigrants in 1984–1988, in Russia 1995–1996, and among Black Hebrews, in Dimona and Chicago, 1992–1999—suggests that Judaic studies and cultural anthropology can benefit from the pursuit of full-bodied ethnography to steer a course aimed at getting beyond the fixity of race and ethnicity.

In New York City in the mid 1980s, my Russian-speaking neighbors and friends, comparing and contrasting themselves with American-Jews-as-category and with me, as I stood, strolled, ate, drank, danced and spoke right there among them, told me that it is blood, genes, and a shared history of suffering that makes one a Jew—nothing more, and nothing less.

During the 1990s, in the dusty Israeli Negev town of Dimona, and in Chicago, America's Second City, the brothers and sisters of the Hebrew Israelite Community told me, as I stood, sat, ate, drank, and danced, interacting with them, that being part of the Jewish people is more than a traceable line of descent or knowledge of Talmudic law. It is in the spirit; it is in the soul. It manifests, so they said, in doing as Abraham did: rejecting a history of misrecognition and mistreatment by coming home to serve the God of Israel in the land of Israel.[1]

In August 2002 when I introduced myself to Gordana, an attorney-turned-café-owner in Eastern Sarajevo, also popularly and contentiously known as Srpsko (Serbian) Sarajevo, and then two years later as I presented my business card to representatives of the ruling Serbian Democratic Party in the town of Pale in the Serbian Republic of Bosnia-Herzegovina, I was told that as a Jew, and an Israeli at that, I should understand their plight better than anyone, that is, that I should understand the threat of Islam. To my request for an explanation of their Party's platform and the division of Bosnia into two ethnic majority entities, the SDS officials looked straight into my eyes and asked, "How is it that you do not understand who we are? We Serbs lost one and a half million, just like your people's terrible loss of six million, during World War II. We were both victims, slaughtered by the same coalition of Croats and Muslims, and Germans, of course." Then one of the spokesmen leaned forward and lowered his voice, "The difference between our peoples is that we Serbs are a poor isolated people. Your people, the Jews, are 15 million strong in the U.S. alone. And they are rich and influential beyond compare: Benjamin Franklin, the Rockefellers, Henry Kissinger, for centuries the leading political and economic figures of the U.S. have all been Jews. You, of all people, should know."[2]

I have presented these vignettes to begin my chapter with drama. These scenes are not straw men conjured up to be deconstructed or torn apart, but dramas that I—mostly inadvertently—elicited through my presence, and in which I consequently participated. I opened with them to demonstrate that amorphous ideas and feelings of belonging—who is who, who should know what, and who should not—often congeal and find expression through the immediacy of face-to-face interaction. These specific vignettes provoke the questions: Who are the Jews and what is Jewishness? How are blood, soul, race, and suffering articulated to define and circumscribe the Jewish people? How do people who define themselves as Jews address these questions? And how do those who are not pose them from without?

This essay results from examining the impact of full-bodied ethnography on issues I have been mulling over for quite some time: the contingent, interpersonal dynamics involved in expressing and making culture. It suggests that sensual propinquity can open up mutual avenues of interaction and inquiry that challenge or confirm taken-for-granted cultural categories, which then leads research in unexpected directions.[3] Once I embraced the comments I had preferred to ignore—remarks about me: my hair, nose, eyes, skin, and height, and my identities as an American, as a Jew, and as a woman—by people who were expressing their own metaphors of group identity, I came to rethink the ethnographic project as embodied, intersubjective negotiations that assert and even produce community and identity, rather than merely elicit *a priori* symbolic or structural codes that the anthropologist then deciphers and interprets.

Full-bodied ethnography—a term I must attribute to Karla Poewe[4]—is all about anthropologists recognizing that in-the-flesh interactions with their hosts make them, as Aaron Turner has suggested, "significant participant[s], insider[s] to the social processes by which practices are developed and gain meaning."[5] Necessarily including a double focus on the embodied subjects of research and the bodies of researchers and the meanings that they express and convey, full-bodied ethnography offers an equalizing but risky research strategy that demands sharing scrutiny and power. At least, that is what I have learned over the years while negotiating my status as an ethnographer, a guest, a friend, a Jew, a woman, an American, and most lately as an Israeli, while conducting research among people who either do or do not define themselves as Jews.

What has vexed me from the start as both a Jewess and as an ethnographer of Jews is the static truth that the Jews, a diverse and dispersed people, are often predefined as a timeless category of humanity.[6] In the words of Harvey Goldberg, "Most basically, being Jewish usually entails a sense of ethnic or communal belonging.... Many Jews also see themselves in religious terms."[7] But, just as basically, Jews have been delineated over the centuries as an ontological given, a race, a nation, a people bound together as much by their refusal of faith as by blood. Jews in Christendom consequently became those soulless, uncanny others that everyone can and does identify when they see, hear, and—in terms of constructions of the Jew's body—smell them.[8]

In the discussion that follows I aim to show through full-bodied ethnography that although united from without and within through metaphors of blood and race and treated as one all-embracing social category excluded in the Western imaginary from grace or soul, the Jews (as real people, a people of history and as cultural symbols) and Jewishness (the practices and attributes attached to Jews that take form within specific historical contexts and in particular nation-states) are startlingly varied.

Contemporary Jews identify each other—and are identified by others—as they play out their Jewishness (or not) between and among embodied actors, including the always specifically aged, raced, gendered, nationed, and sexed ethnographer. During fieldwork, as I became an object of my hosts' curiosity, that, in one way or another represented, elicited, or contradicted their prevailing notions of the Jews or Jewishness, I abandoned the always unstable pose of the invisible and neutral observer-recorder and instead took up the task of ethnographic research as embodied dialogical participation in the social process. That made me a contributor to, as well as a chronicler of, my hosts' expressions of community, identity, and culture.

Ultimately my hope is that in forging a closer link with humanistic anthropology, Jewish studies might benefit from full-bodied ethnography and steer a course parallel to those scholars who strive to get beyond ontological blackness.[9] But first I will pause to develop my case for full-bodied ethnography, particularly as it relates to work about and among the Jews.

Developing Full-Bodied Ethnography

During the last decade of the twentieth century, several scholars directed attention to Judaism and Jews as embodied subjects and objects at different times and places.[10] Moving away from a prima facie understanding of an identity based on the textuality of Judaism (its sacred and rabbinic literature), historians, literary critics, psychologists, and anthropologists have been urging a reexamination of Jews as organic beings, dialectically interacting with—and not just representing or emanating from—religious, literary, and legal texts. Hence Daniel Boyarin ends his book *Carnal Israel* on the price paid for refusing to accept body/spirit dualism and what he sees as the equally high price paid by Christians for embracing it by asking his readers to make use of cultural dialectics to find "solutions to the problems of cultural particularism in a context of human solidarity."[11] Gilman's book, *The Jew's Body,* squarely rooted in recent European history, serves as a chilling reminder to those same readers that while it may seem that the Jews have made it in America,[12] even so, the grotesquely caricatured Jewish body of history may in fact be what Gentiles (and even some Jews) see when real Jewish people who look nothing like those caricatures are standing right before them. The collection edited by Eilberg-Schwartz and Weiss's *The Chosen Body,* it seems to me, are telling their Jewish readers not to feel particularly smug about being a literate, scholarly people because Jews are embodied, and they worry very much about their bodies. In fact, these books point out that much attention in the sacred texts and rabbinical commentaries on them is directed at body care, as well as are those seminal (pun intended) Zionist writings that urged return to the land of Israel. Max Nordau, in particular, stressed the need to get pale, emaciated, flat-footed yeshiva students and their kin out of unhealthy European towns so they could develop robust muscular bodies and take their place in the world, as he advised in *Degeneration* (1895).[13] That desire, now turned to need, for strong, healthy Jewish bodies, Meira Weiss shows, continues in Israel.

While each of these scholars in their concentration on Jewish embodiment has opened a new vista onto the study of Jews and Judaism, I am perplexed that most lack an explicit connection to the embodied Jewish researcher. While reading Gilman's *The Jew's Body* I wanted to know how he could write it so dispassionately. Closer to home, for me at least, how does Riv-Ellen Prell, who has written beautifully about the rage represented in stereotypes of Jewish American Princesses see herself in relation to this category?[14] Does she identify as a "JAP"? If so, why does she write as if she does not; and if not, from what Jewish-female standpoint is she writing?

More broadly, the lack of embodied connections between ethnographers and the people with whom they live during fieldwork has gained attention of late in scholarly, anthropological circles.[15] Informed by the harsh lessons about power and knowledge delivered by Edward Said and Michel Foucault and alarmed by an increasingly logocentric focus in the discipline, some anthropologists have retreated from the theoretical holism of culture to analyze more specific, tangible, cultural products such as music, literature, TV shows, movies, and advertisements. Others, understanding embodiment "as the existential condition of cultural life," have focused on the body.[16]

In response, perhaps, to the postmodern turn in which culture became ever more ephemeral and fragmented as an analytical category, by the mid-1990s it seemed that "the body would appear to be everywhere."[17] This body has been scrutinized and dissected; shown as performing and performed upon; disciplined and resistive; taking pleasure and writhing in pain; described as weighty, opaque, and just about impervious, and as fleeting, fluid, and elusive. Bodies have been portrayed as the live, fleshy material on which culture—or knowledge, power, ideology, fashion—is inscribed, while serving as a key symbol that animates and makes tangible concepts of society, polity, and culture. Yet despite the ubiquity of body studies, with few but striking exceptions, they often remain separated from the reflexivity that has also pervaded ethnography during the last two decades.[18] Aaron Turner attributes this division to the tendency for the reflexive anthropologist to manifest as a disembodied voice commenting on others' bodies as the theorized results of research rather than as an embodied person involved in the social process where bodies—and not only minds and hearts—meet.[19] Even in a volume aimed at breaking taboos, *Taboo, Sex, Identity, and Erotic Subjectivity in Anthropological Fieldwork,* it is telling that Andrew Killick entitled his reflexive essay on "Being White, Straight, and Male in Korea: The Penetrating Intellect," and not, "An Intrusive Body."[20]

Privileging the mind over the body through the I/eye, ethnographers who make other people into the colorful bodily grist for their interpretive mills can lead to misunderstandings rather than clarification, while contributing to an imbalance of power between researchers and the researched.[21] Thus, even when ethnographic knowledge was aimed at or focused on the body, in the 1990s the promise of such knowledge remained shaky. Suggestions for resolving these dilemmas came from many seeking more responsive and responsible research paths.[22] Some, as early as Delmos Jones in 1970, urged limiting ethnographic access to members of the studied population so that the natives really could speak for themselves.[23] But soon after this agenda was laid out, it generated the dilemma of delineating just who native anthropologists are, anyway.[24] What may seem at the outset of a project to be a salient and unifying category, like women, Blacks, gays, or Jews, often turns out to be differently constituted across class lines and nation-states, and native researchers may well find their claims of similitude under assault.[25]

Shaken by these issues, some years ago Michael Ashkenazi and I discussed what we had never written about before and barely mentioned aloud: the embarrassing and risky embodied bulk of our fieldwork. Did we ever feel powerful or privileged as invisible intellects? Hardly! We—or was it our bodies?—had both attracted considerable attention from the people we had come to study—Mike in Japan, myself in New York and urban Israel. To our amazement, we discovered that we had both employed the same strategy—silence—to ease our way out of the personal discomfort and erase the professional anxieties that this attention had caused. Why? Because in the 1980s we understood that our job in the field was to learn about others, not to become the object of our own inquiries. It took me some time under the influence of several brave publications to understand that what had happened to me in fieldwork was an important aspect of the interpersonal dynamics involved in the creation of community and the making of culture.[26]

Based on that preliminary understanding, Michael Ashkenazi and I set out to demystify fieldwork by illuminating it as an ongoing process of negotiations extending far beyond initial entry into the field and establishment of so-called rapport.[27] Accordingly, in the introduction to our edited volume, *Sex, Sexuality, and the Anthropologist,* we issued a call for "historically deep, politically informed 'full-bodied ethnographies' situated in time, space, and emotion between self-aware … ethnographers and their equally self-conscious … field partners."[28] Our volume showed how people in the field gaze at, gossip about, and criticize their ethnographers as particular and often peculiar persons, and often guide them and touch them. These ethnographers are not the all-knowing disembodied analytical consciousness that pervades so many academic texts.[29] Instead, we hoped to show how full-bodied ethnography coupled with the twin strategies of reflexivity and responsibility could offer "a process of intersubjective communications that sometimes work and sometimes do not."[30] Our volume's aim was to provide an alternative to the failed meta-narratives of objectivistic neutrality and the restrictions of class, race, and gender standpoints and thereby revive anthropological fieldwork by revealing how culture is a process grounded in, and not just elicited from, the very intimacy of building and living mindful, soulful, and embodied relationships over time.

Full-Bodied Ethnography: Blood, Soul, Race, and Suffering

In the middle of his retrospective reflections in Jack Kugelmass's pioneering collection of ethnographic essays on American Jewry, Jonathan Boyarin describes for his readers a variety of reactions to the wearing of what he calls his knitted yarmulke (skullcap in Yiddish or *kippah* in Hebrew) in Paris. He writes, "[I]t works effectively, almost dangerously, as a two-way sensor, inducing Jews to present themselves to me and forcing me to try to understand how I am reflected in their eyes."[31] But Boyarin undid the promise of full-bodied ethnography before he could carry it out by writing off the potential importance of these moments of recognition as his fieldwork juvenilia—too superficial or rudimentary, perhaps, to take seriously and pursue further. It is too bad, because I for one would like to know if it is only the crocheted yarmulke on his head that impelled the men he describes to seek contact and identify themselves with him as Jews. Might they have recognized him as Jewish without the skullcap? And how might that recognition be described and interpreted?

I, for one, did not wear a headscarf or a *sheitel* [Yiddish, wig] when I moved to Brighton Beach in Brooklyn New York in January 1984, but the elderly American Jews who remained fixed in that neighborhood had no problem identifying me as one of theirs as soon as I showed up in sweater and jeans. I was not Russian, Puerto Rican, or Korean, and when they announced to my husband and me how great it was to see young people moving back to the area the unspoken words included were "American Jews."

My Russian neighbors, however, were not so sure. Once they ascertained—quite quickly and with astonishment—that I understood and could speak Russian, all kinds of questions were directed my way:

> Boxes and boxes of books, but where is your furniture?
> Where are your parents? Where do they live?
> Were you born in America? Were your parents?
> *Kto Vy po-natsional'nosti?* What is your nationality?

Nationality. Well read, I knew what they were asking and why.[32] What is usually called ethnicity in the United States was and still is referred to in Russia and South-Eastern Europe as nationality.[33] Although my new neighbors had no difficulty recognizing many Americans as Jews, they were not so sure about me. If I had Jewish blood, it certainly was not manifesting in the way that they thought it should:

> You look English, American, Northern European.
> You're too tall.
> Your hair's too straight.
> Your nose goes up.

But I was Jewish all right, and I told them that my grandfather graduated from the Slobodka Yeshiva in Kovno, Lithuania, and had been a rabbi all his life. "Oh, the granddaughter of a rabbi. But you don't look Jewish. Maybe it's something about America." And then, Sasha reminisced about the Moscow Yiddish Theater. Dima told me about the little shul in Odessa where his father had served as the *gabbai* [sexton]; Lyalya recalled childhood gatherings at her grandmother's for gefilte fish and *khremsele* [a filled fried cake made with *matsah* meal] during Passover; Zhenya pondered the irony of how it was that even though her grandparents were devoted communists and enthusiastic atheists, when they died they were buried according to their wishes in a Jewish cemetery with prayers intoned over their graves.

But these recollections did not pour out as one-shot monologues. They were repeated and augmented, interspersed with comments about how American Jews who kept the religion but lost the suffering just do not understand the history of Jews in the Soviet Union. I was told countless times that although Soviet Jews may have lost the religion they never did lose Jewish blood, genes, and intellect—in short, their nationality, and the humiliation, if not discrimination, that went along with it. Indeed, many recalled along with family stories of Jewish belonging how Russian and Ukrainian schoolmates and principals, coworkers, and supervisors made them suffer for having Jewish faces. For ex-Soviet Jews who were cast into an inescapable national category whether they were religious or atheists, being Jewish was an absolute fact. Sometimes, when I was asked once again if I was sure I was Jewish, I wondered if this was not a tiny moment of resistance, maybe even revenge, against all those American Jews at the resettlement agencies and in the streets who, because they were Russian speakers and not overtly religious, dubbed them, in Zvi Gitelman's words, "not Jewish enough."[34] But then, one day, at the funeral of the mother of a mutual friend, as I tied a kerchief over my hair, Sasha, who had been mocking me for more than a year about what he called my shiksa looks, suddenly exclaimed, "Now I can see that you are Jewish! You look like Avital Sharansky!"[35] Was it my covered head? My sad expression? That we were united in the communal chanting of the kaddish, the prayer for the dead? Or did all these factors merge together after a year of friendship—including celebrating Rosh Hashanah (Jewish New Year) with a huge feast, dancing at birthday parties in Russian restaurants, strolling on the boardwalk, sitting on the beach, switching back and forth between English and Russian and throwing in some tangy Yiddish words for good measure that he now saw me in a different light? Had my Americanized body, now in a moment of shared suffering, morphed, if only for a moment, into an absolutely Jewish one?

These embodied interactions—with Sasha, Lina, Zhenya, Dima, Marina, Irina, Misha, and many more—in connection with concerts, parties, funerals, weddings, shopping, gossip exchanges, the food, smells and sounds of the restaurants, and all the people, are what made me, in spite of myself, part of this *Community in Spite of Itself,* to use the title of one of my books. I now regret that my earlier essay on Russian Jewish bat-mitzvahs and funerals was written without me-in-the-text, for everything in its analysis was learned, felt, and enacted in full-bodied ethnography.[36]

Blood and Soul—Separate but Intertwined

About a decade later, I made it to Russia. I spent most days from September 1995 through February 1996 sitting in eleventh-grade classrooms, where I heard Russian teenagers recite poetry and solve mathematical equations for their teachers, followed later by narratives of their life stories for me. The teenagers were in no way thrilled or amazed that I could speak to them in Russian. After all, they were studying English, and sometimes German, French, or Spanish as well. What they did comment upon—girls more frequently than boys—was the ease with which I approached them, and my subdued clothes. And from time to time, one teenager or another would remark that it was easy to talk to me because of my open manner and my warm soulful eyes.

Soul never came up in New York as an expression of Jewish belonging or even in relation to the Russianness that so many of my friends and neighbors valued in linguistic and high cultural forms. Blood and suffering were the key metaphors that expressed their Soviet-Russian-Jewishness. But the young people I met in post–Soviet Russia frequently invoked soul to express a certain way of being in the world, a specific sort of morality or character.[37] They spoke of soul as broad or wide to index generosity, openness, and empathy. And as they articulated their notions of what being Russian means to someone who was not, they hinted that should I understand, appreciate, and, most important, feel in my soul what they were communicating, I too could be Russian. I came to interpret this intimate negotiation of identity and belonging into something larger and politically salient, for in opposition to a loud descent-based counter rhetoric of "Russia for the Russians," it seemed to me that the younger generation extended its malleable notion of soul as an umbrella of Russian belonging to cover all citizens of the Russian Federation.[38] Russianness as soulfulness, however, demands fluent usage and cherishing of the Russian language and its literature while embracing a soulfully Russian way of being in the world. Russian soul and Russian blood frequently combine in the same human bodies, but not always and not necessarily.

Upon returning to Israel I mentioned the teenagers' remarks about my soulful eyes to some of my colleagues. One immediately exclaimed, "You have Semitic eyes!" That may be so, but then I wondered, "Why hadn't my Russian Jewish friends in New York read my eyes that way?" To be honest, I never thought of my eyes as Semitic, nor did my family; we just referred to them as our "droopy eyes." From time to time I would recognize my droopy eyes in the inner sanctums of museums: on Egyptian pyramid murals in the Metropolitan Museum of Art; later, in the Assyrian collection at the British Museum, and more recently on portraits painted by Modigliani, and contemporary sculptures of vanished shtetl Jews. But no one in Russia connected my soulful eyes with the Semites; quite the contrary, many teenagers, their teachers, and their parents, convinced that the connection I had made with them was deeper than what could be expected of Americans, were certain that I had a Slavic soul as well. After all, several pointed out that Marković is a South Slav surname, and reminded me that sometimes the essential connection to soul is soil.

In his thought-provoking book, *Carnal Israel,* Daniel Boyarin describes a key philosophical conflict in first-century Israel that ultimately solidified into an impermeable line of demarcation between Christians and Jews: rabbinic Jews stressed that the human being is a body animated by a soul, whereas for Hellenistic Jews and Greek-speaking Christians, the essence of a human being is a soul, which of necessity is housed in a body. Boyarin explains that this difference manifests even today: when a person declares, "I am not a Christian," she or he is saying something about beliefs and commitments, but when someone declares, "I am not a Jew," she or he is saying something about genealogy.[39] In refusing to accept Jesus as the Christ, Israel remains bound to their particular bodies, unwilling and thus unable to embrace a universal holy spirit and transcend the materialism of this world. Several centuries later, Viktor Kozlov claimed that there is something noble about the Russian soul that eschews materialism for spiritual creativity. Without invoking blood, he states that although Jews may have lived for centuries on Russian soil and speak Russian as the mother-tongue, these Jews can never *be* Russians, for they lack the Slavic soul.[40]

Soul and Race, Race as Soul, Soulfully Jewish?

Russians are not the only people who distinguish themselves from the rest by means of soul as a metaphor of belonging.[41] Soul is widely interpreted as a key signifier of blackness in a White world, while it also expresses the Christian concept of the spiritual potentiality of all humanity to rise above the here and now.[42] As a highly charged symbolic field, soul is powerfully packed with overlapping double messages that index Blacks' specific history of racialized oppression at the very moment that it conjures up transcendence of the oppression necessarily imposed by an embodied color line.[43] And so I wonder, just as Russians-as-Christians necessarily exclude Jews from (their) soul, might not African Americans and Jews be mutually incommensurable?

The African Hebrew Israelite Community (AHIC), better known as the Black Hebrews, offers a provocative milieu for exploring that question. The AHIC is a transnational multi-sited millenarian community centered in Dimona, Israel. Comprising several thousand men, women, and children of African descent who live mainly in the cities of the United States and the Caribbean, as well as in Israel's peripheral south, its central tenet is that most Black people in America are the long-lost descendants of the biblical Israelites. True to biblical prophecy (Deuteronomy 28), as punishment for abandoning God's law they embraced idols of wood and stone, forgot their heritage, and were sold into slavery. To redress the sins of the past and override the depravity of the present, Black people are called on to study the Bible and follow the AHIC's fundamentalist interpretation of it, acknowledge their Judaic roots, and return to their patrimony in Israel. In reconnecting the past with the present, the Hebrew Israelites believe that they will redeem the Black race and ultimately save all of humankind.[44]

Every time I enter the Village of Peace in Dimona—or the Soul Vegetarian Restaurant and Institute of Divine Understanding in Chicago, Atlanta, or Washington, DC—I am immediately recognized as White. Being White here makes me not just a racial Other, for whiteness speaks metonymically for a broader package of social facts: I am an American and an Israeli endowed with a university professorship, all of which carry some measure of authority. The brothers and sisters of the community, who after a long struggle are now legal residents of the land of Israel but not quite citizens of the polity, have at times perceived me as a powerful person with the potential to cause great harm or maybe even bring about some good.[45] But I must admit that I could hardly imagine any connection between what bell hooks has called terrifying whiteness and myself until years of doing fieldwork in discomfort had eased.[46] In America, I am conscious of a profound sense of powerlessness and otherness, and I identify with an *off-White* racial category that does not officially exist. I am not alone; many other Jewish American and Italian American women likewise see themselves that way, and "if anything identify with Black people or people who are other."[47] But I have always kept this feeling in perspective. Unlike Sandra Bernhard, whose provocative one-woman film, *Without You I'm Nothing* (1990), "simultaneously teases and frustrates identifications"[48] because her Black performativity fails to rally support from a Black audience, I have never performed myself as Black. I am well aware that among African Americans my phenotype is read as *White,* which is a marker of privilege in the wider world that excludes me from sharing in their blackness.[49] Many of my Hebrew acquaintances wondered, likewise, if their black skin precluded them from sharing in Jewishness: "Why is it," I have been asked, "that White Jews don't accept us as Jewish and that Israelis know so little about the African American experience of slavery, while we all know about the Holocaust?" Why is it, we wondered together, that the Jews memorialize the Shoah and are rightly recognized for their sufferings, while the descendants of the only people brought to the New World to toil as slaves have not been awarded reparations, praise, or a central place in world history for enduring such trauma? Of what value is the Christian notion of redemptive suffering? What does race have to do with it?

In August 1999, at the end of an invigorating sabbatical year in Chicago, I paid a farewell-for-now visit to Prince Asiel, the international ambassador of the AHIC, who headed the Chicago mission. Out of the blue, or so it seemed to me, in the midst of our conversation Prince Asiel asked me if I had ever been married. Before I could get the words out of my mouth, one of the two other men in the room answered, "Yes, and she was married to a brother." "You mean to a Black man?" asked Prince Asiel. "No," he replied, "to a Jewish brother." "I see," said Prince Asiel as he turned again toward me. "Fran," he said, "I've been looking for a wife with brown hair and soulful eyes." This time I did not hesitate, "Prince Asiel, I am flattered," I said, "But I don't do polygyny."[50] Everyone in the room burst out in laughter and the third man exclaimed, "Neither did we! Try it, you'll like it!" Suddenly race and soul, ethnicity and gender, suffering and humor, came together, reinforced and cancelled out each other in one embodied moment of mutual knowing, respect, and irreverence. Can it be, as Paul Gilroy has suggested, that the centuries' long Black struggle with racialized bodily oppression has paradoxically generated a model of soulful connections that both defines African American identity and is open to all humanity—including the Jews—no matter what the color of their skin?[51]

A Certain People Enters Postmodernity

Who are the Jews in the twenty-first century? Does it make sense to speak of them, en masse, as a certain people? For Charles Silberman, whose book of that name was published in 1985, the answer is clearly, yes.[52] Silberman, as I wrote in 1990, "celebrates the diversity in America that enables Jews to retain names like Shapiro and noses like Streisand's while working as top executive officers and entertainment figures. In addition, Silberman finds that America's atmosphere of pluralism not only tolerates but also encourages retention of Jewish identity and a desire for intragroup social affiliations."[53] While not contesting Jean-Paul Sartre's thesis that it takes Jews to make anti-Semites, Silberman's *A Certain People* quite convincingly demonstrates that it does not take, or no longer takes, anti-Semites to make Jews.[54] In the 1990s, following the publication of his *Modernity and the Holocaust,* Zygmunt Bauman insisted that if the Jews are a certain people it is mainly because they have been categorized and practiced as such during Christianity's two millennia.[55] He suggests that the term "allo-Semitism" best expresses "the practice of setting the Jews apart as people radically different from all others, needing separate concepts to describe and comprehend them and special treatment in all or most social intercourse."[56] "Allo-Semitism," he adds, is an ambivalent term that in its conveyance of the *un*-certainty of the stranger who has come to stay, can take form as either anti-Semitism or philo-Semitism, or remain, as do the Jews for their Christian hosts, ambivalence incarnate—annoying, disruptive, and uncanny. The certain people that Silberman describes and the certainly different uncertain people of Bauman, lead us as ethnographers in divergent directions when researching the Jews.

The certain people are easily found, described, and delineated as specific social groups that vary less among themselves from place to place or over time than they vary from non-Jews. It is therefore not naïveté that underwrites an opening statement by Shalom Staub: "As a Jew and as an anthropologist I wanted to experience the richness of daily, weekly, and yearly rites ... [and i]n the course of my stay I decided to pursue a career in Jewish ethnography."[57] Indeed, most historical, literary, sociological, and anthropological work on Jewish topics takes as its starting point the ontology of the Jews and Jewishness. One does not have to search far and wide to find a Jew, or the Jews; they are a certain people, with a certain look and way of being in the world. That look and way may differ somewhat from place to place and change over the centuries, but the primordial and ultimate certainty of it does not.

Bauman's perspective takes us—or me at least—on a different course. The Jews are inherently negatively marked as Other not only or necessarily because of what they are, but mainly for what they are not. Christian theology would have it that Jews rejected the "true faith," and then, in the nineteenth and twentieth centuries, new ideologies claimed that they continued to challenge European civility as they proliferated while defying the boundaries of nation-states, the new markers of identity in the modern world. For Bauman, the anti-Semitism of the Nazis, brutally enacted in the Shoah, marked the apex of an efficient pseudoscientific campaign against disorder by purging the national body of its weeds—dangerous not only or primarily because they impinge on pure categories, but because they so easily spread everywhere and take over.

Now, more than sixty years after the end of the Holocaust, the Jews continue to live dispersed worldwide, moving within and among nation-states, including Israel. It may well be that the Jewish condition is becoming ever more the rule and not the exception as diasporas spring up and spread throughout the world.[58] Might the mobility, partiality, and transmutability of postmodern identities and the multiplex belongings that derive from increasingly porous state boundaries at long last obviate what Bauman has called "the unbridgeable divide between 'the Jew as such' and the 'Jew next door'"?[59] Yes, Charles Silberman has answered, at least in America, for American Jews. But the words of the Bosnian Serbian Democratic Party spokesmen to me in 2004 should serve as a reminder that the answer may also be no. Jews, they insisted, remain eerily different, for unlike the Serbs and countless other peoples who became victims of powerful aggressors, the Jews have not been vanquished. Even after the destruction of their European communities and the murder of 6 million, they enjoy an enviable economic position and wield considerable influence in the world.

How to explain this? If we are to believe my Serbian interlocutors, no explanation is required; it is part and parcel of the Jews, who have always been able to connect themselves to power and capital. In the latest telling of this story, Jews are portrayed as really Americans, the only nation that emerged from the Cold War as the sole global superpower. Or is it that Americans are really Jews?[60] My bearing, body, and business card made it easy and logical for my hosts to conflate Jewishness and Israeliness with Americanness as they sat with me in Pale in the Serbian Republic of Bosnia and Herzegovina, across a perhaps bridgeable divide.

Conclusion

Michael Herzfeld has urged anthropologists to study nation-states and nationalisms in order to describe the making and entrenchment of static truths.[61] Rejecting ontological Jewishness while recognizing that the Jews as real people and as an uncanny cultural category have existed and persisted for more than three millennia I have taken up this challenge by pursuing full-bodied ethnography to explore the plethora of Jewish possibilities from among those who define as Jews, and those who do not. Blood, race, soul, and suffering continue to serve as key metaphors for delineating, discriminating against, and unifying the Jews. Yet their meanings and nuances come to the fore most saliently through embodied acts. And while these acts make culture, they also help to contest the very categories that lead to the reification and timelessness of race and ethnicity.

Acknowledgments

My thanks go to Misha Galperin and Éva Huseby-Darvas who have heatedly discussed issues of Jewish identity with me over the years, and to Karla Poewe, whose insistence on full-bodied experience and ethical transparency in ethnography continues to inspire. Thanks too to the editors of *Anthropology and Humanism* who graciously agreed to this slightly revised republication of my article that first appeared in *Anthropology and Humanism* 31.1 (2006): 41–56. I am most appreciative of the Society for Humanistic Anthropology's policy to allow unrestricted republication to authors whose work originally appeared in its journal.

Notes

1. The Hebrew Israelites, or the African Hebrew Israelites of Jerusalem (AHIJ), are a transnational, millenarian community that grew out of a Black Hebraic congregation in Chicago during the 1960s. Although far from the sole African American religious group to identify with the biblical Israelites, the AHIJ are the first and only Black Hebraic group to exit North America and establish a community in Israel. Along with the Village of Peace in Dimona, the AHIJ has sizable missions in Atlanta, Chicago, and Washington DC, and a presence in Ghana.
2. Fran Markowitz, *Sarajevo: A Bosnian Kaleidoscope* (Urbana: University of Illinois Press, 2010).
3. Victor Turner and Edward Bruner, eds., *The Anthropology of Experience* (Urbana: University of Illinois Press, 1986).
4. Karla Poewe, "No Hiding Place: Reflections on the Confessions of Manda Cesara," in *Sex, Sexuality, and the Anthropologist,* ed. Fran Markowitz and Michael Ashkenazi (Urbana: University of Illinois Press, 1999), 197–206.
5. Aaron Turner, "Embodied Ethnography, Doing Culture," *Social Anthropology* 8, no. 1 (2000): 55.
6. Michael Herzfeld, *Cultural Intimacy: Social Poetics in the Nation-State* (New York: Routledge, 1997), 10.
7. Harvey E. Goldberg, "Introduction," in *The Life of Judaism,* ed. Harvey E. Goldberg (Berkeley: University of California Press, 2001), 6.

8. See Gilman, *The Jew's Body.*
9. See Victor Anderson, *Beyond Ontological Blackness* (New York: Continuum, 1995); Michael Eric Dyson, *Reflecting Black: African-American Cultural Criticism* (Minneapolis: University of Minnesota Press, 1993); and Gilroy, *Against Race.*
10. Howard Eilberg-Schwartz, ed., *People of the Body: Jews and Judaism from an Embodied Perspective* (Albany: State University of New York Press, 1992); Gilman, *The Jew's Body;* Daniel Boyarin, *Carnal Israel: Reading Sex in Talmudic Culture* (Berkeley: University of California Press, 1993), and Meira Weiss, *The Chosen Body: The Politics of the Body in Israel* (Stanford, CA: Stanford University Press, 2002).
11. Boyarin, *Carnal Israel,* 235.
12. See Charles Silberman's celebratory work, *A Certain People: American Jews and their Lives Today* (New York: Summit, 1985); and Brodkin's more critical *How Jews Became White Folks.*
13. *People of the Body: Jews and Judaism from an Embodied Perspective,* ed. Howard Eilberg-Schwartz (Albany: State University of New York Press, 1992); Weiss, *Chosen Body.* See Presner, *Muscular Judaism* for a cultural historical analysis that links the muscular Jewish body with political regeneration.
14. See Riv-Ellen Prell, "Rage and Representation: Jewish Gender Stereotypes in American Culture," in *Uncertain Terms,* ed. Faye Ginsburg and Anna L. Tsing (Boston: Beacon, 1990), 248–266; and Riv-Ellen Prell, "Why Jewish Princesses Don't Sweat: Desire and Consumption in Postwar American Jewish Culture," in *People of the Body,* ed. Eilberg-Schwartz, 329–359.
15. See George Marcus and Dick Cushman, "Ethnographies as Texts," *Annual Review of Anthropology* 11 (1982): 25–69; James Clifford, "Introduction: Partial Truths," in *Writing Culture,* ed. Clifford and Marcus, 1–26, and Karla Poewe, "Writing Culture and Writing Fieldwork: The Proliferation of Experimental and Experiential Ethnographies," *Ethnos* 61, no. 3–4 (1996): 177–206.
16. See Thomas Csordas, "Embodiment as a Paradigm for Anthropology," *Ethos* 8 (1990): 5.
17. Margaret Lock, "Cultivating the Body: Anthropology and Epistemologies of Bodily Practice and Knowledge," *Annual Review of Anthropology* 22 (1993): 133–155.
18. Some early exceptions are Thomas Belmonte, *The Broken Fountain,* 2nd ed. (New York: Columbia University Press, 1989); Jean Briggs, *Never in Anger* (Cambridge, MA: Harvard University Press, 1970); Nancy Scheper-Hughes, *Death Without Weeping* (Berkeley: University of California Press, 1993); and Michael Taussig, *Shamanism, Colonialism, and the Wild Man* (Chicago: University of Chicago Press, 1986).
19. Turner, "Embodied Ethnography," 52.
20. Andrew Killick, "Being White, Straight and Male in Korea: The Penetrating Intellect," in *Taboo: Sex, Identity, and Erotic Subjectivity in Anthropological Fieldwork,* ed. Don Kulick and Margaret Willson (London: Routledge, 1995), 76–106.
21. See Jill Dubisch, "Lovers in the Field: Sex, Dominance, and the Female Anthropologist," in *Taboo: Sex, Identity, and Erotic Subjectivity in Anthropological Fieldwork,* ed. Don Kulick and Margaret Willson (London: Routledge 1995),

33; and Michael Herzfeld, *Anthropology through the Looking-Glass: Critical Ethnography in the Margins of Europe* (Cambridge, England: Cambridge University Press, 1987), 17.

22. E.g., Moshe Shokeid, "Commitment and Contextual Study in Anthropology," *Cultural Anthropology* 7 (1992): 464–477; Roy A. Rappaport, "Disorders of Our Own," in *Diagnosing America*, ed. Shepard Forman (Ann Arbor: University of Michigan Press, 1994), 234–294; and Nancy Scheper-Hughes, "The Primacy of the Ethical: Propositions for a Militant Anthropology," *Current Anthropology* 36, no. 3 (1995): 409–421.
23. Delmos Jones, "Towards a Native Anthropology," *Human Organization* 29, no. 4 (1970): 251–259.
24. Kirin Nayaran, "How Native Is a 'Native' Anthropologist?" *American Anthropologist* 95 (1993): 671–686.
25. See Linda Carty, "Seeing Through the Eye of Difference: A Reflection on Three Research Journeys," in *Feminism and Social Change,* ed. Heidi Gottfried (Urbana: University of Illinois Press 1996), 123–142; Antonia Chao, "Performing Like a *P'o* and Acting as a Big Sister: Reculturating into the Indigenous Lesbian Circle in Taiwan," in *Sex, Sexuality, and the Anthropologist,* ed. Fran Markowitz and Michael Ashkenazi (Urbana: University of Illinois Press 1999), 128–144; Tom Fitzgerald, "Identity-in-Ethnography: Limits to Ethnographic Subjectivity," in *Sex, Sexuality, and the Anthropologist,* ed. Fran Markowitz and Michael Ashkenazi (Urbana: University of Illinois Press, 1999), 117–127; Shalom Staub, "'Salim's Going to Be Muslim Someday': The Negotiated Identities of an American Jewish Ethnographer, in *Between Two Worlds: Ethnographic Essays on American Jewry,* ed. Jack Kugelmass (Ithaca, NY: Cornell University Press, 1988), 240–264; and Tony Larry Whitehead, "Breakdown, Resolution, and Coherence: The Fieldwork Experiences of a Big, Brown, Pretty-Talking Man in a West Indian Community," in *Self, Sex, and Gender in Cross-Cultural Fieldwork,* ed. Tony Larry Whitehead and Mary Ellen Conaway (Urbana: University of Illinois Press 1986), 213–239.
26. Manda Cesara, *Reflections of a Woman Anthropologist* (New York: Academic Press, 1982); Ruth Behar, *Translated Woman* (Boston: Beacon, 1993); Ruth Behar, *The Vulnerable Observer: Anthropology That Breaks Your Heart* (Boston: Beacon, 1996); and Esther Newton, "My Best Informant's Dress: The Erotic Equation in Fieldwork," *Cultural Anthropology* 8 (1993): 3–23.
27. Compare and contrast Clifford Geertz, "Deep Play: Notes on the Balinese Cockfight," in his *The Interpretation of Cultures* (New York: Basic Books, 1973), 412–413; and William E. Mitchell, "A Goy in the Ghetto: Gentile–Jewish Communications in Fieldwork Research," in *Between Two Worlds,* ed. Kugelmass, 225–239.
28. Michael Ashkenazi and Fran Markowitz, "Sexuality and Prevarication in the Praxis of Anthropology," in *Sex, Sexuality, and the Anthropologist,* ed. Fran Markowitz and Michael Ashkenazi (Urbana: University of Illinois Press, 1999), 10.
29. Turner, "Embodied Ethnography," 52.
30. Ashkenazi and Markowitz, "Sexuality and Prevarication," 10.
31. Jonathan Boyarin, "Waiting for a Jew: Marginal Redemption at the Eighth Street Shul," in *Between Two Worlds,* ed. Kugelmass, 62.

32. During the Soviet era, each citizen's *natsionalnost'* was recorded on line five of his or her internal passport and other related documents. This was particularly damaging for Jews who were exposed to discrimination or prejudice. On Soviet nationality policies and their development, see Robert Conquest, *Soviet Nationalities Policy in Practice* (New York: Praeger, 1967). For work regarding the impact of nationality on the Jews of the former Soviet Union, see Zvi Gitelman, *Jewish Nationality and Soviet Politics: The Jewish Sections of the CPSU, 1917–1930* (Princeton, NJ: Princeton University Press, 1972); and Victor Zaslavsky and Robert J. Brym, *Soviet-Jewish Emigration and Soviet Nationality Policy* (New York: St. Martin's Press, 1983).
33. One of the best, most concise presentations of these ideas is to be found in Tone Bringa, "Nationality Categories, Identification and Identity Formation in 'Multinational' Bosnia," *Anthropology of East European Review* 11, no. 1–2 (1993): 80–88.
34. Zvi Gitelman, "Soviet-Jewish Immigrants to the United States: Profile, Problems, Prospects," in *Soviet Jewry in the Decisive Decade, 1971–80,* ed. Robert O. Freedman (Durham, NC: Duke University Press 1984), 97.
35. He was referring, of course, to the wife of Anatolii Shcharansky (Natan Sharansky) who became religious while her husband was a Prisoner of Zion in a Soviet labor camp.
36. Fran Markowitz, *A Community in Spite of Itself: Soviet Jewish Emigrés in New York* (Washington, DC: Smithsonian Institution Press, 1993); Markowitz, "Rituals as Keys to Soviet Immigrants' Jewish Identity," in *Between Two Worlds,* ed. Kugelmass, 128–147.
37. See Anna Wierbiczka, "Soul and Mind: Linguistic Evidence for Ethnopsychology and Cultural History," *American Anthropologist* 91, no. 1 (1989): 41–58; Dale Pesmen, *Russia and Soul* (Ithaca, NY: Cornell University Press, 2000).
38. Fran Markowitz, "Not Nationalists: Russian Teenagers' Soulful A-politics," *Europe-Asia Studies* 51. 7 (1999): 1183–1198; Markowitz, *Coming of Age in Post-Soviet Russia* (Urbana: University of Illinois Press, 2000).
39. Boyarin, *Carnal Israel,* 7.
40. Viktor Kozlov, *Russkiy vopros: Istoriia tragedii velikogo naroda* [The Russian question: A history of the tragedy of a great people] (Moscow: self-published, 1995).
41. See Dale Peterson, "Justifying the Margin: The Construction of 'Soul' in Russian and African American Texts," *Slavic Review* 5, no. 4 (1992): 749–757.
42. See Ulf Hannerz, *Soulside* (New York: Columbia University Press, 1969), 11; Geneva Smitherman, *Talkin and Testifyin: The Language of Black America* (Boston: Houghton Mifflin, 1977), 55–56; and William Van Deburg, *New Day in Babylon—The Black Power Movement and American Culture, 1965–1975* (Chicago: University of Chicago Press, 1992).
43. See Du Bois, *Souls of Black Folk.*
44. See the writings of the group's messianic leader, Ben Ammi, esp. his *God, the Black Man, and Truth,* 2nd rev. ed. (Washington, DC: Comunicators Press, 1990).
45. See Fran Markowitz, Sara Helman, and Dafna Shir-Vertesh, "Soul Citizenship: The Black Hebrews and the State of Israel," *American Anthropologist* 105, no. 2 (2003): 302–312.

46. bell hooks, *Yearning: Race, Gender, and Cultural Politics* (Boston: South End, 1990); Fran Markowitz, "Creating Coalitions and Causing Conflicts: Confronting Race and Gender through Partnered Ethnography," *Ethnos* 27, no. 2 (2002): 201–222.
47. P. L. Sunderland, "'You May Not Know It, But I'm Black': White Women's Self-Identification as Black," *Ethnos* 62, no. 1–2 (1997): 39.
48. Ann Pellegrini, "Whiteface Performances: 'Race', Gender, and Jewish Bodies," in *Jews and Other Differences: The New Jewish Cultural Studies,* ed. Jonathan Boyarrin and Daniel Boyarin (Minneapolis: University of Minnesota Press, 1997), 131.
49. Contrast Azoulay, *Black, Jewish, and Interracial.*
50. As part of their project to restore the righteous lifestyle of the Hebrew Israelites, community members form families through what they call Divine Marriage. The principles of Divine Marriage are that Man cleaves to Yah (God), woman holds onto the hand of man, and together women and men guide their children. Following the biblical patriarchs and many indigenous African societies, Hebrew Israelite men are allowed and sometimes encouraged to marry more than one woman. See Haraymiel Ben Shaleak, *The Holy Art of Divine Marriage* (n.p, n.d.).
51. Gilroy, *Against Race,* 194.
52. Silberman, *A Certain People.*
53. Fran Markowitz, "Plaiting the Strands of Jewish Identity," *Comparative Studies in Society and History* 32, no. 1 (1990): 182–183.
54. Jean-Paul Sartre, *Anti-Semite and Jew* (New York: Schocken, 1948).
55. Zygmunt Bauman, *Modernity and the Holocaust* (Ithaca, NY: Cornell University Press, 1989); Bauman, "Allosemitism: Premodern, Modern, Postmodern," in *Modernity, Culture and 'the Jew',* ed. Bryan Cheyette and Laura Marcus (Cambridge, England: Polity Press, 1998), 143–156.
56. Bauman, "Allosemitism," 144.
57. Staub, "'Salim's Going to Be Muslim Someday,'" 242; see also Mitchell, "A Goy," 230.
58. See Arjun Appadurai, *Modernity at Large: Cultural Dimensions of Globalization* (Minneapolis: University of Minnesota Press, 1996); and Robin Cohen, *Global Diasporas: An Introduction* (Seattle: University of Washington Press, 1997).
59. Bauman, "Allosemitism," 148.
60. See Slezkine, *The Jewish Century.*
61. Herzfeld, *Cultural Intimacy.*

CHAPTER 15

Jews, Muslims, European Identities

Multiculturalism and Anti-Semitism in Britain

Efraim Sicher

Integration and Difference

The year 1656 is historically known for the resettlement of Jews in England (though the edict of expulsion of 1290 was never formally revoked). The Sephardic Jews who traveled from Amsterdam to England became wealthy and assimilated, but their status as aliens remained anomalous until the second half of the nineteenth century. They were followed from the early nineteenth century by a wave of mainly impoverished German and East European Jews who were racialized and Orientalized before they too became Anglicized by the mid-twentieth century. Today, British Jews are for the most part well integrated and successful. And yet Shalom Lappin, a philosophy professor at King's College London, has concluded that multiculturalism has marginalized the Jews relative to other cultural and ethnic groups.[1] The model of successful integration, admired by some Muslim immigrants to Britain, sometimes exacted a price of conformity to the behavioral norms and cultural codes of a colonialist, nominally Christian society. In today's multicultural Britain, as a new generation reclaims its Jewish ethnic and religious traditions, Jews find themselves subject to a coded discourse based on myths and conspiracy theories. Such beliefs are stronger than personal knowledge and experience.[2] The "Jew" and the "Muslim" in the Western imagination are split between the "good" and the "bad," according to who conforms to societal rules and norms. At the same time, as Others, they are framed by their representation. In other words, as Gil Anidjar has concluded, successful integration is not so much a test of the Other's behavior as of European society's antipathy to or sympathy with their difference.[3] The context in Britain is low-level background racism, such as that vocalized at football matches (the zero-tolerance campaign to stamp out anti-Black and anti-Asian abuse has been extended to anti-Semitic insults directed at the self-styled "Yiddos" of Tottenham Hotspur).[4]

While British Jews have generally enjoyed a benign tolerance, they increasingly experience sporadic physical threats in the streets and desecration of their cemeteries. Physical assaults on Jews and verbal abuse were on the increase in the beginning of the twenty-first century. The figures for 2005 of 454, and in 2006 594 anti-Semitic incidents recorded by the Community Security Trust (CST; a vigilante body of the British Jewish community) indicated a long-term upward trend (there were one hundred cases of physical assault in 2006). Anti-Semitic incidents have been linked with trigger events such as the First Intifada and the Second Lebanon War,[5] and yet the 2007 CST incident report, which covered a period without significant political triggers, while recording a slight decrease in the overall number of incidents, nevertheless showed the second highest level of anti-Semitism in Britain since records were first kept in 1984.[6] The anti-Zionist campaign for delegitimization of Israel and activities of the far right may account for the high level of 929 incidents recorded in Britain in 2009, falling off to 645 in 2010 and 586 in 2011 (compared with 354 that year in France, which has double Britain's Jewish population). In addition, the Jewish community continued to be under threat of both UK-based and foreign terrorist attacks.[7] What was new was that increasingly the attacks and abuse were coming from Muslims (only roughly half the assailants were identified as White in the 2007 incident report,[8] and in 27% of incidents reported in 2011 the perpetrators were identified as South Asian).[9] Around Europe, Muslims and left-wing sympathizers of the Palestine Solidarity Campaign supported boycotting of Israeli goods and harassed pro-Israel speakers on university campuses. Sometimes, as happened on Israel's sixtieth Independence Day in May 2008 and during Operation Cast Lead in December 2008–February 2009, hostility overflowed into attacks on Jewish businesses or residential areas in northeast and northwest London and in Manchester.[10]

While historically anti-Semitism in Britain has not been characterized by the kind of violence seen in Europe, verbal and physical abuse was now coming both from the left, in the guise of an ideological anti-Zionist campaign, and from the right, in a revived nationalistic racism (which did not prevent the British National Party or the English Defence League from attempting to recruit middle-class Jews in the name of a common fear of Islam). By the end of the first decade of the twenty-first-century, anti-Zionism and Judeophobic opinions had become mainstream in British public discourse.[11] Keith Kahn-Harris and Ben Gidley have concluded in their sociological study of the British Jewish community that it has gone from a confidence in its assimilated affluence to a discourse that is concerned with security, anxious for personal safety, and divided on how to ensure continuity.[12] Nevertheless, the often ambiguous discourse about Jews in Britain cannot be clarified without understanding the changing identity politics of the new multicultural society that promised diversity and equal opportunity, but that was becoming a risk society concerned with security, especially following the disturbances in Oldham in 2002 and the July 7, 2005 (7/7), attacks in London, carried out by British jihadists.[13]

In what Amikam Nachmani has termed the "triangle" of Europeans, Muslims, and Jews, European perceptions of Muslims are very often couched in terms of the Holocaust, positing the Muslims as the "new Jews" of Europe, whose mass immigration is perceived to be a far more serious demographic, cultural, and religious threat than was the Jewish presence in Europe in the 1930s. In this racialized discourse, the touchstone of European sensibilities and yardstick of treatment of Muslims is the Holocaust.[14] Anxieties about Islam go back to medieval Christian struggles against Muslim rule in Europe and to the Crusades, while the Muslim and Jew were linked in the medieval imagination as Oriental, alien, and infidel. More recent images of Muslims are politically grounded in American media and mass culture.[15] A study published after 9/11 but relating mainly to press coverage in 1996–1997 showed that the British media tended toward polarization of British Muslims, reverting to an earlier Orientalist discourse and associating them with radical extremism and disloyal behavior.[16] Jews, too, were still being accused of double loyalty in their allegiance to Israel, and the media spread insinuations of the influence of Jewish money in British politics and the economy, while familiar tropes of Jewish conspiracy and world domination have resurfaced, often emanating from left-wing and radical Islamist protests against Israel.

Together with minority rights and the fight against globalization, an anti-racist human rights discourse provides a forum for anti-Israel sentiments where solidarity with Palestinian Arabs is sometimes couched in violent or familiar anti-Semitic language.[17] The historical mutually exclusive claims of Jews and Muslims to the holy sites and heated debates over the Israel–Arab conflict tend to override what the monotheistic faiths have in common, and, despite the work of interfaith groups, there seemed to Michael Nazir-Ali (then Bishop of Rochester and the first Pakistani to hold this office) little cohesive potential as aligned religious minorities in an age of eroded spiritual and moral values.[18] Certainly, the Muslim vote is increasingly significant in Britain (at least in certain constituencies), and, as is true elsewhere in Europe, social pressure for integration is often met by resistance to the consolidation of transnational cosmopolitanism and liberalized views of gender, sexual, and cultural difference. In May 2009 a Gallup poll found that, while overall levels of tolerance were similar among the general European population, Muslims in Britain reported a significantly lower perception of integration (10 percent), compared with France (46 percent) and Germany (35 percent). Moreover, a larger percentage of Muslims in the United Kingdom compared with other European countries believed that religion was important in their lives, whereas fewer among the general British population accorded importance to religion.[19] Investigators have discovered that, despite the slogan "strength in diversity," Britain shows the greatest rift among European countries between a population with generally favorable views of Muslims (characterized by a genteel "live and let live" attitude) and a growing number of Muslims, particularly in the younger age groups, who express resentment toward the host society or embrace extremist views (including support for al Qaeda or for the introduction of sharia law on homosexuality and polygamy).[20] Without going into the reasons for the failure of the liberal state to satisfy the quest it itself has encouraged of "respect and recognition," suffice it to say it is a situation that exacerbates an already tense state of race relations.

However, the picture is complicated by complex shifts in social attitudes and political positions that have altered familiar cleavages between left and right. On the other hand, European governments have made much headway in countering anti-Semitism and other forms of racism; the 2006 interparliamentary commission of inquiry on anti-Semitism in Britain is a case in point. And yet the legacy of racist discourse has not gone away, resurfacing with the mobilizing of support for political platforms and ideological powerbases on both the left and the right and the reawakening of nationalist agendas on the far right feeding on resentment against the mass influx of Muslim immigrants.[21] Across Europe, according to PEW and ADL opinion polls in 2009, anti-Semitic attitudes correlated with hostility to Muslims, though the percentage of those holding stereotyped perceptions was lower in Britain than in other European countries.[22]

This chapter looks at the ambiguous position of Britain's Jews in the racial hierarchy within the tensions of multiculturalism by examining discursive practices in perceptions of Jewish and Muslim communities, with particular reference to the tensions between exclusion and social acceptance in ethnic and national or European identities. The discussion will ask what may be learnt about integration and difference in a Western society from perceptions and representations of Jews, as well as their legal and social status relative to Muslims.

European Identities

At first glance, a secular modern Jewish identity, defined as non-Zionist and voluntarist, might fit in well with a pluralist supranational Europe, just as Jews achieved cultural recognition and were well integrated in the Hapsburg Empire at the turn of the twentieth century.[23] However, in the Hapsburg Empire, multiculturalism did not rule out anti-Semitism. In fact, Europe has not reached an ideal political and social unity, let alone racial and ethnic harmony, while European Jews themselves are diverse and are not unified by any representative body, but see themselves joined by some general *Schicksalgemeinschaft,* a collective fate of persecution and a history of extradition and exile in European countries.[24] And although proposed restrictions to religious practice, such as the campaign in France, Britain, and Holland against ritual slaughter and legal action in Germany and Finland against circumcision, affect both Jews and Muslims, there seems little prospect for a Jewish–Muslim alliance.

Jews, Muslims, and members of other ethnic groups hold varying perceptions of their racial and religious identities, which may range along a salience of multiple affinities. They can no longer be regarded as fixities in the social hierarchy in multicultural Britain, where there has been a reconfiguring of political space and consequently a shift in cultural discourse, for example the use of language codes to assert communal affinity or solidarity in minority group newspapers such as the *Jewish Chronicle*. Stigmatization and negative stereotyping persist in the media (though not without protest), essentializing ethnic and racial difference, while popular culture pushes an agenda of acculturation, critiquing bigotry and ethnic exclusivity on both sides. Ethnic voices, on the other hand, have tended to become more belligerent in asserting their cultural identity.[25]

Among the many changes that have transformed British society since the loss of empire has been the embracing of multiculturalism. Unlike the United States or Canada, which built their economies and societies on mass immigration, the importation of cheap labor into Britain after World War II and the arrival of newcomers from the Commonwealth required a readjustment of the concept of citizenship and its relation to national identity. While in the United States Martin Luther King Jr. and the civil rights movement strengthened respect for ethnic difference and Black consciousness, in Britain foreigners were greeted with hostility as competitors for work and a threat to cultural values.[26] Yet by the time Black consciousness hit Britain, the Black-Jewish civil rights alliance in America had fallen apart and the Jews were no longer recognized as victims of racism and had largely assimilated. Moreover, cultural diversity in Britain has resulted in some dangerous ambiguities that impact on all communal relations, but particularly on mutual perceptions of Jews and Muslims. It should be borne in mind that, whereas in the 1950s race discourse talked of "Coloureds," and later of "Blacks," today we hear more often of "Asians," as binary racial identification according to color has given way to ethnic and cultural identification. And while racism in the postwar period was directed at immigrants from the former colonies, today mainstream hostility toward Jews is generally regarded as separate from hostility toward Muslims and not thought of as racist. Indeed, jihadist propaganda has targeted Jews, while the liberal intellectual left has formed an "anti-War Coalition" with pro-Hamas or pro-Hizbullah groups. The moderate representatives of the Muslim community have on occasion spoken out against extremism and anti-Semitism; indeed, the majority of Muslims are not fundamentalist Islamists, and Islamists themselves are divided by ideologies, intraethnic rivalries, and in-fighting. Nevertheless, among the factions that came together in 1997 in the British Council of Muslims is the Muslim Association of Britain, affiliated with the Muslim Brotherhood, Hamas, and Jamat-e-Islam, opposed to the Middle East peace process and normalization of relations with Israel. Their alliance with the British far left in the Stop the War Campaign and in anti-Zionist platforms is clearly tactical rather than ideological, but it contributes to a common invective which does not always distinguish between anti-Zionism and anti-Semitism.[27] The former British Islamist Ed Husain writes that he had not heard "one single Muslim scholar of any repute" speak out against either suicide bombings or the hijacking of airplanes: "In Muslim political discussions, dominated by Islamists across the globe, killing Jews in Israel was considered to be a means to an end: the annihilation of Israel."[28]

The number of Muslims in Britain is generally estimated at around 1.5 million (some community groups suggest it could be nearer 2 million) out of an estimated 1.5 billion around the world. Moreover, they are the fastest-growing sector of UK population and the least integrated.[29] Their classification as "Asians" is particularly misleading for they may include immigrants and their offspring from African countries and elsewhere, and many are born in Britain. By contrast, the Jewish population of Britain has not changed much since World War II (which means in real terms a near zero growth rate) and stands at under three hundred thousand, of whom a large part are assimilated, but increasingly concentrated in the traditional communities of Manchester and north London.[30] Nasar Meer and Tehseen Noorani have compared the way in which Jewish and Muslim immigrant populations in Britain have negotiated civic rights as religious groups within a post-Enlightenment discourse of integration, noting that neither anti-Semitism nor anti-Muslim sentiment (Islamophobia) have been accorded much attention in studies of British race discourse.[31] Yet their comparison of representation of Muslims in public and media discourse with that of Jewish immigrants at the turn of the twentieth century strikes an analogy between very different social and political situations. Muslim cultural and religious differences are feared and their loyalty questioned, whereas in the past Jewish immigration was restricted despite Jewish efforts at assimilation. In any case, the analogy of Islamist extremists with Jewish anarchists of the turn of the century was clearly unfounded and misleading.[32] Moreover, unlike the former pressure to assimilate to White Christian Englishness, today the debate is over what kind of national values and civic practices a multicultural Britain should adopt and how much difference can be tolerated.

Mixed race families make up around 10 percent of the population in the United Kingdom. Nonetheless, in contrast to the Jewish immigrant pattern, some of the new immigrants, particularly among Muslim youth, tend not to favor assimilatory patterns but instead resist integration into European social behavior.[33] Not all immigrants from Third World countries have been quick to adopt civic values, and media attention invariably focuses on cultural practices (such as forced marriage, funeral pyres, polygamy, or female circumcision) that clash with liberal democratic traditions, gender equality, and human rights. Bhiku Parekh, former head of the Commission on the Future of Multi-Ethnic Britain, has advocated very cautious negotiation between the host society's demand to integrate into the polity and the newcomers' own ethnic and religious identity, bearing in mind that public codes of behavior never form coherent fixed whole but do have constitutional, moral, and social implications.[34]

Muslims as the "New Jews"?

Multiculturalism may mean different things to different people in Britain today: something to be feared or craved, a fig leaf for the fallout of a national culture, a celebration of diversity, or a new brand of intellectual elitism. Yet, if the new multiethnic society celebrated difference, if Britain was redefining itself as a global village in a New Age of a multitude of gods and idols, then there had to be room, within reason, for differing lifestyles, customs, and dress. In France, the Toubon law made compulsory the use of French in public institutions, while in the name of the separation of state and religion a prohibition was introduced on covering the face, and the wearing of visible religious headgear or symbols was banned in schools, including the *hijab*, the yarmulke, and large crosses. The ban quickly became the center of controversy among feminists, human rights activists, and politicians.[35] In Britain, where English did not need defending to the same extent, as it was an international language, street names appeared in Bengali in East London, and accommodation was generally made for needs of minority communities, including the wearing in public places of the *hijab* and *burka,* as well as the Hasidic caftan and the yarmulke (*kippah*). Male police officers were allowed to wear turbans. But nobody seemed to know where the line ran between toleration or respect and separateness, nor was it entirely clear how these related to human dignity and equality.[36]

Integration has always required conformity to rules about language and dress, and until the nineteenth century conformity was required to the state religion as a condition of public office and entry to university. Muslim women may feel that modest dress frees them from the male gaze and ensures a degree of modesty that goes with the outward signs of their ethnic group identity; this may be an issue too for observant married Jewish women and ultra-Orthodox Jewish men. But the *hijab* and *burka* appeared to challenge the very multiculturalism that promised the freedom of difference and choice. The leader of the House of Commons and former British foreign minister, Jack Straw, member of Parliament for Blackburn, where a quarter of the population were Muslims, defended his refusal to receive veiled women in his constituency office hours by writing in the *Lancashire Evening Telegraph* in October 2006 that the veil is a "visible statement of separation and of difference" and was an impediment to better community relations because it prevented the other's face being seen.[37] Like the French who believed (wrongly) that banning religious headdress would encourage secularization of Muslim communities, Straw believed both face-to-face encounter and state support for Muslim schools would stimulate moderate views and stem extremism. There is a peculiar logic at work here that demands that the Other give up difference in the name of recognition of difference. A number of incidents leading to labor court tribunals over unfair dismissal attest to confusion over the boundaries of tolerance and the definition of the permissible among the general population, while the issue of dress was becoming a marker of political allegiance, not just ethnic identity. Indeed, the press coverage of such controversies would seem to be out of proportion to the relative small numbers of Muslims among the UK population.

A widespread perception that the antiterrorist drive created a "politics of fear" played out even in a city as cosmopolitan as London. In *The End of Tolerance: Racism in 21st Century Britain,* Arun Kundnani explains how the Muslim minority in Britain was terrorized by antiterrorist laws, arrest without trial, and threats in the same way the Irish had been "policed" during the IRA bombing campaign of the 1970s.[38] The police were already tainted with alleged racism since the McPherson Report following the murder of Stephen Lawrence in 1993. The mistrust of persons of color in a time of heightened security alerts was illustrated by the police shooting in July 2005 of Brazilian tourist Jean Charles de Menezes. Now, not just skin color, but also religion, was seen as a threat to national security and values.[39] Though Muslim leaders claimed the terror threat was exaggerated, police estimated that some two thousand persons posed a terrorist threat in the United Kingdom in 2007 and concluded that the best that could be done was containment. In January 2009, the MI5 chief Jonathan Evans averred that the terror trials had served as a deterrent, but the threat from al Qaeda remained. Suspects who were British citizens were involved in fundraising or training in Afghanistan and Somalia; three out of four Islamist attacks in Britain had some link to Pakistan (the country of origin of many South Asian immigrants). Their motivation was spurred by distorted or biased media coverage of events in the Middle East, but also domestic and foreign policy and personal circumstances. Lord West, the government's security adviser, declared that Israeli military action was pushing Muslim youth to extremism. This perception forges a direct link between Britain's foreign policy and race relations. Such a top-bottom model of policy decision making anticipates events on the ground and builds in a linkage to the Israeli government's actions when thinking about a large ethnic minority in the United Kingdom.[40] In fact, it was sometimes to extremists that the government turned in order to deal with the perceived threat of violent unrest at home: among those advising the then cohesion minister Hazel Blears and home secretary Jacqui Smith on race relations in Britain were those who openly supported Hamas, such as Dr. Daud Abdullah, deputy director-general of the Muslim Council of Britain, who signed the Istanbul Declaration pledging resistance to any attempts, including those by British troops, to enforce the embargo of terrorist arms to Gaza. Hazel Blears' successor as communities minister, John Denham, who appointed Asim Hafeez, a hard-core Sulafi, as head of intervention in the Office of Security and Counter-Terrorism, brought the stand-off over the Daud Abdullah affair to an end at the beginning of 2010 after the Muslim Council of Britain issued a general statement condemning racism and anti-Semitism. Yet asylum rules did not always make it easy to deport radical Islamist preachers who disseminated hate speech, such as Abu Qatada (convicted in Jordan of terror charges in 1999 and still resident in Britain in December 2012). By March 2009, when the second stage of the war on terror, Contest 2, was launched, the British government was managing diversity by calling on leaders of faith communities for advice, an approach that not only failed to stem extremism, but that also "led to the erosion of anti-racism and the emergence, in its place, of a highly compromised politics of communal identity, in which unrepresentative community organizations lobby for state favours through the promotion of their own inward-looking sense of victimization."[41] As in the previous standoff with the Muslim Council of Britain over its refusal to attend commemoration of Holocaust Memorial Day and again when it boycotted the commemoration in 2009 after Operation Cast Lead, the government managed its relations with the Muslim community by demanding political allegiance from bodies that were not truly representative.[42]

Stigmatization of Muslims as terrorist extremists elicited dismay and anger, and Muslims increasingly spoke of themselves as being treated "like the Jews of Europe,"[43] although British Muslims were certainly not subjected to persecution and genocide. The perception of Muslims as the new "Jews" is nevertheless not uncommon and can in fact facilitate the Muslim's role as the victim of oppression and injustice in the popular imagination, but in a way that erases real Jews. Postcolonial theorists point to the parallel expulsion or forced conversion of Jews and Moors in Spain and Portugal, but also align Zionism with racism and delegitimize Israel as a colonizing nation-state. In the "West versus the Rest" dichotomy Jews are identified no longer as Holocaust victims but as oppressors of Muslims. According to surveys carried out in London, Paris, and Berlin, anti-Semitic views circulate freely among Muslims, or at least are not opposed by the majority, and among the more educated circles anti-Semitic discourse is commonly acceptable.[44]

The stereotyping of Muslims as collectively complicit with terrorism and perceived allegiances with radical Islamism invite hostility and misunderstanding from the host society, as well as from other ethnic groups, including the Jewish community. And we cannot ignore the double-edged antagonism met by some Jews in Britain. They may have an exemplary history of persecution, but are often seen by others as themselves prone to separatism and racism. Thus, they must negotiate their identities in a competition for victimhood, but also must show the correct choice of integration. Asking why Britain seemed not to have matched the American record of success in integrating immigrants, Michael Howard (then Conservative Party leader) evidently subscribed to the common dichotomy in the public mind between Britishness (however defined) and terrorism when he called on Muslims to follow the path of integration that his Jewish parents had chosen. They, he said, knew the difference between integration and assimilation; he also quoted Gandhi who called for Hindus, Muslims, Jews, and others to put their national identity before the exclusivity of religion.[45]

There is another side to the multicultural coin, perhaps no less disturbing. As well as fostering immigrants' cultural traditions, government bodies have rightly shown sensitivity to the needs of ethnic minorities, but this has raised issues of the limits of free speech, censorship, and selective intolerance. For example, a Department of Education–funded report by the Historical Association found that teachers in northern England were dropping lessons about the Holocaust and the Crusades out of consideration for the teachings Muslim pupils received in their homes and mosques that denied the Holocaust or that regarded the Crusades as a holy war against Muslims.[46] It later transpired that fears of a banning of the teaching of the Holocaust were quite unfounded, but the worry that the government had reversed its declared policy of commemorating and teaching the Holocaust combined with other concerns that such sensitivity, however well-intentioned, unduly influenced the decisions of government and public bodies. Religious sensibilities seemed to be on collision course with the principle of free speech and integration into a secular multicultural society in the aftermath of the Rushdie affair, when some segments of the Muslim community called for a ban on Rushdie's novel, *The Satanic Verses,* and there was a book burning in Bradford. At the same time, the right of defense against defamation and incitement to hatred was also something cherished by Jews.[47] Of course, the paradoxes of the liberal state and multiculturalism are not new, and we may look back to the debate over Heinrich von Treitschke's anti-Semitic articles in late-nineteenth-century Germany for examples of the clash between cultural diversity and communal cohesion.[48]

Following the realization that the 7/7 bombers had used the freedoms offered to minority groups to pose a threat to the nation, Prime

Minister Tony Blair made a significant retreat in an eight-year-old policy of multiculturalism when he spoke of respect for difference within a shared space of shared values: "The right to be different. The duty to integrate. That is what being British means. And neither racists nor extremists should be allowed to destroy it."[49] The "duty to integrate" did not cancel the welcoming of diversity, but it now required a commitment to shared values of the nation and a common language, it ruled out separation, and put an end to money being given freely to religious groups if the funds were not being used to promote cohesion and understanding of other faiths. No religious way of life could supersede the rule of law—for example, *medressas* would henceforth be regulated and foreign preachers would be vetted (a regulation that would indirectly though not seriously affect arranged marriages among ultra-Orthodox Jews as well as Israeli rabbis invited to speak or officiate in Britain, whose Jewish community suffers from a dearth of locally trained spiritual leaders). Religious courts could have jurisdiction by consent of the parties, but there would be recourse to English law courts.

This last provision underlines a distinction between Judaism's ruling of *dina demalkhuta dina,* the yielding of halakha to the law of the land in monetary matters, and Muslim calls for sharia to be the law of the land. It was nevertheless to the Jewish *beth din,* which acts as a voluntary court of third-party arbitration in civil disputes, that the archbishop of Canterbury, Dr. Rowan Williams, pointed as a model when he said in a BBC interview that adopting parts of sharia law seemed "unavoidable" if a standoff was to be avoided in a fragmented British society. This was the only way, he argued, to avoid "no-go areas," as bishop Nazir-Ali had earlier called some Muslim communities (a phrase that recalled the worst sectarian violence of Northern Ireland).[50] The archbishop of Canterbury made his remarks after a lecture he gave on "Islam in English Law: Civil and Religious Law in England," on February 7, 2008, in which he spoke for an opening up of the monopoly of secular law to "transformative accommodation." As Bernard Jackson has painstakingly pointed out, Dr. Williams was not proposing parallel jurisdictions or the return of the caliphate (advocated by some radical Islamists), but it was unclear what, practically speaking, he meant by partial acceptance of sharia law, a law that Muslim scholars do not interpret uniformly.[51] These proposals were swiftly rejected by Prime Minister Gordon Brown and the Conservative spokesperson on multiculturalism, the shadow secretary for communal cohesion, Baroness Warsi, herself the first Muslim woman in the House of Lords. It could be that Williams was drumming up support for a greater role for religion in society, following a fall in numbers of worshippers in the Anglican Church. However, the issue at stake here was whether the principle of one law for all squared with ethnic loyalties and religious conscience, something that could reopen a long-standing confrontation in England between Church and State and, instead of benefits which would spill over (as the archbishop put it) into the Jewish community, might spark off competing legal claims in marital and civil rights cases. It is a controversy, moreover, that should be seen in the context of the split in the synod of the Church of England over homosexuality, the ordination of women bishops, and the boundaries of religious debate. At the same time, a call from the evangelical wing of the Anglican Church to declare Christianity the sole path to salvation and to convert Muslims threatened to backtrack on recognition of Judaism and Islam as equal religions and to revert to an older model of Christianity as a fulfillment of the biblical covenant, a messianic dogma that required conversion of the Jews.[52]

Blair's rather naïve ideal of the coexistence and equal value of religions ignored contradictions in outlook and sought to celebrate what was held in common in the Abrahamic heritage (which was a political construction rather than a religious creed).[53] Christian supersession theology denies the Jews are any longer the "Chosen People," and more-recent Protestant replacement theology identifies Arab Palestinians as the "true Israel," since Jesus was a Palestinian (although there was no Palestine at the time of Jesus).[54] Moreover, while not typical of the range of interpretations of Islamic theology, fundamentalist attitudes toward Jews and Christians as *kufr,* who could legitimately be killed, do not seem to quite fit in with Blair's idealism. Muslim leaders responded to Blair's declaration angrily, accusing Blair of putting money into "occupied territories" (presumably Iraq and Israel) instead of investing in deprived social groups (presumably in their view the real cause of extremism).[55]

If in his previous book, *The Dignity of Difference: How to Avoid the Clash of Civilizations* (2003), British chief rabbi Sir Jonathan Sacks (later Lord Sacks) had argued for the benefits of multiculturalism, in 2007 he doubted whether multiculturalism was still desirable: "Multiculturalism has run its course, and it is time to move on."[56] Multiculturalism was supposed to give dignity to difference, to promote integration and not separation. British society had become more open, diverse, and cosmopolitan, but the price was abrasive fracturing instead of tolerance. The murder by an animal-rights activist on May 6, 2002, of controversial gay Dutch politician Pim Fortuyn (just one day after he declared that multiculturalism did not work) was for Sacks symptomatic of the lack of shared social values and the absence of a cohesive national identity.[57] Society was breaking down; there was nothing into which minorities could integrate, least of all any dignity of difference.[58] Sacks wrote from a Lockean tradition of liberal democracy and looked to a vision based on the Jewish concept of *khesed* (altruistic love) that aimed to rebuild society as a home on the ruins of the privileged country house, where Jews were unwanted guests, a home that would replace the bankrupt international hotel, where everyone was a guest.[59] Yet Sacks failed to address the contradiction within integration posed by Islamists who also believed in a religious foundation of a moral vision of society, but who vowed to destroy Western civilization as corrupt and promiscuous and waged war against Israel and the Jews. Tariq Modood has argued that multiculturalism, narrowly redefined as the relation of ethnic and religious pluralism to the polity, could rise to this challenge to secular liberal democracies through educational reform and rethinking of citizenship.[60] For Sacks, modern orthodox Judaism was pledged to *torah 'im derekh erets* (observance of Jewish precepts and Divine commandments while living a Western way of life). Jews had successfully integrated, and so Jews could, like South Asian immigrant communities, maintain their distinctive lifestyle without regarding themselves as other than British.

Immigration was the number one issue in the debate over multiculturalism. This reflected a growing alienation of the White population and their concern over jobs and security, an alienation that threatened to spill into an undercurrent of racism. All over Europe, mass immigration had resulted in pockets of non-White, largely Muslim populations that had no roots in the surrounding culture or common ties to the host nation, whose citizens their children became by right. A few Conservatives seemed to agree that Enoch Powell was right when he made his notorious "rivers of blood" speech in 1968, and many shared the view that a lax immigration policy had changed the character of the nation and exposed it to security risks.[61] Concerns were voiced over the economic and security risks to the nation of continued immigration, as well as consequences for the social and ethnic composition of the nation.[62] The declaration at the Munich security conference in February 2011 by Conservative prime minister David Cameron, reiterating the words of German chancellor Angela Merkel, that multiculturalism had failed, spelled out a hard line on terrorism, but also on ethnic practices that were inimical to democratic values or to respect for equality and for other faiths: "Frankly, we need a lot less of the passive tolerance of recent years and much more active, muscular liberalism."[63] This retreat from a covenant of accommodation with British

Muslims confirms the tensions between integration policies and the wish of ethnic minorities to maintain their difference as well as ties to their country of origin.[64] Baroness Warsi commented that what she said to Islamist organizations operating under cover names such as Muslims against the Crusades (outlawed in November 2011) was, "If you can't live by our values, get off our island." What "our" values were was not clear, but she did reiterate that the fight against Islamophobia was also a fight against anti-Semitism, which was rampant across the political spectrum.[65]

Socialization and Exclusion

One may ask where Jews stand in the multiculturalism debate as well-established offspring of immigrants who have recognizably made significant contributions to Britain's economy and society. They ought to be, one might think, paragons of successful multiculturalism. As a minority group defined both by religion and ethnic identity, they would presumably have everything to gain from faith schools, respect for Sabbath observance at work and in education, and willingness to meet special needs, such as dietary laws, though the law did not always admit grounds of racial discrimination in claims of unfair dismissal because of Jewish religious practice.[66] In the 1990s and early twenty-first century, Jewish culture, art, and music continued to be prominently displayed or performed in London and elsewhere. Paradoxically, "coming out" as Jews was often a self-conscious performance and provoked the question of why Jews felt they were exclusively different or had to be defined by a religion that most of them did not espouse.[67] This may be a response to the new freedom to express ethnicity and explore cultural difference, but these newly conscious or new-born Jews were also coming from a position of pride in their Jewishness after a generation of assimilation and distancing from Jewish cultural roots. On the other hand, the assimilation of the majority of British Jews has rendered them all but invisible in social behavior, dress, and language. Bhiku Parekh has argued that it is precisely assimilation and pressure to conform to a White monist culture that repressed Yiddish among children of Jewish immigrants and Urdu among children of today's Pakistani immigrants, while a pluralist multicultural environment could encourage a return to ethnic language and culture.[68]

The new self-assurance among British Jews, unlike the traditional reserve and low profile of Anglo-Jewry, comes with an attempt to build bridges with the Muslim community in a common search for a pluralistic European identity (interfaith conferences, exhibitions, a joint Jewish-Muslim acting troupe, and a radio station, *Salaam Shalom*). Interfaith dialogue stressed the coexistence of the two communities, using humor to combat the mutual misapprehensions and deeply felt rival allegiances with one side or the other in the Middle East conflict. However, in the 16- to 25-year-old age group, this might be regarded as a minority sport that has to work hard to make headway against stereotypes and a tendency to conflate Israel with all Jews everywhere.[69]

Hasidic Jews in London's Stamford Hill (the only sector of British Jewry that has maintained an upward demographic trend since World War II) are still perceived as beyond the pale of multiculturalism because they do not adopt the rules of civility. They wear strange clothes and separate themselves socially and sexually from the rest of society out of obedience to a "fundamentalist" religious code, which one columnist in a liberal progressive newspaper likened to primitive practices such as female genital mutilation, illegal in Britain but nevertheless carried out on thousands of British girls each year. The "racist" Jews, she believed, were not integrating like the Caribbeans in such classic tales of immigration as Sam Selvon's *Lonely Londoners* (1956) or Zadie Smith's *White Teeth* (2000).[70] The conservative *Daily Telegraph* also voiced concern that Hasidic children in Stamford Hill were not getting a full secular education and thus were not fitted for employment outside the diamond trade, but otherwise praised the community for its ethical standards and close-knit family life, as well as its sticking to age-old traditions, in the face of a promiscuous culture of sex and drugs.[71]

On the one hand, the public space of multiculturalism beckons with its promise of respect for difference, conditional on respect for civil law—and Stamford Hill's Hasidim are exemplary law-abiding citizens. Eric Kaufmann claims that fundamentalist sects tend toward moderation after integration into mixed communities in order to gain recognition and political power. Yet Stamford Hill's Hasidim seem to fit into modern society without compromising their way of life, despite some defections and the growth (rather than diminishing) of a "scholar society" which prioritizes adult study in a *kollel* (higher rabbinical seminary) over employment.[72] On the other hand, their exclusionist separatism is abhorred as racist and patriarchal; integration demands giving up gender segregation and "fundamentalist" modesty, dress, and behavioral codes, as well as compromising on religious intolerance of sexual freedom. The contradiction in the rhetoric of cohesion is evident, especially when different classes in Britain do not share the same social space (do not drink in the same pub or intermarry), or when Jews and Muslims are lumped together as a demographic threat in a declining population.[73]

Schooling is one area where the question of identity has brought the ambiguity in the status of Jewish identity to the fore. A landmark Court of Appeals ruling in June 2009 in the case of M. against the Jews' Free School (JFS, a state-funded comprehensive high school) found that exclusion of a pupil on the grounds of his mother's identity (the mother was a Progressive convert and not recognized halakhically by the court of the chief rabbi as Jewish) contravened the 1976 Race Relations Act, even though the school maintained that its admission policy was based on religion, not on ethnicity or race.[74] The ruling, which was contested and upheld in the new UK Supreme Court, seemed to imply that the Jewish community could be seen as practicing racist discrimination, since rules of exclusion were based on maternal descent, a development that could potentially jeopardize the anomalous (and in some ways privileged) position of the Jewish community. The ruling—a rare decision on discrimination against a Jew as a Jew, but, ironically, in litigation against other Jews[75]—set off further dissension in the Jewish community over the authority of the chief rabbi and over matrilineal identity or religious law as a definition of Jewishness, coming as it did amid controversy around the use of genetics to trace Jewish lineage, which smacked to some of biological racism.[76]

Here it should be remembered that religion has always been regarded as a strictly private matter in England. Historically, as well as constitutionally, religion has been a divisive issue. Jewish faith schools were receiving state support, yet seemed to retain an exclusivist ethnic admission policy under the guise of religious rules (from September 2009, Jewish schools followed Roman Catholic schools' practice in requiring a certificate of synagogue attendance as a condition of enrollment.) A government inspection of faith schools in 2009 reported that most complied with the regulations, but found that some faith schools did not teach about other religions in detail nor did they encourage pupils' interest in a secular society, which might not be surprising since secularity could be seen as undermining the moral values taught in school. The problem seemed partly to be that the government had not clarified what British values were and how they were to be emulated, beyond good citizenship. Moreover, when it came to the Arab–Israeli conflict, inflammatory material was found in some Muslim schools, and in Jewish schools strong emotions seemed inevitable, especially when pupils and teachers had relatives in Israel directly affected by events in the Middle East.[77] Faith schools are one example of government policy that invests in diversity but has occasionally responded critically to the resulting separatism.

Race, Religion, Politics: Local and Global Identities

Were Jews in fact to be regarded as a faith, a racial minority, or honorary White Europeans? The evidence, notwithstanding the boasts of a more open society, suggests some perceptions of Jews have not changed very much, and that, with the rise of secularism and the modern nation-state, the racialization of the Jews has transmuted in the relativistic ethnic identification of minorities. Something in particular was wrong with the sacred cow of multiculturalism and the assumptions underlying the ensuing debate revealed that no easy equivalences could be made between Jews and Muslims.

In Britain, multiculturalism has also privileged minority groups, which may hold hostile views toward Jews, but the unimpeded media onslaught against Israel and the upsurge of anti-Semitism result from the fact that British Jews are unfortunately placed between two hostile forces. On the one hand, a militant Islamism condemns Western civilization and attacks Jews as well as Christians, while a left-Islamist coalition seeks to isolate and delegitimize Israel, which is projected as the central problem of global social unrest and racial tensions. On the other hand, there is a resurfacing of resentment of foreigners in defensive reactions to mass immigration and terrorism. Curiously enough, though, resentment against foreigners did not always include Jews or Israelis who were considered White, predominantly middle-class professionals, and culturally assimilated to the same peer group. It seems religion, race, and color are perceived differently from place to place and from one context to another, but, more significantly, social and economic difference is often perceived, as in the States, along racialized lines.[78] A survey of White and non-White respondents in multiethnic communities in England and Scotland found that foreign Muslims were often excluded from perceptions of national identity, itself torn between English/Scottish and British, but local and native-born non-Whites might not be precluded from the imagined hybrid community that composes the nation: "[W]hilst Englishness is historically racialized as 'White' and closed to phenotypically signified 'Asians,' knowledge of the contemporary 'ethnically mixed' neighbourhood breaks racialized national signifiers. 'Non-whiteness' does not exclude: hybridity interrupts the exclusive racialized role sign of modern ethno-nationality."[79] As in the States, however, assimilated Jews became "White," but then sometimes become blacked as Others because they are perceived as usurpers who make money (presumably in illicit or underhand ways), or are simply resented as belonging to a wealthy class of "toffs."[80]

In contemporary Britain, it should be noted, perceptions of the Jews may differ between Muslim and non-Muslim communities. Indian communities may see in the Jews a kindred ally against a perceived religious threat from Islam, while the Jews' experience of upward social mobility and their renowned business acumen make them a model for acceptance into British society. Muslim youth are themselves torn between pressure to maintain separation and pressure from outside the community to integrate, while radical Islamists take advantage of inadequate religious educational resources in English for British-born Muslims in order to indoctrinate them in a reductionist view of the world, which conflates political enemies in the Middle East with all Jews and Westerners.[81] Much of this rhetoric draws on familiar Western anti-Semitic discourse and feeds back into contemporary discourses about the "Jews."[82]

In today's multicultural societies, the ambiguity of skin color and race has generally confounded identification, leading to misunderstanding and anxiety in the conflict between local and global identities, between a common citizenship and communal or transnational identification with causes and values that may lead to friction between ethnic groups. Witness the shock, in David Baddiel's British film comedy, *The Infidel* (2010), when Mahmud Nasir, a secular Muslim, discovers he was born Solly Shimshillewitz. The movie pokes fun at stereotyping in religious difference and ethnic identity, as well as the mutual misperceptions of Jews and Muslims, but also indulges in its own obsession with what Jews look like and how they behave. Israelis, quips Lenny, the secular American Jew in the movie who plays the role of authentic insider and guide, are not really Jews, because they do not look "Jewish" and do not do the "Jewish thing," which is the shrug, the *gevalt*, the constant self-conscious anxiety about being a Jew (not surprisingly, Lenny's bible is *Portnoy's Complaint*). When Nasir/Solly asks a rabbi to admit him to see the dying man he believes is his biological father, he cannot answer basic questions about Judaism, nor can he tell a Jewish joke successfully at a bar mitzvah celebration. The failure to pass the test (despite being circumcised) questions what Jewish identity is. Nasir discovers that, as a Jew, he is expected to sign on support of Israel, while, on the Muslim side (treated with considerable sympathy and sensitivity), the Islamist radical is dismissed as a deceitful fake, a Cat Stevens–type who uses his charisma to spread fundamentalist dogma. The use of an ethnic minority's view challenges mutual stereotypes, much as British Jewish comedian Sacha Baron Cohen in the character of Ali G. taps into the ambiguities and instabilities of multiculturalism in Britain when he adopts Rastafarian patois and dons a mask of blackness in order to elicit from unsuspecting interviewees their innate prejudices, as well as satirizing culture and politics.[83]

Miscegenation and secrets of origin are favorite comic devices to mock social and racial identities. In the 1992 movie *Leon the Pig Farmer,* for example, a North London Jew discovers he is the son of a Yorkshire pig farmer, a comic device that explores confused identities in a closed-knit community. There is a tendency in comedy to treat all religious and ethnic difference irreverently. Indeed, the mockery in *The Infidel* of both Jewish and Muslim definitions of belonging in terms of religious rules and commitment for or against Israel leaves one wondering what can be said in any meaningful way about Jewish identities in a multicultural society beyond loose definitions of who feels or looks Jewish. The exposure of religion as a sham is also familiar from an assimilationist discourse, which assures ethnic minorities that religious differences are meaningless (or are themselves the cause of needless hatred) and cannot stand in the way of romantic love, as in the 1999 movie *Solomon and Gaenor* about the love affair between a turn-of-the century Jewish traveling salesman and a Welsh daughter of devout Presbyterians.[84] And in the 2003 movie *Wondrous Oblivion* the multicultural message that Eros is bound to overcome racial and ethnic barriers is driven home in the relationship between a German-Jewish refugee's family and the Jamaicans next door, a story set in South London in the 1960s against the background of racism and neo-fascism. The Jamaican teaches the Jewish boy cricket, the quintessential test of Englishness, while the romantic plot underlines the alliance of Jews and Blacks as minorities subject to prejudice and discrimination. When a thug burns down the Jamaican family's home, it is clear that minorities must stick together (even if the Jewish family moves on, up the social ladder, to Hendon).

Conclusion

As we have seen, the multicultural agenda conceals conditions and restrictions that must be considered in any attempt at understanding the perception of Jews in a society where difference is not only perceived in terms of religion, skin color, or race, but also along socioeconomic, cultural, and political lines. The discourse about multiculturalism exposes the tensions between integration and toleration of difference in a society that has been forced by loss of empire and devolution to reassess its national identity and cultural values. The markers of race and color do not always help unravel the confusion of ethnic, religious, and national identities, and the ambivalence toward Jews as Others may revert to older stereotyping in response to unstable discursive boundaries of personal identities and social norms.

This preliminary sketch proposes a rethinking of assumptions about the place of Jews in the racial hierarchy in Britain. The prospect of some common European identity, in which Jews would be exemplary cosmopolitans, is dimmed by the resurgence of anti-Semitism and other forms of racism, on the one hand, and a growing awareness of the need to accommodate regionalism within the European Union, a long-term recession, and social unrest, on the other. What is needed is analysis of discourses about "Jews" circulating in the media, popular culture, and among other ethnic minorities, that can provide indicators of trends in the debate over national identity and multiculturalism, as well as opinion polls among British Muslims that would correlate views of Jews with perceptions of integration and exclusion in a comparative study across Europe.

Acknowledgments

The research for this chapter was funded by the Vidal Sassoon International Center for the Study of Anti-Semitism, Hebrew University of Jerusalem, and by Israel Science Foundation grant 06/233. An earlier version was read at the European Sociology Association, Lisbon, September 2009. I am grateful to Gűnther Jikeli and Linda Weinhouse for comments on the final revision.

Notes

1. Lappin, *This Green and Pleasant Land: Britain and the Jews,* Yale Initiative for the Interdisciplinary Study of Antisemitism Working Paper #2, 2008; http://www.yale.edu/yiisa/lappin_yiisa072.pdf, p. 5.
2. Ben Gidley, "British Jews and Muslims: Two Myths (part 1)," http://www.mus liminstitute.org/blogs/culture/british-jews-and-muslims-two-myths-part-1
3. Anidjar, "Can the Walls Hear?" *Patterns of Prejudice* 43, no. 3–4 (2009): 251–268. Anidjar is addressing colonial rule over Arab populations in North Africa and the Middle East. See also Peter Morey and Amina Yaqin, *Framing Muslims: Stereotyping and Representation after 9/11* (Cambridge, MA: Harvard University Press, 2011).

4. See John Efron, "When is a Yid not a Jew? The Strange Case of Supporter Identity at Tottenham Hotspur," in *Emancipation through Muscles: Jews and Sports in Europe,* ed. Michael Brenner and Gideon Reuveni (Lincoln, NB: University of Nebraska Press, 2006), 235–256.
5. *The Community Security Trust Anti-Semitic Incidents Report 2006* (London: Community Security Trust, 2006); http://www.thecst.org.uk/docs/Incidentspercent5FReport percent5F06.pdf, 4.
6. *The Community Security Trust Antisemitic Incidents Report 2007* (London: CST, 2007), http://www.thecst.org.uk/docs/Incidents_Report_07.pdf
7. *The Community Security Trust Antisemitic Incidents Report 2011* (London: CST, 2012), http://www.thecst.org.uk/docs/Incidents%20Report%202011.pdf; *CST Annual Review 2011,* http://www.thecst.org.uk/docs/Annual_Review_2011.pdf, 9.
8. Michael Whine, "The Liberal Tradition and Unholy Alliances of the Present," 320–321; Whine, "Antisemitism on the Streets," in *A New Anti-Semitism*? ed. Paul Iganski and Barry Kosmin (London: Profile Books, 2003), 23–37.
9. http://www.thecst.org.uk/docs/Incidents%20Report%202011.pdf, p. 23. Michael Whine, "Antisemitism on the Streets," in *A New Anti-Semitism*? ed. Paul Iganski and Barry Kosmin (London: Profile Books, 2003), 23–37; *CST 2007 Incident Report,* http://www.thecst.org.uk/docs/Incidents%20Report%202011.pdf, p. 23.
10. See Whine, "Antisemitism on the Streets," in *A New Anti-Semitism*? ed. Paul Iganski and Barry Kosmin (London: Profile Books, 2003), 23–37; Whine, "The Liberal Tradition and Unholy Alliances of the Present: Antisemitism in the United kingdom," in *Politics and Resentment: Antisemitism and Counter-Cosmopolitanism in the European Union,* ed. Lars Rensmann and Julus H. Schoeps (Leiden: Brill, 2011), 307–327. In the 2001–2004 period 56.9 percent of suspects were identified as White European; 7.2 percent as Arab/Egyptian; 12.3 percent as Indian/Pakistani; 15 percent as African Caribbean; however, some caution is needed in ethnic classification, as categories differ in police statistics and population censuses (Paul Iganski, Vicky Kielinger, and Susan Paterson, *Hate Crimes against London's Jews: An Analysis of Incidents Recorded by the Metropolitan Police Service, 2001-2004* [London: Jewish Policy Research, 2005], 32).
11. See Efraim Sicher, *Antisemitism, Multiculturalism, Globalization: The British Case.* Analysis of Current Trends in Antisemitism #32. Jerusalem: Vidal Sassoon International Center for the Study of Antisemitism, Hebrew University of Jerusalem (2009); Sicher, "The Image of Israel: A View from Britain," *Israel Studies* 16, no. 1 (Spring 2011): 1–25.
12. Keith Kahn-Harris, and Ben Gidley. *Turbulent Times: The British Jewish Community Today* (London and New York: Continuum, 2010).
13. Ben Gidley and Keith Kahn-Harris, "Contemporary Anglo-Jewish Community Leadership: Coping with Multiculturalism," *British Journal of Sociology* 63, no. 1 (2012): 168–187. See Ulrich Beck, *Risk Society: Towards a New Modernity* trans. Mark Ritter (London: Sage Publications, 1992); Ulrich Beck, Anthony Giddens, and Scott Lash, *Reflexive Modernization: Politics, Tradition and Aesthetics in The Modern Social Order* (Stanford: Stanford University Press, 1994). On Muslim perceptions of the multicultural society, see Philip Lewis, *Young, British and Muslim* (London: Continuum, 2007).
14. Amikam Nachmani, "'The Triangle': Europeans, Muslims, Jews," in *Muslim Attitudes to Jews and Israel: The Ambivalences of Rejection, Antagonism, Tolerance*

and Cooperation, ed. Moshe Ma'oz (Brighton: Sussex Academic Press, 2010), 270–275. See also Gűnther Jikeli and J. Allouche-Benayoun (eds.), *Perceptions of the Holocaust in Europe and Muslim Communities. Sources, Comparisons and Educational Challenges* (Dordrecht: Springer, 2012).

15. Peter Gottschalk and Gabriel Greenberg, *Islamophobia: Making Muslims the Enemy* (Boston: Rowman & Littlefield, 2008). See also Jonathan Lyons, *Islam through Western Eyes: From the Crusades to the War on Terrorism.* (New York: Columbia University Press, 2012).
16. Elizabeth Poole, *Reporting Islam: Media Representations of British Muslims* (London: I. B. Tauris, 2002). See Morey and Yaqin, *Framing Muslims.*
17. David Cesarani, "Anti-Zionism in Britain, 1922–2002: Continuities and Discontinuities," in *Anti-Semitism and Anti-Zionism in Historical Perspective,* ed. Jeffery Herf (London and New York: Routledge, 2007), 137–138; Robin Shepherd, *A State Beyond the Pale: Europe's Problem with Israel* (London: Weidenfeld & Nicolson, 2009), 178–179, 182.
18. Michael Nazir-Ali, *Conviction and Conflict: Islam, Christianity, and World Order* (London: Continuum, 2006).
19. Gallup Coexist Foundation, "Gallup Coexist Index 2009: A Global Study of Interfaith Relations with an In-Depth Analysis of Muslim Integration in France, Germany, and the United Kingdom," http://www.muslimwestfacts.com/mwf/File/118267/Gallup-Coexist-Index-2009.aspx
20. Christian Joppke, "Limits of Integration Policy: Britain and Her Muslims," *Journal of Migration and Ethnic Studies* 35, no. 3 (2009): 453–472. See Kundnani, *The End of Tolerance.*
21. Rensmann and Schoeps, eds., *Politics and Resentment.*
22. Lars Rensmann and Julus H. Schoeps, "Politics and Resentment: Examining Antisemitism and Counter-Cosmopolitanism in the European Union and Beyond," in *Politics and Resentment,* ed. Rensmann and Schoeps, 45–46. On comparative attitudes toward Jews and Muslims in various European Union countries see Andreas Zick, Beate Küpper, and Andreas Hövermann, *Intolerance, Prejudice and Discrimination A European Report Forum* (Berlin: Friedrich-Ebert-Stiftung, 2011), 169–173.
23. Steven Beller, *Is Europe Good for the Jews? Jews and the Pluralist Tradition in Historical Perspective* (London: Institute of Jewish Policy Research, 2008).
24. Gideon van Emden, "Relations between the European Jewish Communities, Their Nation States and the Institutions of the EU: The Challenges of Representation," paper presented at a joint symposium of the London-based Jewish Policy Research Institute and Ben-Gurion University of the Negev, Beer-Sheva, June 2009, http://www.jpr.org.uk/discuss/blog.php?id=26
25. Tope Omoniyi, "Discourse and Identity," in *The Continuum Companion to Discourse Analysis,* ed. Ken Hyland and Brian Paltridge (London: Continuum, 2011), 260–276.
26. Tariq Modood, *Multiculturalism: A Civic Idea* (Cambridge, England: Polity Press, 2007), 2–7.
27. Shindler, *Israel and the European Left,* 272–276; Robert Wistrich, *From Ambivalence to Betrayal: The Left, the Jews, and Israel* (Lincoln : University of Nebraska Press, 2012).
28. Ed Husain, *The Islamist: Why I Joined Radical Islam in Britain, What I Saw Inside and Why I Left* (London: Penguin Books 2007), 202.

29. Media perceptions of this trend can be seen in Ruth Dudley Edwards, "Will Britain One Day Be Muslim?," *Daily Mail,* May 5, 2007; Richard Kerbaj, "Muslim Population 'Rising 10 Times Faster than Rest of Society,'" *The Times,* January 30, 2009. The 2011 census of England and Wales showed that religious affiliation was changing too—while there was a decline in self-identifying Christians (down 11% from 2001), practicing Muslims rose by 75%; Buddhists by 71%; Hindus by 48% and Sikhs by 28% (the number of religious Jews remained stable); see Daniel Vulkan, Jonathan Boyd, and David Graham, *2011 Census Results (England and Wales): Initial Insights about the UK Jewish Population* (London: Jewish Policy Research, December 20, 2012) http://www.jpr.org.uk/downloads/2011%20Census%20Initial%20findings%20report%20Final%20Dec%202012.pdf
30. According to the 2011 census the Jewish population of England and Wales was 263,346, only slightly up from the last census in 2001 (Vulkan, Boyd, and Graham, *2011 Census Results*).
31. Nasar Meer and Tehseen Noorani, "A Sociological Comparison of Anti-Semitism and Anti-Muslim Sentiment in Britain," *Sociological Review* 56, no. 2 (2008): 195–215. See also Nasar Meer and Tariq Modood, "Refutations of Racism in the 'Muslim Question'," *Patterns of Prejudice* 43, no. 3–4 (2009): 335–354. On the myth that Islamophobia and anti-Semitism are identical racisms, see Ben Gidley, "British Jews and Muslims: Two Myths (part 2)," http://www.musliminstitute.org/blogs/culture/british-jews-and-muslims-two-myths-part-2; see also Matti Bunzl, *Anti-Semitism and Islamophobia: Hatreds Old and New in Europe* (Chicago: Prickly Paradigm Press, 2007). For a comparative study of Jewish and Muslim immigrations see Anne Kershen, *Strangers, Aliens and Asians: Huguenots, Jews and Bangladeshis in Spitalfields 1660-2000* (London: Routledge, 2005).
32. David Cesarani, "Why Muslims Are Not the New Jews," http://www.thejc.com/comment/comment/21173/why-muslims-are-not-new-jews
33. "21st-Century Britons Are No Longer Either Black or White," *Observer,* January 18, 2009.
34. Bhiku Parekh, *Rethinking Multiculturalism: Cultural Diversity and Political Theory* (Basingstoke: Macmillan, 2000).
35. See Joan Wallach Scott, *The Politics of the Veil: The Public Square* (Princeton, NJ: Princeton University Press, 2007); Bronwyn Winter, *Hijab and Republic: Uncovering the French Headscarf Debate* (Syracuse, NY: Syracuse University Press, 2008).
36. Modood, *Multiculturalism,* 51–58.
37. David Bartlett, "Straw Urges Muslim Women to Take Off Veils," *Lancashire Evening Telegraph,* October 5, 2006.
38. Arun Kundnani, *The End of Tolerance: Racism in 21st Century Britain* (London: Pluto Books, 2007), 172–179.
39. Ibid., 124–128.
40. Richard Norton-Taylor, "'MI5 Chief: Al-Qaida Threat Diminished, But Not Yet Over," *Guardian,* January 7, 2009; Robert Booth, "Minister for Terror: Gaza Will Fuel UK Extremism," *Guardian,* January 28, 2009.
41. Kundnani, *The End of Tolerance,* 183.
42. Morey and Yaqin, *Framing Muslims,* 79–85.

43. "Muslims 'Under Siege Like Jews,'" BBC News, July 4, 2008. http://news.bbc.co.uk/go/pr/fr/-/1/hi/england/bradford/7489392.stm; Maleiha Malik, "Muslims Are Now Getting the Same Treatment Jews Had a Century Ago," *Guardian,* February 2, 2007.
44. Gunther Jikeli, "Anti-Semitism among Young Muslims in Europe," in *Reflections on Anti-Semitism: Anti-Semitism in Historical and Anthropological Perspectives,* ed. V. Tydlitatova and A. Hanzova (Pilsen: West Bohemian University, 2009), 65–69; Jikeli, *Antisemitismus und Diskriminierungswahrnehmungen junger Muslime in Europa* (Essen: Klartext, 2012). For a politicized view see Melanie Phillips, *Londonistan: How Britain is Creating a Terror State Within* (London: Gibson Square, 2006), 132–134. Phillips has frequently been accused of Islamophobia for her statements on Muslims.
45. Michael Howard, "Talk about the British Dream," *Guardian,* August 17, 2005; and see Morey and Yaqin, *Framing Muslims,* 68.
46. Alexandra Frean, "Schools Drop Holocaust Lessons to Avoid Offence," *The Times,* April 2, 2007.
47. Parekh, *Rethinking Multiculturalism,* 295–335.
48. Marcel Stoetzler, "Cultural Difference in the National State: From Trouser-Selling Jews to Unbridled Multiculturalism," *Patterns of Prejudice* 42, no. 3 (2008): 245–279.
49. Tony Blair, "Our Nation's Future—Multiculturalism and Integration," Runnymede Trust Lecture, Downing Street, December 8, 2006, video recording http://www.bbc.co.uk/mediaselector/check/player/nol/newsid_6160000/newsid_6161400?redirect=6161437.stm&bbwm=1&bbram=1&nbwm=1&nbram=1&news=1
50. Rowan Williams, interviewed on "The World at One," BBC Radio 4, February 7, 2008.
51. Bernard Jackson, "'Transformative Accommodation' and Religious Law," *Ecclesiastical Law Journal* 2 (2009): 131–153.
52. Daniel Blake, "Church of England Considers Evangelism of Other Faith Groups," *Christian Today,* October 11, 2006, http://www.christiantoday.com/article/church.of.england.called.to.debate.stance.on.evangelism.of.other.faith.groups/7940.htm; and see Parekh, *Rethinking Multiculturalism,* 23–33.
53. For the origins of "Abrahamic faiths" see Louis Massignon, "Les Trois Prières d'Abraham, Père de Tous les Croyants," *Dieu Vivant* 13 (1949): 20–23. I am grateful to Tina Hamin Dahl for drawing my attention to this reference.
54. Margaret Brearly, "The Anglican Church, Jews and British Multiculturalism" (Posen Papers in Contemporary Antisemitism) (Jerusalem: Vidal Sassoon International Center for the Study of Anti-Semitism, Hebrew University of Jerusalem, 2007).
55. Philip Johnston, "Blair: Paying Religious Groups Is a Mistake," *Daily Telegraph,* December 9, 2006.
56. Jonathan Sacks, *The Home We Build Together: Recreating Society* (London and New York: Continuum, 2007), 3. See also Sacks, *The Dignity of Difference: How to Avoid the Clash of Civilizations,* rev. ed. (London: Continuum, 2003).
57. Sacks, *Home We Build Together,* 4. A more telling example of the post-9/11 turn against multiculturalism was probably the murder in 2004 of right-winger Theo van Gogh by a Muslim assassin (Modood, *Multiculturalism,* 13).
58. Sacks, *Home We Build Together,* 4–5, 25–36.

59. Ibid., 193–203.
60. Modood, *Multiculturalism,* 14–20.
61. "Tory Candidate Quits over 'Powell Was Right' Comments," *Guardian,* November 4, 2007.
62. Phillips, *Londonistan,* 108
63. "State Multiculturalism Has Failed, Says David Cameron," *BBC News,* February 5, 2011, http://www.bbc.co.uk/news/uk-politics-12371994
64. For a comparative history of ethnic relations in local politics see Romain Garbaye, *Getting into Local Power: The Politics of Ethnic Minorities in British and French Cities* (Oxford and Malden, MA: Blackwell, 2005).
65. Baroness Warsi, 2011 European Institute for the Study of Antisemitism Lecture, quoted in Jessica Elgot, "Baroness Warsi: 'We Must Drain the Poison of Antisemitism,'" *JC Online,* November 15, 2011; http://www.thejc.com/news/uk-news/58312/baroness-warsi-we-must-drain-poison-antisemitism
66. On the ambiguous position of Jews under the race relations legislation, see Didi Herman, *An Unfortunate Coincidence: Jews, Jewishness, and English Law* (Oxford: Oxford University Press, 2011), 126–149.
67. Paul Lester, "Have I Got Jews for You: Is it as Awkward for Jewish Musicians to 'Come Out' as it is for Gay Ones?," *Guardian On Line,* February 4, 2008, blogs.guardian.co.uk/music/2008/02/have_i_got_jews_for_you.html
68. Parekh, *Rethinking Multiculturalism,* 204–05. See Stratton, *Coming Out Jewish.*
69. Jason Solomons and Riazat Butt, "Sounds Jewish / Islamophonics," joint podcast, *Guardian On Line,* February 2, 2009, http://www.guardian.co.uk/uk/audio/2009/feb/02/sounds-jewish-podcast-gaza
70. Christina Patterson, "Lessons from Literature—and YouTube—in Immigrant Life," *Independent,* July 24, 2010; and "The Limits of Multi-Culturalism," *Independent,* July 28, 2010. See her response to protests from Muslim and Jewish readers, "We Need to Talk about Integration," *Independent,* August 4, 2010. Patterson defended herself against charges of anti-Semitism by mocking the Simon Wiesenthal Foundation and slamming Israel's record on human rights, while claiming her hatred was not directed against anyone collectively, only individually ("How I Was Smeared as an Anti-Semite," *Independent,* December 23, 2010). British journalist India Knight (of mixed race) also records her anxiety, in response to the furor over wearing veils in public, about Hasidic men in black who avoid her in Golders Green ("Muslims Are the New Jews," *Sunday Times,* October 15, 2006).
71. Mick Brown, "Inside the Private World of London's Ultra-Orthodox Jews," *Daily Telegraph,* February 25, 2011. A BBC2 television documentary about the Jews of Stamford Hill, *A Hasidic Guide to Love, Marriage and Finding a Bride* (May 2011, produced and directed by Paddy Wivell) prized open their secretive world that divided the twenty-first century from the traditions of the eighteenth century by entering the home of a former convict, who served a prison term for money laundering and drug smuggling, thus (perhaps unwittingly) reinforcing the false impression that only the "bad" Jews kept religious laws and outlandish customs strictly (though, to be fair, Wivell could find very few Hasidim willing to talk to the camera).

72. On the "haredization" of Israel and Diaspora Jewish communities, see Eric Kaufmann, *Shall the Religious Inherit the Earth: Demography and Politics in the Twenty-First Century* (London: Profile, 2010), 210–248; and see the review by Kenan Malik, "Eric Kaufmann, *Shall the Religious Inherit the Earth?*" *Observer,* May 2, 2010.
73. Kaufman, *Shall the Religious Inherit,* 161. See Malik, "Eric Kaufmann"; Rafael Behr, "Do Stamford Hill's Jews Need Integration?" *Observer,* June 15, 2008.
74. Simon Rocker, "Jewish School Entry Policies Are Unlawful, Court Rules," *Jewish Chronicle,* June 25, 2009, http://www.thejc.com/articles/jewish-school-entry-policies-are-unlawful-court-rules
75. Didi Herman, "'The Wandering Jew Has No Nation': Jewishness and Race Relations Law," *Jewish Culture and History* 12, no. 1–2 (Summer 2010): 149–154; on the implications of the Jews' Free School case, see Herman, *An Unfortunate Coincidence,* 149–156, 160–172.
76. Gavin Schaffer, "Dilemmas of Jewish Difference: Reflections on Contemporary Research into Jewish Origins and Types from an Anglo-Jewish Historical Perspective," *Jewish Culture and History* 12, no. 1–2 (Summer 2010): 75–94. See in the present volume the foreword by Sander Gilman and chapter twelve by Noa Kohler and Dan Mishmar.
77. *Ofsted Report on Independent Faith Schools,* October 22, 2009, http://www.ofsted.gov.uk/Ofsted-home/Publications-and-research/Browse-all-by/Documents-by-type/Thematic-reports/Independent-faith-schools
78. See Walter Benn Michaels, *The Trouble with Diversity: How We Learned to Love Identity and Ignore Inequality* (New York: Holt, 2007).
79. Christopher Kyriakides, Satnam Virdee, and Tariq Modood, "Racism, Muslims and the National Imagination," *Journal of Ethnic and Migration Studies* 35, no. 2 (2009): 289–307.
80. See Stratton, *Coming Out Jewish,* 57–61; Katya Gibel Azoulay, *Black, Jewish, and Interracial: It's Not the Color of Your Skin, but the Race of Your Kin, and Other Myths of Identity* (Durham: Duke University Press, 1997); Karen Brodkin, *How Jews Became White Folks And What That Says about Race in America* (New Brunswick: Rutgers University Press, 1998).
81. Lewis, *Young, British, and Muslim,* 37–38. See also chapter 1 in this volume.
82. See Robert Wistrich, *A Lethal Obsession: Anti-Semitism from Antiquity to the Global Jihad* (New York: Random House, 2010).
83. See Robert A. Saunders, *The Many Faces of Sacha Baron Cohen: Politics, Parody, and the Battle over Borat* (Lanham, MD: Lexington Books, 2008).
84. See Omoniyi, "Discourse and Identity."

CHAPTER 16

Brothers in Misery

Reconnecting Sociologies of Racism and Anti-Semitism

Glynis Cousin and Robert Fine

Brothers in Misery

There was a time when antiracists like W.E.B. Du Bois and Frantz Fanon sustained an interest in how anti-Semitism and racism articulate with each other. This interest appears to have been downplayed in contemporary studies. Du Bois is often quoted as declaring in 1903, "[T]he twentieth century is the century of the color line."[1] Yet he revised that declaration in the light of his observation of the ill treatment of Poles under German domination and his growing awareness of the horrors of anti-Semitism. In the 1930s, Du Bois made academic visits to Berlin under Nazi rule and witnessed Nazi violence against German Jews, which he compared to the Inquisition and to the European enslavement of Africans, both in terms of its significance and of its scale.[2] Indeed, his eyewitness experiences in Europe revealed to Du Bois the versatility of racism and its reach beyond the Black-White binary. After one particular anti-Semitic episode involving a Jewish traveling companion, Du Bois remarked, it "had never occurred to me until then that any exhibition of race prejudice could be anything but color prejudice."[3] A visit to the Warsaw Ghetto clarified to him "a more complete understanding of the Negro problem" as one that was connected to other forms of racism.[4] Du Bois' experiences in Europe prompted him to deepen his understanding of racism as a form of human hate capable of reaching all sorts of people of all kinds of skin colors: "The ghetto of Warsaw helped me to emerge from a certain social provincialism into a broader conception of what the fight against race segregation, religious discrimination, and the oppression by wealth had to become if civilisation was going to triumph and broaden in the world."[5]

Du Bois ensured that the anti-Semitic passages in his own *The Souls of Black Folk* were edited out of his second edition. As a civil rights activist, he continued to embrace a concern for anti-Semitism alongside racism. He welcomed the active support of Jews for the National Association for the Advancement of Colored People (NAACP), which he cofounded, and he acknowledged both the contribution of Jews to the civil rights movement and their continued vulnerability to racism. While Du Bois appreciated the different forms this vulnerability took, he did not see these as a defense for a radical splitting of racisms.

Like Du Bois, Frantz Fanon was similarly troubled by the persecution of Jews in Europe, though his emphasis was different. While Du Bois' reference point was the legacy of slavery and the denial of equal rights in the United States, Fanon coming from the French colony of Martinique was more exercised by the effects of European colonialism. He shared Du Bois' horror of Nazi atrocities. "Anti-Semitism," he wrote, "hits me head-on: I am enraged, I am bled white by an appalling battle."[6] Fanon was at pains to state his solidarity with the persecuted Jew. His ethical stance was informed by Jaspers's concept of metaphysical guilt: "[I]f he does not stand with his Jewish brother, he stands against him by default." This humanist train of thought prompts Fanon to ask, "Is there in truth any difference between one racism and another? Do not all of them show the same collapse, the same bankruptcy of man?"[7]

Fanon offers an equivocal response to his own question. Despite his evident anguish about the cruelties of anti-Semitism and the shared symbolic meaning he assigns to Jews and Blacks as evil counterpoints to the good Christian, ultimately, he decides, color is what divides Black from Jew: "The Jew can be unknown in his Jewishness. He is not wholly what he is. One hopes, one waits. His actions, his behaviour are the final determinant. He is a White man, and, apart from some rather debatable characteristics, he can sometimes go unnoticed."[8]

In Bryan Cheyette's view, Fanon could locate the predicament of Jews alongside that of Blacks but only within limits set by his perception of Jews as White Europeans. Fanon looked through the twin lens of a Black-White dualism and a homogenizing concept of the West.[9] At a low point he declares the persecution of Jews to be the product of little family quarrels—a comment echoed by some subsequent commentators keen to downplay the significance of European anti-Semitism next to the legacy of European colonialism.[10] His defense of this unfortunate reasoning is that unlike the Black man who is inescapably Black, the Jew "can be unknown in his Jewishness" within a community of Europeans.[11]

Fanon's "The Fact of Blackness" is a moving essay on the devastating effects of a racist White gaze on Black people. "I am the slave," he wrote, "not of the 'idea' others have of me but of my own appearance."[12] To the extent that he sees Jews as White men, he cannot see how they can share his existential agony. He experiences how difficult it is for Black people to hide from a racist gaze, and yet the visibility/invisibility contrast Fanon draws between anti-Black and anti-Semitic racisms is not the whole story. Visible differences are also social constructions.[13] They are not always naturally inscribed on the body. When persecutors, like the Nazis, wanted to mark out a particular group as Other, they enforced the wearing of a yellow star or (in the camps) pink triangle. Sometimes visible differences are self-declared, as when Jews elect to wear distinguishing markers such as a skullcap or Muslim women elect to wear a headscarf. These qualifications do not undermine Fanon's understanding of the fact of blackness, but they temper the contrast with anti-Semitism.

Fanon's critique of European hypocrisy for setting aside human rights when it comes to colonial domination is well taken. Colonialism was rarely about imposing the colonizers' way of life on colonized people; it was based rather on reserving the colonizers' way of life—their freedoms, rights, democracy and material benefits—for themselves and imposing another kind of servitude on the colonized. More questionable, however, is Fanon's identification of Jews simply as White Europeans. Cheyette identifies the symbolic violence of this categorization: because "Jews are ambivalently positioned as both Black *and* White, self *and* other, as both inside *and* outside Western culture" (emphasis in original) their position destabilizes the coherence of these classifications.[14] Once we begin to connect European racism to European anti-Semitism, we may become more inclined to rethink the relation between what Europeans have done to the colonized and what Europeans have done to their own outsiders. Such connections question the category of the West rather than mobilize the West versus the Rest opposition.[15] Fanon himself heeded the connections his professor encouraged him to make between racism against Black people and anti-Semitism: "Whenever you hear anyone abuse the Jews, pay attention, because he is talking about you.' And I found he was universally right—by which I meant that I was answerable … for what was done to my brother. Later I realised that he meant, quite simply, an anti-Semite is inevitably anti-Negro.[16] With hindsight we can see that Fanon's equivocations matter less than the fact that he, like Du Bois, made the connections between racism and anti-Semitism a matter of public discussion and political concern.

In the postwar period, evidence of a continuing concern for integrating questions of racism and anti-Semitism can be found in Hannah Arendt's work on *The Origins of Totalitarianism,* first published in 1951 but now enjoying considerable attention. In the first two sections of *Origins,* those on "Antisemitism and Imperialism," Arendt addresses precisely the ties that bound the rise of political anti-Semitism inside Europe to the spread of new forms of racism that accompanied colonial conquest outside Europe. It is difficult to dismiss as pure coincidence the chronological correspondence between the development of race theories in the last quarter of the nineteenth century and the politicization of anti-Semitism. It was in the 1880s and 1890s that both scientific racism and anti-Semitic political parties were institutionalized in Germany, Austria, France, and to some extent Britain, and racism and anti-Semitism became crossnational ideologies of nationalist and pan movements in Central and Eastern Europe.[17] The age of imperialism was characterized by increasing vulnerability both of conquered peoples outside Europe and of peoples considered to be foreigners within Europe. In relation to the latter, Hannah Arendt observes that political anti-Semitism took off at a time when Jewish communities were losing the degrees of protection they once enjoyed from European nation-states—not least because of the declining significance of Jewish finance. In France, Arendt observes, the Dreyfus Affair exploded not when Jewish banks were at the height of their power in the Second Empire, but when their economic and political significance was in decline.[18]

Racism and Anti-Semitism in Europe

In contemporary Britain, anti-Semitism is discussed in readers on racism and research reports like the Runnymede Trust (1994) study of anti-Semitism, *A Very Light Sleeper,* which also predicted Islamophobia as an upcoming racism.[19] Imagery of the Holocaust and commitment to the slogans "Never Again" were also deployed by various European antiracist movements (such as the Anti-Nazi League and SOS Racisme) to create resonances with new sets of victims. Paul Gilroy has certainly done most to establish connections between racism and anti-Semitism by integrating histories of Europe, Africa, and the Americas through a transnational prism. He argues that the terror of racism for both Black and Jewish people needs to be considered in the same place, proposing that these racisms are in some sort of mutual relation and that a transnational history might provide "precious resources for understanding modernity."[20] The political effect of this transnationalism is to question any competition of victimhood between Blacks and Jews: "The wrangle over which communities have experienced the most ineffable forms of degradation is both pointless and utterly immoral."[21]

Cornell West addresses the linkages between racism and anti-Semitism in the United States, arguing that the presence of anti-Semitism within the ranks of some Black activists, like Louis Farrakhan, compromises the prospects of anti-Black racism as well: "[I]f we fall prey to anti-Semitism, then the principled attempt to combat racism forfeits much of its credibility."[22] Paul Berman also responded to Farrakhan by recalling the genuine popular enthusiasm among liberal Jews in the postwar period for the civil rights movement. He maintains that Jews accounted for almost two-thirds of the White volunteers who went to the South for Freedom Summer in 1964 and that three-quarters of the money raised by the civil rights organizations at the height of the movement came from Jewish contributors. Behind this solidarity, Berman discerned a politics of recognition able to associate slavery and Nazism, lynchings and pogroms, Jim Crow and tsarist anti-Semitism, bigotry and bigotry. Of course, this example of solidarity was not the whole story but, Berman added, "if some kernel of practical self-interest lurked as well—if the higher-ups in the Jewish establishment always knew that people with sheets over their heads were no friends of Jewry either, and Blacks were a good ally to have—that merely shows that idealism and self-interest need not be opposites, in spite of a cheap temptation to assume that they must be."[23] Informing this perceived need to bring racism and anti-Semitism together in the same place was a sense of a connected history that goes right back to the formation of European modernity. Racism and anti-Semitism were linked on the one hand to the formation of homogenous Christian nations within Europe and the exclusion of Jews and Moors, and on the other hand to the colonial conquest of the non-European world and the objectifying treatment of non-Europeans as inferior. The events of 1492 illustrate how connected were these phenomena. The year 1492 marked the victory of Christianity over the Moors and the Jews within the Iberian peninsula and the establishment of Atlantic trade routes with the non-European world. The opening passage from Christopher Columbus' *Journal,* written for the eyes of the king of Spain, exemplifies this conjunction: "So after expelling the Jews from your dominions, your Highnesses, in the same month of January, ordered me to proceed with a sufficient armament to the said regions of India, and for that purpose granted me great favours and ennobled me that henceforth I might call myself Don and be High Admiral of the Sea."[24]

Ella Shohat comments, "European Christian demonology prefigured colonialist racism.... The *Reconquista* policies of settling Christians in the newly conquered areas of Spain, as well as the gradual institutionalisation of expulsions, conversions, and killings of Muslims and Jews in Christian territories, prepared the ground for similar *conquista* practices across the Atlantic."[25] First came the development of the nation at home through the expulsion and persecution of Muslims and Jews; then came slavery and expropriation abroad with the subjugation of indigenous peoples. It was in part out of both forms of violence that the idea of Europe was born. Both Jews and Muslims in Europe and colonized people outside of Europe had cause to cry, in the words of Samuel Usque, the Portuguese Marrano chronicler, writing one generation later, "Now Europe, O Europe, my hell on earth."[26]

Disconnecting Racism and Anti-Semitism

It would appear that the connections between racism and anti-Semitism, which were a subject of curiosity and exploration for Du Bois, Fanon, Arendt, Gilroy, West, Berman, and many others, have become less clear and more contested. In the field of race relations, the emphasis on social disadvantage and discrimination suffered by mainly Black immigrants has contributed to the amelioration of social conditions faced by immigrants as well as to the formation of a more inclusive democracy. The relatively small number of Jews who survived in Europe after the Holocaust did not figure strongly in this framework. In this context, the perception of Jews as White, European, and privileged further removed anti-Semitism from the list of racisms that needed to be addressed. The tendency to measure the gravity of a problem exclusively by its empirical scale deflected attention from the *symbolic* terrain on which racism and anti-Semitism thrived. They are not only conjoint forms of prejudice, but also complementary ways of understanding the world. The kind of racism that targets those collective categories seen as powerful and prosperous—for example, that of Hutu nationalists against Tutsis in Rwanda, or anti-Semites against Jews in Europe—did not easily fit into this way of thinking. Other factors contributed to the emerging split between racism and anti-Semitism. These included the usual imperatives of intellectual specialism. The development of both postcolonial studies and Holocaust studies engendered fruitful research into the workings of colonialism and the

Holocaust, respectively, in the formation and definition of modernity, but it has arguably been at the cost of reifying their separation. As Gilroy argues in relation to the Holocaust, "It is ... essential not to use that invocation of uniqueness to close down the possibility that a combined if not a comparative discussion of its horrors and its patterns of legitimation might be fruitful in making sense of modern racisms."[27] The emergence in some urban situations of social antagonisms between Black and Jewish social actors could make the split between the study of racism and anti-Semitism appear as the expression of practical reality on the ground. The tendency toward disconnection was further reinforced when some Marxist and anti-imperialist writers rationalized the nationalism of the oppressed as the natural way of facing up to the racism of the oppressors. There was considerable debate within Marxist and anti-imperialist circles about whether this approach failed to consider or ruled out more universalist responses.[28]

The division between racism and anti-Semitism may have reflected the separation of expertise in academic discourses, but it became distinctly disfiguring to the extent that it inhibited cross border connections and divided resistance to racism into mutually indifferent or even hostile camps. What started off as a contingent separation could become in these circumstances an intellectually and politically disabling schism. One outcome of situating opposition to racism and opposition to anti-Semitism in distinct camps is that each party could fall prey to an identity politics that presents anti-Semitism as if it were the exclusive concern of Jews, racism as if it were the exclusive concern of Black people, and victim experience as the exclusive source of knowledge construction. This politics encourages singular identity scripts that treat membership of an ethnic or religious group as fundamentally determining of who we are at the cost of all other formative experiences.[29] The only connections it allows for across identities are those made through some notion of intersectionality, that is, within the context of individual experiences or biographies. I may say, "I am a Black, Jewish, North London, gay man," but this form of connectedness is limited to the individual level and remains caught in a world of multiple particularisms. Commitment to a singular identity script may be justified by past experience at certain historic moments, such as in Black Pride movements, but it becomes narrow and rigid if it reduces experience to a victim narrative and places it in competition with other victim narratives.[30] The risk here is of locking people into a framework that situates antiracists and anti-anti-Semites in different camps. In some instances, it can even encourage each camp to relate to the other through homogenizing and stigmatizing typifications.

The splitting of racism and anti-Semitism has been given a temporal reading in some texts.[31] Islamophobia is situated in the here and now in contrast with anti-Semitism, which is seen as now marginalized in the new, post-Holocaust Europe. From this perspective, anti-Semitism is recognized as a terrible stain on Europe's past but is no longer considered a problem for the present. The temptation is to give the story of European anti-Semitism a happy ending and pay tribute to the success of the new Europe in transcending its longest hatred. Anti-Semitism is safely tucked away in history, overtaken by the defeat of Nazism, the fall of the Soviet Union and the rise of the European Union. It is associated with the period of European nationalisms and in particular with the ethnic forms of nationalism that once took hold of Germany and Eastern Europe. The New "postnational" Europe is seen as marking a radically new period in Europe's history—one that spells the end of anti-Semitism as we used to know it. This reassuring narrative looks back to an era in which anti-Semites saw themselves as guardians of the ethnically pure nation-state, but it holds that with the advent of the New Europe, anti-Semitism has become, apart from worrying nationalist throwbacks, a residual trauma or museum piece.

By contrast, it is said that other kinds of racism—especially Islamophobia, racism against Roma, and racism against Black immigrants—are rooted in Europe's colonial history and reiterated in Europe's continuing imperial relation to the non-Western world. The temptation is to see Jews in the post-Holocaust world as having crossed sides and joined the European White elite, an image reinforced by a shift in the discourse from Jews as victims of Nazism to Jews as victimizers of Palestinians. The temporal division of European history into national and postnational periods can, if misapplied, function to exclude anti-Semitism from the list of racisms Europe now has to confront.

The conceptual framework that places anti-Semitism firmly in the past serves to split racism from anti-Semitism in ways not envisaged by the enlightened architects of the new Europe. Among the latter, the school of thought associated with the philosopher Jürgen Habermas has portrayed the European project as bound together by the signs and symbols of Europe's violent past—wars between European nations, colonial conquest of the non-European world, and the murder of the Jews of Europe. It commits the new Europe to teaching each generation the horror lurking beneath the surface of European civilization.[32] Its aim, as the historian Tony Judt once put it, has been to "furnish Europe's present with admonitory meaning and moral purpose."[33] The representation of the Holocaust as a didactic object for all forms of racism and xenophobia remains the official stance of the European Union.

It is, however, rendered fragile by the splitting of anti-Semitism from racism. A periodization of history that situates anti-Semitism in the past renders actual incidents of anti-Semitic abuse or violence harder to see and more amenable to other interpretations—from allusions to Jewish oversensitivity, to displacing the onus of responsibility onto the actions of Jews themselves.[34] It deflects attention from enduring symbolic functions of anti-Semitism in providing an epistemic framework for explaining all manner of social pathologies from wars in the Middle East to financial crises of capitalism and even the power of Arab dictators.[35] The anti-Semitic explanatory framework normally functions through some version of conspiracy, financial power and blood libel. As Naomi Klein has written, "[E]very time I log on to activist news sites like Indymedia.org which practise 'open publishing,' I am confronted with a string of Jewish conspiracy theories about September 11 and excerpts from the *Protocols of the Elders of Zion.*"[36]

Situating anti-Semitism in the past discounts the possibility that anti-Semitism has insinuated itself in our modes of thinking in ways that are as deep as the insinuation of racism against Black people and Muslims. Within the Christian tradition, the usage of the name "Judas" to designate traitor or the existence of Manichaean threads representing Jews as the anti-Christ parallel the association of the color black with darkness and dirt in contrast to the association of white with light and purity. Contextualization is important but it is not everything. The conditioning of language by old anti-Semitic myths can produce an instinctive distrust of Jews (say, for misusing their financial and intellectual powers for self-interested ends) that corresponds to the conditioning of language by old racist myths concerning the incapacity of Black people to achieve moral or intellectual maturity or the incapacity of Muslim men to treat women as equals. The content of these typifications is undoubtedly different—Jews tend to be typified as bearers of an intellectually distorted modernity, Black people as bearers of premodern savagery, Muslims as bearers of an antagonistic civilization—but in all cases the categories of our thought can function to place them on the negative poles of notions of good and evil.

The work of Hannah Arendt and others has successfully dispelled the "eternal anti-Semitism" thesis, which states that anti-Semitism is an unchanging fact of life.[37] This does not mean, however, that the subterranean currents of anti-Semitism in the European world have simply evaporated in the post-Holocaust period. It may be tempting to say that the Holocaust served Europe as a learning experience that by virtue of its horrible extremity taught Europeans a lesson in anti-anti-Semitism. Few people in Europe now proclaim a positive adherence to anti-Semitic ideologies and raising the question of anti-Semitism can meet with emphatic, if not angry, denial.[38] It may *appear*, then, that outside reactive ultranationalist circles, anti-Semitism is an anachronism.[39] However, one of the strengths of the European Union project has been to recognize that the past continues to weigh on the present and recreates afresh the need for every generation to reflect critically on what Europeans have done to one another, to colonized peoples, and to their own minorities. It is an index of the crisis of this project that the project has been converted in the name of civic values from a critical demand for European self-reflection on its own history into an uncritical resource for denouncing others for their regressive nationalism.[40] The temptation facing the enlightened European consciousness is to move from an active and self-reflective radicalism to a renewed endorsement of a moral division of the world between us and them. This slippage establishes the conceptual framework in which the threat of a new anti-Semitism in Europe can find a base and a home.

The Emergence of New Antagonisms

The rejection of connectedness between racism and anti-Semitism can be found on both sides of the divide: both in critical race theories and in new anti-Semitism theories. It may be exemplified on one side by the emergence of a critical race theory in the contemporary Anglophone world that casts doubt on the very possibility of solidarity across this divide.[41] Derek Bell, one of the architects of this paradigm, has argued that Black opposition to anti-Semitism functions not as a genuine expression of solidarity but merely as a means of status enhancement for Blacks in the eyes of Whites.[42] This stance makes solidarity between Blacks and Jews difficult to conceive and challenges the validity of more universalist commitments. It constructs a conceptual universe in which Black and White appear as primary sources of power and inequality, albeit tempered by intersectional factors, and in which there is little space to address questions of anti-Semitism. This is especially the case if Jews are perceived as having become, along with other minorities, advantaged Whites. The construal of White 'elite' solidarity with Black victims of racism exclusively in terms of interest convergence—that is, through the notion that Whites express solidarity *only* when it is in their self-interest—disallows any claim that ethics and self-interest need not be opposites or that some Whites are themselves vulnerable to racism.[43] It declines the humanist stance of the kind expressed in Fanon's observation (quoted above) that racism and anti-Semitism reveal the same bankruptcy of man and in his ethical imperative that those who do not stand with their brother stand against them.

Multiculturalism offers a less skeptical perspective on Black-White solidarity and on the possibilities of Black-Jewish collaboration against racism and anti-Semitism. Multiculturalism has taken many different forms from the corporate to the critical, and has evolved substantially over time.[44] It has played an important role in the struggle against racism by enabling people to become comfortable with difference. By foregrounding respect for difference, it has enabled the construction of rainbow alliances across groups. These alliances have expressed a sense of connectedness through the mutual right both to be different and to play in creative ways with differences. However, if the multicultural approach proposes the celebration of difference as its key response to racism, it also emphasizes what distinguishes us over what we have in common. The temptation of multiculturalism has been to treat every culture as a bounded entity, producing what Amartya Sen has called a mono-multiculturalism in which coexistence trumps connectivity.[45] Sen cautions against imputing to others fixed and rigid differences on the grounds that all human beings are shaped by a complexity of factors that can never be reduced to ethnicity, religion, nationality, and so on. He argues we should assign to others the same ability to be reflective, critical, inventive, and imaginative about themselves as we may wish to assign to ourselves. Kenan Malik goes further in arguing that we need to denature the categories of difference with which multiculturalism operates because of their unwitting affinity with categories of racism: "Challenging the politics of difference has become as important today as challenging racism; this does not mean ignoring the reality of race but seeking rather to transcend the politics of difference, whether promoted by racists or antiracists.... The concept of race is irrational. The practice of antiracism has become so. We need to challenge both, in the name of humanism and of reason."[46]

Critical race theory (to the extent that it is based on the incommensurability of Black and White experiences) and multiculturalism (to the extent that it is based on peaceful cohabitation of different cultures) offer expressions of contemporary antiracism that reveal the difficulty of making connections beyond existing particularisms.

Related problems pertain in relation to anti-Semitism. A common belief expressed under the troubled title of new anti-Semitism theory is that a discriminatory logic has taken hold of significant sections of public opinion in Europe and America. It is argued that Israel is depicted as a uniquely illegitimate state, Zionism as a uniquely noxious ideology, supporters of Israel as a uniquely powerful lobby, and memory of the Holocaust as a uniquely self-serving reference to the past.[47] The fear expressed in new anti-Semitism theory is that behind what passes as criticism of Israel there sometimes—though not always—lies a reconstruction of old anti-Semitic motifs in a new guise: blood libel, global conspiracy, secret power, indifference to the suffering of others, and exclusivity. Israel is represented as the incarnation of all the negative properties the new Europe is allegedly throwing off—racism, colonialism, fascism, ethnic cleansing, and so on—and this projection frames Israel as a vessel that Europeans can fill with all that is bad in Europe's past and by means of which they can preserve the good for themselves. New anti-Semitism theorists express alarm over the range of political forces seen to subscribe to this discriminatory logic, which may include not only fundamentalist groups in the Middle East and ultranationalist parties in Europe, but also sections of liberal and radical European political opinion. Their concern is that otherwise conflicting political forces might unite around hatred of Israel, just as in the past opposing political forces united around hatred of Jews.

The architects and supporters of new anti-Semitism theory do not all speak with one voice. The ultranationalist wing of new anti-Semitism theory imposes its own discriminatory logic. It tends more or less to exaggerate the extent of anti-Semitism in Europe, obscure the existence of other forms of racism, and deny the validity of concepts designed to capture other forms of racism, such as Islamophobia. It threatens to stigmatize entire groups of people—such as the Muslims or the Arabs or the left—as anti-Semitic, to misappropriate the history of the Holocaust by privileging the suffering of Jews over the suffering of others, and to abuse the charge of anti-Semitism in the service of protecting Israel from criticism. In short, the ultranationalist wing of new anti-Semitism theory responds to anti-Semitism with a particularism and exclusivity that can mirror what it opposes.

Two qualifications need to be made. First, there is nothing unique in the phenomenon that opposition to racism can take a nationalistic form. In all kinds of circumstances, people can and do respond to racism against their own group in exclusive terms. Exclusivity is not the defining feature of new anti-Semitism theory any more than it is the defining feature of other forms of antiracism. Second, new anti-Semitism theory is a diverse discourse and there is nothing that intrinsically disconnects resistance to "new" anti-Semitism from resistance to other forms of racism. It contains universalist currents which fully acknowledge the wrong of treating all Muslims or all Arabs as anti-Semitic, or the wrong of disconnecting anti-Semitism from other forms of racism, or the wrong of using the charge of anti-Semitism indiscriminately for political purposes.

Critics of new anti-Semitism theory who slip from a general critique of the limitations of exclusivist forms of opposition to racism to the contention that opposition to the new anti-Semitism is itself exclusivist, mirror the restricted code of what they purport to overcome. Neither new anti-Semitism theory nor its antiracist critics are bound to exclusivity, yet their crystallization into oppositional discourses regrettably encourages not only their disconnection, but also their mutual antagonism.

Conclusion

We would echo the conclusion of Nicole Lapierre to her recent study of *Causes Communes: Des Juifs et des Noirs:* "Empathy ... is not a panacea taking the place of politics, nor a universal key liberating humanity. However, it can humanize political thought and action ... empathy encourages solidarities founded on respect and reciprocity. It is to these solidarities that Frantz Fanon pointed at the end of *Black Skin, White Masks:* 'Why not simply try to touch the other, feel the other, reveal the other in oneself? Is not my liberty given to me to educate the world about You'" (our translation).[48]

Our discussion has sought to raise issues rather than resolve them. We have argued that the integrated study of connections between racism and anti-Semitism should once again be put on the agenda of sociology as part of a wider project of reconstructing an enlarged sociological imagination. We acknowledge that different types of racism have distinctive characteristics and we emphasize that connectedness does not imply the obliteration of differences between racisms. On the contrary, it extends our understanding of racism beyond the particular manifestations with which we are most familiar. It increases reflexivity concerning the racism that immediately concerns us and impels us to take the viewpoint of others.

Sociology is made parochial by the schism between racism and anti-Semitism. While methodological separatism narrows our lens, connectedness impels us to enter into the viewpoint of others. It expands our realm of empathy and our analytical reach. Sociologists of modernity should recognize the role racism and anti-Semitism have together played in the construction of modern society and in the definition of its borders. It is our claim, echoing the insight of Paul Gilroy, that through their connected study—and especially through the critical analysis of the grounds of their disconnection—we can develop our understanding of the deep thought structures of modernity and its constructions of alterity.[49]

Acknowledgments

A different, earlier version of this chapter appeared as "A Common Cause: Reconnecting the Study of Racism and Antisemitism" in *European Societies* 14, no. 2 (2012): 166–185. We should like to thank Claudine Attias-Donfut, Gurminder Bhambra, Daniel Chernilo, Lars Rensmann, and Gurnam Singh for their comments and suggestions.

Notes

1. W.E.B. Du Bois, *The Souls of Black Folk* (Chicago: A.C. McClurg, 1903), 19.
2. Christina Oppel, "W.E.B. Du Bois, Nazi Germany, and the Black Atlantic," *GHI Bulletin Supplement,* 5 (2008): 99–122, http://www.ghidc.org/files/publications/bu_supp/supp5/supp5_099.pdf
3. W.E.B. Du Bois, "The Negro and the Warsaw Ghetto" [1952] in *Social Theory of W.E.B. Du Bois,* ed. Phil Zuckerman (Thousand Oaks, CA: Pine Forge Press, 2004), 45.
4. Du Bois, Ibid., 46.
5. Du Bois, Ibid., 46.
6. Fanon, *Black Skin, White Masks,* 88.
7. Fanon, *The Wretched of the Earth* (Harmondsworth: Penguin, 1967), 86.
8. Fanon, *Black Skin, White Masks,* 115.
9. Bryan Cheyette, "White Skin: Black Masks: Jews and Jewishness in the Writings of George Eliot and Frantz Fanon," in *Cultural Readings of Imperialism: Edward Said and the Gravity of History,* ed. Keith Ansell Pearson, Benita Parry, and Judith Squires (London: Lawrence and Wishart, 1997), 106–25.
10. See Alain Finkielkraut, *Remembering in Vain,* trans. Roxanne Lapidus with Sima Godfrey (New York: Columbia University Press, 1992).
11. Fanon, *Black Skin, White Masks,* 115.
12. "The Fact of Blackness" in ibid., 116.
13. Gilman, *The Jew's Body* (London and New York: Routledge, 1991).
14. Cheyette. "White Skin: Black Masks," 124.
15. Glynis Cousin, "Rethinking the Concept of 'Western,'" *Higher Education Research and Development* 30, no. 5 (2011): 585–594.
16. Fanon, *Black Skin, White Masks,* 122
17. Hannah Arendt, *The Origins of Totalitarianism* [1951] (New York: Harcourt Brace 1979).

18. Ibid., 117–155.
19. Martin Bulmer and John Solomos (eds.), *Racism* (Oxford: Oxford University Press, 1999) and Runnymede Trust, *A Very Light Sleeper: the Persistence and Dangers* of *Anti-Semitism* (London: Runnymede Trust, 1994).
20. See Gilroy, *The Black Atlantic*; and Gilroy, *Between Camps: Nations, Culture and the Allure of Race* (Harmondsworth: Penguin), 2001), 212
21. Gilroy, *Between Camps,* 212.
22. West, *Race Matters,* 110.
23. Paul Berman, "Reflections: The Other and the Almost the Same," *New Yorker,* February 28, 1994, 66.
24. Columbus quoted in Jon Stratton, *Jewish Identity in Western Pop Culture: The Holocaust and Trauma through Modernity* (New York: Palgrave Macmillan, 2008), 10–11.
25. Ella Shohat, "Taboo Memories and Diasporic Visions," in *Performing Hybridity,* ed. Joseph May and Jennifer Fink (Minneapolis: University of Minnesota Press,1999), 136–137.
26. Samuel Usque quoted in Stratton, *Jewish Identity in Western Pop Culture,* 18.
27. Gilroy, *The Black Atlantic,* 214.
28. There seems to have been a greater awareness of these issues in the 1980s in discussions of the relation between nationalist and class politics. See, e.g., contrasting forms of opposition to racism in South Africa arising in labor and nationalist movements in Robert Fine, *Beyond Apartheid: Labour and Nationalism in South Africa 1936-1966* (London: Pluto, 1990), 257–293. Or see contrasting forms of opposition to anti-Arab racism in the Middle East in Max Rodinson, *Marxism and the Muslim World* (New York: Monthly Review Press, 1982). On the wider discussion of nationalist and Marxist responses to racism, see Eric Hobsbawm, "Socialism and Nationalism: Some Reflections on 'The Break-up of Britain,'" in *Politics for a Rational Left* (London: Verso, 1989), 119–142.
29. Amartya Sen, *Identity and Violence: The Illusion of Destiny* (London: Penguin, 2006).
30. Kwame Anthony Appiah, *The Ethics of Identity* (Princeton, NJ: Princeton University Press, 2005).
31. See, e.g., Bunzl, *Anti-Semitism and Islamophobia.*
32. Jürgen Habermas, *The Postnational Constellation: Political Essays,* ed. Max Pensky (Cambridge: MA: MIT Press, 2001); Jürgen Habermas, *The Inclusion of the Other* (Cambridge, MA: MIT Press, 1998).
33. Tony Judt, *Postwar: A History of Europe since 1945* (London: Penguin, 2007), 831.
34. See *Community Security Trust Antisemitic Incidents Report 2010* (London: CST, 2010).
35. Susie Jacobs, "Globalisation, Anti-Globalisation and the Jewish 'Question,'" *European Review of History* 18, no. 1 (2011): 45–56.
36. Naomi Klein cited in Susie Jacobs, "Anti-Semitism and Other forms of Racism: Continuities, Discontinuities (and Some Conspiracies. ...)," *CRONEM: The Future of Multicultural Britain* (London: Roehampton University, 2005), 14–15.
37. Arendt, *Origins of Totalitarianism,* 14.

38. A case in point is to be found in Judith Butler, "The Charge of Anti-Semitism: Jews, Israel and the Risks of Public Critique," in *Precarious Life: The Powers of Mourning and Violence* (London: Verso, 2004), 101–127.
39. Steven Beller, *Anti-Semitism: A Very Short Introduction* (Oxford: Oxford University Press, 2007).
40. Samuel Huntington's *Clash of Civilizations and the Remaking of World Order* (New York: Free Press, 1998) is the most conservative expression of this tendency. However, echoes of this deformation are also to be found in certain forms of radicalism that see the world order in terms of a struggle between civic values and ethnic nationalism. For further discussion, see Robert Fine "The New Nationalism and Democracy: A Critique of *Pro Patria,*" *Democratization* 1, no. 3 (1994), 423–443; and Robert Fine, *Cosmopolitanism* (London: Routledge, 2007), 39–58.
41. Richard Delgrado, *Critical Race Theory* (Philadelphia: Temple University Press, 2000).
42. Derek Bell, *Faces at the Bottom of the Well* (New York: Basic Books, 1992), 114.
43. Bell, *And We Are Not Saved: The Elusive Quest for Racial Justice* (New York: Basic Books, 1989), 122.
44. See the discussions in Goldberg, *Multiculturalism.*
45. See Sen, *Identity and Violence.*
46. Kenan Malik, *Strange Fruit: Why Both Sides Are Wrong in the Race Debate* (Oxford: One World Publications, 2008), 288.
47. Jonathan Judaken, "So What's New? Rethinking the 'New Anti-Semitism' in a Global Age," *Patterns of Prejudice,* 42, no. 4–5 (2008): 531–560.
48. Nicole Lapierre, *Cause Commune: Des Juifs et des Noirs* (Paris: Stock, 2011), 300.
49. For a complementary view of connected sociologies see Bhambra Gurminder, "Sociology after Postcolonialism: Provincialized Cosmopolitanisms and Connected Sociologies," in *Decolonizing European Sociology: Transdisciplinary Approaches,* ed. E. Gutierrez Rodriguez, M. Boatca, and S. Costa (Farnham: Ashgate, 2010), 49–70.

CHAPTER 17

Race by the Grace of God

Race, Religion, and the Construction of "Jew" and "Arab"

Ivan Davidson Kalmar

Race and Religion in the Western Imaginary

Race and religion have each in recent decades been radically rethought. Race is no longer thought of as an objective category, and even as an imaginative construction it no longer depends only on skin color.[1] As for religion, it no longer depends entirely on dogma or even on ritual expressions of faith; it is now commonplace to speak of Western civilization as Christian in the cultural and imaginative, rather than a strictly theological sense. As Jean-Luc Nancy has put it, "The only current atheism is one that contemplates its Christian roots.… Christianity is coextensive with the West."[2] Such cultural practice recalls W.J.T. Mitchell's notion of "double belief," which allows us to rationally reject, while emotionally and imaginatively accepting, all sorts of unverifiable assertions about the world.[3] This surely applies to assertions based on racial perceptions and religious beliefs.[4] It is in this relatively new sense of race as a construction and religion as powerful beyond creed that the general relationship between the two must be rethought. Many scholars have taken this approach in work on identity formation and identity politics. Some have paid attention as well to the related origins of "race" and "religion." My goal is to seek part of those origins in the Bible as the foundational narrative of the Christian West. It is my particular thesis that "Jewish" race and religion are the central figures around which general notions of race and religion are articulated in the Western tradition.

To this general end, I wish to explore, first, the specific relationship between "Jewish" race and "Jewish" religion. And from there I would like to move to "Arab" race and "Arab" religion (i.e., Islam), because Arab race and religion were historically conceived in the West (from the late eighteenth century or even before) as closely related to, and revelatory of, "Jewish" race and religion. The idea that God has chosen one people over others to be his own special folk is, I suggest, a notion that is indispensable to the construction of race in Western cultural history. I will base my argument on the Western belief that "Jewish" race is the mother of all races, of all notions of race, and that it is so by virtue of its association with religion.

In the second half of the eighteenth century, if not before, Jewish peoplehood was reimagined in terms that would in the next century serve the taxonomists of a new racial pseudoscience. But just at the moment that the Jews were invented as a modern race in the Christian West, so were the Arabs. Like "Jewish" race, "Arab" race has been imagined as a religious race, or—which is the same thing—a racialized religion, and in this case the religion is Islam. In many ways, I will be treading on ground explored by Gil Anidjar, who suggests, "Race is religion. The evidence lies in the Semites."[5] However, the twin construction of "Jew" and of "Muslim" or "Arab" goes back much before the nineteenth-century invention of "Semitic race." At the end of this chapter, I briefly and rather programmatically touch on our own period and conclude that recently the Western Christian imagination has lost its interest in the Jews as a racialized religion, leaving the Muslims today as its sole imagined representative, and as such the main imagined racial-theological threat to secularism.

In the long nineteenth century, the term "race" was used broadly to refer to any group imagined as sharing a common descent. It could be a synonym of what we now call "ethnicity" (an equally fuzzy term). But it could also refer to a supraethnic grouping such as "the Celts" or "the Semites," which were determined essentially on the basis of language. And, as the following passage by Emerson shows, it could be related, if rather unsystematically, to religion as well.

> It is a race, is it not? that puts the hundred millions of India under the dominion of a remote island in the north of Europe. Race avails much, if that be true, which is alleged, that all Celts are Catholics, and all Saxons are Protestants; that Celts love unity of power, and Saxons the representative principle. Race is a controlling influence in the Jew, who, for two millenniums, under every climate, has preserved the same character and employments.[6]

In the "White" race (defined primarily by physiognomy) Emerson included the "English" race (ethnic group), but he used religion (Catholic or Protestant, and possibly Jewish) as correlates of race as well. In each case, referring to the imagined descent group as a "race" may have meant giving the categorization what then passed for a scientific veneer. Racial groupings based on language, such as "Celtic" and "Indo-European," or "Semitic," extended the impressive achievements of linguistic taxonomy into the realm of ethnic descent, on the mistaken but then almost universally accepted assumption that linguistic kinship means common descent among the speakers. Race classifications based on color started with a similar overextension of scientific taxonomies, in this case from human physiology, to descent categories, with not only skin color but also head size and shape, facial features, and other characteristics taken as diagnostic.

There were also religious taxonomies, and these too were overgeneralized as racial categories. I will speak presently of Hegel's categorization of Judaism and Islam, together, as "the religion of the sublime," that had a specific, well-defined place in Hegel's clearly formulated taxonomy of religions, arranged on an evolutionary principle from the earliest to the most advanced. Hegel himself identified these different types of religion with different population groups and implied that they were of common descent. For these, he used the term *Volk,* which can be translated as either "people" or "race."

It would be only later that the term *Rasse* came to be widely used in German; where Emerson spoke of the English or Celtic "race," Hegel would employ *Volk.* The term *Volk* continued to be used in many cases as the equivalent of "race," however, even when the more scientific sounding *Rasse* was employed. Infamously, the Nazis would speak of the Jews as both *Volk* and *Rasse.*[7] But although linguistic usage is an important diagnostic tool, our primary concern is not terminology but what it expresses, and in our context the essence of what *Volk, Rasse,* and the English term "race" express is imagined common descent. I am using the word "imagined" in the sense that Benedict Anderson employs in *Imagined Communites*: a group of people who do not know each other face to face, but who are imagined as a community nevertheless. Imagined does not necessarily mean imaginary; referring to a community as imagined makes no judgment about whether the community in some independent sense is or is not real.[8] In a similar way, by "imagined descent group" I mean a group that is imagined as descended from the same ancestor or ancestors, even though the individuals making up the line of descent are not individually known.

And as in the case of imagined community, I make no judgment about whether the group "really" descends from its imagined precursors. For example, typically there are ways to accept newcomers such as immigrants and converts by treating them *as if* they were of the same descent, a fiction that is progressively forgotten in the subsequent generations. Jewish tradition identifies the group as descended from the patriarch Jacob, later known as Israel, and ultimately from Abraham. Converts are called son or daughter of Abraham and Sarah, and their offspring are considered Jews in every respect.

This is in no way to deny that real physiological, linguistic, or religious differences to which racial groupings can and typically are employed in imagining common descent. While physical features, language, and, most importantly for this discussion, religion are not objective and independent criteria of race, they do become very important as specific data that are, in various historical contexts, used in the construction of race as imagined common descent. There are, obviously physiological race markers such as color—typically European, "white" skin, and typically African, "black." But these do not straightforwardly and by themselves determine racial categories. It is, for example, in line with historical and social practice, not nature, that Barack Obama, who is objectively as much of European as of African descent, is habitually categorized as "Black," but never as "White."

The effort to nevertheless define "race" by physiological factors separated from religion reflects the struggle of modernizing states in the West, from the late-eighteenth to the mid-twentieth century, to justify their existence as an expression of the will of the people. The rise of new, ostensibly religion-free, more strictly descent-based notions of race was symptomatic of the need to establish a secular conception for the form of imagined common descent labeled as "the people." Other factors contributed to the rise of "religion" as a concept and a sphere of life separate from others. Talal Asad, in one of the seminal works that examined this issue at the start of the twenty-first century, listed, first, increasing structural differentiation of social spaces resulting in the separation of religion from politics, economy, science, and so forth; second, the privatization of religion within its own sphere; and, third, the declining social significance of religious belief, commitment, and institutions.[9] Increasingly, Asad suggests, "religion" was being moved into the esthetic realm. The Bible was read by the Romantics as a "spiritual poem."[10] While religion was thus being ostensibly depoliticized, "race" moved into the political foreground, as a notion of group descent central to the notion of "the people."

The process through which "religion" was split from the "secular" sphere of life coincided with the formation of capitalist nation-states. This process, Asad explains, differed from state to state because the emerging nation-states were mutually suspicious and had "a collective personality that is differently mediated and therefore differently guaranteed and threatened."[11] I would suggest that the differences were seen in a very different relationship between imagined common descent (essentially, "race") on the one hand, and religion on the other. In the United States, where Black slavery lasted into the second half of the nineteenth century, color-based racial notions affected the civil and legal notions of citizenship very profoundly, but so did religious identities stemming from many of the American settlers' roots in dissenting Protestant and in Catholic communities in the United Kingdom. Religion and race therefore remained important parameters of American identity, in complex ways that found tolerance, for the most part, for religious diversity. In other "White" dominated communities in the New World, such as the Spanish and Portuguese colonies, race had less competition from religion, which the colonial "Creoles" shared with the mother country. Benedict Anderson saw in these Creole communities perhaps the most important source of the modern concept of "nation" as an imagined community, highlighting the career frustrations of local Creole officials, who were regularly bypassed for appointments by nominees from the European metropolis.[12] Hence in these cases religion (overwhelmingly Catholic) played little role in the development of nation-states, and secularism was less of an issue. The Czech petty bourgeoisie, who at the beginning of the nineteenth century staffed the ranks of the burgeoning Austrian army and bureaucracy, may have felt some of the same frustrations as the Latin American Creole officials. Furthermore, in this case the memory of the historic defeat of Bohemia's Protestants by the Catholic Habsburgs ensured that nationalism had not much of a religious element. The situation was completely the opposite in Poland or Ireland, not to speak of the Balkan states, including Greece, under the Ottoman Empire. Here the "people" differed for the most part in religion from their imperial masters, and so religion and "race" were very hard to untangle. In many Muslim lands, such as Algeria or Bosnia, Islam often underwent important transformations as a national consciousness developed, supplementing but not eradicating Muslim religious identity.[13]

Regardless of such important differences, however, the rise of "the secular" was a project that not only produced "religion" as a separate sphere of life, which is what Asad has shown, but also contributed to a new sense of "race," which like "the secular" actually remained entwined with the very same premodern notions of religion that it was meant to replace. In short, the new "secular" notion of "citizenship" was almost never a matter that was independent of either race or religion. I suggest that it is only in the context of the development of modern secular citizenship and its continuing dependence on "religion" that we can understand the development of the modern notion of "race."

Race, the Bible, and Divine Election

The issue of Jewish race and religion, therefore, came up in the history of the modern capitalist nation-state in the context where race and religion were already problematic in the practice and formulation of national identity and citizenship. But the specific case of the Jews was especially prone to bring the general question of the relationship between religion, race, and the nation to a head. Were the Jews only members of a religion, and so part of the same ethnic people or "race" as the rest? Or should race as well as religion be disregarded in the conception of the nation—so a Jew is a citizen regardless of being of a different religion *and* race? To put it more colloquially, were the Jews part of the "people" in spite of their religion, or did their different religion also mean that they were a different "people"? Soon enough Jews asked the same question.

Are the Jews a race, then? In the light of what has just been said, the question cannot be decided on objective grounds. Physical characteristics, language, and religion are irrelevant as objective facts and matter only insofar as they enter into the social construction of the Jewish race. This is so even in the case of recent efforts to determine the genetic heritage of the Jews as a whole or of various Jewish groups. The overall result so far is that there are indeed some genetic features shared by many Jews, but other Jews do not have them while some non-Jews do. As far as that goes, this is no different from physical features such as the "Jewish" or "Semitic" nose. Genetic criteria are equally unsuitable, whatever their other merits may be, for objectively identifying a Jewish race. What does matter is if people have *imagined* the Jews as a race. And that they have.

True, not everyone in the West calls the Jews members of a "race" today. In recent times, the term has acquired the negative connotations of racism, and is avoided in some contexts even when its necessary condition, imagined common descent, is not. Yet, except for some critical scholars and some anti-Zionists, everyone still accepts the notion of the Jews' common descent, if not from the patriarchs Abraham, Isaac, and Jacob, then at least from the people of the biblical land of Israel. In the long nineteenth century, certainly, Jew and Gentile in the West universally imagined the Jews as a race from the Orient. Even the radical assimilationists failed to deny the Jews' distinctive descent, and only argued that it should not matter.[14] As in the Emerson quote, Jews were routinely referred to, by friend and foe, as members of a "race."[15] In this chapter, I will be using the word "race" to mean imagined common descent even in cases where we would no longer use it so; that is, I will be using it in its sense contemporary with the period under investigation. This focus on the signified as opposed to the signifier will also enable us to look beyond the origins of the term "race" itself to the much older history of imagining common descent.

Imagined common descent is the originary principle of human social organization. In spite of great disagreement on detail, there is general agreement among anthropologists that the earliest societies were organized on the basis of kinship, and that kinship was always to at least some extent imagined. Among historically attested hunters and gatherers, kinship was always partly "real," that is, demonstrable by reference to specific progenitors; and partly fictitious, that is, imaginary but treated *as if* real. Fictitious kinship increased with the depth of generations, when the remote ancestors were no longer identifiable. Relatively complex societies were sometimes organized into clans, which are defined by anthropologists as groups who imagine themselves as having a common ancestor, though this descent cannot be independently verified. Northwest American clans reckoned themselves descended from an animal ancestor such as the eagle or the frog. By this definition, the "tribes" of Israel are clans, but so is, at a higher node in the tree of imagined descent, Israel itself as the community descended from Jacob (Israel).

Israel as an imagined descent group differs from other descent groups in that it is imagined, within the Abrahamic imaginary, as the one descent group elected by God. In fact, the election is at first of an even larger descent group. It is declared ritually at the moment discussed in Genesis 7, when God makes a covenant (*brith*) with Abraham, which is recorded by the circumcision of the patriarch and the circumcision of his present and future male offspring. The abstract continuity of the descent group is symbolized in the Hebrew Bible (Gen. 17:7–8) by the metaphor of *zer`a*, translated by the King James Bible as "seed," following the Latin Vulgate's *semen*: "And I will establish my covenant between me and thee and thy seed after thee in their generations for an everlasting covenant, to be a God unto thee, and to thy seed after thee.

And I will give unto thee, and to thy seed after thee, the land wherein thou art a stranger, all the land of Canaan, for an everlasting possession; and I will be their God."

"Seed" sublimates, in the metaphor, the product of the sexual act involving Abraham's circumcised penis, from the literal semen to the generations that it originates. A further sublimation in English translations is to turn the King James version's "seed" into "offspring." Such a demasculinization of the term is, to be sure, in the spirit of some of the biblical text. In Genesis 3:15, humans are described as the *zer`a,* the "seed," of Eve. However, "offspring" obscures the connection, transparent in *zer`a* and the Latin *semen,* to male procreation. The inscription of the *brith* on the male procreative organ is of symbolic significance because the penis is the physical producer of the basic organizing principle of Israelite society, the patrilineage. While membership in Israel as a whole would become matrilineal, kinship structure within Israel was patrilineal.

The blood of circumcision symbolizes the animating principle of procreation, for this part of the body will generate beings who will be members of the people that will belong to God, as well as to their own descent group. The descent group is generated by *semen* rather than, as in the later Christian-Western tradition, by "blood."[16] It is *zer`a* as a metaphoric substance that provides the diachronic link from Abraham to present and future generations of Jews. At the time of their circumcision, male converts, too, mark the *brith* on their procreative member, and thus not only acquire the pedigree of the patriarch, but also are able to pass it on to future generations, that is, to their own *zer`a,* in the same way and subject to the same limitations as men who were born Jewish.

In the biblical narrative, the sacred relation between Abraham's *zer`a* and God is refined through a series of further elections in which the patriarchs Isaac and Jacob are promoted at the expense of their brothers Ismael and Esau, who with their *zer`a* are excluded from the central role in serving God's agenda (Gen. 21:12–14, 25:25–27, 41). But the fact of conversion illustrates that man, too, can play a part in determining the exact membership of a descent group, including God's chosen one. What is true of the form of protoracial grouping labeled as *zer`a* is true of all imagined descent, and therefore remains true of the full-fledged concept of race in the long nineteenth century and beyond. What exists objectively in society is not race—Jewish or other—but racialization, the process of constructing races, and its effects. And it is obvious beyond dispute that, in the modern West at least, the Jews have often if not always been racialized.

Indeed, contrary to the facts just mentioned about color, European and American Jews have in recent times typically been racialized as a monolith: Ashkenazic and White. Racializations of the Jews have always of course taken into account at least the existence of the Sephardim. Christians and Jews have long been talking about Jews in Afghanistan, Africa, China, and New Mexico,[17] while varieties of Black Jews have been under discussion more recently.[18] But these other Jews were interesting just for the reason that they fell outside the prototypical and stereotypical racialization of the Jew as a European resident of Oriental origin. (I am using the word "Oriental" in the old-fashioned, for American English, sense revived by Edward Said, as a near-synonym of Middle Eastern.) These non-European Jews served to reinforce the notion of the Oriental and exotic nature of the Jews who have wandered into Europe. But this does not change the fact that it was the European Jews who were at the focal point of the Western racialization of the Jews.

Before I proceed further, some important disclaimers. I am *not* looking at the notion of the chosen people in Jewish theology, but as it appears in Western—that is to say, essentially Christian—cultural history. I am *not* trying to essentialize the notion of Jewish chosenness as an inflexible given, but believe that what I am about to say holds in spite of the historical changes and local variations in what divine election has meant. Emphatically, I am *not* suggesting that the chosenness of the people of Israel has been the underlying feature of racism throughout the ages. And I am *not* saying that the Bible operates with a notion of race comparable to, say, nineteenth-century notions of race. I think we need to look at this as we might look at stereotypical features of the Jewish physiognomy, such as the hooked nose. These belong to the visual vocabulary of medieval art, linking the images of Jews, monsters, and heretics.[19] Only later does that vocabulary become racial, a kind of building material from which the modern notion of race is constructed.

Most modern ethnic-national groups define themselves by imagined common descent. The Jewish notion of common descent is exceptional because, I argue, it not only contributed to the genesis of the notion of Jewish "race," but also was a major factor in the formation of the Western notion of "race" in general. One of the foundation stones of the Western notion of race is the originally Jewish, then Christian and—*mutatis mutandis*—Muslim, view that God chose for the dramatis personae of history imagined-descent groups. These are called "nations" in the King James Bible, *goyim* in the Hebrew Masoretic text. The Bible and to some extent the Quran present history as unfolding through the interaction of *goyim*. One *goy* is God's chosen.

The biblical term *goy* does not yet mean exactly what "race" would mean later. But Western Christians adopted this biblical concept of *goy* or nation when they needed it for constructing the idea of race. "Race" as a label did not exist in English before 1500, and while it may be a little older in French, Italian, or Portuguese, it is not older there by much. There are many reasons why the notion of race should have germinated in the late Renaissance period. Perhaps the most important is the colonial expansion of European power into the Americas, Africa, and other parts of the world, where populations were treated as less than fully human. This attitude allowed the race-based mass enslavement of Africans imagined as "Black," even during a period of increasing consciousness, in the West, of universal human rights. It may be that the race consciousness of the colonizing Spanish toward the "natives" overseas was related in some way to the racially based persecutions of people of Jewish and Muslim descent in the sixteenth and seventeenth centuries, with the requirement of certificates of so-called pure Christian blood. At any rate, some scholars have claimed, perhaps with justification, that in the hunt of the Inquisition for hidden Jews and Muslims lay the origin of modern racial discrimination.[20] Religion was central to the Spanish construction of "blood." This was not, at least in the case of the Jews as opposed to the Muslim "Moors," a color-based notion. One had pure Christian blood, not pure White blood or pure Spanish or Castillian blood. This fact alone suggests that although the term "race" only dates back to the period following the Reconquista, it is worth exploring its religious roots: not its etymology but its genealogy.

We need to look to the period before some imagined descent groups were labeled "races," to when they were called "nations." As has been mentioned, "nation" was the translation of *goy* in English since the King James Bible, redacted between 1604 and 1611. It follows the Latin Vulgate's *natio*. The literal meaning of *natio* is "something that was born," so the original genetic notion behind the term is clear. "Race," however, would clarify an ambiguity in *natio,* which even in the Middle Ages could refer to not only people of common ancestry but also people born in the same area, or specifically to people born in the noble estate.

The English translations (like the Vulgate) reflect quite faithfully the distinction in the Hebrew Bible between *goy* and *'am*. These are the two main terms by which the Bible refers to Israel and others as imagined communities. To be sure, there is a third term used with much the same significance: *le'om*. In a passage like Genesis 25:23 it seems to function as a synonym of *goy,* while in Genesis 27:29 it appears to be interchangeable with *'am*. In the later books of the Bible, on the other hand, the plural *le'umim* may in some cases be understood to contrast with *'am,* the former referring to Gentile communities and the latter to the people of Israel (e.g., Psa. 57:9, Psa. 67:4). Elsewhere, *le'umim* may be synonymous with *goyim* (Psa. 2:1, Psa. 44:2, 14, Psa. 105:44, Psa. 149:7, Prov. 14:34, Isa. 34:1, Isa. 43:9). It is possible that over time the meaning of *le'umim* as of *goyim* came to focus on the *other* "nations," the Gentiles. In modern Israel, the term *le'om* was chosen to refer to officially recognized identities on citizens' identity cards until 2005, continuing a practice established in Mandatory Palestine, when British-issued identity cards listed "Jew" under "race."

There is far less ambiguity in *goy* and *'am,* and English Bibles consistently translate *goy* as "nation" and *'am* as "people." There is a difference of connotation between the two terms, and perhaps even of denotation. There is no ironclad rule here, but when the Bible speaks of the chosenness of Abraham and of Israel, it prefers *goy.* Just one example: when God commands Abraham to leave his home, he promises, "Ve-'eskha le-*goy* gadol" ("I will make thee a great nation," Gen. 12:2). And, after wrestling with Jacob, God declares, in Genesis 35:10 and 11, "And God said unto him, Thy name [is] Jacob: thy name shall not be called any more Jacob, but Israel shall be thy name: and he called his name Israel. And God said unto him, I [am] God Almighty: be fruitful and multiply; a nation and a company of nations [*goy uqehal goyim*]." God's refusal to describe the Jews as a homogeneous group is significant: this is a nation that is *also* a company of nations, *qehal goyim;* "a company of nations shall be of thee, and kings shall come out of thy loins." Exodus 19:6 commands, "And ye shall be unto me a kingdom of priests, and an holy nation [*mamlekhet kohanim ve-goy qadosh*]." The word *'am* seems to focus more on the community, the social aspect of the imagined descent group. It, rather than *goy,* seems to be the preferred label when God focuses on Israel not as a descent group—that is, not as a proto-race—but as a community defined by their relationship to their sovereign, God. Exodus 33:13 states *'amkha hagoy haze*— (this nation is thy people), meaning this a race, *goy,* whose function is to be your people, *'amkha.* While Israel is only one of many *goyim,* it is unique in being God's chosen *'am.* This is essentially the message when God consoles Abraham upon the eviction of Hagar and Ishmael, promising in Genesis 21:18 that Ishmael will also be a *goy gadol,* a great nation. God does not suggest that Ishmael will also be his *'am.*

Sometimes Israel is actually excluded as a category from *goy,* so that only non-Israelites are *goyim,* as in the common Yiddish usage. Incidentally, the same exclusion is represented by the etymology of the term "Gentiles," which is derived from *gentes,* the common translation in the Latin Vulgate Bible of *goy*. The Vulgate translates as *gentiles* the New Testament *hellenon,* more faithfully translated in the English Bibles as Greeks. Numbers 23:9 reads, "For from the top of the rocks I see him, and from the hills I behold him: lo, the people shall dwell alone, and shall not be reckoned among the nations." [*hen-'am levadad yishkon uvagoyim lo yitkhashav.*] And Deuteronomy 32:43 says, "Rejoice, O ye nations, [with] his people." [*Hareninu goyim 'amo.*] This is not to say that non-Jews are never described as *'am*. In some of the Psalms (Psa. 2:1, Psa. 44:2, 44:14, Psa. 105:44, Psa. 149:7), the King James Bible translates the plural *goyim* as "heathen." These examples suggest that Israel is a "nation" that need not be named as such—as a *goy*—so that *goy* applies only to the others, making the Jews into an unmarked term similar to "White" in modern English racial terminology, where only the others have "color." But of course the privileges of the White group are the very foundation of the color scheme itself, just like the Jews' unique status as the *'am qadosh* who is "*elyon 'al kol ha-goyim*" (Deut 28:1) actually makes the Jewish *goy*, however exceptional, the generative origin of the whole system of constructing other human groups into a constellation of different *goyim*.

The partial separation in the Bible of the race-like concept of common descent, *goy,* from a common identity based on religious purpose as in *'am qadosh* opened up ideologically the possibility that another *goy* than Israel could be *'am qadosh* instead, or as well. A decisive move was that undertaken by Paul of Tarsus, who opened the Jewish sect of Christians to people regardless of which *goy* they belonged to. After a discussion with the church fathers in Jerusalem, Paul obtained full membership in the new community of God's worshippers for Gentiles, who did not have to undergo a ceremony of joining the Jewish people. To be more precise, they did not have to submit to the painful ritual of circumcision, commanded by God to Abraham and his seed as a condition of maintaining the covenant between them. The connection between a ritual affecting the penis and "seed" (*zer`a*) or genetic descent is obvious anthropologically if not theologically. To uncouple seed from the covenant of election meant to open up election to people whose *goy* was not generated by the same *zer`a*.

Mainstream Christians, however, derived their legitimacy from claiming to inherit, rather than reject, Abraham's covenant. Jesus famously declared in Matthew 5:17, "Think not that I am come to destroy the law, or the prophets: I am not come to destroy, but to fulfill." This and similar declarations by Jesus and their interpretation by the early and later doctors of the Church preserved a certain respect for the election of the original Israel. While a few dissidents simply rejected the Old Covenant in favor of the New, for most Christians God's choice of a specific *goy* and *'am* remained a problem, especially since from the Christian point of view the elect rejected the new revelation, through incarnation, of God.

In the Reformation, the problem gained renewed urgency. The reason was the peculiar position of the Reformers on divine grace. The Catholics taught that good deeds, including participating in the sacraments of the Church, could gain the faithful the grace of God. But Luther, Calvin, and other Reformers denied that humans could compel God to grant or withhold his favor. They insisted that the grace of God was not necessarily subject to any humanly discernible criterion. Reason could not advance us to a full understanding of God and his will, but neither could acts performed out of a human sense of justice or even out of the love of God or humanity. The Lutherans and Calvinists took it on faith that God was just and loved us, but they took it on faith alone: they recognized that according to human criteria God might even seem to be unfair and uncaring. God did not owe his grace to anyone, so his grace could not be earned by good works: this was a passionately held and furiously maintained dogma of the Reformers. (Luther stated, "the main point of Christian doctrine" was "that we are justified by faith in Christ without any works of the Law.")[21] The Reformers even more than the Catholics supported their arguments with reference to both testaments of the Christian Bible, and the election of the Jews became for them not only one example of divine grace given without reference to understandable criteria, but its very prototype. Just as God inexplicably (to humanity) chose the Israelite nation above others (and then, many believed, to either all true Christians and even to specific favorite nations such as England), so he chose one individual over another independently of any criteria open to human understanding.[22] Calvin's theory of double destination claimed that each person was predestined for either salvation or damnation. Arising in a period of incipient capitalism, this transfer of divine election to the individual marked the rise of the individual as the main unit of both economic production and intellectual and religious analysis. Similarly proto-capitalist was the view that soon arose among some Protestants that personal wealth was a sign of divine favor. A striking example was the belief among Puritan Calvinists that wealth was one of the visible signs of divine grace.[23] In this sense the Protestant doctrine of divine grace (which had reinterpreted the Augustinian) was an important marker of modernity.

On the other hand, the Reformers' doctrine of grace was the opposite of another modern development: secularism. Secularism is based on the conviction that there are no divine laws that are above human laws. True, as Talal Asad has shown, secularism is not the opposite of religion, and is in fact compatible with religious belief.[24] Theologians can therefore in principle be secularist. For that, however, the theologian must maintain that God rules the world in accordance with principles of reason and justice that are accessible to humanity without reference to God. Crucially, the theologian must affirm that God works by the very principles that underlie the constitution of the modern secular state.

Spinoza or Descartes did not profess to be atheists, but believed that the nature of God and the nature of the world were at some very deep level the same, and that they could be investigated by reference, among other things, to human reason. This belief was developed in a characteristic way by Hegel. For him, in the most advanced, modern stage of history the *Weltgeist* comes to infuse the constitution of the modern state, canceling any principled opposition between God and the world. Likewise, the American revolutionaries believed that their constitution was in complete agreement with their deist conception of the nature of God. There was no contradiction between God's will and the will of the public as expressed by a wise people enlightened by the wisdom of philosophical legislators.

Though typical of Enlightenment thinking and some of its aftermath, this idea was far removed from original Lutheranism and Calvinism. And so, because Renaissance Reformers had insisted that God does *not* dispense his grace in accordance with humanly discernible principles, their heritage was (and is in the much altered form we see in today's evangelicals) in an at least potential conflict with the mainstream secular forms of modern politico theological philosophy. As Christians struggled to reconcile the notions of a religious versus a rational-humanist foundation to the political arrangements of the modern state, Jews and their claim of divine election surfaced once again as a major problem. As long as Jews held on to the traditional form of their religion, which emphasized the divine election of their imagined-descent group, proponents of the modern state often considered them enemies of secularism. They were seen as placing themselves as a people, or in the sense I am using the term, a race, above the laws of the state. For they believed themselves to have been chosen by God in an arbitrary act à la Luther and Calvin—that is, an act separate from and above the common principles of reason, including what Foucault identifies during the period as the emerging notion of raison d'état, or reasons (literally "reason") of state.[25] God's act of election contravened the spirit of individual rather than communal rights emphasized by many Enlightenment political philosophers: first, by choosing a descent group rather than individuals, second, by thereby creating inequality among individuals of different descent, and third, by basing this choice on no humanly discernible, rational grounds.

The famous declaration of the Comte de Clermont-Tonnerre during the French Revolution, "We must refuse everything to the Jews as a nation and accord everything to Jews as individuals," must be understood in this context. In the same speech, Clermont-Tonnerre was arguing that revolutionary France cannot allow the existence of a "nation within a nation" (probably the first time that this phrase was used).[26] As is often the case, however, it is Hegel who takes implicit and half-processed intimations and prejudice, and out of them distills a consistent and explicit system. In *The Philosophy of History* and other works, Hegel arranges religions along an evolutionary scale.[27] In the Jewish stage of religion, the universal spirit or *Geist* is apprehended in the form of a majestic, all-powerful God who is, however, entirely separated from the world: the sublime One compared to whom the world is Nothing. It is inconceivable in this form of religion, which Hegel called the "religion of the sublime" (*Religion der Erhabenheit*), that God would have anything important in common with humans. God is definitely *not* imagined as governed by the rules of reason or the dictates of compassion known to Man.

Arabs, Islam, and Racialized Religion

For Hegel, the religion of the sublime included not only Judaism, but also Islam. And in general, from the eighteenth century on, the Jews, now often referred to explicitly with the term race, are given a companion cousin-race: the Arabs. Both Jews and Muslims are racialized in this period. But while the Jews are racialized under the same name, "Jews," as well as "Hebrews" and "Israelites," the Muslims are racialized under the name "Arabs." It was, of course, quite well known, especially to scholars, that Persians and many South and East Asians were also Muslim, and indeed before the Arabs it was the Turk who was imagined as the generic Muslim. Nevertheless, to nineteenth-century writers Islam was the religion of the Arabs.

Already in the Middle Ages, Islam had often been considered a Judaizing heresy, a throw-back to the Mosaic Law.[28] Noting the similarities between the Hebrew of the Bible and the Arabic of the Quran, eighteenth-century biblical scholars began to expand the Jewish–Muslim affinity from religion to language, and as was the tendency then, from language to what we would call culture and to what they called race. In the first half of the eighteenth century, the great Arabist and biblical scholar Albert Schultens regularly used Arabic philology for understanding the Hebrew Bible.[29] By the early nineteenth century it was widely held that the Bible was a typical Oriental document, and that the study of Semitic texts was useful in uncovering both concrete philological links to the Bible and the general mindset of the Oriental peoples who produced the Holy Script. The book of Job, specifically, was considered the oldest or one of the oldest in the Bible, and it was often said to be the work not of Jews, but their neighbors—some said Idumaeans, others Arabs.[30] In short, biblical philologists believed that Islam and biblical Judaism both sprang from a shared, linguistically conditioned mental universe. This mental universe was increasingly labeled as the racial heritage of, broadly speaking, the Orient, and more specifically of a racial grouping that would eventually be called "Semitic," but that at first appears to have been labeled as simply "Arab."

Hegel claimed, "[T]the proposition that there is only one God [and] he is a jealous God who will have no other gods before him [is] the great thesis of the Jewish, of overall Arab religion of the Western Orient and Africa."[31] We should notice that Hegel speaks here of "Arab," not "Mohammedan" religion, and also that he was able to use "Arab" to include "Jew" in the same sense as one would later use the term "Semitic." Hegel believed that unconditional obedience to an uncomprehended theological Law was not only a Jewish but also an Arab characteristic, and the cultural property of a united West-Asian race.[32] Hegel argued that this Arab-Jewish religion was coextensive with Oriental despotism. One obeys the sublime one without any question, without any search for understanding his providence. This of course posits a source of political authority above secular laws, and therefore is a threat to secularism.

The same broad use of the term "Arab" that we see in Hegel still occurs some decades later in Benjamin Disraeli's fiction.[33] Disraeli, eventually to become the prime minister of Britain, was a baptized Christian of Jewish descent, which for him and most other people was enough to call him a Jew. Like Hegel, he considered a Jewish race to be part of a greater "Arab" race. In fact, in his novel *Tancred* (1847) he made his characters declare, "The Arabs are only Jews upon horseback" and, most astonishingly, "God never spoke except to an Arab."[34] Obviously, he thought that not only Muhammad, but also Abraham, Isaac, Jacob, Moses, and Jesus were "Arabs." This is tantamount to saying that God's chosen race was not just the Jews, but also the Arabs. And indeed Disraeli and many of his contemporaries *also* imagined

Arabs, these racial cousins of the Jews, as a race that carries a religious tradition, and *also* a race that imagines itself as a people of God. The difference, of course, was that many Christians recognized Jewish chosenness, but few, if any, were as generous as Disraeli when it came to the claim of the Muslims, that is, the Arabs. Nevertheless, there was a broad though certainly not universal tendency to think as follows: if modern Christianity was the religion compatible with the modern, liberal, secular state, then Semitic—as it would be called—religion was the typical carrier of theocratic government, of a system where human laws are in conflict with and subordinated to the laws of God. In this way, the old supersessionist thesis about Christianity overcoming the limitations and fulfilling the potential of Judaism was transferred to a racial discourse that even secularist Christians or atheists could affirm. Just as traditional Christian discourse held that Judaism was fulfilled and overcome by Christianity, so this new racial discourse held that a new, rationalist and universalist world view now overcame the old, primitive religion of the Semites, which imagined a God who chose *them* as his own. In Islam, which medieval Christians often imagined as a reversion to Judaism, this Semitic religion found a relatively modern revival, but one that emerged from the same timeless racial depth as Judaism.

The racializing together of Jews and Arabs never functioned without opposition and complications. There was a striving on the part of many Jews and their friends to recognize the Jews as fully European or American. This would, of course, mean distancing the Jews from their Arab racial relatives. This was generally done by stressing that "Jewish" was a religion and not a race. This program, whose origins are in the nineteenth century, was eventually successful—if only after millions of Jews were murdered by racists who opposed the notion of a truly European Jew.

At first, Jews who wished to be seen as only a religious and not a descent group were asked to give up their claims to divine election. Many Reform Jews were indeed prepared to pay this price. Eventually, however, the complexities of international politics and of the Middle East conflict that opposed Jews and Arabs meant that equating Jews with the other Semites lost most of its meaning. With many of Israel's Arab enemies on the losing side of the Cold War, and with Arab terror directed at the West after 9/11, it seemed natural to think of the Jews as *more or less* part of the West. This identification has been reinforced by Israel's emergence from underdevelopment and its portrayal as a blooming democracy isolated, at least until the Arab spring of 2011, in a desert of latter-day Oriental despotism.

As Edward Said remarked long ago, the Jews have been able to shake off this heritage of being regarded as Semites, with all the accruing prejudices that go with this title, but the Arabs have not.[35] Moreover, it seems that recently the naïve racial category of "Arab" has been broadened to include ever more Muslims who are not Arab. Turks and especially Iranians had long been mistaken for Arabs, but what I am speaking about is a broadening that extends to the Muslims of South Asia. Following 9/11 in America, people attacked Sikhs who were wearing turbans because they mistook them for Muslims. This new extended grouping has been vaguely racialized under the label "Middle Eastern" appearance. The term is barely forty years old. Anyone with a Middle Eastern appearance is initially considered a Muslim, akin to the Arabs. As in all racializations, this one too has been naturalized, so that people actually *see* individuals as belonging to this new racial category.

This regrouping of Arabs in popular race terminology with South Asians is, in my view, a new racialization of religion, this time separating Islam from Judaism. There is no more place in this version for the average American or European unrehearsed conception of Jewish race: Diaspora Jews are *not* of Middle Eastern appearance. Of course, this puts non-"White" Jews in a special liminal category. Jews have indeed become White folks.[36] They and the Arabs no longer look alike to Western eyes; Arabs and Indians now do. If once it was the Jews who represented, in the Western popular imagination, the objectionable character of racialized religion, it is now the Muslims. One immensely important difference from the earlier situation is that some Christians recognized then as now the divine election of Israel. Islamophobes, on the other hand, find nothing for the Muslim claim to a special relationship with God but easy, unequivocal, and passionately held rejection.

Notes

1. For some of the varied approaches to race that assume a natural physiologically or genetically given basis for the concept of race, see Juliette Hooker, *Race and the Politics of Solidarity* (Oxford: Oxford University Press, 2009); and Flora Anthias and Nira Yuval-Davis, *Racialized Boundaries: Race, Nation, Colour, Gender and Class and the Anti-Racist Struggle* (London and New York: Routledge, 1993).
2. Jean-Luc Nancy, "The Deconstruction of Christianity," in *Religion and Media*, ed. Hent de Vries and Samuel Weber (Stanford, CA: Stanford University Press, 2001), 113.
3. W.J.T. Mitchell, *What Do Pictures Want: The Lives and Loves of Images* (Chicago: University of Chicago Press), 8.

4. On the genealogy of race and religion, see Craig R. Prentiss, ed., *Religion and the Creation of Race and Ethnicity: An Introduction* (New York: New York University Press, 2003).
5. Gil Anidjar, *Semites: Race, Religion, Literature* (Stanford, CA: Stanford University Press, 2008), 21.
6. Ralph Waldo Emerson, *English Traits* [1856] in *Harvard Classics,* ed. Charles W. Eliot (New York: P.F. Collier & Son, 1909), vol. 5, 13.
7. See Thomas Pegelow, "'German Jews,' 'National Jews,' 'Jewish Volk' or 'Racial Jews'? The Constitution and Contestation of 'Jewishness' in Newspapers of Nazi Germany, 1933–1938," *Central European History* 35 (2002): 195–221.
8. Benedict Anderson, *Imagined Communities,* rev. ed. (London and New York: Verso, 2006), 6.
9. Talal Asad, *Formations of the Secular: Christianity, Islam, Modernity* (Stanford, CA: Stanford University Press, 2003), 181.
10. Ibid., 38.
11. Ibid., 7.
12. Anderson, *Imagined Communities,* chap. 4, "Creole Pioneers."
13. See Ernest Gellner, *Nations and Nationalism,* 2nd ed. (Oxford and Malden, MA: Blackwell, 2006), 70.
14. Moritz Lazarus argued, in *Was heißt National?* (Berlin: Dümmler, 1880), that German Jews were just another German descent group (*Stamm*) such as the Swabians or the Bavarians, even though they were of Oriental origin.
15. John Efron, *Defenders of the Race: Jewish Doctors and Race Science in Fin-de-Siècle Europe* (New Haven, CT: Yale University Press, 1994).
16. Gen. 9:4. This is not the only symbolic use of "blood" in the Bible or in its Jewish and Christian interpretations. See David Biale, *Blood and Belief: The Circulation of a Symbol Between Jews and Christians* (Berkeley: University of California Press, 2007).
17. See, for example, Tudor Parfitt, "The Use of the Jew in Colonial Discourse," in *Orientalism and the Jews,* eds. Kalmar and Penslar, 51–67.
18. See the essays in this volume by Edith Bruder, Bruce Haynes, Steven Kaplan, and Jonas Zianga.
19. Debra Higgs Strickland, *Saracens, Demons and Jews: Making Monsters in Medieval Art* (Princeton, NJ: Princeton University Press, 2003).
20. This idea is discussed, e.g., in Miriam Eliav-Feldon, Benjamin Isaac, and Joseph Ziegler, eds., *The Origins of Racism in the West* (Cambridge: Cambridge University Press, 2009). In particular, see David Nirenberg, "Was There Race before Modernity? The Example of 'Jewish' Blood in Late Medieval Spain," in Eliav-Feldon, Isaac, and Ziegler, *Origins of Racism in the West,* 232–264; and Ronnie Po-Chia Hsia, "Religion and Race: Protestant and Catholic Discourses on Jewish Conversions in the Sixteenth and Seventeenth Centuries," in Eliav-Feldon, Isaac, and Ziegler, *Origins of Racism in the West,* 265–275.
21. Martin Luther, *An Open Letter on Translating.* n.p.: Project Gutenberg, n.d. eBook Collection, http://www.gutenberg.org/ebooks/272, 8. See "Ein Sendtbrief Dr. M. Luthers. Von Dolmetzschen und Fürbit der heiligen," *Dr. Martin Luthers Werke,* Band 30, Teil II (Weimar: Hermann Boehlaus Nachfolger, 1909), 632–646. Luther's tract was first published in 1530.

22. On the Christian supersession of Israel's election, with specific attention to the notion of "race" and its predecessors, see Denise Kimber Buell, *Why This New Race: Ethnic Reasoning in Early Christianity* (New York: Columbia University Press, 2005). On the divine election of the English see, for example, Liah Greenfeld, *Nationalism: Five Roads to Modernity* (Cambridge, MA: Harvard University Press, 1992), 44–59.
23. Edmund S. Morgan, *The Puritan Family: Religion and Domestic Relations in Seventeenth-Century New England* (New York: Harper & Row, 1966).
24. Asad, *Formations of the Secular.*
25. Michel Foucault. *Security, Territory, Population: Lectures at the Collège de France, 1977–1978* (Houndmills and New York: Palgrave Macmillan, 2007).
26. Cited in *The French Revolution and Human Rights: A Brief Documentary History,* ed. Lynn Hunt (Boston/New York: Bedford/St. Martin's, 1996), 86.
27. *Lectures on the Philosophy of World History,* ed. and trans. Robert F. Brown and Peter C. Hodgson (New York and Oxford: Oxford University Press, 2011).
28. Jeremy Cohen, "The Muslim Connection: On the Changing Role of the Jew in High Medieval Theology," in *From Witness to Witchcraft: Jews and Judaism in Medieval Christian Thought,* ed. Jeremy Cohen (Wiesbaden: Harrassowitz, 1996), 141–162; Suzanne Conklin Akbari, "Placing the Jews in Late Medieval English Literature," in *Orientalism and the Jews,* ed. Ivan Davidson Kalmar and Derek J. Penslar (Hanover, NH: University Press of New England, 2005), 32–50.
29. Albert Schultens, *Oratio de Linguæ Arabicæ Antiquissima Origine, Intima ac Sororia cum Lingua Hebræa Affinitate, Nullisque Seculis Præflorata Puritate* (Franeker: Willem Coulon, 1729).
30. Albert Schultens, *Liber Jobi: Cum Nova Versione ad Hebræum Fontem et commentario Perpetuo: In quo Veterum & Recentiorum Interpretum Cogitat Præcipua Expenduntur: Genuinus Sensus ad Priscum Linguæ Genium Indagatur, Atque ex Filo, & Nexu Universo, Argumenti Nodus Intricatissimus Evolvitur* (Leiden: Johannes Luzac, 1737); Robert Lowth, *Lectures on the Sacred Poetry of the Hebrews* (New York: Garland Publications, 1971), 88.
31. Hegel, *Lectures on the Philosophy of Religion* (Berkeley: University of California Press, 1987), vol. 2, 129.
32. Ivan Kalmar, *Early Orientalism: Imagined Islam and the Notion of Sublime Power* (London and New York: Routledge, 2012), 76–87.
33. Ivan Davidson Kalmar, "Benjamin Disraeli: Romantic Orientalist," *Comparative Studies of Society and History* 47, no. 2 (2005): 348–371.
34. Benjamin Disraeli, *Tancred* (London: R. Brimley, 1904), 299, 319.
35. Edward Said, "Arabs, Islam and the Dogmas of the West," *New York Times Book Review,* October 31, 1976; Said, *Orientalism,* 286.
36. Brodkin, *How Jews Became White Folks.*

Selected Bibliography

Abu El-Haj, Nadia. "Jews—Lost and Found: Genetic History and the Evidentary Terrain of Recognition." In *Rites of Return: Diaspora Poetics and the Politics of Memory,* ed. M. Hirsch and N. Miller, 40–59. New York: Columbia University Press, 2011.

———. "The Genetic Reinscription of Race." *Annual Review of Anthropology* 36 (2007): 283–300.

———. *The Genealogical Science: The Search for Jewish Origins and the Politics of Epistemology.* Chicago: University of Chicago Press, 2012.

Adams, Maurianne, and John Bracey, eds. *Strangers and Neighbors: Relations between Blacks and Jews in the United States.* Amherst, MA: University of Massachusetts Press, 2000.

Ahmad, Aijaz, "The Politics of Literary Postcoloniality." *Race and Class* 36, no. 3 (1995): 1–20.

Akbari, Suzanne Conklin. "Placing the Jews in Late Medieval English Literature." In *Orientalism and the Jews,* ed. Ivan Davidson Kalmar and Derek J. Penslar, 32–50. Hanover, NH: University Press of New England, 2005.

Alcalay, Ammiel. *After Jews and Arabs: Remaking Levantine Culture.* Minneapolis: University of Minnesota Press, 1993.

Alexander, Michael. *Jazz Age Jews.* Princeton, NJ: Princeton University Press, 2000.

Anders, Jaroslaw. "Telling the Past Anew: Recent Polish Debates on Anti-Semitism." In *Old Demons, New Debates: Anti-Semitism in the West,* ed. David I. Kertzer, 129–141. New York: Holmes & Meier, 2005.

Anderson, Benedict. *Imagined Communities: Reflections on the Origin and Spread of Nationalism.* Revised ed. London and New York: Verso, 2006.

Anderson, Victor. *Beyond Ontological Blackness.* New York: Continuum, 1995.

Anidjar, Gil. *"Our Place in al-Andalus": Kabbalah, Philosophy, Literature in Arab Jewish Letters.* Stanford, CA: Stanford University Press, 2002.

———. *The Jew, the Arab. A History of the Enemy.* Stanford, CA: Stanford University Press, 2003.

———. "Literary History and Hebrew Modernity." *Comparative Literature Studies* 42, no. 4 (2005): 277–296.

———. *Semites: Race, Religion, Literature.* Stanford, CA: Stanford University Press, 2008.

———. "Can the Walls Hear?" *Patterns of Prejudice* 43, no. 3–4 (2009): 251–268.

Anteby-Yemini, Lisa. *Les Juifs Éthiopiens en Israël: Les Paradoxes du Paradis.* Paris: CNRS editions, 2004.

Anthias, Flora, and Nira Yuval-Davis. *Racialized Boundaries: Race, Nation, Colour, Gender and Class and the Anti-Racist Struggle.* London and New York: Routledge, 1993.

Apel, Dora. "The Tattooed Jew." In *Visual Culture and the Holocaust,* ed. Barbie Zelizer, 300–320. New Brunswick: Rutgers University Press, 2001.

Appadurai, Arjun, *Modernity at Large: Cultural Dimensions of Globalization.* Minneapolis: University of Minnesota Press, 1996.

Appiah, Kwame Anthony. *In My Father's House: Africa in the Philosophy of Culture,* New York-Oxford: Oxford University Press, 1992.

———. "Racisms." In *The Anatomy of Race,* ed. David Theo Goldberg, 3–17. Minneapolis: University of Minnesota Press, 1990.

———. *Cosmopolitanism: Ethics in a World of Strangers.* New York: Norton, 2007.

Arendt, Hannah. *The Origins of Totalitarianism* [1951]. New York: Harcourt Brace 1979.

Asad, Tal. *Formations of the Secular: Christianity, Islam, Modernity.* Stanford, CA: Stanford University Press, 2003.

Ashkenazi, Michael, and Fran Markowitz. "Sexuality and Prevarication in the Praxis of Anthropology." In *Sex, Sexuality, and the Anthropologist,* ed. Fran Markowitz and Michael Ashkenazi, 1–21. Urbana: University of Illinois University Press, 1999.

Ashkenazi, Michael, and Alex Weingrod, eds. *Ethiopian Jews and Israel.* New Brunswick, NJ: Transaction Books, 1987.

Austen, Ralph A. "The Uncomfortable Relationship: African Enslavement in the Common History of Blacks and Jews." *Tikkun* 9, no. 2 (1994): 65–68, 86.

Avikhail, Eliyahu. *Les tribus d'Israël perdues ou lointaines.* Jerusalem: Amishav, 2003.

Azoulay, Katya Gibel. *Black, Jewish, and Interracial: It's Not the Color of Your Skin, but the Race of Your Kin, & Other Myths of Identity.* Durham, NC: Duke University Press, 1997.

Badiou, Alain, and Eric Hazan. *L'Antisémitisme Partout: Aujourd'hui en France.* Paris: La Fabrique, 2011.

Barnstone, Willis. *We Blacks and Jews: Memoir with Poems.* Bloomington: Indiana University Press, 2004.

Barrett, James, and David Roediger. "Inbetween Peoples." *Journal of American Ethnic History* 16, no. 3 (1997): 3–45.

Barzilai, Gad. "Who Is a Jew? Categories, Boundaries, Communities, and Citizenship Law in Israel." In *Boundaries of Jewish Identity,* ed. Susan A. Glenn and Naomi Sokoloff, 27–43. Seattle: Washington University Press, 2010.

Bauman, Zygmunt. "Allosemitism: Premodern, Modern, Postmodern." In *Modernity, Culture and 'the Jew,'* ed. Bryan Cheyette and Laura Marcus, 143–156. Cambridge, England: Polity Press, 1998.

———. "From Pilgrim to Tourist, Or a Short History of Identity." In *Questions of Cultural Identity,* ed. Stuart Hall and Paul Du Gay, 18–35. London: Sage, 1996.

———. *Europe of Strangers.* Oxford: ESRC Transnational Communities Programme, 1998, Working Paper No. 3, 10–11, http://www.transcomm.ox.ac.uk/working%20papers/bauman.pdf

———. *Identity: Conversations with Benedetto Vecchi.* Cambridge, England, and Malden, MA: Polity Press, 2004.

———. *Modernity and the Holocaust.* Ithaca, NY: Cornell University Press, 1989.

Beller, Steven. *Is Europe Good for the Jews? Jews and the Pluralist Tradition in Historical Perspective.* London: Institute of Jewish Policy Research, 2008.

———. *Anti-Semitism: A Very Short Introduction.* Oxford: Oxford University Press, 2007.

Berman, Paul, ed. *Blacks and Jews: Alliances and Arguments.* New York: Dell, 1994.

Bernstein, Lee. "The Avengers of Christie Street: Racism and Jewish Working Class Rebellion." In *The Novel and the American Left: Critical Essays on Depression-Era Fiction,* ed. Janet Galligani Gasey, 118–130. Iowa City, University of Iowa Press, 2004.

Berson, Lenora E. *The Negroes and the Jews.* New York: Random House, 1971.

Bhabha, Homi K. *The Location of Culture.* London: Routledge, 1994.

Biale, David. *Blood and Belief: The Circulation of a Symbol Between Jews and Christians.* Berkeley: University of California Press, 2007.

Biale, David, Michael Galchinsky, and Susan Heschel, eds. *Insider/Outsider: American Jews and Multiculturalism.* Berkeley: University of California Press, 1998.

Birnbaum, Pierre, and Ira Katznelson, eds. *Paths of Emancipation: Jews, States, and Citizenship.* Princeton, NJ: Princeton University Press, 1995.

Bleich, David. *Contemporary Halakhic Problems.* New York: Ktav, 1977.

Bloch, Alice, and John Solomos, eds. *Race and Ethnicity in the 21st Century.* Houndmills and New York: Palgrave Macmillan, 2010.

Bloom, Davida. "White, But Not Quite: The Jewish Character and Anti-Semitism—Negotiating a Location in the Gray Zone Between Other and Not." *Journal of Religion and Theatre* 1, no. 1 (2002), http://www.rtjournal.org/vol_1/no_1/bloom.html.

Boas, Franz. *Anthropology and Modern Life.* New York: Norton, 1962.

———. *The Mind of Primitive Man.* New York: Macmillan, 1938.

Boxwell, D.A. "'Sis' Cat as Ethnographer: Self-Presentation and Self-Inscription in Zora Neale Hurston's *Mules and Men.*" *African American Review* 26, no. 4 (1992): 605–617.

Boyarin, Daniel, *Carnal Israel: Reading Sex in Talmudic Culture.* Berkeley: University of California Press, 1993.

———. *Unheroic Conduct.* Berkeley: University of California Press, 1997.

Boyarin, Jonathan, "Waiting for a Jew: Marginal Redemption at the Eighth Street Shul." In *Between Two Worlds: Ethnographic Essays on American Jewry,* ed. Jack Kugelmass, 57–76. Ithaca, NY: Cornell University Press, 1988.

Boyarin, Jonathan, and Daniel Boyarin, eds. *Jews and other Differences: The New Jewish Cultural Studies.* Minneapolis, MN: University of Minnesota Press, 1997.

Boym, Svetlana. *The Future of Nostalgia.* New York: Basic Books, 2001.

Brackman, Harold. *Ministry of Lies: The Truth behind the Nation of Islam's The Secret Relationship between Blacks and Jews.* New York: Four Walls, Eight Windows Press, 1994.

Brearly, Margaret. *The Anglican Church, Jews and British Multiculturalism* (Posen Papers in Contemporary Antisemitism). Jerusalem: Vidal Sassoon Center for the Study of Anti-Semitism, Hebrew University of Jerusalem, 2007.

Briand, Joseph. *L'Hébreu à Madagascar.* Tananarive: Pitot de la Beaujardière, 1946.

Brettschneider, Marla. *The Family Flamboyant: Race Politics, Queer Families, Jewish Lives.* Albany, NY: State University of New York Press, 2006.

Brodkin, Karen. *How Jews Became White Folks and What That Says About Race in America.* New Brunswick, NJ: Rutgers University Press, 2000.

Brook, Vincent. "American Jews and Television." In *Encyclopedia of American Jewish History.* Vol. 1, ed. Stephen H. Norwood and Eunice G. Pollack, 474–481. Santa Barbara, CA: ABC-Clio, 2008.

———. *Something Ain't Kosher Here: The Rise of the "Jewish" Sitcom.* New Brunswick, NJ: Rutgers University Press, 2003.

Bruder, Edith. *The Black Jews of Africa: History, Religion, Identity.* New York: Oxford University Press, 2008.

Budick, Emily Miller. *Blacks and Jews in Literary Conversation.* Cambridge: Cambridge University Press, 1998.

Buell, Denise Kimber. *Why This New Race: Ethnic Reasoning in Early Christianity.* New York: Columbia University Press, 2005.

Buijs, Gina, "Black Jews in the Northern Province: A Study of Ethnic Identity in South Africa." *Ethnic and Racial Studies* 21, no. 4 (1998): 661–682.

Bulmer, Martin, and John Solomos, eds. *Racism.* Oxford: Oxford University Press, 1999.

Bunzl, Matti. *Anti-Semitism and Islamophobia: Hatreds Old and New in Europe.* Chicago: Prickly Paradigm Press, 2007.

Byers, Michele, and Rosalin Krieger. "Something Old Is New Again? Postmodern Jewishness in *Curb Your Enthusiasm, Arrested Development,* and *The O.C.*" In *You Should See Yourself: Jewish Identity in Postmodern American Culture,* ed. Vincent Brook, 277–297. New Brunswick, NJ: Rutgers University Press, 2006.

Caplan, Marc. *Jew-Hatred as History: An Analysis of the Nation of Islam's "The Secret Relationship."* New York: The Anti-Defamation League, 1993.

Cesarani, David. "Anti-Zionism in Britain, 1922–2002: Continuities and Discontinuities." In *Anti-Semitism and Anti-Zionism in Historical Perspective,* ed. Jeffery Herf, 115–144. London and New York: Routledge, 2007.

Chakrabarty, Dipesh. *Provincializing Europe: Postcolonial Thought and Historical Difference.* Princeton, NJ: Princeton University Press, 2000.

Chaudhuri, Kirti, N. *Asia before Europe: Economy and Civilisation of the Indian Ocean from the Rise of Islam to 1750.* Cambridge: Cambridge University Press, 1990.

Cheyette, Brian. *Constructions of 'the Jew' in English Literature and Society: Racial Representations, 1875–1945.* Cambridge: Cambridge University Press, 1993.

———. "Neither Black nor White: The Figure of 'the Jew' in Imperial British Literature." In *The Jew in the Text,* ed. Linda Nochlin and Tamar Garb, 31–41. London: Thames & Hudson, 1995.

———. "Venetian Spaces: Old-New Literatures and the Ambivalent Uses of Jewish History." *Essays and Studies* 53 (2000): 53–72.

———. "White Skin: Black Masks: Jews and Jewishness in the Writings of George Eliot and Frantz Fanon." In *Cultural Readings of Imperialism: Edward Said and the Gravity of History,* ed. Keith Ansell Pearson, Benita Parry, and Judith Squires, 106–125. London: Lawrence and Wishart, 1997.

Cheyette, Bryan, and Laura Marcus, eds. *Modernity, Culture, and "the Jew."* Cambridge, England: Polity Press, 1998.

Cheyette, Bryan, ed. *Between "Race" and Culture: Representations of "the Jew" in English and American Literature.* Stanford, CA: Stanford University Press, 1996.

Chireau, Yvonne Patricia, and Nathaniel Deutsch. *Black Zion: African American Religious Encounters with Judaism.* New York: Oxford University Press, 2000.

Clifford, James. "Introduction: Partial Truths." In *Writing Culture: The Poetics and Politics of Ethnography,* ed. James Clifford and George E. Marcus, 1–27. Berkeley: University of California Press, 1986.

Cochran, Gregory, Jason Hardy, and Henry Harpending. "Natural History of Ashkenazi Intelligence." *Journal of Biosocial Science* 38, no. 5 (2005): 659–693.

Cohen, Jeremy. "The Muslim Connection: On the Changing Role of the Jew in High Medieval Theology." In *From Witness to Witchcraft: Jews and Judaism in Medieval Christian Thought,* ed. Jeremy Cohen, 141–162. Wiesbaden: Harrassowitz, 1996.

Cohen, Robin. *Global Diasporas: An Introduction.* Seattle: University of Washington Press, 1997.

Conquest, Robert, ed. *Soviet Nationalities Policy in Practice.* New York: Praeger, 1967.

Cooper, Alan. *Philip Roth and the Jews.* Albany: State University of New York Press, 1996.

Cooper, Alanna Esther. *Negotiating Identity in the Context of Diaspora, Dispersion, and Reunion: The Bukharan Jews and Jewish Peoplehood.* Doctoral Thesis, Boston University, 2000. Ann Arbor: UMI, 2000.

Corcos, Alain F. *The Myth of the Jewish Race: The Biologist's Point of View.* Bethlehem, PA: Lehigh University Press, 2005.

Crouch, Stanley. *The All-American Skin Game, or The Decoy of Race: The Long and the Short of It, 1990–1994.* New York: Pantheon, 1995.

———. *Notes of a Hanging Judge: Essays and Reviews, 1979–1989.* New York: Oxford University Press, 1990.

———. *The Artificial White Man: Essays on Authenticity.* New York: Basic Books, 2004.

Davison, Neil. *Jewishness and Masculinity from the Modern to the Postmodern.* New York: Routledge, 2010.

Delgado, Richard, and Jean Stefancic, eds. *Critical Race Theory: The Cutting-Edge.* 2nd ed. Philadelphia: Temple University Press, 2000.

DellaPergola, Sergio, Uzi Rebhun, and Mark Tolts. "Contemporary Jewish Diaspora in Global Context: Human Development Correlates of Population Trends." *Israel Studies* 10, no. 1 (2005): 61–95.

Diner, Hasia. *In the Almost Promised Land: American Blacks and Jews 1915–1935.* Westport, CT: Greenwood Press, 1977.

———. *The Jews of the United States.* Berkeley: University of California Press, 2004.

———. *Lower East Side Memories: A Jewish Place in America.* Princeton: Princeton University Press, 2000.

Donald, James, and Ali Rattansi, eds. *Race, Culture, and Difference.* London: SAGE, 1992.

Du Bois, W.E.B. *The Souls of Black Folk.* Chicago: A.C. McClurg, 1903; republished London: Penguin, 1996.

———. "The Negro and the Warsaw Ghetto." *Jewish Life* (May 1952): 14–15.

Dyson, Michael Eric. *Reflecting Black: African-American Cultural Criticism.* Minneapolis: Minneapolis: University of Minnesota Press, 1993.

Early, Gerald. "The Two Worlds of Race Revisited :A Meditation on Race in the Age of Obama." *Dædalus* (Winter 2011): 11–27.

Efron, John. *Defenders of the Race: Jewish Doctors and Race Science in Fin-de-Siècle Europe.* New Haven, CT: Yale University Press, 1994.

Eilberg-Schwartz, Howard, ed. *People of the Body: Jews and Judaism from an Embodied Perspective.* Albany, NY: State University of New York Press, 1992.

Eisenstadt, Shmuel N. *Jewish Civilization: The Jewish Historical Experience in a Comparative Perspective.* Albany, NY: State University of New York Press, 1992.

Eliav-Feldon, Miriam, Benjamin Isaac, and Joseph Ziegler, eds. *The Origins of Racism in the West.* Cambridge: Cambridge University Press, 2009.

Elliott, Michael A. *The Culture Concept: Writing and Difference in the Age of Realism.* Minneapolis: University of Minnesota Press, 2002.

Entine, Jon. *Abraham's Children: Race, Identity, and the DNA of the Chosen People.* New York: Warner Books, 2007.

Evans, Andrew D. *Anthropology at War: World War I and the Science of Race in Germany.* Chicago: University of Chicago Press, 2010.

Ezrahi, Sidra DeKoven. *Booking Passage: Exile and Homecoming in the Modern Jewish Imagination.* Berkeley: University of California Press, 2000.

Falk, Raphael. *Tzionut vehabiologia shel hayehudim* (Zionim and the Biology of the Jews). Tel Aviv: Resling, 2006.

———. *Genetic Analysis: A History of Genetic Thinking.* Cambridge, England: Cambridge University Press, 2009.

Fanon, Frantz. *Black Skin, White Masks.* Trans. Charles Lam Markman. London: MacGibbon & Kee, 1968.

———. *The Wretched of the Earth.* Harmondsworth: Penguin, 1967.

Fein, Leonard. *The Negro Revolution and the Jewish Community.* New York: Synagogue Council of America, 1969.

Fernheimer, Janice W. *Arguing Black Jewish Identity: Hatzaad Harishon and Interruptive Invention.* Birmingham, AL: University of Alabama Press, 2013.

Fine, Robert. "Fighting with Phantoms: Contribution to the Debate on Anti-Semitism in Europe." *Patterns of Prejudice* 43, no. 5 (2009): 459–479.

———. "Dehumanising the Dehumanisers: The Problem of Reversal in Human Rights." *Journal of Global Ethics* (2010): 179–190. Special Issue on "Critical Theory and the Language of Violence."

Fink, Carole. "Jews in Contemporary Europe." In *Ethnic Europe: Mobility, Identity, and Conflict in a Globalized World,* ed. Roland Hsu, 212–239. Stanford, CA: Stanford University Press, 2010.

Finkielkraut, Alain. *Remembering in Vain.* Trans. Roxanne Lapidus with Sima Godfrey. New York: Columbia University Press, 1992.

Fitzgerald, Thomas K. "Identity-in-Ethnography: Limits to Ethnographic Subjectivity." In *Sex, Sexuality, and the Anthropologist,* ed. Fran Markowitz and Michael Ashkenazi, 117–127. Urbana: University of Illinois Press, 1999.

Foucault, Michel. *Security, Territory, Population : Lectures at the Collège de France, 1977–1978.* Houndmills and New York: Palgrave Macmillan, 2007.

Frank, Gelya. "Jews, Multiculturalism, and Boasian Anthropology." *American Anthropology* 99, no. 4 (1997): 731–745.

Frankenberg, Ruth. *White Women, Race Matters.* Minneapolis: University of Minnesota Press. 1993.

Freedman, Jonathan. "'Who's Jewish?' Some Asian-American Writers and the Jewish-American Literary Canon." *Michigan Quarterly Review* 42, no. 1 (2003): 230–254.

Frenkel, Ronit. "Performing Race, Reconsidering History: Achmat Dangor's Recent Fiction." *Research in African Literatures* 39, no. 1 (Winter 2008): 149–165.

Friedman, Murray. *The Creation and Collapse of the Black–Jewish Alliance.* New York: Free Press, 1995.

Fuchs, Lawrence. *The Political Behavior of American Jews.* Glencoe, IL: Free Press, 1956.

Funderburg, Lise. *Black, White, Other.* New York: W. Morrow, 1994.

Fuss, Diane. *Identification Papers.* New York: Routledge, 1995.

Gebert, Konstanty. "Esau Can Change, But Will We Notice?" In *Old Demons, New Debates: Anti-Semitism in the West,* ed. David I. Kertzer, 115–127. New York: Holmes & Meier. 2005.

Geertz, Clifford. *The Interpretation of Cultures.* New York: Basic Books, 1973.

Gellner, Ernest. *Nations and Nationalism.* 2nd ed. Oxford and Malden, MA: Blackwell, 2006.

Gerber, Israel J. *The Heritage Seekers: American Blacks in Search of Jewish Identity.* Middle Village, NY: Jonathan David, 1977.

Gilman, Sander L. *Franz Kafka, the Jewish Patient.* New York: Routledge, 1995.

———. *Freud, Race, and Gender.* Princeton, NJ: Princeton University Press, 1996.

———. *The Jew's Body.* London and New York: Routledge, 1991.

———. *Jewish Frontiers: Essays on Bodies, Histories, and Identities.* London: Palgrave Macmillan, 2003.

———. *Jewish Self-Hatred: Anti-Semitism and the Hidden Language of the Jews.* Baltimore: Johns Hopkins University Press, 1986.

———. *Multiculturalism and the Jews.* New York: Routledge, 2006.

———. "Private Knowledge." *Patterns of Prejudice* 36.1 (2002): 5–16 (special issue on The New Genetics and the Old Eugenics: The Ghost in the Machine, ed. Sander Gilman).

———, ed. *Race in Contemporary Medicine.* London: Routledge, 2007.

———. *Smart Jews: The Construction of the Image of Jewish Superior Intelligence.* Lincoln: University of Nebraska Press, 1996.

Gilroy, Paul. *After Empire: Melancholia or Convivial Culture?* London: Routledge, 2004.

———. *Against Race: Imagining Political Culture beyond the Color Line.* Cambridge, MA: Harvard University Press, 2000.

———. *Between Camps. Race, Identity and Nationalism at the End of the Colour Line.* London: Penguin, 2000.

———. *The Black Atlantic: Modernity and Double Consciousness.* Cambridge, MA: Harvard University Press, 1993.

———. *There Ain't No Black in the Union Jack.* London: Hutchinson, 1987.

Ginzberg, Eli. "The Black Revolution and the Jew." *Conservative Judaism* (Fall 1969): 3–19.

Gitelman, Zvi. *Jewish Nationality and Soviet Politics: The Jewish Sections of the CPSU, 1917–1930.* Princeton, NJ: Princeton University Press, 1972.

———. "Soviet-Jewish Immigrants to the United States: Profile, Problems, Prospects." In *Soviet Jewry in the Decisive Decade, 1971–80,* ed. Robert O. Freedman, 89–98. Durham, NC: Duke University Press, 1984.

Glaser, Jennifer. "The Jew in the Canon: Reading Race and Literary History in Philip Roth's *The Human Stain." PMLA* 123, no. 5 (2008): 1465–1478.

Glazer, Nathan. *Ethnic Dilemmas: 1964–1982.* Cambridge, MA: Harvard University Press, 1983.

———. "Negroes and Jews: The New Challenge to Pluralism." *Commentary* (December 1964): 29–34.

Glenn, Susan A. "'Funny, You Don't Look Jewish': Visual Stereotypes and the Masking of Modern Jewish Identity." In *Boundaries of Jewish Identity,* ed. Susan A. Glenn and Naomi Sokoloff, 64–90. Seattle: Washington University Press, 2010.

Glick, Leonard B. "Types Distinct from Our Own: Franz Boas on Jewish Identity and Assimilation." *American Anthropologist* 84, no. 3 (1982): 545–565.

Goffman, Ethan. *Imagining Each Other: Blacks and Jews in Contemporary American Literature.* Albany: State University of New York Press, 2000.

Goldberg, David Theo, ed. *Multiculturalism: A Critical Reader.* Cambridge, MA: Harvard University Press, 1994.

———. "Racial Europeanization." *Ethnic and Racial Studies* 29, no. 2 (March 2006): 331–364.

———. *Racist Culture: Philosophy and the Politics of Meaning.* Oxford: Blackwell, 1993.

———. *The Threat of Race: Reflections on Racial Neoliberalism.* Oxford and Malden, MA: Wiley-Blackwell, 2009.

Goldberg, David Theo, and Michael Krausz, eds. *Jewish Identity.* Philadelphia: Temple University Press, 1993.

Goldberg, David Theo, and John Solomos, eds. *A Companion to Racial and Ethnic Studies.* Oxford: Blackwell, 2002.

Goldberg, Harvey and Chen Bram. "Sephardi / Mizrahi / Arab Jews: Anthropological Reflections on Critical Sociology in Israel and the Study of Middle Eastern Jewries within the Context of Israeli Society." *Studies in Contemporary Jewry* 22 (2007): 227–56.

Goldberg, Harvey E., ed. *The Life of Judaism.* Berkeley: University of California Press, 2001.

Goldberg, Rick, ed. *Judaism in Biological Perspective: Biblical Lore and Judaic Practices.* Boulder, CO: Paradigm, 2009.

Goldstein, David B. *Jacob's Legacy: A Genetic View of Jewish History.* New Haven and London: Yale University Press, 2009.

Goldstein, Eric L. *The Price of Whiteness: Jews, Race, and American Identity.* Princeton, NJ: Princeton University Press, 2006.

Gordon, Milton. *Assimilation in American Life.* New York: Oxford University Press, 1964.

Gray, Ahuva. *My Sister the Jew.* New York: Feldheim, 2001.

Greenberg, Cheryl. *"Or Does It Explode?": Black Harlem in the Great Depression.* Oxford: Oxford University Press, 1991.

———. "Negotiating Coalition, Black and Jewish Civil Rights Agencies in the Twentieth Century." In *Struggles in the Promised Land: Toward a History of Black–Jewish Relations in the United States,* ed. Jack Salzman and Cornel West, 253–276. New York: Oxford University Press, 1997.

———. *Troubling the Waters.* Princeton, NJ: Princeton University Press, 2006.

Greene, Daniel. *The Jewish Origin of Cultural Pluralism.* Bloomington: University of Indiana Press, 2011.

Gruber, Ruth Ellen. *Virtually Jewish: Reinventing Jewish Culture in Europe.* Berkeley: University of California Press, 2002.
Guglielmo, Thomas. *White on Arrival.* New York: Oxford University Press. 2004.
Gunning, Sandra. *Race, Rape, and Lynching: The Red Record of American Literature, 1890–1912.* New York: Oxford University Press, 1996.
Gurock, Jeffrey. "The Depth of Ethnicity: Jewish Identity and Ideology in Interwar New York City." *American Jewish Archives Journal* 61, no. 2 (2009): 145–161.
Habermas, Jürgen. *The Inclusion of the Other.* Cambridge, MA: MIT Press, 1998.
———. *The Postnational Constellation: Political Essays,* ed. Max Pensky. Cambridge, MA: MIT Press, 2001.
Halkin, Hillel. *Across the Sabbath River: In Search of a Lost Tribe of Israel.* New York: Houghton Mifflin Harcourt, 2002.
Hall, Stuart. "Cultural Identity and Diaspora." In *Identity. Community, Culture, Difference,* ed. Jonathan Rutherford, 223–237. London: Lawrence & Wishart, 1990.
Harrison-Kahn, Lori. "Passing for White, Passing for Jewish: Mixed Race Identity in Danzy Senna and Rebecca Walker." *MELUS* 30, no. 1 (Spring, 2005): 19–48.
———. *The White Negress: Literature, Minstrelsy, and the Black-Jewish Imaginary.* New Brunswick, NJ: Rutgers University Press, 2011.
Hart, Mitchell B., ed. *Jews and Race: Writings on Identity and Difference, 1880–1940.* Lebanon, NH: University of New England / Brandeis University Press, 2011.
———. *Social Science and the Politics of Modern Jewish Identity.* Stanford, CA: Stanford University Press, 2000.
Haynes, Bruce D. "People of God, Children of Ham: Making Black(s) Jews." *Journal of Modern Jewish Studies* 8, no. 2 (July 2009): 237–254.
Heep, Lynda Hoffman. "Creating Ethnography: Zora Neale Hurston and Lydia Cabrera." *African American Review* 39, no. 3 (2005): 337–353.
Hegeman, Susan. *Patterns for America: Modernism and the Concept of Culture.* Princeton, NJ: Princeton University Press, 1999.
Helmreich, Alan, and Paul Marcus, eds. *Blacks and Jews on the Couch: Psychoanalytic Reflections on Black–Jewish Conflict.* Westport, CT: Praeger, 1998.
Herberg, Will. *Protestant, Catholic, Jew.* Garden City, NY: Doubleday, 1955.
Hill, Herbert. "Black–Jewish Conflict in the Labor Context." *Race Traitor* 5 (Winter 1996): 72–103.
Hirsh, David. *Anti-Zionism and Anti-Semitism: Cosmopolitan Reflections.* YIISA Working Paper No. 1. New Haven, CT: Yale Initiative for the Interdisciplinary Study of Anti-Semitism, 2007.
Hollinger, David A. "Communalist and Dispersionist Approaches to American Jewish History in an Increasingly Post-Jewish Era." *American Jewish History* 95, no. 1 (March 2009): 1–32.
Hödl, Klaus. "The Black Body and the Jewish Body: A Comparison of Medical Images." *Patterns of Prejudice* 36, no. 1 (2002): 17–34.
Hooker, Juliette. *Race and the Politics of Solidarity.* Oxford: Oxford University Press, 2009.
Hoppe, Marcus. "Sub-State Nationalism and European Integration: Constructing Identity in the Multilevel Political Space of Europe." *Journal of Contemporary European Research* 1, no. 2 (2005): 13–28.
Huntington, Samuel. *Clash of Civilizations and the Remaking of World Order.* New York: Simon and Schuster, 1996.

Hutton, Christopher M. *Race and the Third Reich: Linguistics, Racial Anthropology and Genetics in the Dialectic of "Volk."* Cambridge, England: Polity Press, 2005.

Ilona, Remy and Ehav Eliyah, *The Igbo: Jews in Africa? Research Findings, Historical Links, Commentaries, Narratives.* Abuja: Mega Press, 2004.

Isaac, Ephraim. "Jewish Solidarity and the Jews of Ethiopia." In *Organizing Rescue: National Jewish Solidarity in the Modern Period,* ed. Selwyn Ilan Troen and Benjamin Pinkus. London: Frank Cass, 1992, 403–420.

———. "Hearing the Call: Solidarity with Ethiopian Jews." *The Narrow Bridge: Jewish Views on Multiculturalism* ed. Marla Brettschneider. New Brunswick, NJ: Rutgers University Press, 1996, 219–232.

Itzkovitz, Daniel. "Passing like Me." *South Atlantic Quarterly* 98 (1999): 36–57.

———. "They All Are Jews." In *You Should See Yourself: Jewish Identity in Postmodern American Culture,* ed. Vincent Brook, 230–249. New Brunswick, NJ: Rutgers University Press, 2006).

Jackson, Bernard. "'Transformative Accommodation' and Religious Law." *Ecclesiastical Law Journal* 2 (2009): 131–153.

Jacobs, Susie. "Globalisation, Anti-Globalisation and the Jewish 'Question.'" *European Review of History* 18, no. 1 (2011): 45–56.

Jacobson, Matthew Frye. *Roots Too: White Ethnic Revival in Post–Civil Rights America.* Cambridge, MA: Harvard University Press, 2006.

———. *Whiteness of a Different Color: European Immigrants and the Alchemy of Race.* Cambridge, MA: Harvard University Press, 1998.

Jenkins, Richard. *Rethinking Ethnicity: Arguments and Explorations.* London: Sage, 1997.

Jikeli, Gunther. "Anti-Semitism among Young Muslims in Europe." In *Reflections on anti-Semitism: Anti-Semitism in Historical and Anthropological Perspectives,* ed. V. Tydlitatova and A. Hanzova, 65–69. Pilsen: West Bohemian University, 2009.

Jirousek, Lori. "Ethnics and Ethnographers: Zora Neale Hurston and Anzia Yezierska." *Journal of Modern Literature* 29, no. 2 (2006): 19–32.

Johnson, Charles. "The End of the Black American Narrative." *The American Scholar* (Summer 2008); reprinted in *Best African American Essays,* ed. Gerald Early and Randall Kennedy. New York: One World/Ballantine, 2010.

Joppke, Christian. "Limits of Integration Policy: Britain and Her Muslims." *Journal of Migration and Ethnic Studies* 35, no. 3 (2009): 453–472.

Judaken, Jonathan. "So What's New? Rethinking the 'New Anti-Semitism' in a Global Age." *Patterns of Prejudice* 42, no. 4–5 (2008): 531–560.

Judt, Tony. *Postwar: A History of Europe since 1945.* London: Penguin, 2007.

Julius, Anthony. *Trials of the Diaspora: A History of Anti-Semitism in England.* Oxford: Oxford University Press, 2010.

Kahana, Yael. *Achim Shechorim* [Black brothers]. Tel Aviv: 'Am 'Oved, 1997.

Kahn, Susan Martha. "Are Genes Jewish? Conceptual Ambiguities in the Genetic Age." In *Boundaries of Jewish Identity,* ed. Susan A. Glenn and Naomi Sokoloff, 12–26. Seattle: Washington University Press, 2010.

Kahn-Harris, Keith, and Ben Gidley. *Turbulent Times: The British Jewish Community Today.* London, New York: Continuum, 2010.

Kallen, Horace. *Cultural Pluralism and the American Idea.* Philadelphia: University of Pennsylvania Press. 1956.

———. *Culture and Democracy in the United States.* New York: Boni and Liveright, 1924.

Kalmar, Ivan Davidson. *Early Orientalism: Imagined Islam and the Notion of Sublime Power.* London, New York: Routledge, 2012.

———. "Benjamin Disraeli: Romantic Orientalist." *Comparative Studies of Society and History* 47, no. 2 (2005): 348–371.

Kalmar, Ivan Davidson, and Derek J. Penslar, eds. *Orientalism and the Jews.* Waltham, MA: Brandeis University Press / Hanover, NH: University Press of New England, 2005.

Kaplan, Steven. "Black and White, Blue and White, and Beyond the Pale: Ethiopian Immigrants and the Discourse of Colour in Israel." *Jewish History and Culture* 5, no. 1 (2002): 51–68.

———. "Can the Ethiopian Change his Skin? The Beta Israel (Falasha) and Racial Discourse." *African Affairs* 98, no. 393 (1999): 535–550.

———. "If There are No Races, How Can Jews be a 'Race'?" *Journal of Modern Jewish Studies* 3, no. 1 (2003) 79–96.

———, and Shoshana Ben-Dor. *Ethiopian Jewry: An Annotated Bibliography.* Jerusalem, Ben Zvi Institute, 1988.

———, and Chaim Rosen. "Ethiopian Jews in Israel." *American Jewish Yearbook 1994* (1994): 59–109.

———, and Hagar Solomon. *Ethiopian Immigrants in Israel: Experience and Prospect* (London: Institute for Jewish Policy Research, 1998).

Kaufman, Jonathan. *Broken Alliance: The Turbulent Times between Blacks and Jews in America.* New York: Scribner's, 1988.

Kaufmann, Eric. *Shall the Religious Inherit the Earth: Demography and Politics in the Twenty-First Century.* London: Profile, 2010.

Kautke, Egbert. "German 'Race Psychology' and its Implementation in Central Europe: Egon Freiherr von Eickstedt and Rudolf Hippius." In *Blood and Homeland: Eugenics and Racial Nationalism in Central and Southeast Europe 1900–1940,* ed. Marius Turda and Paul J.Weindling, 23–40. Budapest and New York: Central European University Press, 2007.

Kaye/Kantrowitz, Melanie. *The Colors of Jews: Racial Politics and Radical Diasporism.* Bloomington: Indiana University Press, 2007.

Kershen, Anne. *Strangers, Aliens and Asians: Huguenots, Jews and Bangladeshis in Spitalfields 1660–2000.* London: Routledge, 2005.

Kirsh, Nurit. "Genetic Research on Israel's Populations: Two Opposite Tendencies." In *Twentieth Century Ethics of Human Subjects Research: Historical Perspectives on Values, Practices, and Regulations,* ed. V. Roelke and G. Maio, 309–319. Stuttgart: Franz Steiner Verlag, 2004.

———. "Genetic Studies of Ethnic Communities in Israel: A Case of Values-Motivated Research Work." In *Jews and Sciences in German Contexts,* ed. U. Charpa and U. Deichmann, 181–195. Tübingen: Mohr Siebeck, 2007.

Kleiman, Yaakov. *DNA & Tradition: The Genetic Link to the Ancient Hebrews.* New York: Devora Publishing Company, 2004.

Koestler, Arthur. *The Thirteenth Tribe: The Khazar Empire and its Heritage.* London: Hutchinson and New York: Random House, 1976.

Kohn, Marek. *The Race Gallery: The Return of Racial Science.* London: Jonathan Cape, 1995.

Koltun-Fromm, Ken. *Material Culture and Jewish Thought in America*. Bloomington: Indiana University Press, 2010.

Konner, Melvin. *The Jewish Body*. New York: Schocken, 2009.

———. *Unsettled: An Anthropology of the Jews*. New York: Viking, 2004.

Kramer, Michael. "Race, Literary History, and the 'Jewish' Question." *Prooftexts* 21, no. 3 (2001): 287–349.

Kranz, Dani. "Living Local: Some Remarks on the Creation of Social Groups of Young Jews in Present-Day London." *European Review of History* 18, no. 1 (2011): 79–88.

Kruger, Loren. "Black Atlantics, White Indians, and Jews: Locations, Locutions, and Syncretic Identities in the Fiction of Achmat Dangor and Others." *South Atlantic Quarterly* 101, no. 1 (Winter 2001): 111–143.

Krupnick, Mark. *Deep Places of the Imagination*. Madison: University of Wisconsin Press, 2005.

Kugelmass, Jack. "First as Farce, Then as Tragedy: The Unlamented Demise of Bridget Loves Bernie." In *Key Texts in American Jewish Culture*, ed. Jack Kugelmass, 147–160. New Brunswick, NJ: Rutgers University Press, 2003.

Kundnani, Arun. *The End of Tolerance: Racism in 21st Century Britain*. London: Pluto Books, 2007.

Küntzel, Matthias. *Jihad and Jew-hatred: Islamism, Nazism, and the Roots of 9/11*. Trans. Colin Meade. New York: Telos Press, 2007.

Kyriakides, Christopher, Satnam Virdee, and Tariq Modood. "Racism, Muslims and the National Imagination." *Journal of Ethnic and Migration Studies* 35, no. 2 (2009): 289–307.

Lambert, Nick. *Jews and Europe in the Twenty-First Century: Thinking Jewish*. London: Vallentine Mitchell, 2008.

Landing, James E. *Black Judaism: Story of an American Movement*. Durham, NC: Carolina Academic Press, 2002.

Lapierre, Nicole. *Cause Commune: Des Juifs et des Noirs*. Paris: Stock, 2011.

Lappin, Shalom. "This Green and Pleasant Land: Britain and the Jews." YIISA Working Paper No. 2. New Haven, CT: Yale Initiative for the Interdisciplinary Study of Antisemitism, 2008.

Lerner, Michael, and Cornel West. *Jews and Blacks: A Dialogue on Race, Religion, and Culture in America*. New York: Plume/Penguin Group, 1995.

Le Roux, Magdel. *The Lemba: A Lost Tribe of Israel in Southern Africa*. Pretoria: UNISA, 2003.

Lipsitz, George. *The Possessive Investment in Whiteness*. Philadelphia: Temple University Press, 2006.

Liss, Julia, E. "German Culture and German Science in the Bildung of Franz Boas." In *Volksgeist as Method and Ethic: Essays on Boasian Ethnography and the German Anthropological Tradition*, ed. George W. Stocking Jr., 155–184. Madison: University of Wisconsin Press, 1996.

Locke, Hubert G. *The Black Anti-Semitism Controversy*. Selinsgrove, PA: Susquehanna University Press, 1994.

Lopez, Ian Haney. *White by Law*. New York: New York University Press, 1996; reprint 2000.

Lyman, Stanford. *Color, Culture, Civilization*. Urbana: University of Illinois Press, 1995.

Lyons, Len. *The Ethiopian Jews of Israel: Personal Stories of Life in the Promised Land.* Woodstock, VT: Jewish Lights, 2007.

Maiwald, Michael. "Race, Capitalism, and the Third-Sex Ideal: Claude McKay's *Home to Harlem* and the Legacy of Edward Carpenter." *Modern Fiction Studies* 48, no. 4 (2002): 825–857.

Marcus, Jacob Radar. *United States Jewry 1776–1985.* Vol. 3: *The Germanic Period, Part 2.* Detroit, MI: Wayne State University Press, 1993.

Margalit, Gilad. *Germany and Its Gypsies: A Post-Auschwitz Ordeal.* Madison: University of Wisconsin Press, 2002.

Margolick, David. *Strange Fruit: Billie Holiday, Café Society, and an Early Cry for Civil Rights.* Philadelphia: Burning Press, 2000.

Markowitz, Fran. "Creating Coalitions and Causing Conflicts: Confronting Race and Gender through Partnered Ethnography." *Ethnos* 27, no. 2 (2002): 201–222.

———. "Not Nationalists: Russian Teenagers' Soulful A-politics." *Europe-Asia Studies* 51. 7 (1999):1183–1198.

———. "Plaiting the Strands of Jewish Identity." *Comparative Studies in Society and History* 32, no. 1 (1990):181–189.

———. "Rituals as Keys to Soviet Immigrants' Jewish Identity." In *Between Two Worlds: Ethnographic Essays on American Jewry,* ed. Jack Kugelmass, 128–147. Ithaca, NY: Cornell University Press, 1988.

———. *A Community in Spite of Itself: Soviet Jewish Emigrés in New York.* Washington, DC: Smithsonian Institution Press, 1993.

———. *Coming of Age in Post-Soviet Russia.* Urbana: University of Illinois Press, 2000.

Markowitz, Fran, Sara Helman, and Dafna Shir-Vertesh. "Soul Citizenship: The Black Hebrews and the State of Israel." *American Anthropologist* 105, no. 2 (2003): 302–312.

Mayer, Andreas. "Von der 'Rasse' zur 'Menschheit': Zur Inszenierung der Rassenanthropologie im Wiener Naturhistorischen Museum nach 1945." In *Politik der Präsentation: Museum und Ausstellung in Österreich 1918–1945,* ed. Herbert Posch and Gottfried Fliedl, 212–237. Vienna: Turia & Kant, 1996.

Mayer, Egon, Barry Kosmin, Ariela Keysar, eds. *American Jewish Identity Survey.* New York: Center for Cultural Judaism, 2003.

McBride, James. *The Color of Water: A Black Man's Tribute to his White Mother.* New York: Riverhead Books, 1997,

McGee, Daniel J. "Dada Da Da: Sounding the Jew in Modernism." *ELH* 68, no. 2 (2001): 501–527.

McWilliams, Carey. *Brothers under the Skin.* Boston: Little Brown, 1943.

Melnick, Jeffrey. *A Right to Sing the Blues: African Americans, Jews, and American Popular Song.* Cambridge, MA: Harvard University Press, 1999.

———. "Some Notes on the Erotics of 'Black-Jewish Relations.'" *Shofar* 23, no. 4 (2005): 9–25.

———. *Black Jewish Relations on Trial: Leo Frank and Jim Conley in the New South.* Jackson: University of Mississippi Press, 2000.

Meyer, Adam. *Black-Jewish Relations in African American and Jewish American Fiction: An Annotated Bibliography.* Lanham, MD: Scarecrow Press, 2002.

Michaels, Walter Benn. "Plots Against America: Neoliberalism and Antiracism." *American Literary History* 18, no. 2 (Summer 2006): 288–302.

———. *The Trouble with Diversity: How We Learned to Love Identity and Ignore Inequality.* New York: Holt, 2007.

Michaelsen, Scott. *The Limits of Multiculturalism: Interrogating the Origins of American Anthropology.* Minneapolis: University of Minnesota Press, 1999.

Miles, William F. "Black Muslim Africans in the Jewish State: Lessons of Colonial Nigeria for Contemporary Jerusalem." *Issues* 35, no. 1 (1997): 39–42.

Modood, Tariq. *Multiculturalism: A Civic Idea.* Cambridge, England: Polity Press, 2007.

Mohanty, Chandra Talpade. "Under Western Eyes: Feminist Scholarship and Colonial Discourses." In *The Post-Colonial Studies Reader,* ed. B. Ashcroft, G. Griffith and H. Tiffin, 259–263. London: Routledge, 1995.

Mondry, Henrietta. *Exemplary Bodies: Constructing the Jew in Russian Culture since the 1880s.* Boston: Academic Studies Press, 2009.

Moore, Deborah Dash. *At Home in America.* New York: Columbia University Press, 1981.

———. *GI Jews: How World War II Changed a Nation.* Cambridge, MA: Belknap Press of Harvard University Press, 2004.

———, ed. *American Jewish Identity Politics.* Ann Arbor: University of Michigan Press, 2008.

Morawska, Ewa. *Insecure Prosperity.* Princeton, NJ: Princeton University Press, 1996.

Morris-Reich, Amos. *The Quest for Jewish Assimilation in Modern Social Science.* New York: Routledge, 2008.

Most, Andrea. *Making Americans: Jews and the Broadway Musical.* Cambridge, MA: Harvard University Press, 2004.

Mufti, Aamir R. *Enlightenment in the Colony: The Jewish Question and the Crisis of Postcolonial Culture.* Princeton, NJ: Princeton University Press, 2007.

Murphy, Robert F. "Anthropology at Columbia: A Reminiscence." *Dialectical Anthropology* 16, no. 1 (1991): 68–81.

Nahshon, Edna. *From the Ghetto to the Melting Pot.* Detroit, MI: Wayne State University Press, 2005.

Nancy, Jean-Luc. "The Deconstruction of Christianity." In *Religion and Media,* ed. Hent de Vries and Samuel Weber. Stanford, CA: Stanford University Press, 2001.

Nash, Catherine. "Mapping Origins. Race and Relatedness in Population Genetics and Genetic Genealogy." In *New Genetics, New Identities,* ed. P. Atkinson, P.E. Glasner, and H. Greenslade. New York: Routledge, 2007, 77–101.

Nebel, Almut, Dvora Filon, Bernd Brinkmann, Partha P. Majumder, Marina Faerman, and Ariella Oppenheim. "The Y Chromosome Pool of Jews as Part of the Genetic Landscape of the Middle East." *American Journal of Human Genetics* 69, no. 5 (2001): 1095–1112.

Nelson, Alondra. "The Factness of Diaspora. The Social Sources of Genetic Genealogy." In *Rites of Return: Diaspora Poetics and the Politics of Memory,* ed. Marianne Hirsch and Nancy K. Miller, 23–40. New York: Columbia University Press, 2011.

Newton, Adam Zachary. *Facing Black and Jew: Literature as Public Space in Twentieth-century America.* Cambridge: Cambridge University Press, 1999.

North, Michael. *The Dialect of Modernism: Race, Language and Twentieth Century Literature.* New York: Oxford University Press, 1994.

Oded, Arye. *The Bayudaya: A Community of African Jews in Uganda.* Tel-Aviv: Shiloah Center for Middle Eastern and African Studies, Tel-Aviv University, 1973.

Olson, Tamara. *Popular Representations of Jewish Identity on Primetime Television: The Case of The O.C.* Master's thesis. Macalester College, St. Paul, Minnesota, 2006.

Omi, Michael, and Howard Winant. "Racial Formations." In *The Social Construction of Difference and Inequality,* ed. Tracy Ore, 19–29. New York: McGraw Hill, 2003.

———. *Racial Formation in the United States from the 1960s to the 1990s.* 2nd ed. New York: Routledge, 1994.

Oney, Steve. *And the Dead Shall Rise: The Murder of Mary Phagan and the Lynching of Leo Frank.* New York: Pantheon, 1983.

Ostrer, Harry. *Legacy: A Genetic History of the Jewish People.* Oxford: Oxford University Press, 2012.

Parekh, Bhikhu. *Rethinking Multiculturalism: Cultural Diversity and Political Theory.* Basingstoke: Macmillan, 2000.

Parfitt, Tudor. *Journey to the Vanished City.* New York: Vintage Books, 2000.

———. *The Lost Tribes of Israel: The History of a Myth.* London: Phoenix, 2003.

———. *Operation Moses: The Untold Story of the Secret Exodus of the Falasha from Ethiopia.* London: Weidenfeld and Nicolson, 1985.

———. "The Use of the Jew in Colonial Discourse." In *Orientalism and the Jews,* ed. Ivan Davidson Kalmar and Derek J. Penslar, 51–67. Hanover, NH: University Press of New England, 2005.

———. *Black Jews in Africa and the Americas.* Cambridge, MA: Harvard University Press, 2012.

Parfitt, Tudor, and Julia Egorova. *Genetics, Mass Media and Identity: A Case Study of the Genetic Research on the Lemba and Bene Israel.* London: Routledge, 2006.

Parfitt, Tudor, and Emanuela Trevisan Semi. *Judaizing Movements.* London: Routledge Curzon, 2002.

Patai, Raphael; and Jennifer Patai. *The Myth of the Jewish Race.* Revised edition. Detroit: Wayne University Press, 1989.

Pegelow, Thomas. "'German Jews,' 'National Jews,' 'Jewish Volk' or 'Racial Jews'? The Constitution and Contestation of 'Jewishness' in Newspapers of Nazi Germany, 1933–1938." *Central European History* 35 (2002): 195–221.

Pellegrini, Ann. "Whiteface Performances: 'Race,' Gender, and Jewish Bodies." In *Jews and Other Differences: The New Jewish Cultural Studies,* ed. Jonathan Boyarin and Daniel Boyarin, 108–149. Minneapolis: Minnesota University Press, 1997.

Pieterse, Jan Nederveen. "Hybridity, So What? The Anti-Hybridity Backlash and the Riddles of Recognition." *Theory, Culture and Society* 18 (2001): 219–245.

Pinsker, Sanford. "Art as Excess: The 'Voices' of Charlie Parker and Philip Roth." *Partisan Review* 69, no. 1 (2002): 58–74.

———. "Climbing over the Ethnic Fence: Reflections on Stanley Crouch and Philip Roth." *Virginia Quarterly Review* 78, no. 3 (Summer 2002): 472–480.

———. *The Comedy, "Hoits": An Essay on the Fiction of Philip Roth.* Columbia: University of Missouri Press, 1975.

———. "The New Minstreldom, or Why so Much in Contemporary Black Culture Went Wrong." *Virginia Quarterly Review* 79, no. 2 (Spring 2003): 280–286.

Podhoretz, Norman. *Why Are Jews Liberals?* New York: Vintage, 2010.

Popkin, Henry. "The Vanishing Jew of Our Popular Culture." *Commentary* 13 (July 1952): 47–53.

Prell, Riv-Ellen. *Fighting to Become American.* Boston: Beacon, 1999.

Prentiss, Craig R., ed. *Religion and the Creation of Race and Ethnicity: An Introduction.* New York: New York University Press, 2003.

Presner, Todd Samuel. *Muscular Judaism: The Jewish Body and the Politics of Regeneration.* London, New York: Routledge, 2007.

Primack, Karen. *Jews in Places You Never Thought Of.* Hoboken, NJ: Ktav Publishing House, 1998.

Rensmann, Lars and Julus H. Schoeps, eds. *Politics and Resentment: Antisemitism and Counter-Cosmopolitanism in the European Union.* Leiden: Brill, 2011.

Roediger, David. *Toward the Abolition of Whiteness.* New York: Verso. 1994.

———. *Wages of Whiteness.* Rev. ed. New York: Verso, 1999.

———. *Working Toward Whiteness.* New York: Basic Books, 2005.

Rogin, Michael. *Blackface, White Noise: Jewish Immigrants in the Melting Pot.* Berkeley: University of California Press, 1996.

Rothberg, Michael. "Against Zero-Sum Logic: A Response to Walter Benn Michaels." *American Literary History* 18, no. 2 (2006): 303–311.

Rottenberg, Catherine. *Performing Americanness: Gender, Race, and Class in Modern African and Jewish American Literature.* Hanover, NH: University Press of New England, 2008.

Rubin, Gary E. "How Should We Think about Black Antisemitism?" In *Antisemitism in America Today: Outspoken Experts Explode the Myths,* ed. Jerome Chanes. New York: Birch Lane Press, 1995.

Runnymede Trust. *A Very Light Sleeper: The Persistence and Dangers of Anti-Semitism.* London: Runnymede Trust, 1994.

Sabar, Galia. "African Christianity in the Jewish State: Adaptation, Accommodation and Legitimization of Migrant Workers 1990–2003." *Journal of Religion in Africa* 34, no. 4 (2004): 407–437.

Sacks, Jonathan. *The Dignity of Difference: How to Avoid the Clash of Civilizations.* Rev. ed. London: Continuum, 2003.

———. *The Home We Build Together: Recreating Society.* London and New York: Continuum, 2007.

Safran, William. "Ethnoreligious Politics in France: Jews and Muslims." *West European Politics* 27, no. 3 (2004): 423–451.

———. "The Jewish Diaspora in a Comparative and Theoretical Perspective." *Israel Studies* 10, no. 1 (Spring 2005): 36–60.

Said, Edward. "An Ideology of Difference," *Critical Inquiry,* 12, no. 1 (Autumn, 1985): 38-58,

———. *Orientalism.* 25th anniversary edition. New York: Vintage, 1994; republished 2003.

Salamon, Hagar. "Blackness in Transition: Decoding Racial Constructs through Stories of Ethiopian Jews." *Journal of Folklore Research* 40, no. 1 (2003): 3–32.

———. *The Hyena People.* Berkeley: University of California Press, 1999.

———. "Reflections of Ethiopian Cultural Patterns on the 'Beta Israel' Absorption in Israel: The 'Barya' Case." In *Between Africa and Zion,* ed. Steven Kaplan,

Tudor Parfitt, and Emanuela Trevisan Semi, 126–132. Jerusalem: Ben-Zvi Institute, 1994.

Salamon, Hagar, and Steven Kaplan. *Ethiopian Jewry: An Annotated Bibliography 1987–1997.* Jerusalem, Ben Zvi Institute, 1998.

Salzman, Jack. *Struggles in the Promised Land: Towards a History of Black-Jewish Relations in the United States.* New York: Oxford University Press, 1997.

———, ed. with Adina Back and Gretchen Sorin. *Bridges and Boundaries: African Americans and American Jews.* New York: George Braziller, 1992.

Sánchez-Eppler, Benigno. "Telling Anthropology: Zora Neale Hurston and Gilberto Freyre Disciplined in Their Field-Home Work." *American Literary History* 4, no. 3 (1992): 464–488.

Sand, Shlomo. *The Invention of the Jewish People.* Trans. Yael Lotan. London and New York: Verso, 2009.

Santner, Eric L. *On The Psychotheology of Everyday Life: Reflections of Freud and Rosenzweig.* Chicago: University of Chicago Press, 2001.

———. *The Neighbor: Three Inquiries in Political Theology.* Chicago: University of Chicago Press, 2005.

———. *Stranded Objects: Mourning, Memory, and Film in Postwar Germany.* Ithaca, NY: Cornell University Press, 1990.

Sartre, Jean-Paul. *Anti-Semite and Jew.* New York: Schocken, 1948.

Schwarz, Tanya. *Ethiopian Jewish Immigrants: The Homeland Postponed.* London: Routledge/Curzon, 2001.

Seeman, Don. *One People, One Blood: Ethiopian-Israelis and the Return to Judaism.* New Brunswick, NJ: Rutgers University Press, 2009.

Sigelman, Lee. "Blacks, Whites, and Anti-Semitism." *Sociological Quarterly* 36, no. 4 (Autumn 1995): 649–656.

Shain, Milton. "Ethnonationalism, Anti-Semitism, and Identity Politics: The North American and South African Experiences." In *Jewries at the Frontier: Accommodation, Identity, Conflict,* ed, Sander L. Gilman and Milton Shain, 335–350. Urbana: University of Illinois Press, 1999.

Shavit, Yaacov. *History in Black: African-Americans in Search of an Ancient Past.* London: Frank Cass, 2001.

Sheffer, Gabriel. *Diaspora Politics: At Home Abroad.* Cambridge: Cambridge University Press, 2003.

Shepherd, Robin. *A State Beyond the Pale: Europe's Problem with Israel.* London: Weidenfeld & Nicolson, 2009.

Shimoni, Gideon. *Community and Conscience: The Jews in Apartheid South Africa.* Hanover, NH: Brandeis University Press, 2003.

Shohat, Ella. "Taboo Memories and Diasporic Visions." In *Performing Hybridity,* ed. Joseph May and Jennifer Fink, 131–158. Minneapolis: University of Minneapolis Press, 1999.

Sicher, Efraim. *Antisemitism, Multiculturalism, Globalization: The British Case.* Analysis of Current Trends in Antisemitism #32. Jerusalem: Vidal Sassoon Center for the Study of Antisemitism, Hebrew University of Jerusalem, 2009.

———. "The Image of Israel: A View from Britain." *Israel Studies* 16, no. 1 (Spring 2011): 1–25.

Sicher, Efraim, and Linda Weinhouse. *Under Postcoloniaql Eyes: The "jew" in Contemporary British Writing.* Lincoln: Nebraska University Press, 2012.

Silberman, Charles, *A Certain People: American Jews and their Lives Today*. New York: Summit, 1985.

Silberstein, Laurence J. "Mapping, Not Tracing: Opening Reflection." In *Mapping Jewish Identities,* ed. Laurence J. Silberstein, 1–36. New York: New York University Press, 2000.

Sleeper, Jim. *Liberal Racism*. New York: Viking, 1997.

Slezkine, Yuri. *The Jewish Century*. Princeton, NJ: Princeton University Press, 2005.

Smith, Anna Deavere. *Fires in the Mirror: Crown Heights, Brooklyn and Other Identities*. New York: Anchor Books/Doubleday, 1993.

Smitherman, Geneva. *Talkin and Testifyin: The Language of Black America*. Boston: Houghton Mifflin Harcourt, 1977.

Sollors, Werner. "A Critique of Pure Pluralism." In *Reconstructing American Literary History,* ed. Sacvan Bercovich, 250–279. Cambridge, MA: Harvard University Press, 1986.

Sorin, Gerald. *A Time for Building*. Baltimore: Johns Hopkins University Press, 1992.

Sowell, Thomas. *Black Rednecks and White Liberals*. San Francisco: Encounter Books, 2005.

Staub, Shalom, "'Salim's Going to Be Muslim Someday': The Negotiated Identities of an American Jewish Ethnographer." In *Between Two Worlds: Ethnographic Essays on American Jewry,* ed. Jack Kugelmass, 240–264. Ithaca, NY: Cornell University Press, 1988.

Stillman, Norman A. *Jews in Arab Lands: A History and Source Book*. Philadelphia: Jewish Publication Society of America, 1979.

Stoetzler, Marcel. "Cultural Difference in the National State: From Trouser-Selling Jews to Unbridled Multiculturalism." *Patterns of Prejudice* 42, no. 3 (2008): 245–279.

Stratton, Jon. *Coming Out Jewish: Constructing Ambivalent Identities*. London: Routledge, 2000.

———. *Jewish Identity in Western Pop Culture: The Holocaust and Trauma through Modernity*. New York: Palgrave Macmillan, 2008.

Strickland, Debra Higgs. *Saracens, Demons and Jews: Making Monsters in Medieval Art*. Princeton, NJ: Princeton University Press, 2003.

Sunderland, P.L. "'You May Not Know It, But I'm Black': White Women's Self-Identification as Black." *Ethnos* 62, no. 1–2 (1997): 32–58.

Sundquist, Eric J. *Strangers in the Land: Blacks, Jews, Post-Holocaust America*. Cambridge, MA: Harvard University Press, 2005.

Taguieff, Pierre-André. *The Force of Prejudice: On Racism and its Doubles*. Minneapolis: University of Minnesota Press, 2001.

Taschwer, Klaus. "'Lösung der Judenfrage: Zu einigen anthropologischen Ausstellunge im Naturhistorischen Museum Wien." In *Wie ein Monster ensteht: Zur Konstruktion des Anderen in Rassismus und Antisemitismus,* ed. Kirstin Breitnfellner and Charlotte Kohn-Ley, 153–180. Bodenheim: Philos, 1998.

Taylor, Kate. "Hatred Repackaged: The Rise of the British National Party and Anti-Semitism." In *A New Anti-Semitism?* ed. Paul Iganski and Barry Kosmin, 231–248. London: Profile Books, 2003.

Thomas, Mark G., Tudor Parfitt, Karl Skorecki, Haim Ben-Ami, Neil Bradman, and David B. Goldstein. "Origins of Old Testament Priests." *Nature* 394 (1998): 138–139.

Thomas Mark G., Tudor Parfitt, Deborah A. Weiss, Karl Skorecki, James F. Wilson, Magdel Le Roux, Neil Bradman and David B. Goldstein, "Y Chromosomes Travelling South: The Cohen Modal Haplotype and the Origins of the Lemba—the Black Jews of Southern Africa." *American Journal of Human Genetics* 66 (2000): 674–686.

Trachtenberg, Joshua. *The Devil and the Jew.* New Haven: Yale University Press, 1943.

van Emden, Gidon. "Relations between the European Jewish Communities, Their Nation States and the Institutions of the EU: The Challenges of Representation." Unpublished paper presented at a joint BGU-JPR symposium, Ben-Gurion University of the Negev, Beer-Sheva, 2009, http://www.jpr.org.uk/discuss/blog.php?id=26

van Straten, Jits. *The Origin of Ashkenazi Jewry. The Controversy Unraveled.* Berlin and New York: De Gruyter 2011.

Wade, Peter. "The Presence and Absence of Race." *Patterns of Prejudice,* 44, no. 1 (2010): 43–60.

Wagaw, Teshome G. *For Our Soul: Ethiopian Jews in Israel.* Detroit, MI: Wayne State University Press, 1993.

Waligórska, Magdalena. "A Goy Fiddler on the Roof: How the Non-Jewish Participants of the Klezmer Revival in Kraków Negotiate Their Polish Identity in a Confrontation with Jews." *Polish Sociological Review* 4, no. 152 (2005): 367–382.

Walker, Rebecca. *Black, White, Jewish; Autobiography of a Shifting Self.* New York: Riverhead, 2001.

Warren, Kristy. "It's Bigger Than Hip Hop." *Jewish Culture and History* 11, no. 1–2 (2009): 172–183.

Webber, Jonathan, ed. *Jewish Identities in the New Europe.* London: Littman Library of Jewish Civilization, 1994.

Weil, Shalva. *Bibliography on Ethiopian Jewry (1998–2001).* Paris: SOSTEJE, 2001.

———. "Esther David: The Bene Israel Novelist who Grew Up with a Tiger." In *Karmic Passages: Israeli Scholarship on India,* ed. David Shulman and Shalva Weil, 232–253. New Delhi: Oxford University Press, 2008.

———. "On Origins, the Arts and Transformed Identities: Foci of Research into the Bene Israel." In *Indo-Judaic Studies in the Twenty-First Century: A View from the Margin,* ed. Nathan Katz, R. Chakravarti, B.M. Sinha, and Shalva Weil. New York and Houndmills: Palgrave Macmillan, 2007. 147–157

———. "The Place of Alwaye in Modern Cochin Jewish History." *Journal of Modern Jewish Studies,* 8, no. 3 (2009): 319–335.

———. "The Bene Israel Indian Jewish Family in Transnational Context." *Journal of Comparative Family Studies* 43, no. 1 (January–February 2011), 71.

Weiss, Meira, *The Chosen Body: The Politics of the Body in Israel.* Stanford, CA: Stanford University Press, 2002.

West, Cornel. *Race Matters.* Boston: Beacon Press, 1993.

Wexler, Paul. *The Ashkenazic Jews: A Slavo-Turcic People in Search of a Jewish Identity.* Columbus, OH: Slavica, 1993.

Whine, Michael. "Antisemitism on the Streets." In *A New Anti-Semitism*? ed. Paul Iganski and Barry Kosmin, 23–37. London: Profile Books, 2003.

Whitfield, Stephen J. "Black Like Us." *Jewish History* 22 (2008): 353–371.

Wilkerson, Isabel. *The Warmth of Other Suns: The Epic Story of America's Great Migration.* New York: Random House, 2010.

Williams, Vernon, Jr. "Franz Boas's Paradox and the African American Intelligentsia." In *African Americans and Jews in the Twentieth Century: Studies in Convergence and Conflict,* ed. V.P. Franklin, 54–86. Columbia: University of Missouri Press, 1998.

Wirth-Nesher, Hana. *Call It "English": The Languages of Jewish American Literature.* Princeton, NJ: Princeton University Press, 2005.

———. "From Newark to Prague: Roth's Place in the American-Jewish Literary Tradition." In *Reading Philip Roth,* ed. Asher Milbauer and Donald Watson. London: Macmillan, 1988.

———. "Resisting Allegory, or Reading 'Eli, the Fanatic' in Tel Aviv." *Prooftexts* 21, no. 1 (Winter 2001): 103–120.

Wisse, Ruth R. *The Modern Jewish Canon, A Journey Through Language and Culture.* New York: Free Press, 2000.

Wistrich, Robert. *Antisemitism: The Longest Hatred.* London: Thames Methuen, 1991.

———. *A Lethal Obsession: Anti-Semitism from Antiquity to the Global Jihad.* New York: Random House, 2010.

——. *From Ambivalence to Betrayal: The Left, the Jews, and Israel.* Lincoln: University of Nebraska Press, 2012.

Young, Robert J.C. *Colonial Desire: Hybridity in Theory, Culture and Race.* London: Routledge, 1995.

Zackodnik, Teresa. "Fixing the Color Line." *American Quarterly* 53, no. 3 (September 2001): 420–451.

Zaslavsky, Victor, and Robert J. Brym. *Soviet-Jewish Emigration and Soviet Nationality Policy.* New York: St. Martin's Press, 1983.

Zeitz, Joshua. *White Ethnic New York: Jews, Catholics, and the Shaping of Postwar Politics.* Chapel Hill: University of North Carolina Press, 2007.

Zianga, Jonas. *From the Promised Land: Modern Discourse on Africa Jewry.* Beer-Sheva: Ben-Gurion University Press, 2011.

Contributors

Dalit Alperovich is a doctoral student in the School of Cultural Studies at Tel Aviv University, investigating modernist and ethnographic literary constructions of Native American identity in the interwar period. She received a bachelor of arts in psychology, sociology, and anthropology and a master of arts degree in English and American Studies, Tel Aviv University, where she was awarded a Dan David scholarship in 2012. Alperovich teaches courses on ethnicity in America, and on Native American literature. Her fields of interest include twentieth-century ethnic and Native American literature; modernist literature; modern American anthropology; and ethnographic literature.

Edith Bruder is research associate at the School of Oriental and African Studies (University of London), at the French National Center for Scientific Research, Paris, and at the Faculty of Theology's School of Biblical Studies and Ancient Languages, North-West University, South Africa. She is the founding president of the International Society for the Study of African Jewry. Her main subjects of research are African Judaism and religious diasporas, new religious movements, globalization of religions, shifting identities, and marginal religious societies. Dr. Bruder is the author of *The Black Jews of Africa: History, Identity, Religion* (Oxford University Press, 2008), and coeditor of *African Zion: Studies in Black Judaism* (Cambridge Scholars Publishing, 2012).

Glynis Cousin is professor of higher education and director of the Institute for the Enhancement of Learning at the University of Wolverhampton, England. She is a sociologist of education with a focus on questions of equality, diversity, and cosmopolitan approaches. A National Teaching Fellow, she has published a book on qualitative research, *Researching Learning in Higher Education* (Routledge, 2009). She is currently directing two national projects: a seminar series on global citizenship, and an investigation into degree attainment and Black minority ethnic students.

Shlomi Deloia completed his doctorate in the Department of Foreign Literatures and Linguistics at Ben-Gurion University of the Negev, Beer-Sheeva, Israel, in 2011. He works on reading race, whiteness, and cultural identity in the Jewish American immigration novel of the 1920s.

Robert Fine is emeritus professor of sociology at the University of Warwick, England. His current research interests include cosmopolitan social theory, human rights, and anti-Semitism past and present. He is author of *Cosmopolitanism* (Routledge, 2007), *Democracy and the Rule of Law: Marx's Critique of the Legal Form* (Blackburn Press, 2002), *Political Investigations: Hegel, Marx, Arendt* (Routledge, 2001), and *Beyond Apartheid: Labour and Liberation in South Africa* (with Dennis Davis; Pluto, 1990). He was the founding co-convenor of the European Sociological Association Network on Racism and Antisemitism and the Warwick Social Theory Centre. He recently co-edited a special issue of *European Societies* on Racism and Antisemitism and is coeditor of a special issue of the *Journal of Classical Sociology* on Natural Law and Social Theory.

Sander L. Gilman is distinguished Professor of the Liberal Arts and Sciences as well as professor of psychiatry at Emory University. He is also director of the Program in Psychoanalysis and the Health Sciences Humanities Initiative at that university. A cultural and literary historian, he is the author or editor of over eighty books. His *Obesity: The Biography* appeared with Oxford University Press in 2010; his most recent edited volume, *Wagner and Cinema* (with Jeongwon Joe) was published the same year. He is the author of the basic study of the visual stereotyping of the mentally ill, *Seeing the Insane,* published in 1982 (reprinted in 1996), as well as the seminal *Jewish Self-Hatred,* 1986. For twenty-five years, he was a member of the humanities and medical faculties at Cornell University, where he held the Goldwin Smith Professorship of Humane Studies. For six years, he held the Henry R. Luce Distinguished Service Professorship of the Liberal Arts in Human Biology at the University of Chicago, and for four years was a distinguished professor of the Liberal Arts and Medicine and creator of the Humanities Laboratory at the University of Illinois at Chicago.

Cheryl Greenberg is the Paul Raether Distinguished Professor of History at Trinity College. Author of three books and editor of a fourth, she works primarily in the fields of African American history and twentieth-century racial and ethnic relations. Her *Troubling the Waters: Black-Jewish Relations in the American Century,* won the Saul Viener prize in 2007 for best book in American Jewish history. Greenberg has also held fellowships at the W.E.B. Du Bois Institute at Harvard University, the Bicentennial Fulbright Chair at the Renvall Institute at the University of Helsinki and the Charles Warren Center at Harvard. She was Fulbright Fellow at Nankai University, China, in 2010–2011. At present, she is working on the meanings of identity and intermarriage in the African American and Jewish American communities.

Bruce D. Haynes is associate professor of sociology at the University of California, Davis, and an authority on race, ethnicity, and urban communities. He is the author of *Red Lines Black Spaces: The Politics of Race and Space in a Black Middle-Class Suburb* (Yale University Press, 2001) and coeditor of *The Ghetto: Contemporary Global Issues and Controversies* (2011). His essay on Ethiopian Jews, "People of God, Children of Ham: Making Black(s) Jews," appeared in *Journal of Modern Jewish Studies* in 2009. He is currently writing a book about Black Jews in America.

Klaus Hödl is a historian at the Center for Jewish Studies at the University of Graz, Austria. He has published widely on Central and Eastern European Jews, narratives in Jewish historiography, the Jewish body, and Jewish identity. His books include *Die Pathologisierung des Jüdischen Körpers: Antisemitismus, Geschlecht und Medizin im Fin de Siècle* (1997); *Historisches Bewusstsein im Jüdischen Kontext: Strategien-Aspekte-Diskurse* (2004); *Wiener Juden-Jüdische Wiener* (2006); *Kulturelle Grenzräume im Jüdischen Kontext* (2008); *Nicht nur Bildung, nicht nur Bürger: Juden in der Populärkultur* (2012); and *Kultur und Gedächtnis* (2012). He has taught at various universities in Europe and at the Hebrew University of Jerusalem. His current project focuses on Jews in popular culture.

Ivan Davidson Kalmar is professor of anthropology at the University of Toronto. His books include *The Trotskys, Freuds, and Woody Allens: Portrait of a Culture* (Viking/Penguin, 1994), *Early Orientalism: Imagined Islam and the Notion of Sublime Power* (Routledge, 2012) and, as coeditor with Derek Penslar, *Orientalism and the Jews* (2005). His recent articles concern the joint construction of the Jew and Muslim in Western Christian cultural history. His article, "The Rise and Fall of the Semite: Jews, Arabs, and Muslims in the Nineteenth and Twentieth Century," appears in vol. 8 of *The Cambridge History of Judaism,* edited by M. Hart and T. Michels.

Steven Kaplan is professor of African studies and Gail Levin de Nur Professor of Comparative Religion at the Hebrew University in Jerusalem. He is one of the leading modern scholars on the origins of the Beta Israel, or Ethiopian Jews. He was the dean of the Faculty of Humanities at the Hebrew University of Jerusalem from 2004 to 2006. He has been a visiting scholar at Boston University, Harvard University, the University of Hamburg, the University of London, and, most recently, the University of North Carolina at Chapel Hill. Professor Kaplan has held a number of senior administrative positions at the Hebrew University, including director of the Institute for Asian and African Studies, Provost of the Rothberg International School, Dean of the Faculty of Humanities, and Academic Director of the Harry S. Truman Research Institute for the Advancement of Peace.

Noa Sophie Kohler is a graduate of Humboldt University and Freie Universität Berlin; she completed her doctorate at Ben-Gurion University of the Negev, Beer-Sheva, Israel in 2010 in Jewish History. She is currently post-doctoral fellow at the Jacques Loeb Centre for the History and Philosophy of the Life Sciences at Ben-Gurion University, where she is investigating family networking among Ashkenazic Jews by combining population genetics (genome-wide cluster analysis of more than five hundred individuals) with historical research.

Fran Markowitz teaches cultural anthropology at Ben-Gurion University of the Negev, Beer-Sheva, Israel. Her main teaching and research interests focus on ethnicity and racialization, gender and sexuality, migration and diasporas, and heterogeneity and hybridity. She has conducted ethnographic fieldwork in Israel, the United States, Russia, and Bosnia. Her latest books are *Homecomings: Unsettling Paths of Return* (co-edited with Anders H. Stefansson, 2004), and *Sarajevo: A Bosnian Kaleidoscope* (2010).

Dan Mishmar is professor in the Department of Life Sciences, Ben-Gurion University of the Negev, Beer-Sheva, Israel. He has a bachelor of arts in archaeology and a doctor of philosophy in genetics from the Hebrew University of Jerusalem. During his postdoctoral training under the supervision of Professor Douglas C. Wallace (University of

California, Irvine), he focused on investigating human mitochondrial genetics and evolution, a topic that has informed his research since the establishment of his own lab at Ben-Gurion University in 2004.

Amos Morris-Reich teaches in the Department of Jewish History at the University of Haifa, and is the director of Bucerius Institute for Research of German History and Society. He is the author of *The Quest for Jewish Assimilation in Modern Social Science* (Routledge, 2008).

Adam Zachary Newton is University Professor and Ronald P. Stanton Chair in Literature and the Humanities at Yeshiva University, New York, and Chair of the Yeshiva College English Department. He has published *Narrative Ethics* (Harvard University Press, 1995); *Facing Black and Jew: Literature as Public Space in 20th Century America* (Cambridge University Press, 1988); *The Fence and The Neighbor: Emmanuel Levinas, Yeshayahu Leibowitz, and Israel Among the Nations* (State University of New York Press, 2001); *The Elsewhere: On Belonging at a Near Distance* (University of Wisconsin Press, 2005). His new project is called, *"To Make the Hands Impure": Art and Ethical Adventure, the Difficult and the Holy.*

Hannah Adelman Komy Ofir teaches academic writing at Ben-Gurion University of the Negev, Beer-Sheva, Israel and works as an editor and translator. Her doctoral dissertation dealt with memory, trauma, and Jewish identity in the narratives of children of Holocaust survivors and their contemporaries in North America.

Catherine Rottenberg is assistant professor in the Department of Foreign Literatures and Linguistics and the Gender Studies Program at Ben-Gurion University of the Negev, Beer-Sheva, Israel. She is the author of *Performing Americanness: Race, Class and Gender in Modern African-American and Jewish-American Literature* (University Press of New England, 2008) and the editor of *Black Harlem and the Jewish Lower East Side: Narratives Out of Time* (State University of New York Press, 2013). Her articles have appeared in *African American Review, MELUS,* and the *Journal of American Studies.* In 2012 she was awarded the Toronto Prize for Excellence in Academic Research, as well as a Certificate for Excellence in Teaching.

Efraim Sicher teaches English and comparative literature at Ben-Gurion University of the Negev, Beer-Sheva, and researches representation of the Jew in Western culture, the shaping of Holocaust memory, and the nineteenth-century novel. His recent books include *The Holocaust Novel* (Routledge, 2005), *Rereading the City, Rereading Dickens* (AMS Press, 2003; second edition, 2012), *Babel in Context: A Study in Cultural Identity* (2012), and, as editor, *The Complete Works of Isaac Babel* (in Hebrew, 2008–2010). He has coauthored a book with Linda Weinhouse, *Under Postcolonial Eyes: Figuring the "jew" in Contemporary British Writing* (University of Nebraska Press, 2012).

Ibrahim Sundiata has been a faculty member at Brandeis University for two decades. He is an Africanist who has worked on West Africa (Equatorial Guinea and Liberia). More recently, he has worked on comparative race and ethnicity. He has been the recipient of a Fulbright Award to Brazil and has been on the board of the Association for the Study of the Worldwide African Diaspora (ASWAD). Professor Sundiata is also a member of the Council on Foreign Relations. His *Brothers and Strangers, Black Zion, Black Slavery,* was published by Duke University in 2003. His forthcoming book is *Old Dixie, Global Obama: Narratives of Identity, Sexuality and Color in the New Millennium.*

Jonas Zianga is a lecturer in African Studies in the Department of Politics and Government, Ben-Gurion University of the Negev. He has published *From the Promised Land ...: Modern Discourse on African Jewry* (Ben-Gurion University Press, 2011).

Index